Global Algorithmic Capital Markets

Global Algorithmic Capital Markets

High Frequency Trading, Dark Pools, and Regulatory Challenges

Edited by Walter Mattli

OXFORD
UNIVERSITY PRESS

OXFORD
UNIVERSITY PRESS

Great Clarendon Street, Oxford, OX2 6DP,
United Kingdom

Oxford University Press is a department of the University of Oxford.
It furthers the University's objective of excellence in research, scholarship,
and education by publishing worldwide. Oxford is a registered trade mark of
Oxford University Press in the UK and in certain other countries

Published in the United States of America by Oxford University Press
198 Madison Avenue, New York, NY 10016, United States of America

British Library Cataloguing in Publication Data
Data available

Library of Congress Control Number: 2018953894

ISBN 978–0–19–882946–1

Printed and bound by
CPI Group (UK) Ltd, Croydon, CR0 4YY

Contents

Contents

Part 3. Analytical and Regulatory Frameworks

Part 4. Regulatory Agencies and Market Structure Regulation

List of Figures

List of Tables

List of Tables

Notes on Contributors

Daniel Aisen is a co-founder of Investors Exchange (IEX) and the head of the company's Quantitative Strategy team. He was initially responsible for building and evolving the core functionality of IEX as a trading venue. Before co-founding IEX, he was a Vice President at RBC Capital Markets.

Timothy Baikie is Senior Legal Counsel, Market Regulation, at the Ontario Securities Commission, Canada.

Robert Battalio is Professor of Finance at the University of Notre Dame.

Allison Bishop is a quantitative researcher at IEX. She was previously an Assistant Professor of Computer Science at Columbia University and a postdoctoral researcher at Microsoft Research.

Haim Bodek is the Managing Principal and founder of Decimus Capital Markets, LLC, and the author of *The Problem of HFT* and *The Market Structure Crisis*. He is the former CEO of Trading Machines, an independent high frequency trading firm, and has served as Managing Director and Joint Global Head of Electronic Volatility Trading at UBS.

Francis Chung works at IEX, where he designed and developed IEX's matching engine and the query infrastructure underlying much of IEX's internal analytics. Before joining IEX, he traded treasury options at Optiver.

Stanislav Dolgopolov is the Chief Regulatory Officer with Decimus Capital Markets LLC. He was previously affiliated with several law firms and served as an Adjunct Professor teaching classes related to securities regulation at UCLA School of Law.

Stan Feldman is the head of the Business Analytics team at IEX. Prior to joining IEX as a co-founder in 2012, Stan was an analyst on RBC Capital Markets' US equities electronic-trading team.

Thierry Foucault is Professor of Finance at HEC Paris and a research fellow of the Centre for Economic Policy Research.

Merritt B. Fox is Michael E. Patterson Professor of Law and NASDAQ Professor for the Law and Economics of Capital Markets at Columbia Law School.

Tyler Gellasch is Executive Director at the Healthy Markets Association. He is a financial services professional and securities lawyer with senior-level public and private sector experience.

Lawrence R. Glosten is the S. Sloan Colt Professor of Banking and International Finance at Columbia Business School. He is also co-director of the Program in the Law and Economics of Capital Markets at Columbia Law School.

Susan Greenglass is Director of Market Regulation at the Ontario Securities Commission, Canada.

Maureen Jensen is the Chair and CEO of the Ontario Securities Commission, Canada.

Miles Kellerman is a PhD Candidate in International Political Economy at the University of Oxford.

Steffen Kern is Chief Economist and Head of Risk Analysis and Economics at the European Securities and Markets Authority and teaches as Professor of International Finance at the Johannes Gutenberg University Mainz.

Giuseppe Loiacono is a Bank Resolution Expert at the Single Resolution Board and Lecturer in Financial Markets at SciencesPo Paris School of Public Affairs. He co-authored this article in his earlier capacity as Economist at the European Securities and Markets Authority.

Dan Marcus is CEO of Trad-X, the world-leading interest rate swap platform and ParFX, a foreign exchange platform designed to nullify bad market behaviour, as well as co-Head of the Tradition UK Group, a global inter-dealer broker. He is also Global Head of Strategy and Business Development for parent company Tradition.

Greg Medcraft is former Chairman of the Australian Securities and Investments Commission and former Chair of the International Organization of Securities Commissions Board. He is presently Director of the Directorate for Financial and Enterprise Affairs of the OECD. Greg Medcraft's contribution reflects his own opinions, and not those of the OECD or its member countries.

Sophie Moinas is Professor of Finance at Toulouse Capitole University (Toulouse School of Economics and Toulouse School of Management) and a research fellow of the Centre for Economic Policy Research.

Christopher Nagy is co-founder and a board member of the Healthy Markets Association, and CEO of KOR Group, a market structure analytics and advisory firm. He is former Managing Director of Order Routing and Data Strategy at TD Ameritrade.

Gabriel V. Rauterberg is Assistant Professor of Law at Michigan Law School. He is a former research scholar in Capital Markets at Columbia Law School and previously worked as an associate at Cooley LLP and Skadden, Arps, Slate, Meagher & Flom LLP.

Tracey Stern is Manager of Market Regulation at the Ontario Securities Commission, Canada.

Elaine Wah runs the Market Quality team at IEX, where she conducts quantitative research on market structure and monitors the market for potentially manipulative activity.

Yesha Yadav is Professor of Law at Vanderbilt Law School. She worked as a legal counsel at the World Bank and has worked for Clifford Chance LLP in the firm's Financial Regulation and Derivatives group. She is a member of the Commody Futures Trading Commission's Technology Advisory Committee. She also sits on the NASDAQ Hearings Panel.

1

Introduction and Overview

A New Capital Market Reality

Walter Mattli

From New York to London, from Chicago to Tokyo, and from Frankfurt to Sydney, capital markets the world over have undergone revolutionary changes since the last years of the twentieth century.[1] The frenzied activity of traders buying and selling stocks and other financial instruments on the trading floors of the New York Stock Exchange (NYSE), the London Stock Exchange, and the Chicago Board of Trade—traditional icons of global capitalism—has been replaced by algorithmic trading and supercomputers tucked away in gigantic non-descript 'data centres' in out-of-the-way places such as Mahwah (New Jersey), Basildon (outside London), and Aurora (Illinois). Trading has become extraordinarily complex and opaque, with trading speeds no longer measured in minutes or seconds but in time units beyond human perception: milliseconds (a thousandth of a second), microseconds (a millionth), and even nanoseconds (a billionth). By way of comparison, a millisecond is to a second as one second is to 11.6 days; and a nanosecond is to a second as one second is to 31.7 years. The blinking of the human eye takes about 400 milliseconds; and a nerve impulse reaches the brain in about 80 milliseconds—near eternities compared to the speed of modern communications and trading.

Technological advances have scaled up imperceptible and previously irrelevant time differences into operationally manageable and enormously profitable business opportunities for those with sufficient high-tech trading tools. These tools include the fastest private communication and trading lines, the most powerful computers, and sophisticated algorithms ('algos') that are

---

[1] The opening of this introduction is drawn from Walter Mattli, *Darkness by Design: The Hidden Power in Global Capital Markets*. Princeton, NJ: Princeton University Press, 2019.

capable of speedily analysing incoming news and trading data and determining optimal trading strategies in microseconds. High-tech trading also relies on possession of gigantic collections of historic and real-time market data. One Chicago-based market operator is said to possess a collection that contains 'the rough equivalent of approximately 100 times the amount of data included in the Library of Congress.'[2] The storage, management, organization, and analysis of such big data requires enormously costly and complex systems that only a small number of large operators can afford.

Market fragmentation is another central factor that has contributed to the extraordinary complexity of capital markets. At the dawn of the twenty-first century, the NYSE was the world's pre-eminent equity market, listing companies from all over the globe. Today, the NYSE is no longer dominant; from the end of the first decade of this century, its share of the domestic market dropped from 80 per cent to about 20 per cent. Trading in US equity markets is now split between 12 public (also called 'lit') exchanges and many more off-exchange trading venues, including about 40 so-called 'dark pools'—trading platforms that match buy and sell orders but do not display quotations—and over 200 internalizing broker-dealers.[3] This fragmentation is a feature not only of equity markets but also of other markets, including options markets and foreign exchange (FX or forex) markets. And the trend is global—fragmented capital markets are a growing reality in Europe as well as parts of Asia.

In this hyperfast fragmented global marketplace, algos battle algos for trading dominance (i.e. preferential execution position), and the most sophisticated trading supercomputers deal not only in securities but increasingly across asset classes, including futures, fixed income, currencies, and commodities, and across hundreds of markets and dozens of countries. A retired regulator, with a distinguished 15-year record at the helm of two major financial regulatory organizations, recently confessed to me that he no longer understands how these complex capital markets really work. The average investor is even more in the dark about these markets. When an investor sends an order to buy or sell a stock by a click of the mouse, the order may take a lightning journey through a maze of dark pools and exchanges before being filled. How does the investor know that on the journey to execution the order was treated fairly and was filled at the best available price? Adding to market complexity is the extraordinary explosion in order traffic—from millions of orders daily ten years ago to many billions today.

A comprehensive examination of the functioning of these capital markets of today is opportune and should matter to all of us—for the health of these

---

[2] Citadel Inv. Grp., LLC v. Teza Techs. LLC, 924 N.E. 2d 95, 97–98 & n.1 (Ill. 2010).
[3] An internalizing broker-dealer fills a client order by trading with the customer 'internally' or 'in-house' instead of by routing it to an exchange or some other external trading platform.

markets affects our savings and pensions and ultimately has profound implications for the general welfare as well as for equality and justice in society.

The studies presented in this volume make an important contribution to such an examination. Early versions of these studies were presented at a conference in April 2017 at St John's College, Oxford. The purpose of the conference was to bring together about two dozen leading industry experts, regulators, and academics from finance, economics, law, artificial intelligence, and political economy for a focused discussion on the most fundamental equity market structure issues and the most desirable solutions from a broad socio-economic perspective. The discussions were exceptionally lively and generated new insights into how best to approach these problems, assess the strengths and limits of various regulatory and market solutions, and understand the interplay of these solutions.

The chapters selected for publication in this book are organized into four parts. Part 1 presents two topics that are central to the modern algorithmic trading: speed and special order types. Thierry Foucault and Sophie Moinas consider the different meanings of speed. They first discuss the findings of the growing theoretical and empirical literature on trading speed in financial markets. The authors then argue that an increase in trading speed raises adverse selection costs but increases competition among liquidity providers and the rate at which gains from trade are realized. Thus, the effect of an increase in trading speed on market quality and welfare is inherently ambiguous. This observation is important for assessing empirical findings regarding the effects of trading speed and policy-making.

Haim Bodek brings to the discussion the unique perspective of a former high-speed trader and a prominent whistleblower. While much of the public debate surrounding high frequency and algorithmic trading has centred on speed, less has been said about special order types—complex and often non-transparent ways for high frequency traders to interact with exchange markets and other trading venues, allowing them to achieve a favourable execution position, and hence guaranteed economics, at the expense of other market participants. Bodek's chapter documents the special order types used by high frequency traders (HFTs), the absence of adequate disclosure by exchanges, and the problematic interaction between order types designed to accommodate HFT strategies and the order types typically employed by public investors and agency brokers.

Dan Marcus and Miles Kellerman broaden the perspective to consider high frequency and algorithmic trading beyond equity markets, focusing instead on the foreign exchange market. The FX market is by far the largest capital market in the world and, unlike equity markets, remains largely unregulated. Marcus and Kellerman begin by describing the emergence of HFT activity in FX, and show how it bears strong similarity to the trends observed in other capital markets. As is the case elsewhere, rapid developments in execution speed, technology, and market data have created a competitive environment increasingly focused on latency. A growing emphasis on speed and technology has made the market an uneven playing field, to the benefit of HFTs, thereby reducing market transparency and fairness and creating a toxic market ecology that is damaging to the wider trading environment. The last part of the chapter considers possible remedies to these problems.

Part 2 of this book examines quality issues: market quality and best order execution. The chapter by Wah, Feldman, Chung, Bishop, and Aisen suggests that the complex and fragmented nature of the US equities exchange landscape has given rise to structural inefficiencies that have created the potential for inherent conflicts of interest between market participants. The introduction of the Investors Exchange, or IEX, offers an opportunity to evaluate market quality across exchanges with varying design characteristics and fee structures. The authors study four dimensions of market quality—liquidity, execution costs, price discovery, and market stability—and within each, they examine structural mechanics responsible for observed disparities in execution quality. We find that maker-taker exchanges, which dominate the US equities trading landscape, display greater adverse selection, less stability around executions, significantly longer queues at the inside, and a lower probability of execution. This suggests that access fees and rebates perpetuate economic incentives misaligned with the tenets of best execution, and may promote activity detrimental to market quality.

In the next chapter, Battalio examines whether retail brokers make order routing decisions that maximize their customers' execution quality or, instead, maximize their own income from order flow. This chapter identifies retail brokers that seemingly route orders to maximize order flow payments: they sell market orders, and send limit orders to venues paying large liquidity rebates. There are good reasons to suspect that this type of routing may not always be in customers' best interests. For both proprietary limit order data and a broad sample of trades from the NYSE's TAQ database (using data up to the fourth quarter of 2016), the chapter documents a negative relationship between several measures of limit order execution quality and rebate/fee level. This finding suggests that order routing designed to maximize liquidity rebates, which is the norm in today's market, does not maximize execution quality.

Gellasch and Nagy focus on the best execution obligations of brokers but also of investment advisers. While most regulatory agencies have made it clear that investment advisers have best execution obligations, it is not always clear what these responsibilities entail. In this cloudy environment, investment advisers have spent decades developing various strategies to fulfil their duties. These strategies have varied significantly over time and across firms. In recent years, technological advances in markets and trading operations and—still more recently—regulators' expectations have accelerated the evolution of these increasingly sophisticated strategies. Gellasch and Nagy review these developments and survey the current strategies used by investment advisers to meet their best execution obligations in today's increasingly complex and challenging marketplace.

Part 3 of the book is concerned with analytical and regulatory approaches in relation to questionable market practices. Fox, Glosten, and Rauterberg develop an analytical framework, drawing on the tools of microstructure economics and the theory of the firm to provide a overview of the various distinct forms of stock market manipulation, identify those harmed, and evaluate the social welfare effects. Their chapter thus lays the foundation for a renewed understanding of manipulation and its place within securities regulation. The analytical framework can serve as a guide to regulators for successfully prosecuting financial law's most intractable wrong. The authors focus in their chapter on the specific case of 'naked open-market manipulation'.

Yadav argues in her chapter that policy-makers have paid insufficient attention to the interaction of algorithmic trading and automated market mechanics with fundamental legal concepts. The author seeks to fill the gap by surveying eight framework principles critical to regulation and considering how these might apply in an automated marketplace. Specifically, the chapter examines reasonableness; strict liability; foreseeability; contribution; scienter; damage and harm; evidence and proof; and disclosure and information dissemination. This analysis reveals that deeply held assumptions guiding regulatory law sit uneasily in today's complicated and fast-paced markets.

The chapter by Dolgopolov analyses approaches to attaching liability for securities fraud to high frequency traders as primary violators in connection with the current market structure crisis. One of the manifestations of this crisis pertains to inadequate disclosure of advanced functionalities offered by trading venues, as exemplified by the order type controversy. The analysis developed in this chapter is applied to secret deals between trading venues and preferred traders, glitches and gaming, and the reach of the doctrine of market manipulation. Several relevant issues are also viewed from the standpoint of the integrity of the trading process. The chapter concludes by arguing for a balanced approach in interpreting certain problematic practices of high frequency traders as securities fraud.

The conference that produced this book revealed significant differences in design, operating principles, and regulatory cultures across regulatory agencies. Much has been written on the Securities and Exchange Commission (SEC) of the United States. It is a highly politicized regulatory agency suffering from significant levels of capture by the industry (as a result of a persistent 'rotating door' problem and relatively few resources). In sharp contrast to the SEC, the Australian Securities and Investments Commission (ASIC) refuses settlements, stresses regulatory guidance, and is endowed with sophisticated market surveillance technology on a par with the most advanced HFT operations. Such differences naturally have an impact on the regulatory abilities of agencies. In Part 4, the leading regulators from Australia, Canada, and Europe describe their organizations' key features and reflect on their regulatory achievements in three chapters.

This book is intended to reach a wide audience largely ignorant about the inner workings of capital markets. Detailed knowledge about the 'plumbing' of capital markets is confined to a surprisingly small group of equity market structure experts in finance. We want to reach academic colleagues and students in business, law, economics, public policy, and political science. But the topic of how to achieve healthy capital markets is too important to be left only to academic discussions. The book will also be of interest to policy-makers and buy-side market participants (i.e. asset managers, hedge funds, pension funds, trusts) as well as to small investors. Last but not least, we also hope that the findings in this book will have an impact on discussions in regulatory circles at a critical moment of market reform.

Part 1
High Frequency Trading: Key Topics

2

Is Trading Fast Dangerous?

Thierry Foucault and Sophie Moinas

2.1 Introduction

Progress in information and trading technologies have considerably increased the 'speed' at which trading takes place in financial markets, and trading speed is a defining characteristic of high frequency trading firms (hereafter HFTs), such as Citadel, Virtu, Flow Traders, or Jump Trading.[1]

These firms account for a significant fraction of the trading activity in electronic markets. For instance, according to a recent report for the Congressional Research Service,[2] HFTs account for roughly 55 per cent of trading volume in US equity markets (40 per cent in European equity markets), 80 per cent of trading volume in currency futures, and about 66 per cent of trading volume in treasury markets. For 2013 alone, the Tabb Group estimates that investment in fast trading technologies was $1.5 billion, twice the amount invested in 2012. This predominance of high frequency traders and the size of their investment in speed raise concerns about whether high frequency traders use speed at the expense of slower traders (as argued by Lewis in his best-seller, *Flash Boys: A Wall Street Revolt*, 2014) and whether their activity make markets less stable. For instance, analysts have questioned the role played by high frequency traders in several disruptive market events such as the 6 May 2010 flash crash in US stock markets, the 15 October 2014 US treasury flash crash, the 1 January 2016 Shanghai flash crash, or the British pound flash crash of 7 October 2016.[3]

---

[1] The SEC defines high frequency traders as proprietary traders who use 'extraordinary high speed and sophisticated computer programs for generating, routing, and executing orders'.

[2] Miller and Shorter, *High frequency trading*, 2016.

[3] For an analysis of high frequency traders' behaviour during the flash crash of 6 May 2010, see Kirilenko et al., 'The flash crash', 2017.

These concerns have led to several proposals to slow down markets and calls for regulatory interventions. For instance, some trading platforms (e.g. IEX or Alpha) now use 'speed bumps' that extend the time elapsed between the moment at which an order arrives at a trading platform and the moment in which the order enters into the trading platform's matching engine. Alternatively, Budish, Cramton, and Shim[4] proposed switching from continuous electronic order books (the current market organization in many electronic markets) to frequent batch auctions, in which market clearing would take place only at discrete points in time (say, every second).

What is the economic rationale for such regulatory interventions? What are the market failures that they intend to fix? Why should we expect, a priori, the speed of trading to be excessive? Economic analysis of these questions for high frequency trading is nascent. To address them, one must first understand why trading speed is important for high frequency traders and through which channels it can affect liquidity and pricing efficiency. We analyse these issues in Sections 2.2 and 2.3, respectively. Then, in Section 2.4, we discuss possible reasons for which market forces might not generate the socially optimal level of speed and why regulatory intervention might therefore be needed in this area.

2.2 Matching and Informational Speed

One way to assess speed in financial markets is to measure how fast traders (or their algorithms) and trading platforms communicate with each other, i.e. send 'messages' to each other and process these messages. Messages are orders or instructions and reports of various types. For instance, a 'buy market order' is an instruction to buy a given number of shares. A trading platform 'processes' it (i.e. matches the market order against standing sell limit orders) and sends back a message to the original sender confirming receipt and processing of his message. Taking this perspective, one can measure trading speed (e.g. for a given trader and for a given message) by the time elapsed between the moment a message (e.g. the market order to buy shares in our example) is sent to a trading platform and the moment the sender receives feedback from the trading platform (e.g. on the status of his order). This time is often referred to as 'latency'.

Latency has become extremely short in electronic securities markets, close to physical limits. For instance, Baldauf and Mollner[5] report that the average exchange-to-trader latency (the average time elapsed between the moment a message is sent by an exchange to the moment it is received by the firm) is 31 microseconds on average for messages pertaining to the SPDR S&P500

---

[4] Budish et al., 'The high-frequency trading arms race', 2015.
[5] Baldauf and Mollner, 'High-frequency trading', 2017.

Exchange Traded Funds (so called SPY, traded on the NYSE). High frequency traders make investments to minimize the time required to process messages and send messages to exchanges, so presumably their overall latency is also extremely small. For instance, they have invested in fast communication lines between markets, either using fibre optics or microwave transmission (which is 30 per cent faster than fibre optic lines), provided by firms such as Hiberna or McKay brothers.[6] Using microwave transmission, latency between trading platforms based in the Chicago area and those in the New York area is 8.02 milliseconds (ms; source: McKay brothers website), close to the theoretical lower bound (about 7.9ms).

Speed of trading is important for high frequency traders because it is key for the profitability of their strategies, in particular high frequency market making, high frequency arbitrage, and directional trading on very short-lived signals. The role of speed in these strategies is best explained by considering a few examples, as we will do in the subsections below.

2.2.1 *Speed and Trading Strategies*

First, consider a trading algorithm exploiting arbitrage opportunities between an ETF on an index—say, the SPY ETF traded on the NYSE—and a futures on the same index, e.g. the E-Mini futures on the S&P500, traded on the Chicago Mercantile Exchange (CME). When the price of the ETF is high relative to the futures price, the algorithm will send buy marketable orders in the futures market and sell marketable orders in the ETF market. It takes time for these orders to travel between the computer running the algorithm and the trading platforms on which the ETF and the futures are traded (New York and Chicago respectively). Moreover, once these orders have reached these platforms, it takes time for the platforms to execute them against posted quotes, confirm their status (whether they have been fully executed or not), and report the prices at which they have been executed.

The high frequency arbitrageur's profitability is higher if the time elapsed between the moment at which her algorithm sends marketable orders and the moment it gets confirmation of their execution is short, i.e. if trading is fast, for at least two reasons. First, the high frequency arbitrageur faces competition from other arbitrageurs. If competitors are faster, they will take advantage of the arbitrage opportunity before the high frequency trader, and the latter will

---

[6] The first microwave network linking Chicago and New York started operating in 2010 (Shkilko and Sokolov, 'Every cloud has a silver lining', 2016) and is used by traders to obtain fast information on quotes of futures on indexes traded on the Chicago Mercantile Exchange (CME), and information on exchange-traded funds (ETFs) on these indexes traded on equity markets located in the New York area (e.g. trading platforms such as the New York Stock Exchange (NYSE), BATS, or DirectEdge).

end up trading at bad prices.[7] Second, quick feedback from trading platforms is key for risk management. For instance, the buy marketable order placed by the arbitrageur might execute only partially if the arbitrage opportunity vanishes before this order is processed by the CME. In this scenario, the arbitrageur takes the risk of taking a position that is not fully hedged, which in turn requires new quick actions. Chaboud et al., Budish et al., and Foucault et al.[8] provide evidence about high frequency arbitrage strategies.

Consider another example, namely a high frequency trader using price changes in the futures market to forecast price changes in the index constituents. For instance, when the price of the futures increases, the trader buys the index constituents that are the most correlated with the index (e.g. those most heavily weighted in the index).[9] This is a directional trading strategy based on very short-lived signals, i.e. price changes in the futures market. Its profitability depends on the high frequency trader being able to observe and react to these signals *before* the prices of the index constituents adjust to reflect the information contained in futures price changes. This requires very fast access to the futures market data feed and very fast access to trading platforms on which the index constituents are traded. Brogaard et al.[10] provide evidence of such directional strategies on short-lived signals (e.g. macroeconomic announcements or changes in limit order books).

Finally, consider a market maker in one stock traded on two platforms, e.g. BATS Europe (now Cboe) and the London Stock Exchange (LSE). Suppose that a buy market order gets executed on BATS, consuming all the available liquidity at the best ask price in this market. The bid-ask spread on BATS is now wider (say that it increases from 1 cent to 5 cents). Quick information on this event is useful for the market maker for several reasons. First, the arrival of a buy order on BATS is in itself a source of information, which should lead the market maker to revise her quotes upward. The market maker might then optimally decide to update her quotes on the LSE.[11] Second, the new bid-ask spread of 5 cents on BATS might now be too large relative to the competitive level (say, 1 cent). There is therefore an opportunity for submitting new and more competitive sell limit orders on BATS. Again the market maker must be fast to take advantage of this opportunity. Speed matters because if the market

---

[7] For evidence, see Kozhan and Tham, 'Execution risk in high-frequency arbitrage', 2012.

[8] Chaboud et al., 'Rise of the machines', 2014; Budish et al., 2015; Foucault et al., 'Toxic arbitrage', 2017.

[9] See Hendershott and Riordan, 'Algorithmic trading', 2013, and Zhang, 'Need for speed', 2018, for evidence that HFTs use futures prices as a source of information.

[10] Brogaard et al., 'High frequency trading and price discovery', 2014.

[11] This scenario is predicted by models of informed trading, such as Glosten, 'Is the electronic open limit order book inevitable?', 1994; see also Van Kervel, 'Competition for order flow', 2015, for evidence.

maker moves first, she will acquire time priority at the competitive quotes, leaving smaller or no profit to other market makers. Last, suppose that the market maker is the first to set a new competitive bid-ask spread of 1 cent on BATS and that her offer is lifted by another buy market order. The market maker has now a short position. To reduce her position risk, she can place a buy market order on the LSE. The faster this order is filled, the smaller is the risk faced by the market maker. Lescourret and Moinas and Menkveld[12] provide evidence of multi-venue inventory management by high frequency market makers.

High frequency traders do not necessarily specialize in one trading strategy (arbitrage, directional trading, and market making) and might opportunistically use each of them (although empirical evidence suggests that there is some specialization: see Boehmer et al.).[13] Moreover, there are concerns that speed might also be used by some traders for manipulating market prices and deceiving other investors. For instance, the CFTC charged a UK trader (Navinder Singh Sarao) with using a 'layering algorithm' to manipulate prices.[14]

Layering is a manipulative scheme that consists in sending limit orders that are not intended for execution and are therefore quickly cancelled after submission. The goal of this scheme is to distort other traders' beliefs regarding the value of the asset and profit from such distortions. According to the CFTC, N. Sarao's layering algorithm repeatedly submitted large sell limit orders away from the best quotes in the E-Mini S&P500 futures limit order book, without intending these orders to be executed (in fact 99 per cent of them were cancelled). The CFTC claims that these orders artificially depressed the E-Mini S&P500 price and increased its volatility, enabling N. Sarao to make profits by buying the E-Mini S&P500 at depressed prices. Similarly, the French market regulator (AMF) charged Madison Tyler Europe (MTE) (now part of Virtu) with layering in December 2015. However, defining price or market manipulation is difficult, both in legal and economic terms.[15] In particular, as Kyle and Viswanathan[16] point out, it is difficult to distinguish between trading strategies that undermine both price informativeness and liquidity (which they view as manipulative) from trading strategies that just rationally exploit market power and private information.

---

[12] Lescourret and Moinas, 'Fragmentation', 2017; Menkveld, 'High frequency trading', 2013.

[13] Boehmer et al., 'The competitive landscape', 2017.

[14] U.S. Commodity Future Trading Commission vs. Nav Sarao Futures Limited PLC and Navinder Singh Sarao, 2015.

[15] See Fischel and Ross, 'Should the law prohibit manipulation?', 1991; Kyle and Viswanathan, 'How to define illegal price manipulation?', 2008.

[16] Kyle and Viswanathan, 2008.

2.2.2 Matching Speed and Informational Speed

The previous examples show that two types of speeds matter for traders in financial markets (e.g. arbitrageurs, directional traders, or market makers): (1) 'informational speed', i.e. the speed at which traders receive information (about their own trades, changes in quotes, others' transactions, etc.) from trading platforms and (2) 'matching speed', i.e. the speed at which orders are processed and filled by the trading platform. Conceptually, matching and informational speeds are different, e.g. a trading platform which is fast in executing incoming market orders could be slow in providing information to traders. In practice, however, they are bundled and difficult to disentangle.

For instance, consider co-location, i.e. the possibility for traders to locate their algorithms in close proximity to a trading platform's server. Co-location is a way to reduce latency by minimizing the physical distance between traders' algorithms and the trading platform. It increases both the speed at which the orders sent by an algorithm are received and processed by a trading platform (matching speed) and the speed at which the algorithm receives information from the trading platform (informational speed).[17] For example, NASDAQ OMX offers three different types of co-location: basic, premium, and 10G (10 gigabytes). The premium co-location reduces the latency for order entry (matching speed) and order book information retrieval (informational speed), while the 10G co-location reduces the time from order submission to order confirmation for traders' algorithms.[18]

The dramatic increase in informational speeds in recent years is just the terminal point of a long historical process. Astute speculators and exchanges have always sought to speed up the transmission of information on trades and quotes using new information technologies (such as carrier pigeons, the telegraph, the telephone, the ticker, etc.). The first undersea transatlantic cable between Europe and the US dates back to 1866 and was quickly used to arbitrage price differentials between Wall Street and the City.[19] Stock tickers were introduced in 1867, and the Boston Stock Exchange and the NYSE were linked by the telegraph in 1889 to speed up the transmission of information on trades and prices between these two markets. Similarly, speculation on advance access to news (public information) is in no way novel. For instance, around 1835, the reporter Daniel Craig started selling advance access to news from Europe arriving in the US by steamships. Steamships stopped in Halifax,

---

[17] Some market participants may exploit only some aspects of co-location that best suit their trading or investment strategies. For instance, some active funds may choose to be co-located when they rebalance their portfolio in order to execute their trades in different stocks simultaneously and minimize their price impact.

[18] Brogaard et al., 'Trading fast and slow', 2015.

[19] Garbade and Silber, 'Technology', 1978; Hoag, 'Atlantic telegraph cable', 2006.

allowing Craig's agents to read the news and deliver them in Boston through carrier pigeons *before* the steamships arrived in America. Craig was charging $500 for each hour of advance access to the news.[20]

In sum, the value of informational speed has long be recognized by traders and the various strategies exploiting informational speed (cross-market arbitrage, directional trading, and market making) are not new. More novel is the scale at which high frequency traders can deploy these strategies. To leverage their investments in informational speed, high frequency traders typically trade in a large number of stocks, and at any given point in time they process a very large amount of data. Thus, they must automate information processing and the order submission process ('algorithmic trading'). In turn, the automation of order submission requires order processing by exchanges to be automated as well. Thus, informational and matching speeds are complementary and they have been feeding on each other (the automation of matching engines by stock exchanges began in the 1970s[21]). This complementarity is important for regulatory interventions, as one can affect the profitability of high frequency trading by reducing informational or matching speeds or both.

2.3 Effects of Informational and Matching Speeds: Theory and Evidence

There are four channels through which a change in traders' informational and matching speed can affect costs of liquidity provision and gains from trade: (1) search, (2) inventory risk, (3) adverse selection, and (4) competition among liquidity providers.

2.3.1 Search

Speed enables traders to find a counterparty faster. Pagnotta and Philippon[22] show how an exchange's matching speed allows buyers and sellers to be matched and to realize gains from trade more quickly. Biais et al.[23] argue that, in fragmented markets, informational speed allows traders to detect trading platforms with the best quotes, and thereby to complete their desired trades, faster. For instance, investors can buy fast access to exchange data feed to receive accurate information on posted quotes, or use smart routers that instantaneously compare quotes across trading venues to split their

---

[20] *Wall Street Journal*, 'Wall Street, 1889', 2014.   [21] Jain, 'Financial market design', 2005.
[22] Pagnotta and Philippon, 'Competing on Speed', 2018.
[23] Biais et al., 'Equilibrium fast trading', 2015.

orders across platforms optimally. Similarly, as shown in Foucault et al.[24] and Bongaerts et al.,[25] a trader's likelihood of trading increases in the speed with which he observes posted quotes. In all these models, trading faster shortens the time required to realize gains from trade. We are not aware of any direct empirical evaluation of this (potentially first-order) benefit of trading speed.

2.3.2 Inventory Risk Management

Speed helps market makers to better manage their inventory risk. Ait-Sahalia and Sağlam[26] analyse theoretically the optimal pricing behaviour of a high frequency market maker. The market maker receives buy or sell market orders at random points in time and bears inventory holding costs. In choosing his quotes, the market maker optimally balances bid-ask spread revenues with his inventory holding cost.[27] For instance, after accumulating a long position, the market maker optimally stops quoting on the bid side (or shades his bid price) to reduce his inventory. Ait-Sahalia and Sağlam[28] characterize the market maker's optimal pricing policy and show that his bid-ask spread is smaller on average when he is faster. It is intuitively clear that trading faster enables the market maker to revise his quotes more frequently and thereby to better manage his inventory position (e.g. to shade his bid more quickly after accumulating a long position).

Brogaard et al.[29] find evidence for the inventory risk channel. Indeed, they show that traders who buy the fastest co-location services on NASDAQ OMX are predominantly market makers. Moreover, these market makers hold their inventory for a longer period of time after buying the fastest co-location service, which suggests that their inventory holding cost is smaller when they are faster. Consistent with this conjecture, Brogaard et al.[30] also find that fast market makers' quotes are less sensitive to an increase in their inventory positions than slow ones.

2.3.3 Adverse Selection

Speed allows traders to get information and use it faster, possibly at the expense of slower traders. For instance, consider the arrival of positive news for the S&P500 index. Dealers in the E-Mini futures mark up their quotes, while liquidity providers in ETFs on the S&P500 are slow in doing so. In this scenario, a high frequency trader who observes the quote update in the E-Mini

[24] Foucault et al., 'Liquidity cycles', 2014.
[25] Bongaerts et al., 'Trading speed competition', 2016.
[26] Ait-Sahalia and Sağlam, 'High frequency market making: Optimal quoting', 2017.
[27] As, e.g. in Ho and Stoll, 'Dynamics of dealer markets', 1983.
[28] Ait-Sahalia and Sağlam, 2017.   [29] Brogaard et al., 2015.   [30] Ibid.

futures can make a profit by buying the ETFs at stale quotes. This profit is obtained at the expense of dealers in the ETFs' market.

This source of adverse selection (known as 'picking off', 'sniping', or 'free option' risk) is due to differentials in speeds of reaction to news. It is by no way specific to modern markets. Speculators buying advance information on news from Daniel Craig in the nineteenth century (see Section 2.2.2) were already exploiting a faster access to news.[31] However, automation of the trading process and the considerable increase in the speed at which traders can react to news has made picking off risk for liquidity providers much more acute. Accordingly several theoretical papers have analysed how the acceleration of access and reaction to news (broadly defined, i.e. including quote updates for instance) affects adverse selection costs in financial markets.[32]

Liquidity providers can reduce their exposure to picking off risk by better monitoring the flow of news and cancelling their quotes when they become stale, before they are lifted by other traders ('quote snipers'). News arrival is therefore followed by a race between traders attempting to lift stale quotes before they are cancelled and liquidity providers attempting to cancel their quotes before they are picked off. This race is one reason why cancellations-to-trade ratios have considerably increased in recent years and has been one driver of the massive investment in speed observed in the industry.[33]

Consequently the net effect of an increase in trading speed on adverse selection costs depends on whether it makes liquidity providers relatively faster than quote snipers (directional traders or arbitrageurs) or vice versa. For instance, in Foucault et al.,[34] an increase in arbitrageurs' speed *relative* to dealers raises adverse selection costs, while a decrease in their relative speed decreases adverse selection costs.

Ultimately, which effect dominates is an empirical question. Several empirical papers present support for the prediction that an increase in trading speed can raise adverse selection costs. Chakrabarty et al.[35] consider the SEC ban on unfiltered market access (so called 'naked access'). This ban is a negative shock on high frequency traders' speed of access to the market because unfiltered access enabled them to directly connect to exchange servers, thereby bypassing brokerage controls. Moreover, it did not affect traders registered

---

[31] See Copeland and Galai, 'Information effects', 1983, and Foucault et al., 'Market making', 2003, for other examples and models of the picking off risk that predate the development of high frequency trading.

[32] Hoffman, 'Dynamic limit order market', 2014; Biais et al., 'Equilibrium fast trading', 2015; Budish et al., 2015; Jovanovic and Menkvel, 'Middlemen', 2016; Foucault et al., 'News trading and speed', 2016; Foucault et al., 'Toxic arbitrage', 2017; Menkveld and Zoican, 'Need for speed?', 2017.

[33] For models of investements in speed, see Foucault et al., 'Market making with costly monitoring', 2003; Biais et al., 'Equilibrium fast trading', 2015; Budish et al., 2015; Foucault et al., 'Toxic arbitrage', 2017.

[34] Foucault et al., 'Toxic arbitrage', 2017.

[35] Chakrabarty et al., 'Speed of market access', 2015.

as broker-dealers. Hence, a ban on naked access most likely affected high frequency traders that are not specialized in market making. Consistent with the view that fast trading by HFT can raise adverse selection costs, Chakrabarty et al.[36] find that the unfiltered access ban is associated with a significant drop in adverse selection costs and accordingly a drop in trading costs. Foucault et al.[37] consider a technological change that increases arbitrageurs' relative speed in the foreign exchange market and find that this shock results in an increase in adverse selection costs. In a similar vein, Shkilko and Sokolov[38] show that rain precipitation, which slows down the microwave transmission of information between Chicago and New York, result in a decrease in adverse selection costs in ETFs traded in New York. Again, this finding suggests that slowing down arbitrageurs or directional traders who are exploiting lagged adjustments of prices across markets reduces adverse selection. Brogaard et al.[39] show that high frequency traders' short selling activity has a negative effect on liquidity because high frequency traders raise adverse selection for other market participants.

There is also evidence that improving the speed at which liquidity providers can cancel their quotes is associated with improvements in liquidity and a reduction in adverse selection costs. For instance, Hendershott, Jones, and Menkveld[40] find that the introduction of Autoquote on the NYSE (which allows liquidity suppliers to become more quickly informed about changes in the limit order book) is associated with an improvement in liquidity. Brogaard et al.[41] show that market makers become significantly better at avoiding adverse selection after upgrading their co-location with NASDAQ OMX. Biais et al.[42] also find that fast traders provide liquidity without making losses.

2.3.4 Competition

Speed intensifies competition among liquidity providers. Indeed, fast feedback on the state of the limit order book allows market makers to quickly identify profitable trading opportunities for two reasons. First, time priority has value in limit order book markets. Indeed, price discreteness (a non-zero tick) implies that limit orders placed ahead of the queue at a given quote in the book are more profitable than limit orders placed further in the queue, as implied by models such as Glosten, Parlour and Seppi, and Foucault and

---

[36] Ibid.   [37] Foucault et al., 'Toxic arbitrage', 2017.   [38] Shkilko and Sokolov, 2016.
[39] Brogaard et al., 'High frequency trading and the 2008 Short Sale Ban', 2017.
[40] Hendershott et al., 'Does algorithmic trading improve liquidity?', 2011.
[41] Brogaard et al., 'Trading fast and slow', 2015.
[42] Biais et al., 'Who supplies liquidity?', 2015.

Menkveld.[43] Thus, after a transient increase in the bid-ask spread due to the arrival of one market order, liquidity suppliers have an incentive to race to be first to supply liquidity at price points at which liquidity has vanished. Faster traders are more likely to win this race and to pocket the rents associated with time priority.[44] The value of time priority is higher in stocks with larger tick sizes (as predicted by models such as Glosten, Parlour and Seppi, Foucault and Menkveld, and Foucault et al.).[45] Thus, high frequency market makers should be particularly active in stocks with large tick size. Consistent with this prediction, Yao and Ye[46] find that HFTs provide a larger fraction of liquidity in stocks with relatively large tick sizes.

Second, and relatedly, fast reaction to a change in the limit order book enables market makers to undercut their competitors' quotes more quickly. Thus, when market makers receive quicker feedback on the state of the book (e.g. because they can observe it more frequently), quotes become competitive more quickly.[47]

In sum, an increase in the speed at which liquidity providers react to the limit order book should intensify competition among liquidity providers and thereby improve liquidity. There is yet little empirical evidence on this channel. Brogaard et al.[48] find that constraints on short selling activity by high frequency traders *increases* competition among liquidity providers, which goes against the idea that their presence enhances competition. More empirical research is needed on this question.

2.3.5 Net Effects on Market Liquidity and Efficiency

Overall, evaluation of these channels suggests that the effects of speed on the costs of liquidity provision are complex. An increase in speed can increase adverse selection costs for liquidity suppliers while increasing competition among liquidity providers and reducing their inventory holding costs. Empirical studies should therefore carefully analyse the effects of changes in trading speeds (due for instance to technological upgrades) on *each* component of bid-ask spreads separately.[49] Theory predicts that the effect on adverse selection

---

[43] Glosten, 1994; Parlour and Seppi, 'Liquidity-based competition', 2003; Foucault and Menkveld, 'Competition for order flow', 2008.

[44] See, for instance, Foucault and Menkveld, 2008, Section V.B.

[45] Glosten, 1994; Parlour and Seppi, 2003; Foucault and Menkveld, 2008; Foucault et al., 'Liquidity cycles', 2014.

[46] Yao and Ye, 'Why trading speed matters', 2017.

[47] Cordella and Foucault, 'Minimum price variations', 1999; Bongaerts and Van Achter, 'High-frequency trading', 2016.

[48] Brogaard et al., 'High frequency trading and the 2008 Short Sale Ban', 2017.

[49] Bid-ask spreads in financial markets can be split into three components: (1) adverse selection costs, (2) inventory costs, and (3) order processing costs. See Foucault et al., *Market Liquidity*, 2013, Chapter 5, for empirical techniques used to estimate each cost.

costs should be positive, while the effect on inventory holding costs and order processing costs (which also include rents for liquidity providers) should be negative. Hence, the net effect on transaction costs is theoretically ambiguous and might vary across samples. This might explain why conclusions of empirical studies regarding the effect of high frequency trading on liquidity are not clear-cut.

Speed can also affect the pricing efficiency of securities markets. It is intuitively apparent that accelerating the flow of information on trades and prices help to make markets better integrated, i.e. it brings prices more quickly in line with no arbitrage relationships. Garbade and Silber[50] show that the introduction of the telegraph in the US had exactly this effect. In a similar vein, Chaboud et al.[51] show that the introduction of algorithmic trading on foreign exchange trading platforms has made triangular arbitrage opportunities in currencies markets more short-lived. Brogaard, Hendershott, and Riordan[52] also find that high frequency traders' orders tend to reduce noise in prices, making the latter closer to a random walk.

The social benefit of the gains in pricing efficiency brought up by super-fast communication lines between markets is not clear, however. Price differentials for identical assets across markets suggest that gains from trade are not exploited. For instance, if a trader is willing to buy an asset in market A at a price higher than the price at which the asset is offered by another trader in market B, both traders should trade together. By buying the asset in market B and selling it in market A, arbitrageurs correct the price differential and help traders located in different markets to realize gains from trade.[53] Doing so at the 'speed of light' is valuable only if traders highly discount the time required for realizing gains from trade. More evidence is needed on this question.

Moreover, although high frequency trading makes prices more efficient, it does not necessarily make prices more informative. In fact, high frequency traders' ability to quickly extract signals from order flows (trades and price changes) could increase the rate at which informed investors' informational advantage ('alpha') decays. If this is the case, then high frequency trading might reduce the profitability of producing fundamental information and thereby make asset prices less informative about firms' future cash-flows in the long run.[54] Consistent with this prediction, Weller[55] finds a negative association between algorithmic trading activity in a stock and the informativeness of the stock price about future earnings.

---

[50] Garbade and Silber, 1978.   [51] Chaboud et al., 2014.

[52] Brogaard et al., 'High frequency trading and price discovery', 2014.

[53] Foucault et al., 'Toxic arbitrage', 2017.

[54] See Dugast and Foucault, 'Data abundance', 2017, and Draus, 'High frequency trading', 2017, for formal analyses of this possibility in the broader context of automated information processing.

[55] Weller, 2017.

2.4 Are Financial Markets Too Fast or Too Slow?

Concerns about the speed at which trading takes place in financial markets has triggered several proposals to slow down trading in financial markets (see the Introduction to this chapter). Implicit in these proposals is the view that market forces alone cannot set the right level of trading speed and that trading speed is excessive for social welfare. Hence, regulatory intervention is needed. What are the market failures that justify such intervention?

This is a difficult question. As explained previously, investment in speed by some traders generates gains for these traders, possibly at the expense of other traders. For instance, traders who get faster access to information make profits at the expense of liquidity providers who are slow to update their quotes when new information arrives. Market makers who are fast in obtaining time priority capture a larger fraction of the rents associated with time priority at the expense of slower market makers. In these examples, investment in speed redistributes trade gains from slow to fast traders. However, per se, this transfer is not sufficient to conclude that fast traders should be slowed down, unless one takes the view that slow traders' welfare is more important than that of fast traders.

A stronger case for regulating speed in financial markets requires us to ask (1) why market forces will not lead to the optimal level of speed from a social welfare viewpoint and (2) whether markets are too fast or too slow relative to this social optimum. These are complex questions. To address them, one must develop economic models endogenizing both the demand for speed by investors and the supply of speed by trading platforms, information sellers (such as Bloomberg or Thomson-Reuters), or infrastructure providers (e.g. providers of antennas for microwave transmission). Some recent models, discussed below, have made progress in this direction but more research is needed in this area.

Pagnotta and Philippon[56] is a good example of such a model. They analyse how trading platforms compete on speed. In their model, the speed of trading on a platform determines the rate at which buyers and sellers are matched. Thus, Pagnotta and Philippon[57] focus on the provision of matching speed and on the search benefit of speed. They show that trading platforms relax competition by choosing different speed levels, thereby attracting different clienteles (as in models of vertical differentiation). The equilibrium is such that the levels of speed chosen by competing platforms is in general too *low* compared to the level that would maximize welfare. The reason is that choosing a low speed is a way for a trading platform to differentiate from a faster market and

---

[56] Pagnotta and Philippon, 2018. [57] Ibid.

retain market power. Pagnotta and Philippon's model,[58] however, does not consider the role of informational speed.

Biais et al. and Budish et al.[59] develop models in which traders can make investments to increase their speed of access to information. In Biais et al.,[60] traders differ in their private valuations for a risky asset, so that gains from trade exist. Each trader can choose, before learning his private valuation for the asset, to invest in a trading technology to obtain (1) fast access to information about the payoff of the asset (e.g. incoming news about earnings for a stock) and (2) fast access to trading opportunities. That is, the trading technology enables traders to acquire both informational and matching speed. In this setting, an increase in the mass of fast traders has an ambiguous effect on aggregate welfare. On the one hand, speed has a search benefit: it enables fast traders to find a counterparty more quickly.[61] This is valuable because traders are impatient, so that they value more gains from trades realized earlier than later. On the other hand, as the mass of fast traders increases, adverse selection increases. As a result, bid-ask spreads charged by liquidity providers become larger and, for this reason, some traders optimally abstain from trading (to avoid trading costs). This is a social loss that adds to the real costs of the trading technology. The socially optimal level of investment in speed balances the search benefit of speed with the adverse selection cost of speed and the technological cost. This level is in general strictly positive (i.e. allowing some traders to trade fast is socially optimal).

However, the equilibrium level of investment in speed exceeds the socially optimal level. Indeed, in making their decision to invest in speed, traders balance the speculative and search benefits they can obtain by becoming fast with the cost of being fast (e.g. co-location fees, technological investments, etc.) but they do not internalize the negative externality of their decision (their effect on adverse selection cost) on other traders. This negative externality generates a welfare loss because higher adverse selection costs ultimately lead more investors to abstain from trading.

In sum, Biais et al.[62] suggest two market failures that can justify the regulation of trading speed in securities markets. First, asymmetric information raises adverse selection costs and thereby prevents traders from maximizing gains from trade. Second, investors do not internalize the negative externality that their investment speed imposes on other market participants. So there is excessive investment in speed from a social standpoint. Budish et al.[63] reach a similar conclusion in a model in which speed is only a way to get quicker

[58] Ibid.   [59] Biais et al., 'Equilibrium fast trading', 2015; Budish et al., 2015.
[60] Biais et al., 'Equilibrium fast trading', 2015.   [61] As in Pagnotta and Philippon, 2018.
[62] Biais et al., 'Equilibrium fast trading', 2015.   [63] Budish et al., 2015.

access to information. In this framework, speed has no social value and any investment in speed is excessive.

As regulatory intervention, Biais et al.[64] propose a Pigovian tax on investment in speed as a way to align private decisions with the social optimum. By contrast, Budish et al.[65] propose a change in the organization of electronic markets, moving from continuous limit order books to batch auctions (uniform double-sided price auctions) run at frequent points in time (e.g. every second). They show that such a shift reduces incentives to invest in speed for the sole purpose of picking off ('sniping') stale quotes after news arrival. As a result, liquidity is improved and investment in speed is closer to the social optimum (zero in their model).

2.5 Conclusion

Theory and evidence suggest that informational speed (fast access to information) can be harmful for market quality and welfare: it raises adverse selection costs for slow traders, leading to less trading and potentially to wasteful investments in speed. However, theory also suggests that trading speed has benefits: it intensifies competition among liquidity providers, lowers their inventory holding costs, and expedites the search for trading counterparties.

Evidence on the magnitude of these benefits is scarce so far. It is often claimed that high frequency traders have reduced trading costs. However, direct empirical evidence that this is the case is limited and, in any case, the exact channels (inventory holding costs, monitoring, competition, etc.) through which this happened are still not well understood.[66]

One reason is due to specific data challenges. Consider inventory holding costs first and the conjecture that they are smaller for high frequency traders, other things being equal (i.e. holding inventory size constant). Ideally, one would like to estimate inventory holding costs for high frequency and non-high frequency market makers and compare them (again, other things being equal). Estimating inventory holding costs, however, requires data on dealers inventories.[67] Unfortunately, to our knowledge, there is yet no long time series of individual inventories for a cross-section of high frequency and non-high frequency market makers. Indeed, one would need to observe all

---

[64] Biais et al., 'Equilibrium fast trading', 2015.   [65] Budish et al., 2015.

[66] Moreover, some channels can simultaneously have positive and negative effects on trading costs. For instance, entry by high frequency traders can both increase competition between liquidity suppliers (which reduces trading costs) and raise adverse selection costs for slower traders (which increases adverse selection costs). In order to have a good understanding of high frequency trading, therefore, it is very important to measure each effect separately.

[67] For estimations of inventory holding costs for non-high frequency market makers, see Hendershott and Menkveld, 'Price pressures', 2014, and references therein.

the trades made by each market maker in all the different platforms to be able to compute the consolidated inventory. It is not clear that market makers (whether slow or fast) would be willing to provide such data to researchers. Now, consider competition among liquidity providers. Ideally, one would like to analyse how entry by high frequency market makers intensifies competition among liquidity providers and reduces bid-ask spreads. However, identifying the causal impact of such entry is difficult because high frequency traders endogenously choose to be active or not in a given market or under specific market conditions. Empiricists must therefore rely on 'natural experiments', i.e. events that trigger 'exogenous' entries or exits of high frequency traders (i.e. entries or exits unrelated to unobserved variables that could also affect liquidity or price efficiency). Good experiments of this type are rare.[68] In either case (inventory costs or competition), researchers should also be able to identify high frequency traders and non-high frequency traders. Some existing datasets allow such identification to some extent but for limited periods of time.

A second, maybe more serious, problem is that some of the benefits of high frequency trading, in particular the utility benefit of reduction in search time, are intrinsically difficult to measure in electronic limit order markets. In contrast to liquidity or price efficiency, there are no easily observable proxies for improvements in gains from trade due to reduction in search frictions in electronic markets. Moreover, it is not even clear that standard measures of liquidity such as bid-ask spreads and market depth constitute good proxies for gains from trade.[69] To overcome this problem, researchers could rely on structural estimation of models of trading in limit order markets.[70] This approach could potentially allow empiricists to quantify the welfare gains or costs of increasing trading speed in securities markets and to propose regulatory actions to control it.

References

Ait-Sahalia, Yacine, and Mehmet Sağlam. 'High frequency market making: optimal quoting'. Available at: https://ssrn.com/abstract=2674767. Working paper, Princeton University, 2017.
Baldauf, Markus, and Joshua Mollner. 'High-frequency trading and market performance'. Available at: https://ssrn.com/abstract=267476. Working paper, 2017.

---

[68] For examples, see Brogaard and Garriott, 'High frequency trading competition', 2018; Breckenfelder, 'Competition among high frequency traders', 2017.
[69] Dugast, 'Inefficient market depth', 2017.
[70] As, for instance, Hollifield et al., 'Estimating the gains', 2006.

Biais, Bruno, Fany Declerck, and Sophie Moinas. 'Who supplies liquidity, how and when?' Working paper, Bank for International Settlements, 2015.

Biais, Bruno, Thierry Foucault, and Sophie Moinas. 'Equilibrium fast trading'. *Journal of Financial Economics* 116, no. 2 (2015): 292–313.

Boehmer, Ekkehart, Dan Li, and Gideon Saar. 'The competitive landscape of high-frequency trading firms'. Forthcoming *Review of Financial Studies*.

Bongaerts, Dion, and Mark Van Achter. 'High-frequency trading and market stability'. Available at: https://ssrn.com/abstract=2698702. Working paper, 2016.

Bongaerts, Dion, Lingtian Kong, and Mark Van Achter. 'Trading speed competition: Can the arms race go too far?' Available at: https://ssrn.com/abstract=2779904. Working paper, 2016.

Breckenfelder, Johannes. 'Competition between high frequency traders, and market quality'. Working paper, European Central Bank, 2017.

Brogaard, Jonathan, and Correy Garriott. 'High frequency trading competition'. *Journal of Financial and Quantitative Analysis*, forthcoming (2018).

Brogaard, Jonathan, Björn Hagströmer, Lars Nordèn, and Ryan Riordan. 'Trading fast and slow: Colocation and liquidity'. *Review of Financial Studies* 28, no. 12 (2015): 3407–43.

Brogaard, Jonathan, Terrence Hendershott, and Ryan Riordan. 'High frequency trading and price discovery'. *Review of Financial Studies* 27, no. 8 (2014): 2267–306.

Brogaard, Jonathan, Terrence Hendershott, and Ryan Riordan. 'High frequency trading and the 2008 Short Sale Ban'. *Journal of Financial Economics* 124, no. 1 (2017): 22–42.

Budish, Eric, Peter Cramton, and John Shim. 'The high-frequency trading arms race: Frequent batch auctions as a market design response'. *Quarterly Journal of Economics* 130, no. 4 (2015): 1547–621.

Chaboud, Alain, Benjamin Chiquoine, Erik Hjalmarsson, and Clara Vega. 'Rise of the machines: Algorithmic trading in the foreign exchange market'. *Journal of Finance* 69, no. 5 (2014): 2045–84.

Chakrabarty, Bidisha, Pankaj K. Jain, Andriy Shkilko, and Konstantin Sokolov. 'Speed of market access and market quality: Evidence from the SEC naked access ban'. Working paper, Wilfrid Laurier University, 2015.

Copeland, Thomas E., and Dan Galai. 'Information effects on the bid-ask spread'. *Journal of Finance* 38, no. 5 (1983): 1457–69.

Cordella, Tito, and Thierry Foucault. 'Minimum price variations, time priority, and quote dynamics'. *Journal of Financial Intermediation* 8, no. 3 (1999): 141–73.

Draus, Sarah. 'High frequency trading and fundamental trading'. Working paper, Paris Dauphine University, 2017.

Dugast, Jérôme. 'Inefficient market depth'. Available at: https://ssrn.com/abstract=3075940. Working Paper, 2017.

Dugast, Jérôme, and Thierry Foucault. 'Data abundance and asset price informativeness'. *Journal of Financial Economics*, forthcoming.

Fischel, Daniel, and David Ross. 'Should the law prohibit manipulation?' *Harvard Law Review* 105 (1991): 503–53.

Foucault, Thierry, and Albert Menkveld. 'Competition for order flow and smart order routing systems'. *Journal of Finance* 63, no. 1 (2008): 119–58.

Foucault, Thierry, Johan Hombert, and Ioanid Rosu. 'News trading and speed'. *Journal of Finance* 71, no. 1 (2016): 335–82.

Foucault, Thierry, Ohad Kadan, and Eugene Kandel. 'Liquidity cycles and make/take fees in electronic markets'. *Journal of Finance* 68, no. 1 (2014): 299–341.

Foucault, Thierry, Roman Kozhan, and Wing Wah Tham. 'Toxic arbitrage'. *Review of Financial Studies* 30, no. 4 (2017): 1053–94.

Foucault, Thierry, Marco Pagano, and Ailsa Röell. *Market Liquidity: Theory, Evidence, and Policy*. New York: Oxford University Press, 2013.

Foucault, Thierry, Ailsa Röell, and Patrik Sandås. 'Market making with costly monitoring: An analysis of the SOES controversy'. *Review of Financial Studies* 16, no. 2 (2003): 345–84.

Garbade, Kenneth, and William Silber. 'Technology, communication and the performance of financial markets: 1840–1975'. *Journal of Finance* 33, no. 3 (1978): 819–32.

Glosten, Lawrence. 'Is the electronic open limit order book inevitable?' *Journal of Finance* 49, no. 4 (1994): 1127–61.

Hendershott, Terrence, and Albert Menkveld. 'Price pressures'. *Journal of Financial Economics* 114, no. 3 (2014): 405–23.

Hendershott, Terrence, and Ryan Riordan. 'Algorithmic trading and the market for liquidity'. *Journal of Financial and Quantitative Analysis* 48, no. 4 (2013): 1001–24.

Hendershott, Terrence, Charles Jones, and Albert Menkveld. 'Does algorithmic trading improve liquidity?' *Journal of Finance* 66, no. 1 (2011): 1–33.

Ho, Thomas, and Hans Stoll. 'The dynamics of dealer markets under competition'. *Journal of Finance* 38, no. 4 (1983): 1053–74.

Hoag, Christopher. 'The Atlantic telegraph cable and capital market information flows'. *Journal of Economic History* 66, no. 2 (2006): 342–53.

Hoffman, Peter. 'A dynamic limit order market with fast and slow traders'. *Journal of Financial Economics* 113, no. 1 (2014): 298–302.

Hollifield, Burton, R. A. Miller, Patrick Sandås, and J. Slive. 'Estimating the gains from trade in limit order markets'. *Journal of Finance* 61, no. 6 (2006): 2753–804.

Jain, Pankaj K. 'Financial market design and the equity market premium: Electronic versus floor trading'. *Journal of Finance* 60, no. 6 (2005): 2956–85.

Jovanovic, Boyan, and Albert Menkvel. 'Middlemen in limit-order markets'. Available at: https://ssrn.com/abstract=1624329. Working paper, 2016.

Kirilenko, Andrei, Albert S. Kyle, Mehrdad Samadi, and Tugkan Tuzun. 'The flash crash: High-frequency trading in an electronic market'. *Journal of Finance* 72, no. 3 (2017): 967–98.

Kozhan, Roman, and Wing Wah Tham. 'Execution risk in high-frequency arbitrage'. *Management Science* 58, no. 11 (2012): 2131–49.

Kyle, Albert S., and S. Viswanathan. 'How to define illegal price manipulation?' *American Economic Review* 98, no. 2 (2008): 274–9.

Lescourret, Laurence, and Sophie Moinas. 'Fragmentation and strategic market-making'. Available at: https://ssrn.com/abstract=2498277. Working paper, 2017.

Lewis, Michael. *Flash Boys: A Wall Street Revolt*. New York: W.W. Norton & Company, 2014.

Menkveld, Albert. 'High frequency trading and the new market makers'. *Journal of Financial Markets* 16, no. 4 (2013): 712–40.

Menkveld, Albert, and Marius Zoican. 'Need for speed? Exchange latency and liquidity'. *Review of Financial Studies* 30, no. 4 (2017): 1188–28.

Miller, Rena S., and Gary Shorter. *High Frequency Trading: Overview of Recent Developments*. Congressional Research Service, 2016.

Pagnotta, Emiliano, and Thomas Philippon. 'Competing on speed'. Forthcoming *Econometrica*.

Parlour, Christine, and Duane Seppi. 'Liquidity-based competition for order flow'. *Review of Financial Studies* 16, no. 2 (2003): 301–43.

Shkilko, Andriy, and Konstantin Sokolov. 'Every cloud has a silver lining: Fast trading, microwave connectivity and trading costs'. Available at: https://ssrn.com/abstract=2848562. Working paper, 2016.

U.S. Commodity Future Trading Commission vs. Nav Sarao Futures Limited PLC and Navinder Singh Sarao. *Complaint for injunctive relief, civil monetary penalties, and other equitable relief*. Available at: https://www.cftc.gov/sites/default/files/idc/groups/pub lic/@lrenforcementactions/documents/legalpleading/enfsaraoorder110916.pdf, 2015.

Van Kervel, Vincent. 'Competition for order flow with fast and slow traders'. *Review of Financial Studies* 28, no. 7 (2015): 2094–127.

Wall Street Journal. 'Wall Street, 1889: The telegraph ramps up trading speed'. *Wall Street Journal*. Available at: https://www.wsj.com/articles/wall-street-1889-the-telegraph-ramps-up-trading-speed-1404765917. 7 July 2014.

Weller, Brian M. 'Does algorithmic trading deter information acquisition?' *Review of Financial Studies* 31, no 6 (2018): 2184–226.

Yao, Chen, and Mao Ye. 'Why trading speed matters: A tale of queue rationing under price controls'. *Review of Financial Studies* 31, no. 6 (2017): 2157–83.

Zhang, Sarah. 'Need for speed: Hard information processing in a high-frequency world'. *Journal of Futures Markets* 38, no. 1 (2018): 3–21.

3

A Case Study in Regulatory Arbitrage and Information Asymmetry

High Frequency Trading and the Post Only Intermarket Sweep Order

Haim Bodek

3.1 Introduction

For nearly a decade, the high frequency trading (HFT) industry successfully obfuscated the essential role played by regulatory arbitrage, by the exploitation of grey areas of regulation, and even by nontransparent advantages based on selectively disclosed features that resulted in the success of many of its key strategies, and apparently convinced the rest of the industry, the financial press, and academia that the HFT 'edge' was purely technological in nature and based on the much-touted quantitative prowess and speed.

When I approached the US Securities and Exchange Commission (hereinafter SEC) in the summer of 2011 alleging that several exchanges had accommodated HFT strategies by introducing special order types and order matching engine features that enhanced profits with artificial advantages, I did not fully recognize that my contribution would extend far beyond alerting the regulators to the tricks of the trade, so to speak. The order type controversy, as it is now generally known, ended up sparking a market reform debate that to date has resulted in a multi-year special order type investigation of every major equities exchange by the SEC, extensive coverage by the *Wall Street Journal*, two record-tying fines against securities exchanges, a major—and still ongoing—class action lawsuit against a group of exchanges, and hundreds of pages of order-type-related disclosures in the Federal Register.

Nearly seven years later, one big question looms about the significance of the order type controversy. How did the relatively obscure topic of special order types, which many have considered to be mere nuances of market plumbing, unfold into a mix of regulatory changes, legal actions, and even a matter of interest to the general public? What was so compelling and controversial about features that high frequency traders (HFTs) were able to obtain, if not demand, from major exchanges, as implemented in their trading systems? Certainly, many observers have viewed these issues as 'first world' problems, perhaps indicative of the maturity, success, and sophistication of our markets compared to those of less financially developed countries. However, as the order type controversy has continued to expose deep asymmetries in the US equity markets, regulators in Australia, Canada, Germany, and other nations have started to question the unintended consequences of Regulation NMS (SEC 2005),[1] a pivotal regulation governing equities markets in the United States, as well as the ability of the US regulators to rein in what I have called the 'problem of HFT'. And, finally, a central question remains: has the order type controversy been resolved in a satisfactory manner?

From my perspective, the order type controversy is best understood as a cautionary tale of how regulations that were meant to serve and protect the investing public were systematically undermined by self-regulating and yet deeply conflicted exchanges that sought to provide advantages to their highest-volume HFT customers, which in some cases were equity holders or held board positions on such exchanges. As the groundbreaking SEC action against Direct Edge's HFT-oriented order types in 2015 demonstrates, HFT firms, with exchange assistance, had created an artificial edge by distorting the very regulations aimed at protecting the investing public against such an edge.

What was the role of the US regulators in the order type controversy, including its origins, the circulation of information, and the regulatory response to it? The 'revolving door' phenomenon involving the regulatory community and the industry has certainly played a role. Securities lawyers, many of them with an SEC pedigree, were certainly at the centre of the action. Ex-regulators hired by top HFTs or those inside exchanges themselves who were submitting rule filings with what arguably amounted to misrepresentations of introduced features are largely to blame for the extensive list of undocumented order type features and order matching engine practices that I provided to the SEC. At the regulatory agency itself, there were champions both in the Division of Enforcement and the Office of Compliance Inspections and Examinations who sought to pull back a decade of HFT manoeuvring. On the other hand, the

---

[1] SEC, *Regulation NMS—Final Rule*, 2005.

Division of Trading and Markets, another key unit at the SEC that handles, among other things, approval of exchange rulemaking, appeared to have been heavily influenced by the arguments made by industry in the course of the order type investigations, at times giving its stamp of approval to rules that retroactively legitimized exchange features that had operated on an undisclosed basis to the benefit of HFTs for a number of years.

In the end, given a hard-to-ignore request by SEC Chairman Mary Jo White to the exchanges to proceed with 'appropriate rule changes to help clarify the nature of their order types and how they interact with each other, and how they support fair, orderly, and efficient markets',[2] hundreds of features were ultimately disclosed by the exchanges in 'clarifications' submitted as rule filings. Of the problematic features I had alerted the SEC about, only a few were required to be backed out or were voluntarily retired by the exchanges while under investigation. It appears that it was not impermissible to have highly technical advantages built into the market for preferred HFT customers: these advantages just could not be hidden. Even Direct Edge's infamous 'Hide Not Slide' functionality was censured not for 'queue-jumping' or the other advantages built into it to benefit two HFTs that designed its features, but simply for 'failing to file proposed rules and proposed rule changes that completely and accurately described [the relevant functionalities]' and for 'not complying with [the exchanges'] own rules'.[3] As it turned out, the SEC essentially determined that it was not improper for an exchange to favour one type of participant over another in the mechanics of its market structure: it just had to disclose the relevant mechanics and present them for regulatory approval.

3.2 The Order Type Controversy

As I have noted, in 2011 I approached the SEC detailing the advantages based on order types and making the claim that the exchanges were providing undisclosed advantages to HFTs by introducing undocumented features into inadequately disclosed order types, particular with regard to interaction between HFT orders and orders typically used by institutional investors. Following my contact with the SEC, all major exchanges were investigated from 2011 to 2015. The SEC investigation conducted by the Division of Enforcement was initially reported by the press in 2012. The extent of the investigations reaching BATS, Direct Edge, and HFT firms Getco and Tradebot was publicly announced by the *Wall Street Journal* on 23 March 2012,[4]

---

[2] SEC, *Speech by Mary Jo White*, 2014.
[3] SEC, *Order . . . in the Matter of EDGA Exchange*, 2015, 18.
[4] Patterson and Eaglesham, 'SEC probes rapid trading', 2012.

the morning of the infamously botched BATS IPO (initial public offering), though this piece of news on the investigation was certainly overshadowed by the IPO's failure. The investigations of NASDAQ and NYSE were revealed just a few months later.[5] A parallel investigation conducted by the SEC's Office of Compliance Inspections and Examinations was reported by the press in late 2012.[6]

Although the order type controversy made traction as a market reform issue, it was discouraging to watch it unfold, as the intricacies of order type practices were not immediately understood by wider industry circles and other constituencies. The exchanges and HFTs alike were surely relieved that the sheer complexity of the issues and the extent of technical expertise required to dig into the substance—compounded by informational asymmetries—served as obstacles to articulating a coherent narrative. Even the financial press encountered some impediments in its quest to get answers from exchange officials.[7] One HFT executive, who attempted to convince me to abandon my 'crusade', told me that I could disclose all the details and the buy-side still would fail to 'do their homework' and consequently would neither understand the extent of abuses nor modify their execution behaviour in response. A year later, after a public debate with him on order types at a market structure conference, I told him offline that he was completely right about the industry. The response of sell-side brokers and buy-side investment firms who were on the losing end of the special order type abuses was muted at best, and the industry debate on the significance of special order type advantages was further complicated by the misleading public relations efforts of exchanges and HFT firms that were under investigation.

Over this period, apparent internal disagreements between the SEC's two key units, the Division of Trading and Markets and the Division of Enforcement, on the significance of the order type investigations sent mixed messages to the public, as evident from the following passage:

> A source at the SEC said the most sophisticated exchange users go to great pains to figure order types out. Even if some may benefit certain participants more than others, 'I don't know that there's necessarily fire there', the source said.[8]

However, the tone changed in 2014 when the SEC's leadership started publicly expressing concerns about order type practices and requested the exchanges to evaluate and clarify them through additional disclosure, which greatly intensified the internal cleanup process and led to the pipeline of massive rule filings.

---

[5] Patterson and Strasburg, 'For superfast stock traders', 2012.
[6] Patterson and Eaglesham, 'Exchanges get closer inspection', 2012.
[7] Scotti, 'Exchange order types', 2014.   [8] Lash, 'Complaints rise', 2012.

As another landmark, in early 2015, BATS settled with the SEC for a record $14 million for some of its exchanges' failure to describe orders types accurately while selectively disclosing information to preferred traders. A number of passages from the SEC order are illuminating as an illustration of symbiotic relationships between trading venues and its key customers and the extent of HFT involvement in crafting order types:

> Trading Firm A explained to Direct Edge that in order to generate profits from its trading strategy, which was designed to capture spreads and/or collect rebates offered by trading centers for providing liquidity, it required a high degree of certainty that it could enter and exit individual trades at its intended prices. Trading Firm A informed Direct Edge that one of the ways it sought to achieve such certainty was through its queue position.... Trading Firm A further advised Direct Edge that implementation of such an order type would likely cause it to increase the order flow that it sent to Direct Edge from 4–5 million orders per day to 12–15 million orders per day. Additional order flow would be beneficial to Direct Edge because it would increase its market volume and its revenue.[9]

One of the most important manifestations of the order type controversy is the Post Only ISO (intermarket sweep order), the 'queen bee' of HFT special order types, and the one whose operation for a number of years could not even be verified on the basis of official documentation provided by trading venues. It may seem unusual that Post Only ISOs have not resulted in a perceptible regulatory response, given the existence of numerous regulatory developments, but this situation is not that much different from the multitude of other hidden or inaccurately documented functionalities that simply disappeared without any repercussions or got legitimized ex post with additional disclosure. To date, in the context of market structure oreder types issues, my analysis has contributed to now public and successful enforcement actions against the BATS/Direct Edge[10] and NYSE[11] with the latter being more removed from the HFT space. However, one might note that some enforcement actions against alternative trading systems, a category of non-exchange trading venues that includes 'dark pools', have addressed order type practices as well, such as the settlement with UBS.[12]

At the same time, the same order type practices are currently being targeted by a class action lawsuit against the leading securities exchanges,[13] and this lawsuit has cleared several key procedural hurdles, getting through these exchanges' regulatory immunity and demonstrating the viability of stated allegations.

---

[9] SEC, *Order... in the Matter of EDGA Exchange*, 2015, 7.   [10] Ibid.
[11] SEC, *Order... in the Matter of New York Stock Exchange*, 2018.
[12] SEC, *Order... in the Matter of UBS Securities*, 2015.
[13] City of Providence v. Bats Global Markets, 2017.

Importantly, the allegations in this lawsuit have included an extensive discussion of the Post Only ISO order type and its use by individual exchanges.

3.3 High Frequency Trading and Special Order Types

The implementation of Regulation NMS in 2007 served as the inflection point for the rapid growth of HFT strategies in the US equities space. To properly assess the intimate relationship between the growth of HFT strategies, the regulatory regime change, and the features that exchanges and HFTs introduced into the market in order to gain undisclosed advantages, it is essential to understand the inner workings of HFT strategies and the impact of regulation on their operation. HFTs rely on electronic execution advantages to get an edge over other participants. These advantages include (a) lower-latency access and reaction to changes in market information, (b) the ability to achieve superior queue position in an exchange order book, (c) low-latency detection of trading activity and execution (i.e. assisting in rapid cancellation on market moving events), and (d) superior fee economics as represented in the maker-taker pricing model prevalent in equities.

Simply stated, in the US equities trading environment, HFTs want to be able to place their orders at the top of the book queue, thereby establishing a new price eligible for a rebate under the maker-taker pricing model. Such orders have the highest likelihood of trading, as intended by HFTs, in neutral or favourable conditions. More generally, HFTs seek to avoid adverse selection or being 'picked off'. Naturally, an exchange that provides an environment where HFTs can execute in such conditions is rewarded with increased trading activity. Interestingly, Regulation NMS interfered with HFT order placement into such favourable conditions. However, under competitive pressure, the exchanges addressed these deficiencies by introducing special features that circumvented Regulation NMS in a manner that permitted HFTs to get the advantages they sought. The mechanism through which this goal was accomplished is represented by special order types designed for HFTs.

Regulation NMS's Rule 610 required exchanges to prohibit 'its members from engaging in a pattern or practice of displaying quotations that lock or cross any protected quotation in an NMS stock',[14] which in essence meant prohibiting the acceptance of orders that established a new bid when another exchange was offered at that bid price or lower. However, the precise time to try establishing a high queue position is to place an order to buy at a higher price on an exchange that is not displaying the best offer when the offer price

---

[14] SEC, *Regulation NMS—Final Rule*, 2005.

is 'crumbling' (i.e. the visible liquidity is rapidly diminishing on other exchanges). In other words, HFTs have to lock market or appear to lock market (in the view of slower participants and exchanges' order matching engines) for their strategies in order to achieve a higher queue position. Thus, we have a paradox. Rule 610 effectively prohibits an exchange from accepting orders that aggressively improve the price in its market in precisely the conditions in which HFT signals dictate that it would be beneficial to send such orders to achieve a high queue position. To comply with Rule 610, an exchange must either reject such orders or 'reprice' them to a worse price, both thoroughly unacceptable scenarios for HFTs. In response, HFTs developed 'spam and cancel' strategies that used post-only orders (which are rejected when they would take liquidity) in rapid succession to repeatedly attempt to execute at the same price until it is accepted with a post-only condition, effectively polling the exchange in question at the desired price and tolerating rejections until acceptance. Later on, the exchanges created price-sliding orders that effectively acted as a 'reservation' at the new price, and which would leap ahead of other orders when the HFT's intended price no longer violated Rule 610. The motivation behind this feature was not a secret, although perhaps not obvious to most market participants in the late 2000s:

> BATS, being particularly aggressive with the adoption of special order types that 'hide and light,' summed up quite elegantly the appeal of such order types: 'Display-Price Sliding eliminates the need for traders to retry orders multiple times in rapid succession trying to be high in priority at the next NBBO [National Best Bid and Offer] price.'[15]

Some of these orders provided HFTs with hidden perks such as queue-jumping (i.e. sidestepping price-time priority) which permitted HFTs to leap ahead of price-sliding orders typically used by institutional investors even in cases where an HFT order arrived later in time. Some variations even assisted in converting institutional orders resting on the book from orders eligible for rebates to orders that paid taker fees due to the opaque mechanisms through which various orders interacted with one another during locked market conditions. In fact, when one realizes that all orders in a post-Regulation NMS environment utilized some variation of price-sliding or reject mode to handle orders that did not comply with Rule 610, it becomes apparent that the internal workings of exchange order matching engines were slippery at best, at least when it came to the issue that each exchange had assumed significant discretion over price setting and therefore execution quality.

Rule 610 was not the only inconvenience arising from Regulation NMS. Rule 611 and its trade-through rule had the impact of requiring exchanges to

---

[15] Bodek, *The Problem of HFT*, 2013, 36.

block orders resulting in trade-throughs, i.e. executions at inferior prices compared to the best alternative on other trading venues, unless there was a specific exception provided by that rule. One of the exceptions was the so-called intermarket sweep order (ISO). Originally intended for large institutions with immediacy needs, ISOs were provided for by Regulation NMS for firms that aimed to hit multiple levels of the order book, thus assessing liquidity in an instantaneous manner that would otherwise register as a trade-through.[16]

Although the most basic ISO was associated with the 'immediate or cancel' time-in-force condition, the concept of a Day ISO was also introduced, which allowed a firm to sweep the liquidity and then post at the order limit price. To use a Day ISO, a broker-dealer is required either (a) to show it is not locking or crossing away markets or (b) to sweep markets displaying prices that would otherwise lock or cross. Thus, the Day ISO functionality addresses conditions in which Regulation NMS puts constraints on an order to simultaneously satisfy the ban on locked markets stipulated by Rule 610 and the trade-through rule stipulated by Rule 611.

To grasp the importance of these two prohibitions, one must understand that HFTs use low-latency market data to trade and/or post on the right side of market price movements. If such orders actually or apparently trade through the prevailing market price, Rule 611 would require an exchange to reject such orders. It is not much use paying for an inherently faster direct data feed if your orders are rejected as being in violation of Rule 611. More generally, Rule 611 and the prohibition of trade-throughs interfered with HFTs aiming to execute trades aggressively in fast-moving market conditions when the official consolidated feeds would lag the direct data feeds. Thus Rule 611 hindered the ability of HFTs to access liquidity in the direction of market momentum, as well as their ability to post aggressive prices that appeared to trade-through a stale price on the 'official' data feed provided by the Security Information Processor (SIP).

It should come as no surprise that Rule 611 was transformed from an HFT impediment into an HFT advantage. The exchanges and the SEC permitted the expansion of Rule 611 beyond its initial scope with the concept of *self-determination*, which permitted HFTs to avoid the inconveniences described above that otherwise would have stifled their low-latency advantages. If a firm subscribed to more timely data than the SIP, it was able to utilize the ISO exception and execute at prices that would normally be rejected by exchanges as impermissible, provided it recorded its own 'constructed NBBO' using the direct data feeds, which was presumed to be more accurate than the SIP.

---

[16] To use an ISO, a broker-dealer must attest to compliance with the ISO requirements and sweep out the NBBO on all exchanges using ISOs. A broker-dealer also assumes liability for ensuring that trade-throughs that result from using ISOs in fact qualify for that exception.

This concept of self-determination of a constructed NBBO permitted HFTs to leverage their own calculations of the NBBO and avoid interference from an exchange that would otherwise reject HFT orders when enforcing Rule 611 due to the usage of a less timely NBBO. With this novel concept of self-determination commingled with the ISO exception, HFTs were free to utilize low-latency market data to execute orders on exchanges at prices that other market participants were in fact prohibited from executing at. Thus the ISO order type became an essential part of the HFT order type arsenal.

Hence, HFTs exploit ISOs for regulatory arbitrage purposes to get ahead of slow SIP feeds, a practice outside the scope that was originally anticipated in the definition of the ISO exception. HFTs step ahead of the slow SIP by using ISOs and self-determination of a 'constructed' NBBO that is faster than the SIP based on the best bids and offers from individual exchanges. ISOs permit HFTs to get orders accepted that would otherwise be rejected due to trade-through or locked market restrictions. The ISO exception is especially important in fast-moving market conditions when the SIP lags even more behind the direct data feeds. In many cases, HFTs determine that ISOs can be utilized without sending any marketable orders to away exchanges, a notion completely orthogonal to the original construction of the ISO definition. If those benefits were not enough, the Day ISO order type is in fact more powerful than hide-and-light/reservation orders due to its ability to queue-jump such orders by establishing (i.e. 'lighting') a new price.

Thus, the primary order types useful for HFT strategies are the hide-and-light/reservation order types that incorporate post-only and price-sliding features and the Day ISO and its more complex variations. The hide-and-light order type navigates the problem of Rule 610 and often embeds a reservation feature that permits such orders to light a new price or otherwise queue-jump other market participants, as Direct Edge's 'Hide Not Slide' functionality had accomplished. The second category centred on complex ISO order types that allow an HFT to establish a new aggressive price at the top of the queue (locking or crossing away markets) and also to 'light' (e.g. to activate a displayed price) any hide-and-light orders waiting in a hidden reservation mode.

Latency still matters quite a bit with these order types. To set a new price with a Day ISO, one has to be first, because the Day ISO order type lights the hide-and-light orders prior to the acceptance of the second-fastest Day ISO sent by another market participant, which is placed at the back of the queue behind the first Day ISO and all the lit hide-and-light orders. One problem with the Day ISO is that while it is guaranteed to get to the top of the queue when it sets a new price, it is implemented as a 'sweep and post' order, paying taker fees with any liquidity with which it interacts, such as hidden liquidity which may represent institutional orders or opposing hide-and-light orders. Thus, the Day ISO has a significant penalty in terms of the underlying fee structure risk, as well as an adverse selection bias when it trades against informed parties on the contra side of the trade, participants that tend to use hidden orders and/or hide-and-light orders which may not be displayed at the execution price. As shall be seen in the subsequent sections of this chapter, this material deficiency in the Day ISO was addressed with the Post Only ISO, a more advanced order type that effectively merges two categories of special order types into a super-charged combination. This functionality was discreetly introduced into the market without sufficient regulatory oversight.

The original formulation of Rule 610 and Rule 611 should have resulted in diminished HFT volumes in the US equities market, given the significant interference such regulation should have had with the operation of HFT strategies. However, it is in 2007, which marked the implementation of Regulation NMS, that one can observe an inflection point in the growth of HFT volume which ultimately peaked at approximately 70 per cent. Certainly, Rule 610 and Rule 611 did not interfere with HFTs, but rather dramatically contributed to their edge through the very means by which the exchanges assisted in undermining the purpose and intent of such rules by adopting special order types and order matching engine mechanisms that virtually eliminated the inconveniences presented by Regulation NMS. While the rest of the market naively let their orders be impeded by Rule 610 and Rule 611, HFTs utilized orders that were essentially immune to harmful effects of being denied access to liquidity precisely in the scenario when the market is moving away from a trader's limit price.

3.4 Exchange Conflicts of Interest

When I was first introduced to HFT-oriented features by an exchange representative who encouraged me to utilize them in order to avoid systematic execution slippages, I was struck by the precision with which exchange order matching abuses had been implemented. Not only were HFT order types advantaged in an absolute sense, but significant attention had been put into the interaction between HFT order types and order types typically utilized by institutional traders. This interaction virtually assured that, on average, execution costs (i.e. fees, adverse selection, and slippage) were transferred from HFTs to institutional traders. The order matching engine abuses associated with HFT special order types, some of which I was led to by a hint from that exchange representative, included (a) unfair order handling practices that permitted HFTs to step ahead of investor orders; (b) unfair rebooking and repositioning of investor orders to the back of order book queues; (c) unfair conversion of investor orders eligible for maker rebates into unfavourable executions incurring taker fees; (d) conflicted order matching engine modifications that increased the frequency of HFT intermediation between legitimate customer-to-customer matching; and (e) unfair and discriminatory treatment of investor orders in the order matching process during sudden price movements.

As one technologist who worked for top electronic communication networks (ECNs) and exchanges described the process of accommodating HFTs, 'We spent a tremendous amount of money trying to meet their needs.... It's all about what functionality can I offer the HFT that they can take advantage of. We are going after guaranteed economics.'[17] This was seconded by another insider at a trading venue:

> We created all these different order types to accommodate how they wanted to trade. We tweaked how the order would interact with our book according to what they wanted. A lot of the unique orders were created at the request of a customer, typically a high frequency customer. You had to be a sophisticated customer to learn how to use it.[18]

The advantages built into HFT-oriented special order types shift the execution performance distribution toward a positive mean, which enhances a strategy's consistent profitability over a large number of transactions. These advantages shift fee structures toward rebate capture, convert a greater proportion of stop-loss trades into scratch-outs (exclusive of fees), and reduce adverse selection associated with an inferior queue position. Overall, these features assist in achieving neutral to favourable queue ranking (i.e. avoidance of disadvantaged price sliding). When used as intended, the special order type features and order matching engine practices permit HFTs to access liquidity at prices that would otherwise be inaccessible on the momentum side of a price movement.

The efforts that exchanges put into accommodating HFT strategies is astonishing, resulting in highly complex exchange programming interfaces that were constructed to assist a relatively small number of high-volume HFT firms in setting the best price in the market at the top of the queue, which is the order placement most likely to result in a favourable trade. Post-only orders were provided by these exchanges for 'spam and cancel' strategies that engage in polling with HFT-oriented order types, testing price points between the market bids and offers to see whether an order is price-slid or accepted in an effort to set a new price at the top of the queue. The exchanges subsequently introduced hide-and-light order types that were permitted to lock an away market with a hidden state that would 'light' at the top of the queue when the displayed price was permissible. Day ISO order types were provided to leverage the ISO exception so that HFTs could post aggressive orders during price

---

[17] Patterson, *Dark Pools*, 2013, 204.   [18] Ibid., 205.

changes and 'light' at the top of the queue. These developments were contrary to the broad mandate of Regulation NMS to protect the investing public. In fact, in the adopting release, the SEC emphasized that 'one of the most important goals of the equity markets is to minimize the transaction costs of long-term investors'[19] and pointed to 'the largely hidden costs associated with the prices at which trades are executed [which] often can dwarf the explicit costs of trading' for such investors.[20] Moreover, the regulatory agency articulated the following general principle: 'In those few contexts where the interests of long-term investors directly conflict with short-term trading strategies, we believe that, in implementing regulatory structure reform, the Commission has both the authority and the responsibility to further the interests of long-term investors.'[21]

In sum, the modern electronic marketplace was shaped to create a two-tier ecosystem bifurcating institutional order types that were constrained by Regulation NMS and HFT order types that effectively circumvented the regulatory framework with active exchange assistance. In other words, HFTs did not wait for best bids and offers at all exchanges to move to prices that would ensure compliance with the regulations prohibiting locked and crossed markets or trade-throughs before they placed aggressive orders, as Regulation NMS would have naturally required under Rule 610 and Rule 611. Instead, HFTs were able to exploit the newly created arsenal of complex order types whose ultimate purpose was to overcome the inconvenience of such constraints. In fact, HFTs utilized such order types prior to a tick move to reserve a top-of-the-queue position during price movements using the distorted regulatory framework, all the while attributing their success to speed.

3.5 The Post Only ISO

The Post Only ISO is a super-charged order type that is self-contradictory at best. It embeds the post-only property, which prevents an order from executing in the conditions in which it would act as a liquidity taker and thus incur a fee, either price-sliding the order or rejecting it altogether. At the same time, the Post Only ISO embeds the ISO exception, which Regulation NMS stipulates must meet the following execution requirement:

> Simultaneously with the routing of the limit order identified as an intermarket sweep order, one or more additional limit orders, as necessary, are *routed to execute against* the full displayed size of any protected bid, in the case of a limit order to sell, or the full displayed size of any protected offer, in the case of a limit order to buy,

---

[19] SEC, *Regulation NMS—Final Rule*, 2005, 37, 499.   [20] Ibid., 37, 501.
[21] Ibid., 37, 603.

for the NMS stock with a price that is superior to the limit price of the limit order identified as an intermarket sweep order. These additional routed orders also must be marked as intermarket sweep orders.[22]

Given that the post-only property of the Post Only ISO prevents that order from meeting its obligation to 'execute against the full displayed size of any protected bid [or] protected offer',[23] this feature is clearly a distortion of the purpose and intent of Rule 611. The contradiction between the post-only and ISO properties is blatant, and a common reaction of market participants, when first introduced to this order type, was to deny the very possibility of such an order type in light of these contradictory features. The controversial nature of the Post Only ISO is compounded by the fact that this order type was not disclosed in any meaningful capacity by the exchanges. In some cases, the existence of this order type was denied altogether by exchange employees who were at best unaware that such a functionality had been introduced into their exchanges' trading systems in an effort to appease HFT customers.

The Post Only ISO protects against incurring taker fees and ensuring the post-only property by either price-sliding (i.e. ticking the order back to a permissible price) or rejecting the order altogether if it would have incurred a taker fee by trading against displayed or hidden liquidity. If the order is accepted at its limit price, it can light the new price setting the most favourable queue position. A more sophisticated version, such as that available on NYSE, acts as a reservation order and waits until hidden or displayed liquidity evaporates before jumping ahead to the next price to get to the top of the queue. The Post Only ISO is designed to get to the top of the queue while leveraging self-determination and the 'lighting' behaviour of Day ISOs, all while protecting HFTs from paying taker fees when colliding with resting orders.

The irony is that the Post Only ISO seemingly can pretty much do anything except actually 'sweep' a price, a core principle built into the ISO definition in Regulation NMS. Was the Post Only ISO even evaluated and approved by the regulators? As discussed below, this order type was not comprehensively documented by several exchanges until it had been operational on nearly all exchanges for a number of years, with most of them not complying with basic regulatory approval requirements when this order type was first rolled out. One outcome of the order type controversy is that the first sufficiently documented filing was put forth by NYSE, at that time the only major exchange that did not support the Post Only ISO. For all practical purposes, this filing has been interpreted by other exchanges as giving carte blanche to widespread use of Post Only ISO functionality.

---

[22] Ibid., 37, 621–2 (emphasis added).   [23] Ibid.

At this point—and putting the aside blatant contradictions within this order type—it should be clear that the Post Only ISO was specifically designed to achieve HFT goals of leveraging distortions of Rule 610 and Rule 611 in a single order type. The Post Only ISO is the ultimate 'have your cake and eat it too' order type available in the HFT order type arsenal. I became aware of the Post Only ISO's existence only *after* having operated for some time in a whistleblower capacity on the subject of HFT order types, and I could not until much later verify that the order had been supported on nearly every major exchange. I contend that the Post Only ISO serves as the primary example of an undocumented and selectively disclosed order type in the US equity market during the HFT 'Wild West' era. A posthumous assessment of the Post Only ISO is a fitting endpoint for evaluating the operation of the US equities regulatory regime.

3.5.1 *The Post Only ISO: A Timeline*

I initially became aware of Post Only ISOs during my review of equity market venues in late 2011, first identifying the Post Only ISO order type as being supported on NYSE Arca and shortly thereafter identifying support for that order type on Direct Edge. Although it is hard to determine the exact date of rollout, it is possible that Post Only ISOs were in fact available for use on Direct Edge in 2009, i.e. even before Direct Edge became a registered securities exchange. Over the course of 2012, I revisited source materials at various exchanges, including NYSE Arca, Direct Edge, CHX, NSX, and Lava ECN, in order to determine why the significance of Post Only ISOs had eluded me despite my focus on order types.

Although I had identified support for the Post Only ISO on NYSE Arca and Direct Edge based on their application protocol interface (API) materials, I was unable to confirm that Post Only ISOs were supported on NASDAQ and BATS during this period and in fact received contradictory and misleading information from both exchanges. As subsequently described, I learned in 2013 that both NASDAQ and BATS indeed supported the Post Only ISO order type when these exchanges revealed such support in their order types statistics reports. At the time, it appeared that NASDAQ had provided these order type statistics based on the SEC's investigation into order types. NASDAQ did not formally disclose the operation of the Post Only ISO in any regulatory filing until its 2015 clarification on order types.[24] Similarly, I believed that BATS, just like NASDAQ, had provided its order type statistics based on the SEC's investigation into order types. BATS did not reference the Post Only ISO in its technical

---

[24] SEC, *Notice of a Proposed Rule Change*, 2015, 16, 058.

documentation until September 2014, when it disclosed the 'Post Only Day ISO' in its presentation on order types.[25] Based on my current review of existing materials, it still appears that BATS continued to remain deficient in providing a regulatory filing or adequate technical documentation detailing the functionality of the Post Only ISO.

In the meantime, starting in 2012 and intensifying rather dramatically in 2014, the industry had witnessed 'the phenomenon of comprehensive order-type focused rule filings by equities exchanges', which in fact involved every single exchange, often marketed under the banner of clarification and simpli-fication.[26] As mentioned earlier, a significant number of order type filings related to special order types appear to have been driven at least in part by regulatory scrutiny resulting from the order type investigations. At the same time, the order type settlement with BATS in connection with the pre-merger activities of Direct Edge was concluded and, according to some observers, had resulted in a clean bill of health provided by the regulators,[27] a concerning development when considered in light of the significant volume associated with the opaque and undocumented nature of Post Only ISOs on BATS itself. As will be discussed, the SEC did in fact 'normalize' the Post Only ISO by approving rule filing introduced by the exchanges as self-regulatory organiza-tions, starting with NYSE's rule filing.[28] These actions retroactively provided undeserved legitimacy to what I consider to be the most secretive and power-ful order type provided to HFTs over the period in question.

3.5.2 Regulatory Precedents on NSX and CHX

My research efforts in 2012 led me to the peculiar filings by NSX approved on 24 July 2008[29] and by CHX approved on 6 July 2009,[30] filings which at that time were the only ones I could find that fulfilled exchange obligations to seek regulatory approval for the Post Only ISOs. Given the lack of any regulatory filings concerning the Post Only ISO on NASDAQ, NYSE Arca, BATS, or Direct Edge in 2012, and in conjunction with the verified support of Post Only ISOs on Direct Edge and NYSE Arca, I concluded that the Post Only ISO had been designed much earlier than I had previously been led to believe and that in addition to CHX and NSX, one or more of the major exchanges or other trading venues may have introduced Post Only ISOs even before 2009.

---

[25] BATS, *Order Type Guide*, 2014, 29.
[26] Bodek and Dolgopolov, *The Market Structure Crisis*, 2015, 57–8.
[27] SEC, *Letter from Kathryn A. Pyszka*, 2017.
[28] SEC, *Order Approving Proposed Rule Changes by New York Stock Exchange*, 2014.
[29] SEC, *Notice of Filing . . . National Stock Exchange*, 2008.
[30] SEC, *Notice of Filing . . . Chicago Stock Exchange*, 2009.

The Post Only ISO order types available on NSX and CHX are relatively simple versions that do not incorporate the much more sophisticated price-sliding capability available for NYSE's recent Post Only ISO. Additional colour on the origins of the Post Only ISO is provided by the CHX regulatory filing approved on 6 July 2009, which sought to appeal to precedent. CHX did not explicitly indicate which exchange(s) supported the Post Only ISO in its attempt to gain approval through precedent. Instead, the filing states: 'CHX notes that order types similar to the proposed Post Only and Post Only ISO order types are already in use by other market centers', referring explicitly to NSX, BATS, and NYSE Arca.[31] Perhaps due to its inability to cite any regulatory filing for the major equities exchanges and the possibility that the Post Only ISO was being provided by a major equities exchange venue in 2009 without regulatory approval, CHX chose language which obscured the venues on which the Post Only ISO order type operated or originated and which it sought to reference as precedent, and its references to specific rules of other exchanges commingled traditional Post Only and Post Only ISO order types.

BATS is a more likely candidate of the two major exchanges mentioned by the CHX filing to have had the Post Only ISO order type operational in 2009; there is no public record of when BATS introduced the Post Only ISO into its marketplace. As will be discussed, NYSE Arca appears to have introduced the Post Only ISO in 2010; but it is conceivable that it may have supported it earlier. It is difficult to determine when each of the major exchanges actually released the Post Only ISO in its respective marketplace, given the lack of regulatory filings and the tendency for exchanges to introduce this order type into the marketplace without adequate announcement and circulars.

More interestingly, in 2013—and in the midst of the order type scrutiny— CHX repealed its Post Only ISO order type as being 'simply a limit order marked Post Only and BBO ISO and not a distinct order modifier' and thus 'redundant and unnecessary'.[32] This development is especially concerning in light of the fact that Post Only ISOs are in practice the most advanced and complicated order types in the US equities market, especially when considered in the context of potentially contradictory features in both order handling instructions and regulatory requirements. This fact is thoroughly attested to by the NYSE rule filing in June 2014,[33] which aimed to introduce its own Post Only ISO. Although the Post Only ISO functionality as such was not eliminated, CHX peculiarly sought approval *not to document* the functionality by withdrawing prior documentation through the official rulemaking process, despite the fact that it took place during a period of significant regulatory scrutiny of order types.

---

[31] Ibid.   [32] SEC, *Notice of Filing . . . Chicago Stock Exchange*, 2013, 28, 673.
[33] SEC, *Notice of Filing New York Stock Exchange*, 2014.

Regardless of the validity of CHX's withdrawal of documenting the Post Only ISO in its regulatory filing, it should be noted that both the CHX and NSX versions of the Post Only ISO are simple forms of the order type that incorporate a 'cancel back' response and would require less disclosure in comparison to more sophisticated versions of the Post Only ISO that incorporate price-sliding. The exchanges that support sophisticated versions of the Post Only ISO over this period (apparently NASDAQ and Direct Edge) have a higher burden of regulatory disclosure than exchanges that did not incorporate complex order handling in the Post Only ISO.

3.5.3 *NYSE Arca*

NYSE Arca's Post Only Day ISO Limit order type is an advanced version that incorporates price-sliding features, specialized interactions of aggressively priced orders, and minimum lot size requirements. The Post Only Day ISO Limit order type enjoys a significant presence on NYSE Arca. In December 2017, it was utilized for approximately 4 per cent of matched volume as reflected in NYSE Arca's order type statistics.[34]

According to NYSE Arca API change logs and technical specifications, it appears that the Post Only ISO order type was introduced into the market in early 2010, at which time it was called the PNP ISO ALO order type, which was a basic version of this class of order type that would be rejected if it would take liquidity. However, I have not been able to locate any circular or regulatory filing to support the release of the PNP ISO ALO on NYSE Arca. Furthermore, though I actively traded on NYSE Arca at the time of the rollout, I was not made aware of this release through any communications provided by NYSE Arca despite frequent interactions with its representatives at that time. Admittedly, the technical specifications provided by NYSE Arca on the PNP ISO ALO are significantly more thorough when compared to examples of technical disclosure of Post Only ISOs found on other exchanges. Regardless, NYSE Arca appears to have violated its regulatory obligation to adequately disclose and gain approval for an order type of this sophistication through a regulatory filing and does not appear to have adequately informed its market participants with a technical circular. Irrespective of NYSE Arca's standing relative to other exchanges, my experience and research strongly suggest that NYSE Arca did not comply with its regulatory filing obligations over this period with regard to the Post Only ISO order type. Furthermore, and despite numerous filings on order types, NYSE Arca remained deficient in its regulatory filings for the Post Only ISO for roughly five years.

---

[34] NYSE Arca, *Order Type Usage*, 2018.

It was not until early 2015 that the first mention of the NYSE Arca Post Only ISO order type occurs in regulatory filings with the terse and incomplete description: 'The Exchange further notes that all functionality associated with PNP Orders, including the ability to be designated ISO, are applicable to PNP Orders that are designated ALO.'[35] It is interesting to note that NYSE Arca had already provided significant order type clarifications in 2014 that did not address the Post Only ISO and that NYSE Arca remained delinquent in providing regulatory filings adequately disclosing of the Post Only ISO throughout 2014. Moreover, it was only later in 2015 that NYSE Arca sufficiently disclosed its Post Only ISO in regulatory filings, indicating that it would introduce significant changes to the operation of this order type:

> The Exchange proposes substantive differences for a Day ISO ALO in Pillar to provide that such order would not be rejected if marketable against orders on the NYSE Arca Book and would instead re-price, consistent with how the proposed ALO Order would function in Pillar.[36]

A later rule filing added additional logic to address order interaction of aggressive prices to match the functionality of other exchanges:

> The Exchange proposes to make two substantive changes to how ALO Orders would operate on Pillar: An ALO Order that crosses the working price of any displayed or nondisplayed orders would trade with the resting order(s); and [a]n ALO Order that locks the price of any-sized display order would be re-priced.[37]

To accompany this change, the applicability to the Post Only ISO was addressed as well:

> [T]he Exchange proposes to [provide] that an arriving Day ISO ALO to buy (sell) may trade through or lock or cross a protected quotation that was displayed at the time of arrival of the Day ISO ALO, and would be re-priced or trade, or both.[38]

As will be subsequently highlighted, the issue of interaction of aggressive prices in such scenarios can lead to queue-jumping/price-time priority abuses in connection with the Post Only ISO, an issue that needs to be specifically addressed, as this was done by BATS and NASDAQ during the height of SEC's investigations into order type practices in 2012.

Lastly, given my focus on NYSE Arca order types from 2009 onward, interactions with exchange and industry contacts, and observation of continued deficiencies with regard to regulatory filings and documentation, I believe that

---

[35] SEC, *Notice of Filing . . . NYSE Arca, Inc. to Eliminate Additional Order Type Combinations*, 2015, 12, 539.
[36] SEC, *Notice of Filing . . . NYSE Arca, Inc. Adopting New Equity Trading Rules*, 2015, 45, 037.
[37] SEC, *Notice of Filing . . . NYSE Arca, Inc. Amending Equities Rule 7.31P(e)*, 2016, 35, 416.
[38] Ibid., 35, 418.

the release and introduction of the original version of the Post Only ISO on NYSE Arca, the PNP ISO ALO, was selectively disclosed by NYSE Arca to preferred customers without requisite regulatory filings. More generally, I contend that the exchanges overwhelmingly failed to disclose to all market participants how their respective Post Only ISO order types could be utilized in a manner compliant with Regulation NMS.

3.5.4 Direct Edge

Direct Edge's Post Only ISO order type was originally a complex version incorporating a variety of configurable price-sliding features, but it appears to have been defeatured after the BATS acquisition of Direct Edge. Regardless, the Post Only ISO order type enjoys a significant presence on Direct Edge. In December 2017, it was utilized for approximately 4 per cent of executed orders as reflected in order type statistics based on a combined view of BATS and Direct Edge exchanges.[39]

According to Direct Edge's API materials, it appears to have introduced the Post ISO in 2009 with very limited detail on its operation. It was not until 2014 that Direct Edge clarified the functionality of its Post Only ISO as being similar to NSX, but it also incorporated advanced price-sliding capability which it chose not to elaborate beyond the following excerpt:

> An ISO with a Post Only and TIF [time-in-force] instruction of GTT [good-'til-time] or Day will be rejected without execution if, when entered, it is immediately marketable against an order with a Displayed instruction resting on the EDGX Book, unless the User included on the ISO a Price Adjust, Hide Not Slide, or the Single Re-Price instruction.[40]

In a footnote, it was also stated that

> [t]he operation of an ISO with a TIF instruction of Day is similar to the Post ISO order on the [NSX], but for the NSX stating that it will reject a Post ISO if it is immediately marketable against a displayed order on the NSX Book, while the Exchange retains such orders where they include a Price Adjust, Hide Not Slide, or Single Re-Price instruction.[41]

This content is the totality of documentation on Direct Edge' Post ISO until the merger with BATS, when all the order matching engines were migrated to the BATS platform. The final development in the narrative is the description of the Direct Edge Post Only ISO in its order type guide, which documented the order as such after the merger: 'Post Only Day ISOs will not remove contra

---

[39] Cboe Global Markets, *Order Type Usage Summary*, 2018.
[40] SEC, *Notice of Filing EDGX Exchange*, 2014, 44, 537.   [41] Ibid., 44, 537 n.64.

liquidity on the receiving exchange [and] [w]ill not be posted at their limit price if displayed contra liquidity is present.'[42] Of course, this incomplete description fails to explain how Direct Edge would actually handle such an order when displayed contra liquidity is present. Moreover, this issue is further complicated by BATS's decision to retire the Hide Not Slide functionality and tweak other price-sliding functionalities on Direct Edge,[43] the significance of which for the Post Only ISO was disclosed in Direct Edge's prior regulatory filing. Notably, the Hide Not Slide functionality was at the heart of the record settlement with the SEC in connection with inadequate disclosure by Direct Edge, and the regulators specifically pointed to that very filing by Direct Edge as finally referencing 'the [Hide Not Slide], Price Adjust and Single Re-Price order types [with] a description of how they operate'.[44]

Overall, the disclosure of Direct Edge's Post Only ISO order type has been deficient in technical and regulatory filings since it was introduced in 2009 or earlier and currently remains so. With regard to the current operation of the order type after it was migrated to the BATS platform, the degree to which price-sliding features still impact the order type is not possible to determine from the source material.

3.5.5 *BATS*

The BATS Post Only ISO order type is likely one of the first instances of this class of order type introduced into the market, incorporating a reject mode if the order would take liquidity as well as specialized interactions for aggressively priced orders. The BATS Post Only ISO order type enjoys a significant presence on BATS. In December 2017, it was utilized for approximately 4 per cent of executed orders as reflected in order type statistics based on a combined view of BATS and Direct Edge exchanges.[45] Note, however, that at the time BATS initially released its order statistics report and two years prior to the disclosure of the BATS Post Only ISO in regulatory filings, the volumes of associated with the BATS Post Only ISO order type were materially different. In January 2013, the BATS Post Only ISO accounted for over 9 per cent of executed orders on BATS, an astonishing proportion of trading for an undocumented order type.[46]

In 2012, in the course of my research efforts into special order types, I attempted to make indirect inquiries at BATS about its support for the Post Only ISO. I did not want to interact with BATS directly, given my recent

---

[42] Direct Edge, *Order Type Guide*, 2014, 28.   [43] SEC, *Notice of Filing...EDGX Exchange*, 2015.
[44] SEC, *Order...in the Matter of EDGA Exchange, Inc., and EDGX Exchange, Inc.*, 2015, 17.
[45] Cboe Global Markets, *Order Type Usage Summary*, 2018.
[46] BATS, *Order Type Usage Summary*, 2013.

exposure in the *Wall Street Journal* as a whistleblower related to the SEC's investigations covering that exchange, but I thought that my contact could assist me with my research efforts. By that time, I had concluded that the BATS documentation on the ISO and Post Only modifiers was difficult to interpret with regard to the Post Only ISO and had surmised that the Post Only ISO order type might indeed be supported on BATS, albeit in an undocumented manner. Intuitively, I found it hard to believe that Direct Edge and NYSE Arca had both provided an order type of such powerful capability and obvious relevance to HFTs without the same order type also being part of the functionality offered on BATS. At the same time, my indirect inquiries indicated that BATS had denied support for the Post Only ISO order type, and its personnel even questioned the very purpose of combining the Post Only and ISO modifiers to create such an order type. This response certainly illustrates the point that without adequate disclosure any sophisticated user would naturally believe that the Post Only ISO is an 'oxymoron' order type that would not be expected to be supported by an exchange.

Notably, BATS order type statistics, which appeared in the second quarter of 2013, provided information from January 2013 onward and indicated that the BATS Post Only ISO constituted 9.1 per cent of executed orders in January 2013.[47] Until the BATS Order Type Guide with a reference to this order type was released in September 2014,[48] these statistics served as the primary evidence that BATS indeed supported the Post Only ISO. In late 2012, when I could not even confirm the existence of the BATS Post Only ISO, it is likely that the BATS Post Only ISO was not only in use on BATS, but probably ranked as the fifth most significant order type by execution volume. I continue to be perplexed by the absence of regulatory filings and technical disclosure for the BATS Post Only ISO, given that BATS finally provided some technical information on the Post Only ISO in its September 2014 order type guide, almost two years after denying that they supported the order type. To date, it still appears that just one slide in the above-referenced outdated presentation is the extent of documentation of the Post Only ISO on BATS, which implies that this version is similar to the one operational on CHX, given that it embeds a reject mode.

Moreover, it is unknown why BATS trading activity historically associated with its Post Only ISO has been so significant with that order type being limited as such, which is unlikely to be the case prior to 2012. Given the history of regulatory filings, there is a real likelihood that undocumented order type properties that were embedded in the original instantiation of BATS Post Only (BOPO) order type, which was operational prior to 2012,

---

[47] Ibid.   [48] BATS, *Order Type Guide*, 2014, 29.

were likely incorporated into the Post Only ISO on BATS at the time of its introduction into the market without adequate disclosure. In 2012, BATS closed a loophole that permitted BOPO orders to be accepted at prices that were multiple ticks through the NBBO and to be handled in an undocumented manner.[49] This order matching engine behaviour had operated for a number of years, which was not disclosed by BATS prior to or at the time of modification to the BOPO order type. At the time, other exchanges would execute such orders in a manner that would incur taker fees and BATS proposed to adopt similar functionality. Prior to the implementation of this rule change, BATS would accept overly aggressive BOPO orders and handle them in an undisclosed manner. Though the exact details of how queue priority was addressed for BOPO orders prior to this rule filing is difficult to determine, the order handling approach most consistent with this regulatory filing is that BATS held an internal queue of BOPO orders that would 'light up' at more aggressive prices when permissible, and this functionality would be similar to NYSE's order type filing for Post Only and Post Only ISOs.[50] Thus the 2012 rule change appears to have eliminated order type asymmetries relating to order handling of aggressive Post Only orders that were previously exploited by HFTs. I believe that this change of the treatment of aggressive Post Only orders could have impacted the handling of Post Only ISOs on BATS, although that rule filing did not disclose the Post Only ISO order type and its remaining controversial properties, let alone the relevant changes applied to that order type.

The most likely scenario—consistent with the documentation, communications with my contact, order type statistics disclosure, and continued failure to adequately disclose the Post Only ISO through technical documentation and regulatory filings—is that BATS was an early adopter of the Post Only ISO, selectively disclosing it to preferred customers and perhaps just to a small circle of its own staff. When I finally became aware that BATS supported the Post Only ISO in 2013 through its disclosure of the Post Only ISO order type statistics, I concluded that this order type had been central to the aberrant HFT success on BATS in particular and hypothesized that it was an ongoing focus of the SEC's order type investigations. I have since come to believe that the BATS Post Only ISO was instrumental to the unusual performance of specific HFT firms on BATS, and that each benefited from either selective disclosure of the order type altogether, the loophole in the BATS order matching engine described above, or some combination thereof.

Overall, the failure of BATS to provide clarification of the BATS Post Only ISO in any regulatory filings and the terse language describing it in its limited

---

[49] SEC, *Notice of Filing . . . BATS Exchange*, 2012.
[50] SEC, *Notice of Filing . . . New York Stock Exchange*, 2014.

technical materials, as well as a history of selective disclosure, the inability to determine when the Post Only ISO was introduced into the BATS marketplace, the order type achieving close to 10 per cent of exchange matched orders at its peak, and alterations to the order type in 2012 that modified undocumented features, and the fact that such issues remain outstanding, collectively illustrate a systematic failure in the regulatory response to resolving the order type controversy.

3.5.6 NASDAQ

The NASDAQ Post Only ISO incorporates sophisticated price-sliding features and specialized interactions of aggressively priced orders. It is likely that NASDAQ's Post Only ISO order type enjoys a significant presence on NASDAQ. Even in early 2013, it was utilized for approximately 3 per cent of executed orders as reflected in NASDAQ's order type statistics.[51] More current statistics for this order type are not available due to NASDAQ's decision to cease the provision of order type statistics reports.

I conducted an order type review on NASDAQ in 2012, which involved frequent interaction with NASDAQ's technical support personnel. At the time, I specifically investigated available order type functionalities relying on communications with NASDAQ and explicitly inquired whether the Post Only ISO was supported by NASDAQ, as it was not disclosed in any technical documentation or regulatory filing. I could find no evidence that Post Only ISOs were supported on NASDAQ at the time, and I recall double-checking with NASDAQ's technical support personnel. As I have suggested with regards to BATS, not only is it likely that the Post Only ISO was selectively disclosed to preferred customers, but it is also likely that the order type was selectively disclosed internally among NASDAQ staff. Thereafter, despite a rigorous review of NASDAQ's technical documentation, regulatory filings, and interactions with exchange staff, I arrived at the erroneous conclusion that NASDAQ did not support the Post Only ISO. Furthermore, it appears that the only way to discover NASDAQ's support for the Post Only ISO prior to 2013—without being the beneficiary of selective disclosure—would be to explore the order handling of a combination of post only and ISO order modifiers in a production environment, an ill-advised endeavour given the significant regulatory and compliance risks involved.

When NASDAQ eventually provided order type statistics in early 2013,[52] I was astonished to find that it indicated support for Post Only ISOs. Up until its comprehensive order type filing in March 2015,[53] this odd form of

---

[51] NASDAQ, *NASDAQ OMX Equity Order Type Usage*, 2013. [52] Ibid.
[53] SEC, *Notice . . . NASDAQ Stock Market*, 2015.

disclosure appears to be the only piece of evidence that Post Only ISOs were provided by NASDAQ. Furthermore, this odd disclosure evident in the order type statistics was later withdrawn when NASDAQ stopped publishing order type statistics reports on its website and eliminated the previously available reports (apparently in early 2014). NASDAQ's withdrawal of its order type statistics effectively withheld knowledge of NASDAQ's support for the Post Only ISO from a broader group of market participants for the remainder of 2014, a period when NASDAQ clearly failed its obligations to disclose the Post Only ISO in regulatory filings and technical documents. Without the order type statistics released in early 2013, a typical market participant could not have been reasonably expected even to know that the Post Only ISO order type was permissible and supported on NASDAQ.

I am of the opinion that it is impossible to determine from publicly available information when NASDAQ had rolled out its Post Only ISO. In light of NASDAQ's disclosure of the Post Only ISO in its order type statistics in early 2013, NASDAQ most likely introduced the Post Only ISO in 2012 or earlier without any technical disclosure, circular, or regulatory filing. Interestingly, NASDAQ appears to have first disclosed the existence of the Post Only ISO in 2014 in a regulatory filing requested by the SEC for enhanced disclosure of its usage of data feeds. This initial disclosure in a terse passage indicated a number of repricing scenarios applied to the Post Only ISO.[54] It was not until NASDAQ's regulatory filing in March 2015 that it disclosed the Post Only ISO in a form that met reasonable disclosure requirements, indicating the exchange's support of a sophisticated version of the Post Only ISO that incorporated various conditions of price-sliding operating in a range of scenarios:

> [A] Post-Only Order designated as an ISO that locked or crossed an Order on the Nasdaq Book would either execute at time of entry or would have its price adjusted prior to posting. Accordingly, the System would not interpret receipt of a Post-Only Order marked ISO that had its price adjusted prior to posting as the basis for determining that any Protected Quotation at the Order's original entered limit price level had been executed for purposes of accepting additional Orders at that price level.[55]

For these reasons, and in conjunction with information provided to me by an executive of an HFT firm that heavily uses Post Only ISOs who is a former employee of NASDAQ, I believe that NASDAQ selectively disclosed the Post Only ISO to preferred customers over a prolonged period, while deliberately withholding required and essential information from the market as a whole and from the SEC.

---

[54] SEC, *Notice of Filing NASDAQ Stock Market*, 2014, 44, 957 n.9.
[55] SEC, *Notice NASDAQ Stock Market*, 2015, 16, 058.

3.5.7 *NYSE*

The NYSE Post Only ISO is the most recent and one of the most sophisticated versions of the Post Only ISO across the entire marketplace, incorporating price-sliding, multiple-tick reservation/queue-jumping properties, and hidden order detection capabilities. The Post Only Day ISO Limit order type enjoys a significant presence on NYSE. In December 2017, it was utilized for approximately 2 per cent of matched volume as reflected in NYSE's order type statistics.[56] Interestingly, matched volume for this order type apparently peaked in September 2015 when it was reported as being responsible for roughly 6.5 per cent of NYSE's matched volume.[57]

At the time of NYSE's rulemaking proposal, I was particularly concerned that the SEC approval supported NYSE's criticism of the arguments I had made in my comment letter,[58] which I felt had been misrepresented. In some cases, the SEC utilized NYSE's language near-verbatim to dismiss the content of my comment letter in a way that was favourable to NYSE's position. This outcome was especially important to me because of NYSE's interpretation of my statements, which I found self-serving and contradictory to my knowledge of this matter. For better or worse, the SEC's approval of the NYSE Post Only ISO in October 2014 was a significant development because it was the first comprehensive order type filing that described the operation of the Post Only ISO even though NYSE was actually the *last* exchange to introduce the Post Only ISO order type. The effect was naturally to 'normalize' the undocumented order type that was already in use on every other major equity exchange.

I continue to believe that the sheer volume of the Post Only ISO trading activity indicated by the order type statistics provided by the major exchanges is irreconcilable with the limited scope of applicable usage conditions in which this order type can be used in a compliant manner. Consider, for example, the limited usage case presented in NYSE's response to my comment letter, which articulates two usage scenarios in which the Post Only ISO can be used compliantly, both of which assume that traditional Day ISOs (i.e. orders that incur taker fees) are simultaneously sent to away exchanges while a 'Day ISO with ALO modifier' is sent to NYSE when the best price on NYSE is inferior to the NBBO. I believe that the limited scope of permissible usage implied in NYSE's response obfuscates the more extensive set of usage scenarios likely envisioned by NYSE. Such usage scenarios would be more consistent with the significant volumes associated with the Post Only ISO on major equities

---

[56] NYSE, *Order Type Usage . . . July–December 2017*, 2018.
[57] NYSE, *Order Type Usage . . . August 2015—January 2016*, 2016.
[58] Bodek, *Comment Letter to the SEC*, 2014.

exchanges, which is perhaps alluded to in NYSE's claim that its submission offers 'order type functionality that is consistent with Regulation NMS and used on all other equity exchanges'.[59]

I am particularly concerned that the features of NYSE's Post Only ISO are similar in nature to possibly queue-priority and 'reservation' features associated with aggressive Post Only orders (and, by extension, the features associated with undocumented Post Only ISOs) that appear to have been exploited by HFTs on NASDAQ and BATS prior to being corrected through order matching engine changes as a result of the intense regulatory scrutiny of order types. As previously mentioned, a regulatory filing by BATS in 2012 addressed an order matching engine asymmetry by penalizing aggressively-priced Post Only orders typically used by HFTs.[60] Likewise, a 2012 NASDAQ announcement penalized aggressively priced Post Only orders and normalized undocumented price-sliding differences between OUCH and FIX interfaces.[61] The modifications proposed in these filings with regard to the treatment of aggressive Post Only orders suggest that these two exchanges eliminated undocumented (and presumably abusive) queue-priority and reservation advantages for Post Only orders—and by extension Post Only ISOs orders— with these changes.

Anecdotally, after this order type had been released, it had a disruptive effect on the floor broker community. Not only did the order type effectively queue-jump floor brokers' orders, but NYSE had actually clarified its policy that '[r]outing of ALO and ISO orders directly to the Broker Systems will not be supported',[62] which might be explained by the sheer difficulty for such market participants to comply with the ISO requirements without having access to low-latency technology.

NYSE's versions of Post Only and Post Only ISO functionalities provide for treatment of aggressively-priced orders in a manner that appears to be more consistent with the (insufficiently documented) functionality of Post Only ISOs apparently in operation in some form on BATS and NASDAQ (and eliminated with the 2012 modifications on both of these exchanges). I am concerned that NYSE's Post Only ISO, presumably designed with the assistance of NYSE customers using Post Only ISOs on competing exchanges and/or concerned about inquiries with regard to compliant usage of Post Only ISOs on such exchanges in prior years, might in effect have served as a precedent, retroactively legitimizing advantages provided through insufficiently documented order handling practices.

---

[59] NYSE, *Letter to the SEC*, 2014, 9 (emphasis added).
[60] SEC, *Notice of Filing…BATS Exchange*, 2012.
[61] NASDAQ, *Equity Technical Update #2012–24*, 2012.
[62] NYSE, *Expansion of ALO Modifier*, 2014, 1.

In NYSE's response to my comment letter concerning the Post Only ISO, NYSE does not address my concern that the ISO designation of a Post Only ISO might be used in an abusive manner, thereby falsely attesting to 'satisfying' ISO routing obligations mandated by Rule 611 to execute against away markets, when in fact such compliance cannot be achieved by an order with the post only designation. Furthermore, I allude to the possibility of NYSE's Post Only ISO being designated with overly-aggressive prices which, despite NYSE's rebuttal referencing the implicit price-sliding protection of the Day ISO ALO, would not in fact protect against all potential violations of the trade-through rule by this order type's usage. In fact, NYSE does not define non-compliant usage of the Post Only ISO in its rebuttal to my criticism, nor does it appear to commit to any adequate plan of surveillance to ensure that market participants comply with Regulation NMS and NYSE rules in a manner that addresses the unique differences between Day ISOs and Day ISO ALO orders.

While the Day ISO ALO introduced on NYSE in 2014 is actually the first example of a sufficiently documented version of the Post Only ISO in the US equity markets, it also serves as an example of the pro-industry perspective of the SEC's Division of Trading and Markets. The degree to which this particular version validated and normalized previously inadequately documented or undocumented Post Only ISOs operating on other exchanges, as well as the deference accorded by the Division of Trading and Markets to the inaccuracies of NYSE's arguments, amounted to approving features contradictory to the purpose and probably even the letter of Regulation NMS. Notably, in the process of NYSE's Post Only ISO submission, the 'revolving door' phenomenon is likely to have informed the involved parties about the nature of particular features that NYSE sought to get approved, as well as the negative impact on the industry if the Post Only ISO incarnations running on other exchanges were deemed impermissible by the regulators. With the approval of NYSE's proposal by the Division of Trading and Markets, the issue of Post Only ISOs was ultimately resolved in the industry's favour.

3.5.8 *The Post Only ISO: Unresolved Matters and Summary of Allegations*

I believe that sophisticated trading firms have been abusing the scope of permissible and compliant use of the Post Only ISO order type with tacit approval of exchanges, including the use of the ISO designation beyond its acceptable scope and relying on exchange order handling (e.g. price-sliding) to submit Post Only ISOs with non-compliant prices and sizes. Furthermore, I believe that exchanges are supplying compliance guidance and endorsing usage cases for the Post Only ISO that violate exchange rules, Rules 610 and 611 of Regulation NMS, or a combination thereof. At a minimum, given the information provided to me by an HFT executive, some exchanges appear to have advised HFT firms on compliant use of the Post Only ISO without seeking SEC approval for such functionalities through the appropriate regulatory approval process.

Hence, the unresolved matters and outstanding allegations against the major exchanges concerning the Post Only ISO are summarized in the following.

a. The exchanges failed to submit regulatory filings or gain regulatory approval for the Post Only ISO, one of the most sophisticated and controversial order types provided by the trading venues.

b. The exchanges that supported sophisticated versions of the Post Only ISO would have had a higher burden of regulatory disclosure than the exchanges that did not incorporate complex order handling in the Post Only ISO.

c. The exchanges had a duty to provide circulars and communications indicating that they were releasing the Post Only ISO order type into the marketplace.

d. The exchanges had a duty to provide accurate technical documentation indicating that the Post Only ISO was supported, how it operated, and how one could use the Post Only ISO in a compliant manner.

e. The exchanges were required to abstain from a practice of selective disclosure, particularly with regard to disclosing nonpublic information to sophisticated traders with regard to the existence, support, operation, and compliant use of the Post Only ISO.

f. The exchanges were required to provide truthful and accurate information in response to technical inquiries concerning their support of the Post Only ISO.

g. It is likely that major HFTs have utilized the Post Only ISO in a manner contrary to the limited scope of compliant use approved more recently by the SEC.

h. The exchanges were required to correct material deficiencies in their regulatory filings and technical documentation concerning the Post Only ISO to comply with the SEC's mandate for increased order type transparency through clarifications made through the rulemaking process.

3.6 Conclusion

In order to appease their highest-volume HFT customers, several leading equities exchanges circumvented the regulatory regime governing the US equities markets by introducing the Post Only ISO without proper regulatory approvals and compliance with Regulation NMS. However, this advantage could not have remained hidden forever in light of the broader scrutiny, both public and regulatory, of order type practices. From 2011 to 2015, the SEC conducted comprehensive order type investigations for every major exchange. Moreover, the exchanges submitted hundreds of pages of regulatory filings 'clarifying' their order type functionalities as mandated by the SEC. Over the period of 2013–14, the manoeuvring by the exchanges to develop regulatory precedents and indirect disclosures of the Post Only ISO appears to have been influenced by the order type investigations. Moving forward, the exchanges, now not being able to bypass the SEC's approval process but having to rely on the regulators' (at least nominal) involvement, aimed to retroactively approve the Post Only ISO. This tacit move to 'normalize' the Post Only ISO order type was only accomplished after it had been running in the majority of equities exchanges in an undocumented/unapproved manner and to the benefit of HFT insiders who received an unfair advantage over other investors.

Over the period from 2012 to 2014, the SEC's review of rule submissions by the exchanges in fact succeeded in 'normalizing' and, for all practical purposes, retroactively legitimizing the Post Only ISO. The most important normalizing rule filing was for the NYSE Post Only ISO, against which I wrote a detailed comment letter.[63] After positive press coverage of my comment letter citing some industry support for my position,[64] I was surprised to learn that the SEC had summarily approved NYSE's Post Only ISO without addressing the substance of my comment letter and, at the same time, regurgitating NYSE's self-serving misinterpretations of my arguments and echoing NYSE's rebuttals.

In 2014, I met with an HFT executive to discuss NYSE's Post Only ISO rule filing, who had been concerned with my arguments critical of that order type. By the time I met with this executive, NYSE's proposal had already been approved. The executive told me I should I have 'known better' that the SEC could not make an order type illegal if it was already operational on the vast majority of exchanges, despite any of my arguments on technical violations or contradictory properties of such order types. When I countered that this order type had not been documented in any meaningful capacity and that there was no guidance on how to use the Post Only ISO in a compliant manner, this executive told me 'it wasn't your fault', pointing out that I did not have the right contacts and that the exchanges had advised his firm and others on compliant usage of the Post Only ISO.

---

[63] Bodek, *Comment Letter to the SEC*, 2014.   [64] Byrne, 'New whistleblower joust', 2014.

To date, the only enforcement action that the SEC has taken in connection with the Post Only ISO has been the 2015 settlement with Latour Trading, and that particular action was focused on violations of exchange rules themselves rather than the substance of those rules and the self-contradictory nature of the order type in question: 'Latour violated exchange rules adopted under Rule 610 of Reg NMS that require exchange members to reasonably avoid displaying, and prohibit them from engaging in a pattern or practice of displaying, orders that lock or cross protected quotations.'[65] Interestingly, this enforcement action is possibly the only regulatory precedent that provides some guidance on compliant usage of the Post Only ISO. Given the successful manoeuvring by the industry, the approval of particular exchange rule filings, and the normalization of the Post Only ISO through the SEC oversight function, it appears that an ex post regulatory review of this order type from the standpoint of liability exposure is unlikely, although it perhaps lingers on as a market reform and private litigation issue, including concerns about potentially persisting informational asymmetries. This observation is a final reflection on a notable example of failure for the US market structure regulation and enforcement for an order type associated with roughly 4–5 per cent of trading activity on the US equities exchanges.

References

BATS. *Order Type Usage Summary—January 2013*. Available at: https://markets.cboe.com/us/equities/market_statistics/order_type_usage/?year=2013&month=01, 2013.

BATS. *Order Type Guide*. Available at: http://www.brainshark.com/DCS/vu?pi=zHTzdnPSpz3QRKz0, 2014.

Bodek, Haim. *The Problem of HFT: Collected Writings on High Frequency Trading & Stock Market Structure Reform*. CreateSpace Independent Publishing Platform, 2013.

Bodek, Haim. *Comment Letter to the SEC on Securities Exchange Act Release No. 72,548-15 September*. Available at: https://www.sec.gov/comments/sr-nyse-2014-32/nyse201432-1.pdf, 2014.

Bodek, Haim, and Stanislav Dolgopolov. *The Market Structure Crisis: Electronic Stock Markets, High Frequency Trading, and Dark Pools*. Decimus Capital Markets, LLC, 2015.

Byrne, John Aiden. 'New whistleblower joust over high-speed trades'. *New York Times*. Available at: https://nypost.com/2014/09/21/new-whistleblower-joust-over-high-speed-trades/, 21 September 2014.

Cboe Global Markets. *Order Type Usage Summary—December 2017*. Available at: http://markets.cboe.com/us/equities/market_statistics/order_type_usage/?year=2017&month=12, 2018.

---

[65] SEC, *Order . . . in the Matter of Latour Trading*, 2015, 9.

City of Providence v. Bats Global Markets, Inc. *878 F.3d 36 (2d Cir. 2017)—No. 15-3057*. Available at: https://cases.justia.com/federal/appellate-courts/ca2/15-3057/15-3057-2017-12-19.pdf?ts=1513697407, 2017.

Direct Edge. *Order Type Guide*. Available at: http://www.brainshark.com/DCS/vu?pi=zGwzPWcfUz3QRKz0, 2014.

Lash, Herbert. 'Complaints rise over complex U.S. stock orders'. Reuters. Available at: https://www.reuters.com/article/us-exchanges-ordertypes/analysis-complaints-rise-over-complex-u-s-stock-orders-idUSBRE89I0YU20121019, 19 October 2012.

NASDAQ. *Equity Technical Update #2012–24*. Available at: http://www.nasdaqtrader.com/TraderNews.aspx?id=ETU2012-24, 2012.

NASDAQ. *NASDAQ OMX Equity Order Type Usage—February 2013*. Available at: https://web.archive.org/web/20130825130953/http://nasdaqtrader.com/content/marketstatistics/FebOTU.pdf, 2013.

NYSE. *Expansion of ALO Modifier and Day Time in Force for ISOs—15 October*. Available at: https://www.nyse.com/publicdocs/nyse/markets/nyse/ALO_Customer_Notice_Final.pdf, 2014.

NYSE. *Letter to the SEC in Response to Comment Letters for Securities Exchange Act Release No. 72,548—30 September*. Available at: https://www.sec.gov/comments/sr-nyse-2014-32/nyse201432-3.pdf, 2014.

NYSE. *Order Type Usage (Percentage of Matched Volume)—August 2015—January 2016*. Available at: http://www.smallake.kr/wp-content/uploads/2016/02/NYSE-Order-Type-Usage.pdf, 2016.

NYSE. *Order Type Usage (Percentage of Matched Volume)—July–December 2017*. Available at: https://www.nyse.com/publicdocs/nyse/markets/nyse/NYSE-Order-Type-Usage.pdf, 2018.

NYSE Arca. *Order Type Usage (Percentage of Matched Volume)—July–December 2017*. Available at: https://www.nyse.com/publicdocs/nyse/markets/nyse-arca/NYSE_Arca_Order_Type_Usage.pdf, 2018.

Patterson, Scott. *Dark Pools: The Rise of the Machine Traders and the Rigging of the U.S. Stock Market*, rev. edn. New York: Crown Publishing Group, 2013.

Patterson, Scott, and Jean Eaglesham. 'Exchanges get closer inspection'. *Wall Street Journal*. Available at: https://www.wsj.com/articles/SB10001424127887323622904578129210389143-012, 20 November 2012.

Patterson, Scott, and Jean Eaglesham. 'SEC probes rapid trading'. *Wall Street Journal*. Available at: https://www.wsj.com/articles/SB10001424052702304636404577297-840134760650, 23 March 2012.

Patterson, Scott, and Jenny Strasburg. 'For superfast stock traders, a way to jump ahead in line'. *Wall Street Journal*. Available at: https://www.wsj.com/articles/SB10000872396390443989204577599243693561670, 19 September 2012.

Scotti, Michael. 'Exchange order types may finally get sunlight'. *Buy Side Trader*. Available at: http://buysidetrader.com/tag/exchange-order-types/, 30 April 2014.

SEC (US Securities and Exchange Commission). *Regulation NMS—Final Rule*. 70 Fed. Reg. 37496. Available at: https://www.gpo.gov/fdsys/pkg/FR-2005-06-29/pdf/05-11802.pdf. Release No. 34–51808; File No. S7–10–04– codified at 17 C.F.R. pts. 240 & 242, 2005.

SEC. *Notice of Filing and Immediate Effectiveness of Proposed Rule Change by the National Stock Exchange, Inc. to Provide for a Post Intermarket Sweep Order.* 73 Fed. Reg. 44305. Available at: https://www.gpo.gov/fdsys/pkg/FR-2008-07-30/pdf/E8-17412.pdf. Release No. 34–58217; File No. SR–NSX– 2008–12, 2008.

SEC. *Notice of Filing and Immediate Effectiveness of a Proposed Rule Change by the Chicago Stock Exchange, Inc. Adding the Post Only and Post Only ISO Order Types.* 74 Fed. Reg. 33494. Available at: https://www.gpo.gov/fdsys/pkg/FR-2009-07-13/pdf/E9-16449. pdf. Release No. 34–60243; File No. SR–CHX–2009–09, 2009.

SEC. *Notice of Filing and Immediate Effectiveness of a Proposed Rule Change by BATS Exchange, Inc. to Amend BATS Rules Related to the Operation of BATS Post Only Orders and Match Trade Prevention Functionality.* 77 Fed. Reg. 33798. Available at: https:// www.gpo.gov/fdsys/pkg/FR-2012-06-07/pdf/2012-13765.pdf. Release No. 34–67093; File No. SR–BATS– 2012–018, 2012.

SEC. *Notice of Filing and Immediate Effectiveness of a Proposed Rule Change by the Chicago Stock Exchange, Inc. to Consolidate All Order Types, Modifiers, and Related Terms Under One Rule and to Clarify the Basic Requirements of All Orders Sent to the Matching System.* 78 Fed. Reg. 28671. Available at: https://www.gpo.gov/fdsys/pkg/FR-2013-05-15/ pdf/2013-11453.pdf. Release No. 34–69538; File No. SR–CHX– 2013–10, 2013.

SEC. *Notice of Filing and Immediate Effectiveness of Proposed Rule Change by NASDAQ Stock Market LLC to Disclose Publicly the Sources of Data Used for Exchange Functions.* 79 Fed. Reg. 44956. Available at: http://www.gpo.gov/fdsys/pkg/FR-2014-08-01/pdf/2014-18119.pdf. Release No. 34–72684; File No. SR– NASDAQ–2014–072, 2014.

SEC. *Notice of Filing of a Proposed Rule Change by EDGX Exchange, Inc. Relating to Include Additional Specificity Within Rule 1.5 and Chapter XI Regarding Current System Functionality Including the Operation of Order Types and Order Instructions.* 72 Fed. Reg. 44520. Available at: https://www.gpo.gov/fdsys/pkg/FR-2014-07-31/pdf/2014-17989.pdf. Release No. 34–72676; File No. SR–EDGX– 2014–18, 2014.

SEC. *Notice of Filing of Proposed Rule Change by New York Stock Exchange LLC Amending Rule 13 to Make the Add Liquidity Only Modifier Available for Additional Limit Orders and Make the Day Time-In-Force Condition Available for Intermarket Sweep Orders.* 79 Fed. Reg. 40183. Available at: https://www.gpo.gov/fdsys/pkg/FR-2014-07-11/pdf/2014-16191.pdf. Release No. 34–72548; File No. SR–NYSE–2014–32, 2014.

SEC. *Order Approving Proposed Rule Changes by New York Stock Exchange LLC and NYSE MKT LLC Amending Exchange Rule 13 to Make the Add Liquidity Only Modifier Available for Limit Orders, and Make the Day Time-in-Force Condition and Add Liquidity Only Modifier Available for Intermarket Sweep Orders.* 79 Fed. Reg. 62223. Available at: http://www.gpo.gov/fdsys/pkg/FR-2014-08-01/pdf/2014-18119.pdf. Release No. 34–73333; File Nos. SR–NYSE– 2014–32 and SR–NYSEMKT–2014–56, 2014.

SEC. *Speech by Mary Jo White, Chairman of the U.S. Securities and Exchange Commission: Enhancing Our Equity Market Structure.* Available at: https://www.sec.gov/news/ speech/2014-spch060514mjw#.VRs_khz38yg. Sandler O'Neill & Partners, L.P. Global Exchange and Brokerage Conference, 5 June 2014.

SEC. *Notice of a Proposed Rule Change by NASDAQ Stock Market LLC to Amend and Restate Certain Nasdaq Rules That Govern the Nasdaq Market Center.* 80 Fed. Reg. 16050.

Available at: https://www.gpo.gov/fdsys/pkg/FR-2015-03-26/pdf/2015-06891.pdf. Release No. 34–74558; File No. SR– NASDAQ–2015–024, 2015.

SEC. *Notice of Filing and Immediate Effectiveness of a Proposed Rule Change by EDGX Exchange, Inc. to Rules 11.6, 11.8, 11.9, 11.10 and 11.11 to Align with Similar Rules of the BATS Exchange, Inc.* 80 Fed. Reg. 43810. Available at: https://www.gpo.gov/fdsys/pkg/FR-2015-07-23/pdf/2015-18034.pdf. Release No. 34–75479; File No. SR–EDGX–2015–33, 2015.

SEC. *Notice of Filing of a Proposed Rule Change by NYSE Arca, Inc. Adopting New Equity Trading Rules Relating to Orders and Modifiers and the Retail Liquidity Program to Reflect the Implementation of Pillar, the Exchange's New Trading Technology Platform.* 80 Fed. Reg. 45022. Available at: https://www.gpo.gov/fdsys/pkg/FR-2015-07-28/pdf/2015-18277.pdf. Release No. 34–75497; File No. SR– NYSEARCA–2015–56, 2015.

SEC. *Notice of Filing of a Proposed Rule Change by NYSE Arca, Inc. to Eliminate Additional Order Type Combinations and Delete Related Rule Text and to Restructure the Remaining Rule Text in NYSE Arca Equities Rule 7.31.* 80 Fed. Reg. 12537. Available at: https://www.gpo.gov/fdsys/pkg/FR-2015-03-09/pdf/2015-05291.pdf. Release No. 34–74415; File No. SR– NYSEArca–2015–08, 2015.

SEC. *Order Instituting Administrative and Cease-And-Desist Proceedings ... Making Findings and Imposing Remedial Sanctions and a Cease-And-Desist Order ... in the Matter of EDGA Exchange, Inc., and EDGX Exchange, Inc.* Available at: https://www.sec.gov/litigation/admin/2015/34-74032.pdf Securities Exchange Act of 1934, Release No. 74032, 2015.

SEC. *Order Instituting Administrative and Cease-And-Desist Proceedings ... Making Findings and Imposing Remedial Sanctions and a Cease-And-Desist Order ... in the Matter of Latour Trading LLC.* Available at: http://www.sec.gov/litigation/admin/2015/34-76029.pdf. Securities Exchange Act of 1934, Release No. 76029, 2015.

SEC. *Order Instituting Administrative and Cease-And-Desist Proceedings ... Making Findings and Imposing Remedial Sanctions and a Cease-And-Desist Order ... in the Matter of UBS Securities LLC.* Available at: http://www.sec.gov/litigation/admin/2015/33-9697.pdf. Securities Act of 1933, Release No. 9697–Securities Exchange Act of 1934, Release No. 74060, 2015.

SEC. *Notice of Filing and Immediate Effectiveness of a Proposed Rule Change by NYSE Arca, Inc. Amending Equities Rule 7.31P(e) Regarding ALO Orders.* 81 Fed. Reg. 35415. Available at: https://www.gpo.gov/fdsys/pkg/FR-2016-06-02/pdf/2016-12891.pdf. Release No. 34–77934; File No. SR– NYSEArca–2016–80, 2016.

SEC. *Letter from Kathryn A. Pyszka, Assistant Regional Director, Chicago Regional Office SEC, to to Eric Swanson, General Counsel, BATS Global Markets, Inc.* Available at: http://cdn.batstrading.com/resources/regulation/SEC_BATS_Closeout_Letter.pdf. 12 January 2017.

SEC. *Order Instituting Administrative and Cease-And-Desist Proceedings ... Making Findings and Imposing Remedial Sanctions and a Cease- And-Desist Order ... in the Matter of New York Stock Exchange LLC, NYSE American LLC, and NYSE Arca, Inc.* Available at: https://www.sec.gov/litigation/admin/2018/33-10463.pdf. Securities Act of 1933, Release No. 10463—Securities Exchange Act of 1934, Release No. 82808, 2018.

4

The FX Race to Zero

Electronification and Market Structural Issues in Foreign Exchange Trading

Dan Marcus and Miles Kellerman

4.1 Introduction

Since the publication of Michael Lewis's *Flash Boys*, discussions of high frequency trading (HFT) issues and accusations that 'the market is rigged' have focused almost entirely on equities.[1] What is less widely known is that similar issues have existed and continue to exist in spot foreign exchange markets (FX or forex). In many ways, this particular asset class presents even greater opportunities for speed to provide certain market participants with significant economic advantages. FX is a highly commoditized asset traded in enormous volumes. Further, currency trading takes places on a continuous, global, and significantly fragmented market with various modes of trading (bilateral, multilateral, last look, wholesale, retail) and different levels of pre- and post-trade transparency ('dark' vs 'lit' markets). These characteristics are very attractive to computer algorithms. And, because FX trading takes place across such a fragmented landscape of execution venues, there are ample opportunities to take advantage of asymmetrical access to speed and information.

The potential implications of market structural issues in FX are monumental. As of April 2016, FX was the second largest financial market in the world after interest rate swaps in terms of value added, equating to an average daily volume of USD 5.1 trillion.[2] Approximately USD 1.7 trillion of that daily total is in 'spot FX', i.e. standard currency trading with (generally) two-day settlement

---

[1] Lewis, *Flash Boys*, 2014.   [2] BIS, 'Triennial central bank survey', 2016.

periods. The fundamental purpose of FX trading is to allow firms that (a) are involved in cross-border business and/or (b) buy or sell goods or services in more than one currency to hedge the risk associated with currency fluctuations. Traditionally, such firms will assess their current and future currency exposure and subsequently hedge on a forward basis (usually by trading directly with, or contracting the agency services of, large banks). If market structural issues make it more expensive to do so, firms are faced with an unnecessary and non-trivial cost. Further, the creation or exacerbation of flash crashes in particular currencies, such as the sudden 9 per cent drop and recovery in the price of GBP sterling in 2016, could materially impact fund performance and discourage retail investor participation.[3] The Swiss National Bank's decision to remove their cap on the Swiss franc in 2015 demonstrates the potential impact of such market events. The resulting volatility forced multiple market makers into liquidation.[4] And stock of FXCM, then one of the largest FX brokers in the US, fell more than 90 per cent, forcing the company to pursue an emergency loan.[5]

In this chapter, we contribute to the debate over high frequency trading and market structure by demonstrating that the issues widely recognized in equities markets are also prevalent in FX. Further, we provide an example of a latency-based arbitrage opportunity and discuss how randomized delays can disrupt such opportunities.[6] In so doing, this work sheds light on market structural issues in FX that have received far too little theoretical or empirical attention. We also present a discussion of relevant national and international regulations. This includes an identification of key gaps in forthcoming legislation that will be of direct interest to regulatory practitioners.

This chapter will proceed in the following order. We begin in Section 4.2 with a review of the small but growing literature on structural issues and electronic trading in FX markets. Section 4.3 follows with an examination of how electronic communication methods and algorithmic trading have affected the structure of currency markets. In Section 4.4 we outline what we believe are the key issues in today's FX markets. This begins with a discussion of arbitrage techniques and questionable trading practices. We then examine

---

[3] Hunter and Mackenzie, 'Pound's plunge', 2016.

[4] Bird, 'Foreign-exchange brokers', 2015.

[5] Egan, 'Swiss shock'. In 2017, the US Commodity Futures Trading Commission banned FXCM from operating in the United States. FXCM was found to have misled customers and the National Futures Association about its undisclosed interest in a market maker that consistently received large shares of the company's trading volume. That market maker, in turn, was taking positions against FXCM's retail customers. See CFTC, 'CFTC orders', 2017.

[6] ParFX, of which one of this chapter's co-authors is Chief Executive Officer, assisted in providing access to certain data for comparison purposes. ParFX is an FX trading platform designed to eliminate the advantages of speed by applying, *inter alia*, a meaningful randomized pause to all order submissions, amendments, and cancellations. It is a subsidiary of Compagnie Financière Tradition SA, an inter-dealer broker.

two of the most concerning outcomes of these practices: the liquidity mirage and flash crashes. This is followed by an analysis of how trading venues have facilitated these developments by (a) monetizing access to speed and information and (b) paying for order flow. We conclude this section with an examination of 'last look', an FX-specific feature not present in equities markets. Section 4.5 discusses current and forthcoming attempts to regulate these issues in the United Kingdom, the European Union and the United States. We specifically focus on the regulation of spot FX. This is followed by a discussion of recent industry-led initiatives to create best practices for algorithmic traders and venue operators. We conclude with a discussion of potential avenues for future research in Section 4.6.

4.2 Previous Work on Structural Issues in Foreign Exchange Markets

In comparison to that on equities, the literature on market structural issues in FX in the era of electronic trading is fledgling. With the exception of a few notable studies, including those by certain international financial institutions, there is very little academic work on how algorithmic trading in FX has affected market quality and market conduct. Empirical works, in particular, are few and far between. We attribute this to two primary factors. First, FX trade data is largely proprietary, opaque, and not reported to national regulators to the same extent as data on other asset classes. Therefore, it is very difficult to access. And second, by comparison with equities markets, there is simply less awareness that the issues brought to public attention by Michael Lewis' *Flash Boys* are equally if not more pervasive in currency trading. In the remainder of this section, we provide a brief review of the literature on FX market structure and electronic trading.

The contemporary study of FX market structure can be traced back to the early 1970s.[7] In response to the perceived failures of existing models, a small but active group of scholars began to ask new questions about how FX markets operate.[8] These questions derived from three key observations.[9] First, not all information in currency markets is publicly available. Certain participants have access to better information than others and/or receive that information at quicker speeds. In other words, FX markets feature significant informational

---

[7] Lyons, 'Microstructure approach', 2002, 3.

[8] King, Osler, and Rime, 'Market microstructure approach', 2013, 97.

[9] Lyons, 'Microstructure approach', 4. Originally, scholars were focused on the determination of exchange rate movements. Over time, however, academic work on FX market structure has expanded to address a significantly wider set of outcomes.

asymmetries. Second, market participants are heterogeneous. Therefore, the incentives of, for example, global banks and small trading outfits may differ. And, finally, institutions matter; differences in the design of trading mechanisms and market structures may affect distributional outcomes.

These observations pointed to numerous new avenues for research. How, for example, do informational asymmetries affect distributional outcomes and the quality of currency markets? Early work sought to address this question by analysing the interplay between asymmetric information, order flow, and the behaviour of market makers.[10] One of the key observations of existing research is that centralized price information alleviates operational inefficiencies.[11] In contrast, decentralized markets with high informational asymmetries are *privately* efficient for market participants with informational advantages.[12] Researchers have explored these relative advantages by, for example, analysing the capacity of large market makers to 'sell' each other information about their transactions with outside counterparties by trading in the dealer-to-dealer market.[13] Academics have also sought to better understand informational advantages in the context of specific market events. Phylaktis and Chen, for example, find that global banks possess an informational advantage over other FX market participants when it comes to news announcements.[14] Further, there is evidence to suggest that algorithmic trading has the capacity to exacerbate these asymmetries. One study finds, for example, that algorithmic trading improves price discovery efficiency but increases adverse selection costs for slower traders.[15] These results imply that informational asymmetries in FX have important distributional consequences.

And, indeed, the impact of electronic trading on currency markets is an important new area of research. Osler and Wang contend, for example, that electronic trading has transformed the industrial organization of FX, providing opportunities for economies of scale that favour increased concentration of market power.[16] Another group of scholars trace how the introduction of electronic trading has altered the structure of currency markets.[17] Particular emphasis is placed on the proliferation of new, electronic-based trading mechanisms (e.g. electronic communication networks and retail aggregators) and the entrance of HFT. The Bank for International Settlements (BIS) has played a particularly important role in this conversation by releasing tri-annual survey

---

[10] See, for example, Lyons, 'Private beliefs', 1991.

[11] See, for example, Flood, 'Market structure', 1994.

[12] Perraudin and Vitale, 'Interdealer trade', 1996, 74. See also Ito et al., Lyons, and Melvin, 'Is there private information?', 1998; Lyons, 'Simultaneous trade model', 1997.

[13] Perraudin and Vitale. Also see Sarno and Taylor, 'Microstructure', 2001, 40–2.

[14] Phylaktis and Chen, 'Asymmetric information', 2010.

[15] Chaboud et al., 'Rise of the machines', 2014.

[16] Osler and Wang, 'Microstructure', 2013.   [17] King et al., 2011.

data on the size, composition, and nature of FX markets.[18] The conclusions of these studies are largely consistent: advances in computational power have significantly altered the structure of currency markets by facilitating HFT and the creation of new, electronic trading venues.

Relatively little work has been performed, however, on how these changes have affected market quality and conduct in FX trading. One notable exception is an analysis of EBS's decision to reduce its tick size (the minimum incremental price movement a trading instrument can experience) from four decimal points to five decimal points in March 2011.[19] The authors' working conclusion, consistent with the widely-held belief that smaller decimal sizes favour algorithmic strategies, is that this reduction in tick size enabled high frequency traders to front-run human counterparties.[20]

These preliminary empirical findings are largely consistent with the themes of this chapter. But much more analysis is needed in order to enable policy-makers and market participants to make an informed decision on whether and to what extent further regulation and/or changes to market practices are necessary. By outlining in detail the primary structural and conduct-related issues associated with algorithmic and high frequency trading in FX, we hope to encourage further research. We return to this topic in Section 4.6, outlining a number of avenues (and challenges) for future empirical work.

4.3 FX Market Structure and Electronic Trading

The FX market trades 24 hours a day, five-and-a-half days a week. Currency trading has historically been decentralized and highly fragmented. This contrasts with equities, which originally developed to facilitate trading only on certain recognized exchanges within pre-defined time periods (though, as addressed throughout this volume, equities have experienced significant fragmentation over the last 15 years). In recent years, however, the market for *spot* FX has shown signs of becoming more similar to that for equities. A significant proportion of trading is now undertaken on electronic platforms or through large banks that internalize order flow via single-dealer platforms.[21]

This change is due in part to the commoditized nature of spot FX and its amenability to algorithmic trading. Approximately 41 per cent of global FX trading involves just two currency pairs: EUR v USD and USD v JPY.[22] Spot FX

---

[18] For an analysis of market structural developments based on this data, see Rime and Schrimpf, 'Anatomy', 2013.

[19] Mahmoodzadeh and Gençay, 'Human vs. high frequency', 2017.

[20] On the relationship between tick size and algorithmic trading, see Bessembinder, 'Trade execution COSTS', 2003.

[21] Golden, 'OTC FX trading', 2016.   [22] BIS, 'Triennial central bank survey', 2016, 5.

also has a relatively small average trade size of USD 1–2 million.[23] And, finally, spot FX is more straightforward than complex instruments such as FX swaps (few transactions in finance are as simple as the trade of, for example, one USD for one Euro). In sum, the relative simplicity, high liquidity, and small average trade size of spot FX is well suited for electronic trading and HFT. As a result, spot FX has been at the forefront of the transition to electronic trading in currency markets.

Electronic execution methods in FX have been predominant for only about 20 years. In the early 1990s, bank-to-client and bank-to-bank activity was still generally carried out over the phone. This changed later in the decade, when two electronic platforms, Reuters Dealing 2000 and EBS, established dominance, handling a combined 85 per cent of inter-dealer activity as of 2005.[24] The trend toward electronic trading has continued: one study concluded as early as 2012 that the proportion of market participants trading FX electronically in the US, the UK, and continental Europe was 82 per cent, 82 per cent, and 75 per cent, respectively.[25] Spot FX is, in effect, a wholly electronic market. Any remaining voice trading is largely restricted to abnormally large trades (e.g. by high net worth individuals) and for transactions in more exotic (i.e. less commonly traded) currency pairs.[26]

As the spot FX market has become more electronic, a number of additional corresponding trends have occurred. First, average trade sizes have decreased. One study finds that the average trade size in spot FX has declined from approximately USD 3.6 million in 2005 to USD 1.4 million in 2009, a decrease of almost 40 per cent in four years.[27] It is no accident that the prevalence of algorithmic trading and HFT in FX significantly increased during the same period. Data from the BIS indicates that the percentage of average daily spot FX trading volume attributable to 'other financial institutions', which includes algorithm-driven hedge funds and proprietary trading firms specializing in HFT methods, rose from approximately 21 per cent in 1998 to 56 per cent in 2016.[28] The 'prime broker' model of trading access largely facilitated this change. The prime broker model allows customers to establish lines of credit and utilize the prime broker's connectivity infrastructure for market access. As a result, customers can transact with a wider set of counterparties more quickly, and, in some cases, maintain anonymity by trading under the name of their prime broker.

---

[23] Moore et al. 'Downsized FX markets', 2016, 49.
[24] Sager and Taylor, 'Under the microscope', 2006.
[25] Greenwich Associates, 'Trading slowdown', 2013.
[26] Edelen, 'Is FX voice trading dead?', 2012.
[27] Zubulake and Lee, *High Frequency Game Changer*, 2011, 92.
[28] Numbers calculated from BIS, 'Triennial central bank survey', 1998; BIS, 'Triennial central bank survey', 2016.

Table 4.1. Top ten firms by total FX volume, 2016

Ranking	Firm	Total market share
1	Citibank	12.91%
2	J.P. Morgan	8.77%
3	UBS Bank	8.76%
4	Deutsche Bank	7.86%
5	Bank of America Merrill Lynch	6.40%
6	Barclays Bank	5.67%
7	Goldman Sachs	4.56%
8	HSBC	4.56%
9	**XTX Markets**	**3.87%**
10	Morgan Stanley	3.19%

Source: Euromoney, 'All Change', 2016.

The increase in trading volume for 'other financial institutions' has come primarily at the cost of what the BIS terms 'reporting dealers', meaning global banks that have traditionally dominated the provision of liquidity in FX markets.[29] And, indeed, non-bank liquidity providers (i.e. proprietary trading firms specializing in HFT methods) have begun to encroach directly on this territory. One consultancy estimates that non-bank liquidity providers account for 15–35 per cent of volume in spot FX and developed listed equities markets.[30] And in a recent survey conducted by *Euromoney*, a non-bank liquidity provider (XTX Markets) broke into the list of top 10 firms by overall FX market share for the first time in history (see Table 4.1).

The ability of non-bank liquidity providers to make such gains over global banks is largely attributable to two factors. First, these firms are able to access significant funds via their prime broker(s) without the costs and complexities of providing the full suite of traditional banking services. Second, non-bank liquidity providers (particularly HFT-focused hedge funds) have proven more adept at recruiting top technology talent and adjusting quickly in response to industry changes.

In sum, today's wholesale spot FX markets are electronic, feature smaller average trade sizes (most commonly the equivalent of USD 1 million), and are heavily influenced by non-bank liquidity providers. Electronic trading methods do have efficiency advantages over traditional voice trading. But, notably, these changes have also facilitated the development of new structural issues in the FX market.

[29] Ibid. See also Rime and Schrimpf.
[30] Graseck et al., 'World turned upside down', 2017, 28.

4.4 Market Structure Issues in Foreign Exchange Trading

Like all asset classes, FX has always been vulnerable to different forms of market abuse and perverse incentives. The era of electronic trading has, however, created new problems (or exacerbated existing problems), raising questions about whether the existing regulatory landscape is sufficient. In this section we discuss the primary structural, market quality, and conduct-related issues in FX.

4.4.1 *Speed and Latency Arbitrage*

As processing power improved during the electronification of the spot FX market, sophisticated hedge funds and a new breed of proprietary trading firms found opportunities to achieve 'alpha' (industry terminology for active return on investment in excess of a market index). This was largely predicated upon the ability of algorithms to trade at extremely high frequencies within very short time frames. Trading quickly and frequently is not inherently bad. What has created issues, however, is the ability of certain firms to acquire faster access than others to trading venue servers and market data.

In order to understand how this works, it is important to note that, in simplified terms, requests to buy or sell currencies on trading venues are 'filled' in the order that they are received. Therefore, if a participant can send their requests more quickly than others, they are more likely to receive the best possible price. Often the difference in price is very small (pennies on the dollar, or even less). But when trading at extremely high frequencies, these differences add up.[31] Billions of dollars have been invested in creating a complex network of data centres, underground cables, and microwave signals, typified by Spread Networks and Seaborn Networks' 2017 launch of a submarine fibre optic cable system from data centres in Carteret, New Jersey to BM&F Bovespa Stock Exchange in São Paulo, Brazil.[32] The goal of these investments is to reduce 'latency' (i.e. the time that passes between electronic messages) so that customers can execute, amend, or cancel orders as quickly as possible.

The proliferation of electronic trading venues and data centres, combined with the ability to purchase faster access and information, has created an asymmetry between more and less-informed participants. One of the most common methods of exploiting this asymmetry is to engage in what is widely referred to as 'latency arbitrage'. Although there are various types of latency

---

[31] HFT giant Virtu Financial is the most commonly cited example of how profitable these small advantages can be. In its initial public offering document, Virtu acknowledged that it lost money on just one day from 2009 to 2014. Virtu, 'Form S-1', 2015.
[32] Spread Networks, 'Spread Networks and Seaborn', 2017.

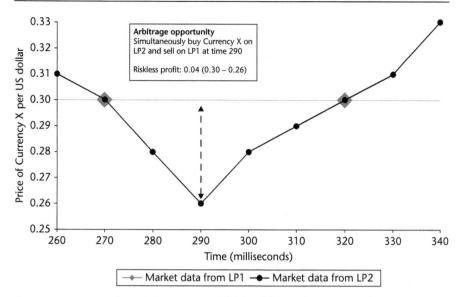

Figure 4.1. Arbitrage opportunity presented by differential price feeds

Note: the markers represent the moments at which each feed (LP1 and LP2) updates price information for Currency X. Because LP1 updates less frequently than LP2, there are instances (e.g. at time 290) in which LP1's displayed price is out-of-date (i.e. 'stale').

arbitrage, the term usually refers to the exploitation of price differences in identical or similar financial instruments across multiple trading venues. One group of scholars constructed and examined a real-life opportunity to engage in latency arbitrage in Apple Stock, finding that a fast trader with access to proprietary data feeds could make a profit of USD 32,510 in one day.[33] And in a recent working paper using data from 11 US equities exchanges, Wah estimates that the total realizable profit from latency arbitrage in S&P 500 stocks was more than USD 3 billion in 2014.[34]

Latency arbitrage is also highly prevalent in FX markets. Here we provide a worked example of an arbitrage opportunity in FX (Figure 4.1). This example is based on hypothetical market data from two different platforms/liquidity providers (LP1 and LP2) that provide data on the price of a particular currency at different frequencies. As discussed at greater length in Section 4.4.4, numerous FX platforms provide customers with the option to pay for superior data provided at faster speeds. Therefore, this hypothetical example is representative of a common, real-life arbitrage opportunity.

Here we see significant fluctuation in Currency X in less than 80ms. The price feeds (LP1 and LP2) follow the same trend line but provide information at different frequencies. If one were to have access only to price information

---

[33] Ding et al., 'How slow is the NBBO?', 2014.   [34] Wah, 'How prevalent?', 2016.

from LP1, one would not be aware that Currency X was actually experiencing significant fluctuation between the posted prices. More importantly, one would not be aware that the price one is viewing at, for example, the 290ms mark is stale (i.e. out-of-date). This provides a riskless arbitrage opportunity for market participants with access to both trading venues and data streams. Specifically, an HFT algorithm can buy Currency X on LP2 at the 290ms mark at $0.26 and instantaneously sell at $0.30 on LP1. The $0.04 difference is riskless arbitrage profit. An algorithm can be programmed to identify and execute such opportunities hundreds or thousands of times per day.

If, however, a randomized delay is applied, the arbitrage opportunity may be eliminated. For example, if a delay of 30ms is applied (Figure 4.2), the orders placed by the HFT algorithm at the 290ms mark will not be filled instantaneously. After the application of the delay, the desired buy and sell prices are no longer available. Instead, the order is filled at the 320ms mark when the prices displayed by LP1 and LP2 are the same. As a result, the riskless arbitrage opportunity is no longer available. Further, the threat of a randomized delay introduces an element of uncertainty that may deter the pursuit of said opportunities.

Latency is also integral to the use of first-in first-out (FIFO) order stacking. In HFT, FIFO order stacking refers to a method in which orders are placed at every potential price level possible before any other counterparty places orders. These orders are small (no more than the equivalent of USD 1 million) and are generally referred to as 'feelers'. They allow the HFT firm to acquire information

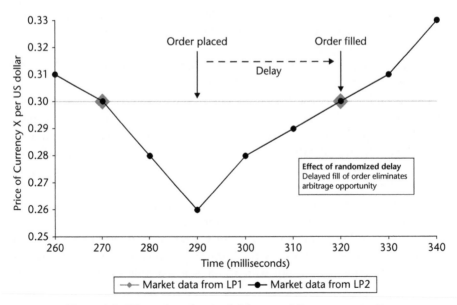

Figure 4.2. Effect of randomized delay on arbitrage opportunity

on impending opportunities and take advantage ahead of other markets participants. Further, they allow the firm to more accurately gauge the cause of a particular price movement (e.g. aggressive trading versus more mundane adjustments in response to external information).

Many venues also provide an execution report to counterparties before confirmation of the trade is made available to the public via market data feeds pulsing information at different frequencies. By stacking orders, an HFT algorithm can acquire this information before other market participants. These advantages are so significant that certain participants may attempt to stack orders across the market in order to 'cut' the line (queue-jump) ahead of other participants. Such actions are referred to as 'walking' the market. They allow the 'walker' to ensure they receive information and/or execution first and, in certain circumstances, provide the impression of increased liquidity.

4.4.2 *Market Manipulation and Questionable Trading Practices*

A particularly concerning byproduct of electronification in FX is the ability to engage in high frequency market behaviour that may negatively impact market integrity and/or other participants. In this subsection, we examine front-running and two types of abuse based on order cancellation: spoofing/layering and quote stuffing. Some of these practices are actually old types of abuse dressed in new clothes. What differentiates the current period, however, is the pace and frequency at which nefarious market participants are able to take advantage of low-latency techniques at the cost of other traders.

Front-running occurs when a market participant trades based on advance knowledge of pending orders from another market participant, allowing him or her to profit from that knowledge. Take, for example, a situation in which Trader A knows in advance that Trader B wants to buy British pounds (GBP) in exchange for US dollars (USD) at an exchange rate of 1.3215. With this knowledge in hand, Trader A can execute the same trade before Trader B. Trader A is then able to turn around and sell the currency to Trader B at an inflated price. Trader A's front-running profit is the difference between the original price and the price at which the currency is sold back to Trader B.

In 2016, the US Department of Justice charged the head of global foreign exchange cash trading at HSBC Bank plc with conspiracy to commit wire fraud by front-running a client's order.[35] The complaint alleges that in the course of executing a USD 3.5 billion conversion related to the planned sale of a client's foreign subsidiary, certain individuals at the bank purposely drove up the price of sterling in advance, resulting in approximately USD 8 million in illicit

---

[35] DOJ, 'Global head', 2016.

profits at the client's expense. Front-running does not, however, always involve such large sums. The ability of certain firms to acquire faster access to venues has made it possible to obtain data on other firms' trading intentions (known as 'information leakage'). Access to this data, in conjunction with the ability to trade faster than other participants, provides certain firms with a significant advantage. Firms can exploit this advantage by, for example, trading before slower, less-informed participants within extremely small time-periods (milliseconds or microseconds) and in a manner that is difficult to detect. Further, this allows firms to front-run FX orders undertaken to hedge against the currency risk associated with trades of other asset types (e.g. equities, bonds, or commodity derivatives). The latter method is what one might call 'second order' front-running. Each move may generate only a very small profit, but when repeated hundreds (or thousands) of times, the gains add up.

A number of additional forms of high-speed manipulation are based on the cancellation of orders. Spoofing, for example, occurs when a market participant submits a flurry of orders to buy or sell a financial instrument in order to create the illusion of market liquidity. Once other market participants react to this apparent activity and the price changes as a result, the spoofer quickly cancels their orders and trades against those market participants, profiting at their expense. Layering is a similar tactic in which traders place and cancel orders on both the buy *and* sell sides to create the illusion of general market activity in the particular currency. Not every strategy, however, is designed to give the appearance of liquidity. Quote stuffing, for example, is a method by which algorithms flood the market to overwhelm data feeds and create delays. The ensuing confusion creates opportunities to mask activity. In 2015, the New York attorney general's office issued subpoenas to a number of broker-dealers in relation to accusations of spoofing in FX.[36] This followed a landmark criminal case in which a former trader was sentenced to three years in prison for spoofing in various asset classes, including Euro FX and pound FX futures.[37]

Anecdotal evidence collected by the authors suggests, however, that enforcement actions do not necessarily capture the extent of morally ambiguous trading behaviour by participants using latency-driven strategies. This is due, in part, to the difficulty of recognizing and categorizing such behaviour as potentially manipulative. It is extremely challenging to accurately set thresholds for what constitutes potentially suspicious behaviour. Equally difficult is the legal hurdle of establishing intent to manipulate the market or other participants.[38] Some firms have experimented with alternative methods

---

[36] Chon and Stafford, 'New York's top prosecutor', 2015.
[37] DOJ, 'High-frequency trader convicted', 2015.   [38] Yadav, 'Insider trading', 2016.

of preventing such activities. ParFX has (*inter alia*) implemented a randomized delay in order to introduce an element of execution uncertainty. This uncertainty is designed in order to, in part, undermine the capacity of nefarious algorithms to anticipate opportunities for front-running or spoofing. The Toronto Stock Exchange's TSX Alpha has also implemented a randomized delay in respect to equities.[39]

4.4.3 *The Liquidity Mirage and Flash Crashes*

As a result of the increase in order cancellation and nefarious practices discussed above, FX has also experienced the infamous 'liquidity mirage' widely recognized in equities markets.[40] The liquidity mirage in FX refers to the illusion of liquidity created by the tremendous number of prices placed but ultimately cancelled. At any moment in time, there may be only one price and one level of liquidity in a currency pair in the wholesale market. This information is proliferated across multiple dealing channels as a data point. The mirage appears when there is an over-extension of that price by counterparties who are not in the genuine business of assuming or transferring risk. In other words, speculative participants submit multiple orders on multiple venues based on the same data point, giving a false impression of the demand/supply for that particular currency at that particular price.

This may reflect nefarious activity or simply legitimate strategies that involve cancelling or amending orders. Regardless, it often makes it difficult for market participants to execute at their desired price or full order size. The situation is adeptly summarized by Andrew Haldane, former Executive Director for Financial Stability at the Bank of England: 'With HFT firms serving as de-facto market-makers, but with the vast majority of their orders cancelled, many on-screen quotes may not actually be executable. This creates a potentially misleading picture of market resilience, a mirage of liquidity.'[41] The liquidity mirage is a factor in FX markets, challenging efforts to obtain the best possible execution quality.

In addition, the electronification of FX markets has been associated with a rise in so-called flash crashes. Table 4.2 lists notable currency flash crashes in recent years.

Further, FX markets have experienced mini flash crashes, or what one group of scholars terms 'ultra-fast extreme events'.[42] There is no agreed-upon definition of mini flash crashes, but they generally refer to sharp movements in the

---

[39] TMX, 'Overview', 2016.
[40] This term was popularized by Lewis. For additional discussion with specific reference to FX, see King and Rime, 'Algorithmic trading', 2011; Heath and Whitelaw, 'Electronic trading', 2011.
[41] Haldane, 'Financial arms races', 2012, 5.   [42] Johnson et al., 'Abrupt rise', 2013.

Table 4.2. Recent flash crashes in foreign exchange markets

Date	Currency	Fluctuation in price
March 2015	USD	3.0%
October 2016	GBP	9.0%
May 2017	GBP	0.8%

Source: Nanex, 'U.S. Dollar Flash Crash', 2015; Badkar and Wigglesworth, 'Another Pound Flash Crash?', 2017; BIS Markets Committee, 'The Sterling "Flash Event"', 2017.

price of a security within extremely small periods of time. Unlike normal flash crashes, these fluctuations tend to rebound at equally extreme speeds, and therefore are not normally apparent to human traders. A recent study by Pragma Securities has attempted to define a currency flash crash as a large price move (13 times normal volatility) with a strong reversion in price (more than 70 per cent) and a widened spread (more than two times normal spread).[43] In a sample size of 313,000 price movements in 11 currency pairs, this definition captured 69 flash crash events from 2015 to 2016, including those widely publicized in the press such as the October 2016 sterling flash crash. This exercise also demonstrates, however, the technical difficulties of defining flash crashes. Very small changes in the pre-set thresholds may significantly affect the number of flash crashes recognized and, therefore, our perception of whether such events have increased or decreased over time.[44] Further investigations into the prevalence of this phenomenon in FX and its implications for market efficiency would be an excellent avenue for future research.

4.4.4 *Perverse Incentives Facing FX Trading Venues*

FX market participants will, understandably, pursue opportunities for profit wherever they might be found. And as we have noted in previous subsections, FX trading venues have provided plenty of new opportunities. In the era of electronification, the great majority of said venues have succumbed to a perverse incentive to monetize informational asymmetries. Here we discuss two of the primary methods by which they do so. First, they allow users to pay extra money to acquire superior trading data before other market participants. They do so by letting firms (a) place their servers next to that of the trading venues ('co-location') and (b) purchase subscriptions to higher-quality data. Second, they pay certain participants to direct trades toward their venue,

---

[43] Pragma Securities, 'Defining the FX flash crash', 2017, 5.

[44] In the sample period studied, the researchers found no clear upward or downward trend in the number of flash crashes over time. Ibid., 6.

commonly referred to as 'payment for order flow'. Regardless of intent, these practices indirectly facilitate the structural issues discussed above.

4.4.4.1 CO-LOCATION AND DIFFERENTIAL DATA ACCESS

In order to pursue latency-driven strategies, firms naturally need to have faster access to trading venues than the competition.[45] They can acquire this access by purchasing the option to 'co-locate' their servers next to those of the venue. Initially, trading venues provided this opportunity by hosting customer systems in their own data centres. More recently, third-party providers (e.g. Equinix) host both venue technology and customer technology in independent sites, enabling low-cost access to markets at very low latency.

The proximity to the matching engine of a venue enables the HFT firm to place an order very quickly and, importantly, to amend or remove that order quickly. Many exchanges and third-party data centres offer co-location to numerous market participants and coil their cables to ensure that clients have equal latency advantages regardless of the physical position of their servers within the warehouse. Nevertheless, there remains a significant speed asymmetry between firms that have acquired limited co-location spaces and those that have not.

In addition, FX trading venues provide superior trading data to firms for extra fees. Firms executing HFT strategies benefit from having access to faster and higher-quality market data than other counterparties. The subsequent informational asymmetry provides a significant trading advantage. Venues have, over time, recognized that selling superior data presents a sustainable source of non-volatile revenue (i.e. revenue not based on trading volume). There is, of course, the fee itself. But some venues will also create certain conditions for accessing superior data. EBS, for example, allows participation in their 'Live Ultra' data feed only if participants deal as price makers for at least $200 million per day and for at least 40 per cent of their weekly traded volume.[46] The Live Ultra feed updates at 5ms intervals, as opposed to EBS's other interval rates of 20ms and 100ms.[47] Therefore, in return for providing superior data at faster speeds to large market participants, the venue receives not just additional revenue but also a valuable source of liquidity provision.

One might argue that superior access to trade data is no different from paying for a Bloomberg terminal. But this is a false equivalence. The superior trade data that FX trading platforms provide can be used to pursue low-latency strategies that result in direct losses for less informed and less wealthy

---

[45] Further, firms focusing on HFT strategies need the round-trip time of messaging to and from venues to be as deterministic as possible to ensure that their trading algorithms can accurately predict the time such messages are submitted to, and acted upon by, the venue.

[46] Finextra, 'EBS BrokerTec', 2016.   [47] Abdel-Qader, 'EBS's super-fast data feed', 2017.

participants. In addition, if firms purchase access to superior data and/or speed in order to *avoid* such losses, this represents an unnecessary cost that is particularly burdensome for (a) smaller players and (b) entities that need to hedge their own currency exposure and whose prime motivation is not based on latency arbitrage/alpha opportunities.

4.4.4.2 PAYMENT FOR ORDER FLOW

Numerous FX platforms incentivize and/or pay for order flow through schemes that may be specific to a participant or offered to all participants. This usually takes the form of rebates for sending orders and trades to their venue. Firms are normally rebated according to their average daily volume (ADV) on the platform in question. Naturally, the rebate increases commensurately with ADV. Alternatively, exchanges may simply reward higher ADV with reduced fees. The Chicago Mercantile Exchange's transaction fee for standard FX futures, for example, starts at $0.32 for ADV of 0–6,500 but reduces to $0.11 for ADV in excess of 65,000.[48]

Venues provide these rebates and fee reductions in order to make their market look more liquid than it actually would be in perfect competition. The more liquid a market looks, the more likely it is to attract additional participants. But paying for order flow can create a conflict of interest, particular when participants are directing orders to the venue on behalf of clients.[49] Brokers can become incentivized to direct orders to whichever venue pays the best rebate, rather than where the best price is offered. This non-optimal execution translates into a direct loss for clients. This is particularly concerning in FX given the rapidly growing retail FX market. The BIS found that in April 2013 retail FX trading accounted for, on average, 3.8 per cent of total daily spot FX turnover, equating to approximately USD 78 billion per day.[50]

4.4.5 *Last Look*

Unlike equities, FX markets also face the problem of 'last look'. Last look refers to the capacity of FX market makers (generally global banks) to have a final review of a matched order before it executes. This ability to cancel pending orders is not available to other counterparties. Last look originally developed to protect market makers against volatility and manipulation.[51] But it has

---

[48] CME, 'Fees for trading', 2016. This specific rebate is available only to Corporate Equity Members.
[49] FSA, 'Finalised guidance', 2012.   [50] BIS, 'Retail trading', 2013.
[51] Bank of England, HM Treasury, and Financial Conduct Authority, 'Fair and effective', 2015, 31.

come under substantial criticism, as it also allows market makers to abuse this power by rejecting unprofitable trades in a systematic manner.

And, indeed, Barclays was fined USD 150 million in 2015 for doing just that.[52] Specifically, the New York Department of Financial Services (NYDFS) found that Barclays was automatically rejecting trades that would be unprofitable as a result of price swings during the last look 'holding' period (i.e. the milliseconds between an agreed trade and Barclays' final opportunity to 'have a last look' before execution). When clients asked why their orders were receiving an abnormal number of cancellations, Barclays staff were instructed to blame other factors such as latency or general market volatility rather than mentioning the profitability of the trades in question.[53] Barclays managers also instructed staff to hide the existence of their last look capability from sales staff: 'avoid mentioning the existence of the whole BATS Last Look functionality. If you get enquiries just obfuscate and stonewall.'[54]

Numerous segments of the industry have argued that last look is an outdated practice. An important example is the FX Global Code recently released by the Foreign Exchange Working Group (FXWG). The FXWG is sponsored by the central banks of major industrialized states and features both public and private representatives from each member country. The Code states that liquidity providers should be transparent about how they use last look.[55] It specifically emphasizes transparency around how market makers use the information they obtain in the course of cancelling transactions.[56] But without explicit regulatory prohibition, last look continues to be used, often inconsistently. It is possible that the industry will eliminate last look without regulatory interference. XTX Markets, the world's largest non-bank liquidity provider, has moved in this direction with the introduction of zero-latency holding periods to its direct client feeds.[57] Although not an outright elimination of last look capability, the change is indicative of greater industry awareness of, and concern with, last look abuse.

4.5 Regulation of Foreign Exchange Markets

Regulators in multiple jurisdictions have acknowledged the market structural issues discussed in this chapter. FX markets feature prominently in the UK's Fair and Effective Markets Review. And in the United States the Commodity Futures Trading Commission (CFTC) has taken steps to implement FX-specific provisions introduced by the Dodd-Frank Wall Street Reform and Consumer

---

[52] NYDFS, 'NYDFS announces', 2015.   [53] Ibid.   [54] Ibid.
[55] GFXC, 'FX Global Code', 2017, 20.   [56] Ibid.
[57] Golovtchenko, 'Breaking', 2017. Further, ParFX does not permit the use of last look.

Protection Act (Dodd-Frank) and the Food, Conservation and Energy Act of 2008.[58]

Nevertheless, these acknowledgements have translated into only a limited number of explicit regulatory requirements when it comes to spot FX. These gaps are due, in part, to the difficulties of coordinating national regulatory policies to address what is a truly global FX market. But, as will be discussed in more detail in Section 4.5.1, it is also a result of direct industry lobbying. In this section, we analyse the regulation of spot FX in two significant national jurisdictions: the UK/European Union and the US. We then go beyond state legislation and examine the role of private standard-setting bodies.

4.5.1 *Regulation of Spot FX in the UK and European Union*

Spot FX is very lightly regulated in the UK and the European Union (EU). As stated by Edwin Schooling Latter, Head of Markets Policy at the UK Financial Conduct Authority (FCA):

> ... spot FX sits in an interesting place on what we call our regulatory perimeter. Spot FX trading is only within the perimeter in certain circumstances, for example where a spot trade is ancillary to a transaction in a regulated 'financial instrument' (for example, when buying currency to purchase a bond), or where manipulation of prices on spot FX markets impacts the prices on regulated markets such as those for FX derivatives, or impacts on a benchmark. Most other FX trading is, in formal terms, outside our perimeter.[59]

As Latter notes, spot FX is excluded from the list of financial instruments subject to the EU's Market Abuse Directive II (commonly referred to as the Market Abuse Regulation, or MAR), which came into effect in July 2016. MAR explicitly defines and prohibits various types of low-latency abuse, including spoofing, layering, and quote stuffing.[60] MAR also imposes a requirement on trading venues, proprietary trading firms, and brokers to implement a system for detecting and reporting potentially suspicious activity. Spot FX is excluded from these rules, unless orders or transactions in spot FX result in the manipulation of financial instruments or benchmarks that *are* captured by MAR. The FCA has nevertheless indicated that they expect firms to engage in appropriate market conduct in relation to spot FX and have publicly supported implementation of the FX Global Code.[61] But the absence of formal rules has created confusion within the industry, and may be incentivizing

---

[58] See, for example, CFTC, 'CFTC releases final rules', 2010.   [59] Latter, 'Conduct risk', 2016.

[60] ESMA, Commission Delegated Regulation 2017/565, 2017, Annex III. Notably, however, it does not provide specific prescriptions of how to set parameters for the detection of those potentially suspicious behaviours.

[61] Latter.

firms to disregard (or delay) MAR's provisions when it comes to their spot FX business.[62]

Spot FX is also largely absent from the largest financial regulatory regime ever introduced in Europe, the Markets in Financial Instruments Directive II (MiFID II). This was not for lack of consideration. The European Securities and Markets Authority (ESMA) queried spot FX in the course of designing MiFID II and the European Markets Infrastructure Regulation (EMIR). The latter concerns the regulation of derivatives, central counterparties and trade repositories. The EU found significant variation in the way different member states define FX spot and forward contracts.[63] Ultimately, it was concluded that a spot contract was any contract for the exchange of one currency for another with delivery schedules within two trading days, and that these contracts would be excluded from the definition of a 'financial instrument' under MiFID II.[64] This was allegedly the result of lobbying efforts by certain segments of the industry that were concerned about the cost of increased trade reporting requirements.[65]

Firms that trade or match orders in spot FX generally also do so in FX forwards and other types of derivatives contracts. Therefore, many firms and venues engaged in spot FX will be subject to MiFID II despite its exclusion. But the gap provides an avenue for firms to legally dis-apply certain provisions of MiFID II to spot contracts. Within MiFID II there are numerous new requirements that would contribute to the amelioration of the problems identified above. These include requirements to robustly test trading algorithms, establish risk limits, and maintain the capacity to instantly stop trading through the use of so-called 'kill switches' (Article 17).

Spot FX may, however, benefit from the effort of MiFID II to transition over-the-counter trading in financial instruments to exchanges and exchange-like platforms. The Directive creates a new legal category of trading venue called Organised Trading Facilities (OTFs) and expands requirements for the existing categories of Multilateral Trading Facilities (MTFs) and Systematic Internalisers (SIs). The specific differences between these types are not necessary for the purpose of this chapter. The key point is that they will capture (and therefore impose new requirements on) many FX single-dealer and multi-dealer platforms. Those platforms may end up applying the same standards to spot FX as part of a risk-based approach.

The legislation does attempt to address the market structural issues discussed in this chapter. MiFID II requires venues to monitor its participants'

---

[62] Golden, 'More clarity', 4 August 2016.
[63] ESMA, 'Impact Assessment on Delegated Acts Implementing Directive 2014/65/EU', 2016, 124.
[64] ESMA, Commission Delegated Regulation 2017/565, 2017, Article 10.
[65] Khalique, 'FX players', 25 April 2014.

order-to-trade ratios and punish firms that exceed pre-set thresholds.[66] The goal is to discourage order-driven strategies that contribute to disorderly markets, such as quote stuffing. These rules do not, however, prescribe just how large that punishment should be. This may provide trading venues with an opportunity to set relatively trivial penalties, undermining the effectiveness of order-to-trade ratios as a deterrence mechanism. And, as noted above, there is no regulatory prohibition of last look practices.

4.5.2 Regulation of Spot FX in the United States

Before the late 20th century, FX trading was largely unregulated in the United States. This changed with the passage of the Commodity Futures Trading Commission Act of 1974, which created the CFTC and brought exchange-traded derivatives (including FX derivatives) under its regulatory jurisdiction. Over-the-counter FX Trading was excluded, based on the US Treasury Department's reasoning that FX market participants knew what they were doing and were already subject to oversight by the Federal Reserve and Comptroller of the Currency.[67] This exclusion was reinforced in numerous court decisions, at one point preventing the CFTC from bringing enforcement actions against FX 'bucket shops' that were defrauding retail investors.[68] In response, Congress provided the CFTC with jurisdiction over retail FX transactions in the Commodity Future Modernization Act of 2000 (CFMA).

FX trading between institutional investors finally came into scope as part of Dodd-Frank, which also created new, complicated trade reporting requirements and specific provisions for the protection of retail FX participants. Like MiFID II, Dodd-Frank inspired an intense debate over the exact definition of certain derivatives contracts, in this case swaps. The final rules confirmed that non-exempt swaps would include foreign currency options, currency swaps, cross-currency swaps, and non-deliverable forward contracts involving foreign exchange.[69]

Notably, however, none of these rules cover spot FX. Exchanges of one currency for another with standard two-day settlement periods are excluded from CFMA, and do not form part of the definition of a retail FX transaction under the Commodity Exchange Act.[70] The CFTC does, however, maintain the ability to enforce against market manipulation and fraud in spot FX despite its general exclusion from regulation. This is based on the agency's wide interpretation of its anti-manipulation powers over 'any commodity in

---

[66] ESMA, Commission Draft Delegated Regulation C(2016) 2775 Final, 2016.
[67] Carruthers, 'Credit ratings', 2016, 338.   [68] Aron et al., 'Regulation', 2017, 3.
[69] WSGR, 'Fourth update', 2014.
[70] Latham & Watkins, 'Regulation', 2013; SEC, Final Rule, 2013; Winston & Strawn LLP, 'Dodd-Frank', 2013.

interstate commerce'.[71] And like MAR, the CFTC and the Financial Industry Regulatory Authority (FINRA) expect certain firms to have controls in place to detect and report suspicious transactions. The agencies' most high-profile FX-related enforcement actions thus far have, however, related to the spoofing of FX futures and the manipulation of FX benchmarks rather than to spot contracts.

The CFTC has also introduced preventative measures that share certain characteristics with new MiFID II rules. For example, Designated Contract Markets (DCMs), which captures trading venues, are required to have risk control mechanisms to prevent and reduce the risk of market disruptions, including trading halt mechanisms that resemble what ESMA refers to as 'kill switches'.[72] Like MAR and MiFID II, it is not clear that spot FX falls within the realm of instruments to which these preventative rules apply (despite the CFTC's clear ability to enforce against manipulation and fraud in instruments outside regulation). But, also like MAR and MiFID II, numerous firms are likely to apply such preventative measures regardless in order to mitigate regulatory risk. More concerning is that existing restrictions in the United States do not address the fundamental structural issues identified in this chapter. As long as it remains legal and standard industry practice for venues to sell differential access to speed and data, the market is vulnerable to high frequency manipulation. There are signs that the latter may be more amenable to change than the former. As noted above and mentioned in more detail within this chapter, numerous exchanges (e.g. IEX and ParFX) are experimenting with alternative business models that purposefully mitigate the benefits of speed.

4.5.3 *Private Standard Setting and Best Practices*

Public regulation is not the only method of encouraging industry change; there are also private-led initiatives. The FICC Markets Standards Board (FMSB), for example, was established by the private sector in 2015 as a response to the Bank of England's Fair and Effective Markets Review.[73] The FMSB focuses on fixed income, currencies and commodities (FICC), and was inspired by conduct-related issues in all three markets since the 2008 financial crisis. The FMSB, whose membership includes most of the largest global banks and broker-dealers, is, at the time of writing, working on standards for algorithmic trading and trading venue practices that provide more detailed guidance on implementation than do existing public regulations.

There are a number of areas where the FMSB could provide additional guidance on existing regulations and address spot FX. With regard to

---

[71] Aron et al., 11.   [72] CFTC, 'Concept release', 2013, 24.

[73] Daniel Marcus is a member of the FMSB Electronic Trading and Technology Committee.

algorithmic trading, the FMSB could, for example, encourage firms to create specific lines of accountability for individual algorithms and outline what parameters can be set by human employees. It could also recommend that firms disclose to customers how routing preferences may be determined in order to address any potential conflicts of interest presented by payment for order flow programs. Further, the FMSB could provide recommendations on what types of tests should be considered when firms update their order execution software. This level of detail would go beyond UK and European regulatory provisions, which generally refrain from prescribing the exact form of testing and risk management algorithmic traders should be using. In this sense, the FMSB has the opportunity to complement regulatory efforts.

In addition, the FMSB should, through the creation of industry standards, encourage venue operators to be transparent regarding all key aspects of their trade execution processes. This should include disclosing all available order types and the manner in which bids and offers are filled. The FMSB should also build on the work of the FX Global Code of Conduct and address last look in more detail by recommending that customers be provided with a full account of how liquidity providers are using information obtained in the course of rejecting trades. The FMSB could also directly address potential conflicts of interest associated with fee structures and rebate schemes. Specifically, the FMSB could recommend that said structure and schemes are not designed in a manner that could encourage market misconduct or disorderly trading conditions. Although firms are not legally obliged to comply with FMSB recommendations, national regulators may be encouraged to reference firms to FMSB standards as a benchmark for compliance. There is precedent for doing so. The Joint Money Laundering Steering Group, for example, is an association of trade groups whose guidance on anti-money laundering is highly influential.

4.6 Concluding Thoughts and Avenues for Future Research

The academic analysis of high frequency trading in spot FX is in its infancy. This is due to a number of factors, not least the overwhelming focus of researchers on equities markets. The *FX Flash Boys* book has yet to be written (despite a large potential market for book sales!), and therefore researchers have largely ignored the extent to which such market structural issues exist in currency trading.[74] In *Flash Boys*, Michael Lewis argued that markets are rigged by virtue of the fact that sophisticated investors can use an asymmetry of data

---

[74] For a historical narrative of electronic trading and FX, see Rodgers, *Why Aren't They Shouting?*, 2016.

and execution access to ensure that they always win. The same issues are highly prevalent in spot FX. As Virtu has demonstrated, a losing day is like a blue moon.[75] The quality of HFT firms' technical capabilities, in conjunction with the possibility of paying for superior speed and information, provides ample opportunities for riskless profit.

As stated in this chapter, there are regulatory nods to policing HFT more effectively, particularly in MiFID II. But the efforts of legislators and regulators are undermined by a lack of empirical research. Does HFT improve markets by tightening bid/offer spreads, or are these benefits outweighed by the costs of the FX liquidity mirage? Exactly how prevalent is spoofing and layering, and what is the aggregate economic cost of these abusive strategies? How common are 'mini flash crashes' in currency markets, and what are the welfare implications? In this chapter, we have outlined these (and other) market structural issues and have endeavoured to provide data where possible. But significantly more empirical analysis is needed to provide any conclusive answers to these questions. Policy-makers rely on such analyses to determine appropriate regulatory responses, and therefore we strongly encourage further empirical research on high frequency trading in FX markets.

Conducting such research is particularly difficult due to the fact that spot FX, and the venues that provide access to it, have historically been lightly regulated and, therefore, do not provide national authorities with transactional data equivalent to that available on equities. Further, FX is a global product traded across venues on a fragmented basis, and hence a golden copy (i.e. an official, master record of data) is required to ensure that results are not misleading. Creating such a database is (far) easier said than done. But if regulators or private sectors actors assist the academic community and/or public institutions with collecting and standardizing information on currency trading, policy-makers will be in a much better position to objectively evaluate the costs and benefits of FX HFT.

Public regulation is not, however, the only option for addressing the structural issues discussed in this chapter. In equities trading, there is increasing support of IEX's goal of eliminating the advantages of speed and mitigating conflicts of interest. For example, a number of major venues (e.g. the New York Stock Exchange) have considered implementing IEX-like 'speed bumps' to slow down market access and eliminate the advantages of low-latency strategies.[76] Similarly, the FX market is engaged in a process of self-healing. There is widespread recognition within the industry that changes are needed

---

[75] For those keeping track, the US National Aeronautics and Space Administration (NASA) finds that a 'blue moon' (i.e. a month in which there are two full moons as opposed to the regular one because of calendar fluctuations) occurs, on average, every 2.5 years. Phillips, 'NASA – Blue Moon', 2004.

[76] Bullock, 'NYSE wins approval', 2017.

in order to ensure that FX markets remain fair and effective in the face of rapid technological advances and market structural changes. This desire to provide industry-led solutions has largely inspired the ParFX model and the efforts of the FMSB. Such 'change from within' initiatives can complement well-designed regulations, and, hopefully, reduce the perverse incentives that drive the FX race to zero.

References

Abdel-Qader, Aziz. 'EBS's super-fast data feed now pumps out price updates at 5ms intervals'. *Finance Magnates*. Available at: https://www.financemagnates.com/institutional-forex/technology/ebss-super-fast-data-feed-now-pumps-price-updates-5ms-interval/, 1 February 2017.

Aron, David, P. Georgia Bullitt, and Jed Doench. 'Regulation of U.S. currency transactions'. *Futures and Derivatives Law Report* 37, no. 5. Available at: http://www.willkie.com/~/media/Files/Publications/2017/06/Regulation of US Currency Transactions.pdf, 2017.

Badkar, Mamta, and Robin Wigglesworth. 'Another pound flash crash?' *Financial Times*. Available at: https://www.ft.com/content/8dcbf067-e645-362e-ac42-e104d57f3605, 18 May 2017.

Bank of England, HM Treasury, and Financial Conduct Authority. 'Fair and Effective Markets Review'. Available at: http://www.bankofengland.co.uk/markets/Documents/femrjun15.pdf, 2015.

Bessembinder, Hendrik. 'Trade execution costs and market quality after decimalization'. *Journal of Financial and Quantitative Analysis* 38, no. 4 (December 2003): 747.

Bird, Mike. 'Foreign-exchange brokers are getting wiped out by the Swiss franc's surge'. *Business Insider*. Available at: http://uk.businessinsider.com/foreign-exchange-brokers-are-getting-wiped-out-by-the-swiss-francs-surge-2015-1, 16 January 2015.

BIS (Bank for International Settlements). 'Triennial central bank survey of foreign exchange—statistical annexes'. Available at: https://www.bis.org/publ/r_fx98statanx.pdf, 1998.

BIS. 'Retail trading in the FX market'. Available at: http://www.bis.org/publ/qtrpdf/r_qt1312z.htm, 2013.

BIS. 'Triennial central bank survey of foreign exchange'. Available at: https://www.bis.org/publ/rpfx16fx.pdf, 2016.

BIS Markets Committee. 'The sterling "flash event"of 7 October 2016'. Available at: https://www.bis.org/publ/mktc09.pdf, 2017.

Bullock, Nicole. 'NYSE wins approval for "speed bump" in trading'. *Financial Times*. Available at: https://www.ft.com/content/eed7f77a-3a8a-11e7-821a-6027b8a20f23, 17 May 2017.

Carruthers, Bruce. 'Credit ratings and global economic governance: Non-price valuation in financial markets'. In *Contractual Knowledge: One Hundred Years of Legal*

Experimentation in Global Markets, ed. Grégoire Mallard and Jérôme Sgard, 324–50, Cambridge: Cambridge University Press, 2016.

CFTC (Commodity Futures Trading Commission). 'CFTC releases final rules regarding retail forex transactions'. Available at: http://www.cftc.gov/PressRoom/PressReleases/pr5883-10, 2010.

CFTC. 'Concept release on risk controls and system safeguards for automated trading environments'. Available at: https://www.federalregister.gov/documents/2014/01/24/2014-01372/concept-release-on-risk-controls-and-system-safeguards-for-automated-trading-environments, 2013.

CFTC. 'CFTC orders Forex Capital Markets, LLC (FXCM), its parent company, FXCM Holdings, LLC and FXCM's founding partners, Dror Niv and William Ahdout, to pay a $7 million penalty for FXCM's defrauding of retail forex customers'. Available at: http://www.cftc.gov/PressRoom/PressReleases/pr7528-17, 2017.

Chaboud, Alain P., Benjamin Chiquoine, Erik Hjalmarsson, and Clara Vega. 'Rise of the machines: Algorithmic trading in the foreign exchange market'. *Journal of Finance* 69, no. 5 (2014): 2045–84.

Chon, Gina, and Philip Stafford. 'New York's top prosecutor probes brokers over forex spoofing'. *Financial Times*. Available at: https://www.ft.com/content/48cb693e-9202-11e5-bd82-c1fb87bef7af, 23 November 2015.

CME (Chicago Mercantile Exchange). 'Fees for trading FX futures and options'. Available at: http://www.cmegroup.com/, 2016.

Ding, Shengwei, John Hanna, and Terrence Hendershott. 'How slow is the NBBO? A comparison with direct exchange feeds'. *Financial Review* 49, no. 2 (2014): 313–32.

DOJ (United States Department of Justice). 'High-frequency trader convicted of disrupting commodity futures market in first federal prosecution of "spoofing"'. Available at: https://www.justice.gov/usao-ndil/pr/high-frequency-trader-convicted-disrupting-commodity-futures-market-first-federal, 2015.

DOJ. 'Global head of HSBC's foreign exchange cash-trading desks arrested for orchestrating multimillion-dollar front running scheme'. Available at: https://www.justice.gov/opa/pr/global-head-hsbc-s-foreign-exchange-cash-trading-desks-arrested-orchestrating-multimillion, 2016.

Edelen, Candyce. 'Is FX voice trading dead?' *TABB Forum*. Available at: http://tabbforum.com/opinions/is-fx-voice-trading-dead, 3 December 2012.

Egan, Matt. 'Swiss shock crushes US currency broker'. *CNN Money*. Available at: http://money.cnn.com/2015/01/16/investing/swiss-currency-fxcm/index.html,16 January 2015.

ESMA (European Securities and Markets Authority). Commission Draft Delegated Regulation C(2016) 2775 Final. Available at: https://ec.europa.eu/transparency/regdoc/rep/3/2016/EN/3-2016-2775-EN-F1-1.PDF, 2016.

ESMA. Impact Assessment on Delegated Acts Implementing Directive 2014/65/EU of 15 May 2014 on Markets in Financial Instruments and Amending Directive 2002/92/EC and Directive 2011/61/EU(recast) and Regulation (EU) No 600/2014 of 15 May 2014 on Markets in Financial Instruments and Amending Regulation (EU) No 648/

2012. Available at: http://ec.europa.eu/smart-regulation/impact/ia_carried_out/docs/ia_2016/swd_2016_0157_en.pdf, 2016.

ESMA. Commission Delegated Regulation 2017/565, Official Journal of the European Union. Available at: http://eur-lex.europa.eu/legal-content/EN/TXT/PDF/?uri=CELEX:32017R0565&from=DE, 2017.

Euromoney. 'All change in the 2016 Euromoney FX Rankings'. *Euromoney*. Available at: https://www.euromoney.com/article/b12kp9ksqdg9gl/all-change-in-the-2016-euromoney-fx-rankings, 2016.

Finextra. 'EBS BrokerTec launches EBS Live Ultra'. *Finextra*. Available at: https://www.finextra.com/pressarticle/66302/ebs-brokertec-launches-ebs-live-ultra/wholesale, 28 September 2016.

Flood, Mark D. 'Market structure and inefficiency in the foreign exchange market'. *Journal of International Money and Finance* 13, no. 2 (1994): 131–58.

FSA (Financial Services Authority). 'Finalised guidance on the practice of "payment for order flow"'. Available at: https://www.fca.org.uk/publication/finalised-guidance/fg12-13.pdf, 2012.

GFXC. 'FX Global Code'. Available at: http://www.globalfxc.org/docs/fx_global.pdf, 2017.

Golden, Paul. 'More clarity needed on impact of MAR on Spot FX'. *Euromoney*. Available at: https://www.euromoney.com/article/b12kpl59bb140d/more-clarity-needed-on-impact-of-mar-on-spot-fx, 4 August 2016.

Golden, Paul. 'OTC FX trading becomes "exchange-like"'. *Euromoney*. Available at: https://www.euromoney.com/article/b12kp3zljw20cj/otc-fx-trading-becomes-exchange-like, 21 April 2016.

Golovtchenko, Victor. 'Breaking: XTX markets takes charge to reform last look holding window'. *Finance Magnates*. Available at: https://www.financemagnates.com/institutional-forex/brokerage/breaking-xtx-markets-takes-charge-reform-last-look-holding-window, 10 August 2017.

Graseck, Betsy L., Magdalena L. Stoklosa, Bruce Hamilton, Michael J. Cyprys, Anil Sharma, Vishwanath Tirupattur, Christian Edelmann, James Davis, Dylan Walsh, Mariya Rosberg, Patrick Hunt, Harriet Roberts, Aaron Sonenfeld, and David Selman. 'The world turned upside down'. New York: Oliver Wyman / Morgan Stanley. Available at: http://www.oliverwyman.com/content/dam/oliver-wyman/v2/publications/2017/mar/Oliver Wyman Morgan Stanley 2017.pdf, 2017.

Greenwich Associates. 'Trading slowdown can't stop the electronification of FX'. Available at: https://www.greenwich.com/press-release/trading-slowdown-cant-stop-electronification-fx, 2013.

Haldane, Andrew G. 'Financial arms races' (speech given at Institute for New Economic Thinking, Berlin). Available at: http://www.bis.org/review/r120426a.pdf, 2012.

Heath, Alexandra, and James Whitelaw. 'Electronic trading and the Australian foreign exchange market'. *Bulletin* [Sydney]. Available at: https://www.rba.gov.au/publications/bulletin/2011/jun/pdf/bu-0611-6.pdf, 2011.

Hunter, Michael, and Michael Mackenzie. 'Pound's plunge joins growing list of "flash crashes"'. *Financial Times*. Available at: https://www.ft.com/content/b214e822-8c5f-11e6-8cb7-e7ada1d123b1?mhq5j=e3, 7 October 2016.

Ito, Takatoshi, Richard K. Lyons, and Michael T. Melvin. 'Is there private information in the FX market? The Tokyo experiment'. *Journal of Finance* 53, no. 3 (1998): 1111–30.

Johnson, Neil, Guannan Zhao, Eric Hunsader, Hong Qi, Nicholas Johnson, Jing Meng, and Brian Tivnan. 'Abrupt rise of new machine ecology beyond human response time'. *Scientific Reports*, 3 (2013).

Khalique, Farah. 'FX players lobby Brussels for spot FX concession'. *Euromoney*. Available at: https://www.euromoney.com/article/b12kkrt202csm5/fx-players-lobby-brussels-for-spot-fx-concession, 25 April 2014.

King, Michael, and Dagfinn Rime. 'Algorithmic trading and FX market liquidity'. *CFA Magazine*. Available at: https://www.cfapubs.org/doi/pdf/10.2469/cfm.v22.n3.5, 2011.

King, Michael R., Carol L. Osler, and Dagfinn Rime. 'The market microstructure approach to foreign exchange: Looking back and looking forward'. *Journal of International Money and Finance* 38 (2013): 95–119.

Latham & Watkins. 'Regulation of foreign currency transactions: The intersection of the treasury determination, swaps regulation and the retail foreign exchange rules overview'. Available at: https://www.lw.com/thoughtLeadership/US-Treasurys-Regulation-of-Foreign-Currency-Transactions, 2013.

Latter, Edwin. 'Conduct risk in FX Markets'. In *FX Week Europe*. London: Financial Conduct Authority. Available at: https://www.fca.org.uk/news/speeches/conduct-risk-fx-markets, 2016.

Lewis, Michael. *Flash Boys*. New York: W.W. Norton & Company, 2014.

Lyons, Richard K. 'Private beliefs and information externalities in the foreign exchange market'. *National Bureau of Economic Research Working Paper Series* No. 3889. Available at: http://www.nber.org/papers/w3889.pdf, 1991.

Lyons, Richard K. 'A simultaneous trade model of the foreign exchange hot potato'. *Journal of International Economics* 42, no. 3 (1997): 275–98.

Lyons, Richard K. 'The microstructure approach to exchange rates (a review)'. *Financial Analysts Journal* 58, no. 5 (2002): 101–3.

Mahmoodzadeh, Soheil, and Ramazan Gençay. 'Human vs. high frequency traders in the interbank FX Market, role of tick size'. Available at: http://www.systemicrisk.ac.uk/sites/default/files/images/Tick Size.pdf, 2017.

Moore, Michael, Andreas Schrimpf, and Vladyslav Sushko. 'Downsized FX markets: causes and implications'. Available at: https://www.bis.org/publ/qtrpdf/r_qt1612e.pdf, 2016.

Nanex. 'Nanex – 18-Mar-2015 – U.S. dollar flash crash'. *Nanex*. Available at: http://www.nanex.net/aqck2/4689.html, 2015.

NYDFS (New York Department of Financial Services). 'NYDFS announces Barclays to pay additional $150 million penalty, terminate employee for automated, electronic foreign exchange trading misconduct'. Available at: https://www.dfs.ny.gov/about/press/pr1511181.htm, 2015.

Osler, Carol, and Xuhang Wang. 'The microstructure of currency markets'. In *Market Microstructure in Emerging and Developed Markets*, ed. Kent Baker and Halil Kiymaz, 79–99, Hoboken, NJ: John Wiley & Sons, 2013.

Perraudin, William, and Paolo Vitale. 'Interdealer trade and information flows in a decentralized foreign exchange market'. In *The Microstructure of Foreign Exchange*

Markets, ed. Jeffrey A. Frankel, Giampaolo Galli, and Alberto Giovannini, 73–106, Chicago: University of Chicago, 1996.

Phillips, Tony. 'NASA – Blue Moon'. Available at: https://www.nasa.gov/vision/uni verse/watchtheskies/07jul_bluemoon.html, 2004.

Phylaktis, Kate, and Long Chen. 'Asymmetric information, price discovery and macro-economic announcements in FX market: Do top trading banks know more?' *International Journal of Finance and Economics* 15, no. 3 (2010): 228–46.

Pragma Securities. 'Defining the FX flash crash'. Available at: https://www.pragmatrading. com/resource/defining-fx-flash-crash-december-2017/, 2017.

Rime, Dagfinn, and Andreas Schrimpf. 'The anatomy of the global FX market through the lens of the 2013 triennial survey'. *BIS Quarterly Review*, 2013.

Rodgers, Kevin. *Why Aren't They Shouting? A Banker's Tale of Change, Computers and Perpetual Crisis*. New York: Random House Business, 2016.

Sager, Michael J., and Mark P. Taylor. 'Under the microscope: The structure of the foreign exchange market'. *International Journal of Finance and Economics* 11, no. 1 (2006): 81–95.

Sarno, Lucio, and Mark P Taylor. 'The microstructure of the foreign-exchange market: A selective survey of the literature'. *Princeton Studies in International Economics* 89 (2001): 1–58.

SEC (Securities and Exchange Commission). Final Rule: Retail Foreign Exchange Trans-actions, Pub. L. No. 17 CFR Part 240. Available at: https://www.sec.gov/rules/final/ 2013/34-69964.pdf, 2013.

Spread Networks. 'Spread Networks and Seaborn team up to provide SeaSpeed: Brazil's first dedicated ultra-low latency subsea route'. Available at: http://newswire.tele comramblings.com/2017/05/spread-networks-seaborn-team-provide-seaspeed-brazils-first-dedicated-ultra-low-latency-subsea-route, 8 May 2017.

TMX. 'Overview of TSX Alpha Exchange'. Available at: https://www.tsx.com/resource/ en/1190/overview-of-tsx-alpha-exchange-2016-01-27-en.pdf, 2016.

Virtu. 'Form S-1 with the United States Securities and Exchange Commission'. Available at: https://www.sec.gov/Archives/edgar/data/1592386/000110465915025092/file name2.pdf, 2015.

Wah, Elaine. 'How prevalent are latency arbitrage opportunities on U.S. stock exchanges?' Available at: https://papers.ssrn.com/sol3/papers.cfm?abstract_id=2729109, 2016.

Winston & Strawn LLP. 'Dodd-Frank: Recent relief from business conduct rules in respect of FX transactions'. *Lexology*. Available at: https://www.lexology.com/ library/detail.aspx?g=4f798cd1-0594-4b9d-a99d-86a79663a75f, 2013.

WSGR (Wilson Sonsini Goodrich & Rosati). 'Fourth update: Dodd-Frank rules impact end-users of foreign exchange derivatives'. Available at: https://www.wsgr.com/pub lications/PDFSearch/wsgralert-fourth-update-dodd-frank-rule.pdf, 2014.

Yadav, Yesha. 'Insider trading and market structure'. *UCLA Law Review* 63 (2016): 968–1033.

Zubulake, Paul, and Sang Lee. *The High Frequency Game Changer: How Automated Trading Strategies have Revolutionized the Markets*. Hoboken, NJ: John Wiley & Sons, 2011.

Part 2
Market Quality and Best Order Execution

5

A Comparison of Execution Quality across US Stock Exchanges

Elaine Wah, Stan Feldman, Francis Chung,
Allison Bishop, and Daniel Aisen

5.1 Introduction

On 17 June 2016, the US Securities and Exchange Commission (SEC) approved the Investors Exchange (IEX) after a highly contentious application process, during which the SEC received over 500 comment letters over a 10-month period.[1] Not only is IEX the first new US equities exchange in six years, but also key differences in its design offer a distinct alternative to the other exchanges. The introduction of IEX's unique exchange model to the equities trading landscape provides a valuable opportunity to compare its market quality to that of the other US stock exchanges, as well as to examine the structural characteristics and inefficiencies driving disparities in performance. In this chapter, we evaluate execution quality along four dimensions: liquidity, execution costs, price discovery, and market stability. We employ a publicly available dataset (Daily TAQ) in an effort to facilitate replication of our metrics, via which market participants can independently evaluate execution quality across various venues.[2]

The US equities markets have undergone a metamorphosis over the past few decades, with IEX's entrance coming at a time in which trading is highly fragmented and the most sophisticated market participants compete with

---

[1] SEC, *In the Matter of the Application of Investors' Exchange*, 2016.
[2] The authors are grateful to Walter Mattli and Robert Battalio for their helpful comments and feedback.

Table 5.1. Average market share as reported by Cboe Global Markets (2017), both including and excluding off-exchange trades (which are reported to the Trade Reporting Facilities, or TRFs) for US stock exchanges operational during the first quarter of 2017

Exchange	Market share	Ex-TRF market share
NYSE Arca	9.6	15.5
NASDAQ BX	2.7	4.3
Cboe BYX Exchange	4.4	7.1
Cboe BZX Exchange	6.0	9.6
Chicago Stock Exchange (CHX)	0.4	0.7
Cboe EDGA Exchange	2.3	3.7
Cboe EDGX Exchange	6.5	10.6
Investors Exchange (IEX)	2.0	3.2
NYSE American (MKT)	0.2	0.3
NASDAQ Stock Market (NSDQ)	14.0	22.6
National Stock Exchange (NSX)	0.0	0.0
New York Stock Exchange (NYSE)	12.9	20.8
NASDAQ PSX	0.9	1.5

Note: market share numbers are based on volume in all sample securities, even those that do not trade on a given venue. NSX ceased operations on 1 February 2017. Fees are given for Tape A symbols, which are traded by all exchanges other than NYSE American (MKT). As of 3 April 2017, NYSE American traded only Tape B symbols. These fees and rebates are for displayed volume only.

each other on speed[3] and the ability to predict market moves.[4] We begin with a bird's-eye view of the rich and variable landscape of equities trading. There are a dozen exchanges and more than 30 alternative trading systems (ATSs) operating at any given time. In terms of overall market share, the exchanges represent approximately 60 per cent of the US equities market, while the remaining 40 per cent trades off-exchange and is reported to the NASDAQ and New York Stock Exchange (NYSE) Trade Reporting Facilities. More precise statistics for each exchange are provided in Table 5.1.

Within the exchanges, the most dominant entities are the NASDAQ Stock Market (NSDQ), NYSE, and NYSE Arca, which each have a market share near or above 10 per cent. The next tier is comprised of Cboe EDGX Exchange and Cboe BZX Exchange, which each have a market share between 5 per cent and 8 per cent. IEX falls within a third cluster of exchanges with market share of approximately 2 per cent to 5 per cent. This cluster also includes Cboe BYX Exchange, NASDAQ BX, and Cboe EDGA Exchange. The fourth cluster of exchanges typically averages below 1 per cent and includes NASDAQ PSX, NYSE American (MKT), and the Chicago Stock Exchange (CHX).

US equity trading is governed by Regulation National Market System (NMS), which lays out rules intended to ensure that trades occur at the best available

[3] Biais and Foucault, 'HFT and market quality', 2014; Budish et al., 'High-frequency trading arms race', 2015; Goldstein et al., 'Computerized and high-frequency trading', 2014; Laughlin et al., 'Information transmission', 2014.

[4] Hirschey, 'Do high-frequency traders anticipate?', 2018.

prices.[5] This is meant to protect a market participant from entering into a sub-optimal trade on one venue merely because they are not aware of (or cannot readily access) a better price available elsewhere. To translate this intention into a clear rule, Regulation NMS establishes the concept of a 'protected quotation', which is a quote displayed on an exchange that is immediately and broadly accessible.

Trading centres are also mandated by Regulation NMS to prevent 'trade-throughs' where trades are executed at prices worse than the protected quotations. However, market participants are permitted to use intermarket sweep orders, or ISOs, to trade through orders on other exchanges, provided that additional ISOs, as needed, are also routed to execute against the full displayed size of any better-priced protected quotes. Only the top-of-book (i.e. the highest-priced buy order and lowest-priced sell order) prices on each exchange are considered protected, and market participants using ISOs are assuming the responsibility of interacting with each protected quote.

Since Regulation NMS decrees that trades cannot occur at prices that are inferior to this best available price, the regulation can thus be seen as supporting the obligation of brokers to route orders for *best execution*, which is both an investor protection requirement and an obligation to 'obtain the most advantageous terms for the customer'.[6] Factors to consider in assessing best execution include but are not limited to the speed, likelihood of execution, and *price improvement*, which is the opportunity for an order to execute at a better price than what is currently quoted.

These protected quotations are made available in a consolidated form known as the Security Information Processor (SIP), a real-time data feed that includes all updates to protected quotes. At any given moment in time, a market participant can determine the best price available among protected quotations by reference to the SIP. The public price quote generated by the SIP is called the 'National Best Bid and Offer' or NBBO, and represents the highest-priced buy order (i.e. bid) and lowest-priced sell order (i.e. offer) across all exchanges. The SIP also reports trade executions.

While the SIP creates a common reference that all market participants can rely upon, it does not eliminate asynchrony in the dissemination of market data. The same information that is disseminated through the SIP is also available through the proprietary direct feeds offered by exchanges, and participants have several options for accessing these various data sources. Geographic distances affect the latency of these connections, and the co-location and technology services offered by some exchanges (discussed in Chapters 2 and 4) exacerbate the resulting differences between participant capabilities.

---

[5] SEC, *Regulation NMS*, 2005.   [6] FINRA, *Guidance on Best Execution Obligations*, 2015.

Another important consideration for market participants is a venue's access fees and rebates. To attract order flow, many exchanges pay market participants a per-share rebate to provide liquidity by sending resting orders (which wait on the bid or offer for potential executions). In this pricing model, the liquidity provider, i.e. *maker*, receives a rebate when its order eventually executes, and the *taker* that trades against the resting order pays an access fee to the exchange. Brokers typically do not pass these rebates back to their customers, and these fees are capped at 30 mils per share, or $0.003 per share.[7] Pricing can depend on a market participant's volume on a given venue, and achieving the most favourable, top-tier rebates is feasible only if the participant exceeds certain volume thresholds. In contrast to the maker-taker model, some venues have adopted an *inverted*, or taker-maker, fee structure. Inverted venues assess a fee to provide liquidity and pay a rebate to remove liquidity. Such venues include BYX and BX. EDGA offered an inverted pricing structure until 1 June 2017, when it switched to a flat fee structure.[8] Since the underlying data we analyse spans the first quarter of 2017, references here to 'inverted' exchanges include EDGA. Industry reports have estimated that there are over 800 different pricing tiers—structured to attract incremental order flow from brokers—available across exchanges today.[9] We summarize only

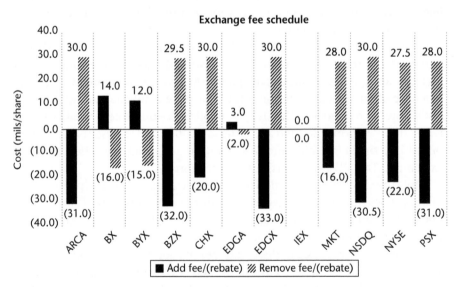

Figure 5.1. Top-tier exchange access fees and rebates for shares executed at or above $1, by exchange, as of 3 April 2017

---

[7] SEC, *Maker-Taker Fees*, 2015.   [8] Cboe Global Markets, *Press Release*, 2017.
[9] Popper, 'Stock exchange prices grow', 1 March 2016.

the top-tier access fees and rebates for the first quarter of 2017 in Figure 5.1, as this is the time period analysed in our study.

Market participants must be diligent in navigating this complex ecosystem and seeking out favourable execution opportunities, but comprehensively evaluating the quality of executions on each market centre can be challenging. Execution quality comprises a number of different aspects, such as execution price, quantity filled, and cost savings relative to the public price quote. Venue performance can be difficult to assess as it depends in part on brokers' trading or routing strategies and their subsequent interactions with a venue. Another important consideration is market structure, as the fragmented exchange landscape has led to increased market complexity. For instance, each exchange has its own fee structure (as discussed above) as well as its own trading dynamics, which only further complicate the calculus of routing decisions. These access fees and rebates may create conflicts of interest for brokers, who must reconcile their own economic incentives with their fiduciary duty to seek the best execution possible for their customers—but best execution is primarily a principles-based rather than objectively verifiable requirement, and there is no well-defined industry standard when it comes to determining how brokers should route to obtain the most favourable terms of execution, especially when considering passive limit orders. The role of the stock exchange in trading has also undergone a transformation. Exchanges have become increasingly reliant on revenue from tiered access and proprietary market data fees, which segment market participants into those who possess the sufficient level of technological sophistication both to justify such fees and to process and respond to the transmitted data with the requisite speed, and those who do not.[10] Based on these fee and structural differences, each exchange attracts different populations of market participants.

Clearly, execution quality on a stock exchange cannot be examined independently of equity market structure. Therefore, we take a holistic view: we study execution quality along four dimensions, which we describe below.

Liquidity: the Securities Exchange Act of 1934 states, 'It is in the public interest and appropriate for the protection of investors and the maintenance of fair and orderly markets to assure an opportunity ... for investors' orders to be executed without the participation of a dealer.' In this spirit, we interpret liquidity to mean the availability of opportunities for natural investors to trade with counterparties at stable prices—without the need for a professional intermediary. We compare liquidity across exchanges via proxy measures for natural investor interaction such as overall volume,

---

[10] Goldstein et al., 'Computerized and high-frequency trading', 2014.

block volume (i.e. trades of at least 10,000 shares of stock or at least $200,000 of notional value), midpoint volume, and average queue size.

Execution costs: the cost of trading reflects the ease with which market participants can execute transactions. Our primary metric of execution costs is trade markouts—effectively equivalent to realized spread—which capture the potential gains realizable after a trade for executions where the resting order can be identified. We also evaluate the likelihood and amount of price improvement, which occurs when a marketable order receives a better price than what is currently quoted.

Price discovery: incorporating new information smoothly into prices is a critical function of any market. While we do not explicitly measure each venue's contribution to price discovery, as a proxy measure we determine each exchange's time at the inside quote. In other situations, such as when the best buy price on one exchange is equal to or exceeds the best sell price on another (i.e. during locked and crossed markets), the price formation process is essentially frozen, so we analyse time at the inside quote during these scenarios to determine the degree to which each exchange may be impeding price discovery in this way.

Market stability: we characterize a stable market as one where market participants can execute significant volume without excess price fluctuations. Market stability both promotes efficient price discovery and reflects a market participant's ability to trade at accessible prices. To assess each venue's contribution towards NBBO stability (or instability), particularly around trades, we analyse the post-trade price movement of midpoint trades, and the percentage of volume executed immediately prior to a quote change.

We are particularly interested in how market quality on IEX compares to the incumbent US exchanges. Much of the controversy prior to IEX's approval revolved around unique features of its market model, such as the IEX point-of-presence or so-called 'speed bump', which adds a 350 microsecond delay to all incoming and outbound order messages. IEX also offers several pegged order types—primary peg, midpoint peg, and discretionary peg—which are non-displayed with prices that update (up to the limit price, if specified) in response to changes in the NBBO.[11] IEX consumes direct data feeds from other exchanges

---

[11] Primary peg orders are pegged one minimum price variant outside the NBBO (one tick lower than the National Best Bid, or NBB, for buy orders, and one tick higher than the National Best Offer, or NBO, for sell orders) but can exercise discretion to trade at the quote, except in instances where the IEX crumbling quote signal predicts an immediate price transition. Midpoint peg orders are pegged to the midpoint of the NBBO. Discretionary peg orders are pegged to the quote (NBB for buy orders, NBO for sell orders) but can also exercise discretion to trade at a more aggressive price up to the midpoint of the NBBO, except in instances where the IEX crumbling quote signal predicts an immediate price transition.

in order to update these pegged orders. The direct feeds are not subject to the speed bump, which allows IEX to update the prices of resting pegged orders before incoming orders reach the matching engine. Primary peg and discretionary peg orders are enriched with IEX's crumbling quote signal, which employs a probabilistic model to detect impending quote changes. When the crumbling quote signal predicts an imminent price change, the signal becomes 'active', thereby preventing primary peg buy (sell) orders from trading at the NBB (NBO) and discretionary peg buy (sell) orders from trading at prices more aggressive than the NBB (NBO). These components of the IEX model work in concert to deter certain types of predatory trading, in which market participants may exploit advantages in speed and access in order to execute at stale or soon-to-be stale prices to the detriment of the resting order. In addition, unlike most other exchanges, IEX does not segregate access by fees or tiers: it offers a flat fee schedule of 3 mils per share for displayed trading[12] and 9 mils per share for non-displayed executions.

We note that many other analyses of execution quality depend in part on proprietary data from one broker or a handful of brokers. Whether such results can be generalized to the broader market is indeterminable. For example, typical venue analysis conducted by a Transaction Cost Analysis (TCA) provider relies on a specific client's trading data. This type of comparison is subject to biases based on the client's strategies and trading behaviour on different venues. For this reason, we base this study on publicly available Daily Trade and Quote (TAQ) data, which is accessible by both academics and industry participants. This renders a comparison of execution quality across all venues readily reproducible. To further facilitate replication, we include our source code for each metric (written in the array processing language Q) in an appendix. Our hope is that market participants, in particular institutional investors and brokers who make decisions regarding venue selection, apply our methods to independently evaluate execution quality on the various exchanges.

Overall, we find that IEX's market model promotes both rich midpoint liquidity and a stable market by protecting orders from executing at an imminently stale NBBO. IEX also offers the most cost-effective executions, with positive trade-to-mid markouts, low effective spread, and the greatest potential for half-spread price improvement. We observe that fee structure plays a large role in performance disparities across exchanges, which suggests that access fees and rebates perpetuate economic incentives misaligned with the tenets of best execution. Our results are summarized in Table 5.2.

This chapter is organized as follows. We survey related work in Section 5.2, and describe our dataset in Section 5.3. Section 5.4 discusses our findings on

---

[12] Prior to 2 January 2018, IEX offered free displayed trading.

Table 5.2. Overview of our analyses comparing execution quality across US stock exchanges

Feature	Metric	Section of this chapter	Results
LIQUIDITY	Block volume	5.4.1	The largest exchanges by market share (i.e. NASDAQ, NYSE, Arca, EDGX) also have the largest average daily block volume
	Midpoint volume	5.4.2	Approximately 60% of IEX volume trades at the midpoint, thereby receiving half-spread price improvement; NASDAQ and IEX rank highest in average daily midpoint volume
	Midpoint block volume	5.4.2	IEX attracts the most midpoint block volume, which is concentrated primarily in stocks rather than ETFs
	Queue size	5.4.3	Average queue sizes are generally stratified by fee structure, with the shortest queues on IEX and the inverted exchanges
EXECUTION COSTS	Markouts (realized spreads)	5.5.1	IEX and the inverted exchanges offer the most favourable trade-to-mid markouts, indicating higher potential profit for resting orders, whereas traders on maker-taker exchanges are at greater risk of adverse selection
	Price improvement	5.5.2	IEX offers the greatest potential for price improvement, most notably relative to the inverted venues which offer rebates to liquidity takers
	Quoted and effective spreads	5.5.3	The maker-taker exchanges offer the narrowest quoted spreads, but IEX offers the lowest effective spread and effective-to-quoted spread ratio
PRICE DISCOVERY	Time at inside	5.6.1	NASDAQ and Arca contribute the most time and size at the inside, followed closely by most of the other maker-taker venues
	Locked and crossed markets	5.6.2	Maker-taker exchanges spend the most time at the inside during locked and crossed markets; in contrast, IEX and the inverted exchanges are at the inside quote less than 5% of the time in locked markets, and less than 12% of the time in crossed markets
MARKET STABILITY	Post-trade midpoint movement	5.7.1	In wider-spread symbols, IEX has the highest percentage of midpoint volume with no price change based on snapshots at various times after the trade
	Quote instability	5.7.2	IEX and the inverted exchanges provide more stability around trades, with IEX offering the lowest percentage of midpoint volume within 2ms of an NBBO quote change

liquidity across venues. Section 5.5 presents our results on execution costs. We describe our analyses on price discovery and market stability in Sections 5.6 and 5.7, respectively. We present our conclusions in Section 5.8.

5.2 Related Work

This chapter compares market quality on IEX to that on other exchanges, and furthermore explores the broader structural mechanics behind certain observed disparities in execution quality. To our knowledge, no previous work has compared execution quality across the US stock exchanges since the approval of IEX as an exchange.

While there is substantial literature on the impact of algorithmic trading (i.e. the use of computerized algorithms to automate the process of making trading decisions) on overall market quality,[13] these studies generally do not compare performance across venues. Much of the previous work comparing US stock exchanges analyses only a subset of symbols or exchanges.[14]

However, there are a number of prior studies that evaluate execution quality under different fee structures. Battalio, Corwin, and Jennings[15] analyse the impact of access fees and rebates on limit order execution quality. They focus on various measures of execution quality, including likelihood of a fill, speed of fills, realized spread, and quoted depth, finding that limit order traders face longer wait times on maker-taker venues than on the inverted exchanges. Their results suggest that routing orders to capture the maximum rebate is detrimental to limit order execution quality. In a related study, Cardella, Hao, and Kalcheva[16] employ cross-sectional regression analysis at the exchange level to show that exchange volume is inversely correlated to the net fee. They also find that volume on a venue is more sensitive to changes in the taker fee versus the maker rebate, consistent with the theoretical results of Foucault and Menkveld.[17] Ye and Yao[18] examine the impact of relative tick size on liquidity on the inverted venues, finding that slower traders enter taker-maker markets more frequently than high frequency traders, as the former do not have the speed advantages necessary to compete for position at the front of the queue on

---

[13] Cardella et al., 'Computerization', 2014; Biais and Foucault, 'HFT and market quality', 2014; Brogaard et al., 'High-frequency trading', 2014; Goldstein et al., 'Computerized and high-frequency trading', 2014; Hasbrouck and Saar, 'Low-latency trading', 2013; Hendershott et al., 'Does algorithmic trading improve liquidity?', 2011; Zhang, 'Effect of high-frequency trading', 2010.

[14] Bessembinder and Kaufman, 'Cross-exchange comparison', 1997; Bessembinder, 'Issues in assessing', 2003; Boehmer, 'Dimensions of execution quality', 2005; Huang and Stoll, 'Dealer versus auction markets', 1996; Peterson and Sirri, 'Order preferencing', 2003.

[15] Battalio et al., 'Can brokers have it all?', 2016.

[16] Cardella et al., 'Liquidity-based trading fees', 2017.

[17] Foucault and Menkveld, 'Competition for order flow', 2008.

[18] Ye and Yao, 'Tick size constraints', 2015.

maker-taker venues. Harris[19] discusses the agency problem between brokers and their customers perpetuated by maker-taker pricing, and finds that the primary effect of maker-taker is to narrow quoted spreads. Malinova and Park[20] explore the impact of maker-taker pricing on liquidity and volume by analysing data around the introduction of a maker rebate on the Toronto Stock Exchange. Their results are consistent with Angel, Harris, and Spatt,[21] who posit that competition induces prices to adjust to offset any increase in the maker rebate: quoted bid-ask spreads are narrowed artificially as traders post quotes in pursuit of liquidity rebates and avoid marketable orders so as not to pay access fees, and ultimately the net prices are the same on average as without a maker-taker pricing model.

Other previous work explores a variety of structural features in the exchange landscape and their impact on market quality, such as the effect of fragmentation[22] or market latency.[23] Jain[24] examines the impact of institutional characteristics on venue performance, finding across a dataset comprised of 51 stock exchanges from around the world that exchange-design features are the major determinants of liquidity, as measured via spreads, volatility, and trading turnover.

5.3 Data

The majority of our analyses employ trade and quote data from Daily TAQ.[25] This is by design—our goal is to facilitate the reproducibility of our metrics, as TAQ data is both an industry standard and publicly available across academic and government institutions.[26] For supplemental analyses or where a statistic cannot be determined using TAQ data alone, we rely on internal IEX data.

[19] Harris, *Maker-taker Pricing Effects*, 2013.

[20] Malinova and Park, 'Subsidizing liquidity', 2015.

[21] Angel et al., 'Equity trading in the 21st century', 2011; Angel et al., 'Equity trading in the 21st century: An update', 2015.

[22] Bennett and Wei, 'Market structure', 2006; Foucault and Menkveld, 'Competition', 2008; O'Hara and Ye, 'Market fragmentation', 2011.

[23] Riordan and Storkenmaier, 'Latency', 2012.   [24] Jain, 'Institutional design', 2003.

[25] A potential alternative to TAQ data is the data that market centres make available under SEC Rule 605. Rule 605 reports provide a summary of various market statistics, aggregated by security, order marketability buckets, and order size buckets. Statistics that underlie Rule 605 reports are calculated for all executions belonging to a particular order. Given the way these executions are aggregated and bucketed, as well as the timestamps used, the reliability of Rule 605 is limited, especially when it comes to producing trade-based metrics versus order-based metrics. Rule 605 reports also have several key exclusions, such as non-exempt short sales, orders of 10,000+ shares, and odd lots. Non-exempt short sales potentially exclude non-trivial market-maker activity, as their sell orders are more likely to be marked short. Excluding orders of 10,000+ shares may disproportionately exclude institutional activity. Given these considerations, we use TAQ data for our analysis, as its structure, granularity, and included information are more suitable for our purposes.

[26] We note that although publicly available, Daily TAQ data is not free of charge. At the end of the first quarter of 2017, ongoing Daily TAQ data cost $3,000 per month (Intercontinental Exchange, *Daily TAQ*, 2017).

As of the end of the first quarter of 2017, there are 12 national stock exchanges in operation. About 8000 symbols are traded on any given day across all of these venues. These symbols are divided into three groups, called tapes, based on where they are listed. Securities that are NYSE-listed belong to Tape A, securities that are NASDAQ-listed belong to Tape C, and all the remaining securities (listed on Arca, MKT, or BZX) belong to Tape B. In the first quarter of 2017, the New York Stock Exchange traded only Tape A securities, whereas NYSE American traded only Tape B securities. In our metrics, unless broken out by tape, any percentages are based on all symbols in the dataset, not just those traded on a given exchange.

Table 5.3. Percentage of total volume and number of symbols eligible, ineligible, and ineligible if disregarding auctions from Daily TAQ data for the first quarter of 2017

Panel A: Percentage of volume eligible/ineligible				
Exchange	Shares eligible	% eligible	% ineligible	% non-auction ineligible
ARCA	31,682,334,580	78	22	16
BX	11,063,526,974	97	3	3
BYX	18,049,417,237	97	3	3
BZX	22,432,423,088	88	12	12
CHX	281,725,922	16	84	84
EDGA	9,289,449,412	96	4	4
EDGX	24,181,876,853	87	13	13
IEX	8,030,880,425	94	6	6
MKT	563,221,505	62	38	7
NSDQ	46,576,106,472	78	22	11
NSX	19,175,637	86	14	14
NYSE	35,995,661,049	66	34	7
PSX	3,463,121,214	89	11	11

Panel B: Number of symbols eligible/ineligible			
Exchange	No. eligible	No. ineligible	No. non-auction ineligible
ARCA	8,458	9	9
BX	8,162	3	3
BYX	8,285	6	6
BZX	8,317	8	8
CHX	4,117	60	60
EDGA	8,204	7	7
EDGX	8,370	11	11
IEX	8,138	7	7
MKT	396	0	0
NSDQ	8,425	23	21
NSX	3,363	62	62
NYSE	3,225	3	3
PSX	7,147	11	11

Note: percentages are based on our filters for the trades and quotes most representative of a typical trading experience during regular market hours.

We apply a number of filters (described in the following subsection) to the TAQ data in order to best capture the trades and quotes representative of the typical trading experience on a venue while including as broad a swath of activity as possible. Table 5.3 summarizes the percentage of volume and the number of symbols eligible for inclusion in our full dataset, and demonstrates that our filters preserve the vast majority of both volume and unique symbols on each venue. The National Stock Exchange ceased operations on February 1,[27] and we therefore exclude it from our dataset. We also exclude both NYSE American and CHX from our analyses due to concerns about sample size and data robustness: NYSE American traded Tape B securities exclusively in the first quarter of 2017, and a significant portion of CHX's volume is comprised of Contingent Trades which are not representative of continuous market trading activity.

5.3.1 TAQ

We use Daily TAQ data, in which quotes and trades are timestamped to the microsecond. Our dataset includes 8522 symbols, of which 1773 are exchange-traded funds (ETFs) and 6749 are corporate equities. The time period of the dataset is the first quarter of 2017 (3 January 2017 through 31 March 2017). We exclude quotes and trades outside of regular market hours (9:30 a.m. to 4:00 p.m. Eastern Time) and during the opening and closing auctions. We omit quotes and trades during locked and crossed markets unless otherwise specified, as measurements of market quality are not meaningful during these 'economically nonsensical states'.[28] To filter out abnormal quotes for metrics benchmarked to the NBBO, we include only quotations for which the NBO is within the range $[\frac{1}{3}NBB, 3NBB]$, where NBB is the national best bid and NBO is the national best offer. We also omit instances where either the bid or offer price is 0 or missing.

We include in our dataset executions that are generally representative of typical trading activity. To that end, we remove trades with correction indicators not equal to 0 or 1, as well as those with sale condition codes B, C, G, H, L, M, N, O, P, Q, R, T, U, V, W, Z, 4, 5, 6, 7, 8, or 9. We also omit symbol BRK.A (Berkshire Hathaway Class A stock) from our analyses, as it is atypical in both price and quantity traded. As a final filter to remove potentially erroneous executions, we omit trades more than 10 per cent outside the NBBO: in other words, where the price is not within the range $[NBB - 0.1M, NBO + 0.1M]$, where $M = \frac{1}{2}(NBB + NBO)$ is the NBBO midpoint at the time of the trade in question. In order to assess the full spectrum of standard continuous market

---

[27] SEC, *Notice of Filing*, 2017.
[28] Holden and Jacobsen, 'Liquidity measurement problems', 2014.

trading activity, we do not omit midpoint trades or trades initiated by inter-market sweep orders.[29]

Trade-signing algorithms serve to classify individual trades as initiated by a marketable buy or sell order, which facilitates identification of the resting order. When the initiating direction of an execution is necessary, we sign trades by determining whether the trade occurred at the quote (either the bid or the offer) or inside the NBBO spread. For trades inside the quote, we avoid making assumptions about the side of midpoint trades, but otherwise sign based on whichever side is closer (e.g. an execution inside the spread and strictly less than the midpoint would be signed as a resting buy order that executed against a liquidity-removing seller). We do not compute statistics that require assumptions about which side is adding liquidity in a midpoint trade, but instead develop alternative metrics to assess the execution quality of midpoint executions.

Finally, our analysis includes securities in the Tick Size Pilot Program,[30] which widened the minimum quoting increment in approximately 1200 symbols to 5 cents starting 3 October 2016. We do so in order to more comprehensively represent the aggregate trading experience on exchanges. Given that the majority of our statistics are volume-weighted, and the tick pilot securities are generally thinly traded, the inclusion of these symbols is unlikely to have a significant impact on our qualitative results.

5.3.2 IEX Stream

IEX maintains a record of messages that have passed through its trading system dating back to its launch as an ATS on 25 October 2013. This data store includes but is not limited to information on new order messages, order cancellation requests, execution reports, market data received from other exchanges, and child orders sent by the router to other exchanges. All these messages are sequenced and processed by all applications within the IEX trading system in a consistent, deterministic order. While this data would be sufficient to conduct many of the analyses contained in this chapter, we choose to use public data sources wherever possible in order to facilitate reproduction of our statistics.

We supplement our TAQ-based analyses with one metric computed using internal IEX data: price improvement via the IEX router (Section 5.5.2). For this metric, we restrict our analysis to fill messages for liquidity-removing orders sent to the IEX router. The included date range is the first quarter of 2017. To match the TAQ data as closely as possible, we omit trades outside of

---

[29] Our results hold when intermarket sweep orders are excluded, so we present only our analyses on the full trades dataset, inclusive of midpoint trades and ISOs.
[30] SEC, *Order Approving*, 2015.

regular market hours, we exclude BRK.A, and we filter out trades more than 10 per cent outside the NBBO, as defined above. We apply the same constraints regarding locked and crossed markets, and well-defined bid and offer prices.

5.4 Liquidity

The liquidity available on a market is a crucial reflection of its properties. A fair and healthy market should attract natural trading interest, and one can see strong indications of this by examining its liquidity. A venue's market share (Table 5.1) is a passable starting benchmark, since 'liquidity begets liquidity'. However, given the fee structures present in equities, in which traders are incentivized by rebates to add liquidity on certain venues over others, in order to evaluate comparative market quality it is necessary to consider liquidity not only in quantity but also in quality.

In this section, we examine several features of the liquidity on IEX as compared to other markets. We find that the nature of IEX's liquidity is in certain respects unique. It is characterized by a relatively high prevalence of large trades (discussed in Section 5.4.1) and a concentration of midpoint trading (Section 5.4.2). We believe these are positive indications that natural trading interest is well-represented on the IEX platform. Finally, we analyse average queue size to determine the accessibility of liquidity on each venue (Section 5.4.3).

5.4.1 *Block Volume*

A trade is classified as a *block* trade if it consists of at least 10,000 shares of stock or at least $200,000 of notional value. Block trading represents an opportunity for investors to make large-scale transactions in a stock while minimizing the number of executions required to do so. In Figure 5.2, we compare block trading on IEX to block trading on other exchanges. Our analysis is restricted to block-sized executions, rather than attempting to isolate trades that originated from block-sized orders. We find the largest quantity of block volume on the largest exchanges (NASDAQ, NYSE, Arca, and EDGX), but IEX has the same block ADV (average daily volume) as BZX, a venue with approximately triple its market share.

There is one technical caveat that complicates this comparison as well as other metrics that focus on large trades. In the TAQ database, NYSE trades are 'bunched' when reported, meaning that several trades are aggregated into one report. This occurs when a larger order arrives and trades against several smaller orders resting on NYSE's order book. For example, a buy order for 500 shares at $10 may arrive and trade separately against two sell orders each

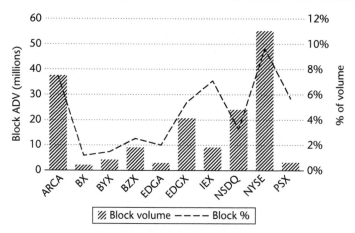

Figure 5.2. Average daily block volume and block volume as a percentage of total volume, by exchange

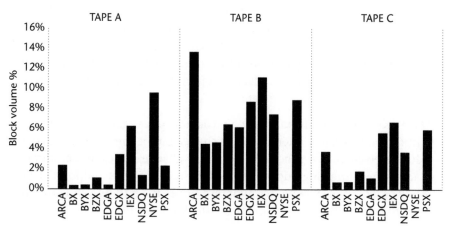

Figure 5.3. Block volume as a percentage of total volume, by tape and exchange
Note: NYSE trades only Tape A securities, as of the first quarter of 2017.

for 200 shares at $10 and another sell order for 100 shares at $10. This activity will be reported as a 500 share trade at $10 at NYSE, whereas the other exchanges will report each individual trade (i.e. two trades of 200 shares each and one trade of 100 shares). This practice obscures the sizes of the individual trades and artificially inflates trade sizes on NYSE as compared to other venues. This distortion should therefore be kept in mind when interpreting the data.

In Figure 5.3, we break down symbols by tape and examine what percentage of volume on each venue in each tape is comprised of blocks. For Tape A symbols, NYSE is notably higher than other exchanges, but as discussed above, this may not be representative of their true block volume percentage due to bunching. Arca has a higher block percentage in Tape B, whereas IEX and PSX have comparably high block volume percentages in Tape C securities. We observe that in general, blocks constitute a larger fraction of volume on venues such as IEX and EDGX, in contrast to BYX and BX.

5.4.2 Midpoint Volume

Given the non-displayed nature of resting midpoint liquidity, midpoint trading provides a useful option for large investors to opportunistically source liquidity without revealing to the broader market their intention to buy or sell. Therefore, trading at the midpoint can be an effective way for investors to obtain fills without either having to cross the full spread or having to reveal their trading interest to market participants.

The design of IEX includes many features that facilitate healthy and robust midpoint trading. Orders resting at the midpoint on IEX are protected by the speed bump in the sense that new market information (i.e. a change in the NBBO) is reflected in the resting prices of such orders on par with or faster than the fastest market participants—in other words, before informed incoming traders can interact with these orders. This prevents a phenomenon known as stale quote arbitrage, which we define below.

> **Stale quote arbitrage** is trading at a favourable price against a resting order in the brief window after an NBBO change but before the market centre has received and/or processed the NBBO change: for example, immediately after witnessing a down-tick, selling stock against a midpoint pegged buy order at the stale higher midpoint price on a trading venue that has yet to receive the information of the stock's down-tick.

However, changes in the NBBO often appear as a multi-step process: venues at the inside may desert the NBB one by one, for example, until it finally ticks downward. Other market participants may observe this shuffling and may probabilistically predict price changes before these movements actually occur. This enables them to submit liquidity-taking orders at soon-to-be-stale prices before any venue (even one with a speed bump) can process the still-pending price change, as in crumbling quote arbitrage, which is defined below.

> **Crumbling quote arbitrage** is trading at a favourable price against a resting order by recognizing that the NBBO is very likely in the process of changing (but has not actually changed yet): for example, immediately after witnessing 5 of 6 bids disappear across the market in close succession, attempting to sell stock against a midpoint pegged buy order at the soon-to-be-stale midpoint price.

To enhance protection against this kind of adverse selection, IEX developed its own probabilistic model, called the crumbling quote signal, for predicting when a price change is imminent. When the model predicts that a price change is likely to occur, the crumbling quote signal becomes 'active'. This period lasts for 2ms following the prediction and affects only trading at the current price level and side, so it effectively ends when either the price changes or the 2ms window expires, whichever comes first. The crumbling quote signal is embedded into the IEX discretionary peg order type and prevents a resting buy order, for example, from 'stepping up' to the midpoint while the signal is active at the current price. During these scenarios, the order may still trade at the near side of the NBBO (NBB for buy orders, NBO for sell orders), but it will not exercise discretion in trading at any price more aggressive. This kind of protection has recently been extended to primary peg orders. Functionality is analogous to the discretionary peg order, except primary peg orders are prevented from stepping up to the near side during periods when the signal is active.

Considering that these tools are in place to enable successful midpoint and other non-displayed trading, it is no surprise that a large share of midpoint trading across the market occurs on IEX, as evidenced in Figure 5.4(a). In terms of midpoint average daily volume (ADV), IEX is the second largest exchange. If we consider the percentage of each exchange's volume that trades at the midpoint, we see that IEX has the largest percentage. Of course, trades at the midpoint invariably represent non-displayed liquidity. Given the relative prevalence of non-displayed volume on IEX, it is not surprising that IEX outperforms in midpoint volume compared to other exchanges.

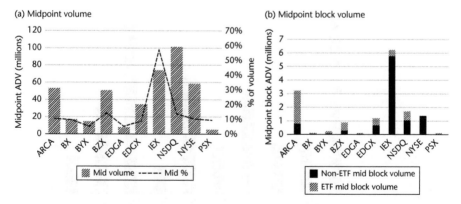

Figure 5.4. Average daily midpoint volume and midpoint volume as a percentage of total volume, by exchange (left); average daily midpoint block volume, by exchange and whether stock versus ETF (right)

Another promising feature of midpoint trading on IEX is that it often attracts large blocks. If we consider midpoint block volume by exchange during the continuous session, IEX has the highest volume overall, as shown in Figure 5.4(b). Notably, the composition of large midpoint volume on IEX is dominated by stocks rather than ETFs, which may reflect the presence of large natural investor interest on IEX.

5.4.3 Queue Size

Another component of liquidity is the probability of execution, which depends in large part on two factors: the *queue size* or the aggregate quantity available at a price level, and the economics of the liquidity remover. The larger the queue, the longer it will take for an order joining the end of the queue to begin receiving fills. The higher the fee charged to the liquidity remover on an exchange, the lower the probability that a remover will choose that exchange. All things being equal, a trader would prefer to post an order on a venue with a shorter queue to one with a longer queue.

TAQ data does not offer order-level information, but what we can see are the aggregate sizes available, by venue, at the inside quote. In order to estimate queue size with a statistic that is reproducible with publicly available data, we compute the quoted depth, or the average size available during the day at the NBBO. More specifically, we take the average of the quoted size at the National Best Bid and the quoted size at the National Best Offer, for each venue.

Figure 5.5 illustrates the average queue size at the NBBO by exchange. We note that since our queue size statistic is based on all symbols in our dataset,

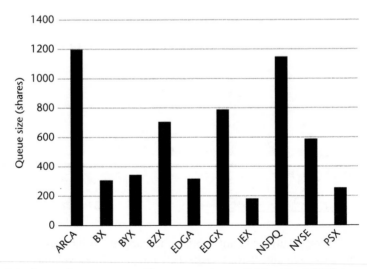

Figure 5.5. Queue size, as measured by average size available at the NBBO, by exchange

and NYSE trades Tape A securities exclusively, this measure underestimates the queue size on NYSE in Tape A symbols. Regardless, we find a direct relationship between fee structure and queue size. In line with the quoted depth results from Battalio, Corwin, and Jennings,[31] the queue sizes on the inverted venues and IEX are significantly smaller than those on the maker-taker exchanges—with the sole exception of PSX, which is most likely due to its size given that it is the smallest venue by market share. Still, despite being a fraction of BX, BYX, and EDGA, PSX's queue size is comparable.

Shorter queue sizes generally reflect less competition at the inside, which means that IEX and the inverted exchanges should be desirable for market participants who prioritize probability of execution for limit orders. Our findings indicate that market participants are choosing to join a longer line, with an accordingly lower probability of fill. We observe that the longest queues to buy or sell shares are at the exchanges that offer the highest rebates (and in turn charge the highest fees to remove liquidity). This suggests that rebates may induce brokers to direct passive order flow to the standard maker-taker exchanges, even when those venues are already densely populated with resting orders and consequently offer a lower probability of execution.

5.5 Execution Costs

Execution costs are an important indicator of market quality on a venue, as they reflect both the ease with which market participants can complete trans-actions, and the profits potentially achievable after executions. We start our discussion of execution costs by surveying the explicit cost of trading. Due to the current fee-rebate paradigm, per-share trading cost of a given venue is largely dependent on the active-to-passive ratio of market participants. In the context of this discussion, a participant is considered active 100 per cent of the time if all its traded shares removed liquidity. Conversely, if all its traded shares added liquidity, the participant is 100 per cent passive.

The rate at which market participants add or remove liquidity determines how expensive or inexpensive a venue may be for them to use. For example, for a participant that removes liquidity 100 per cent of the time, the cheapest venue is the one with the lowest cost to take. Conversely, for a participant that adds liquidity 100 per cent of the time, the cheapest venue is the one with the highest rebate.

To evaluate the cost of a venue, we estimate the *blended cost* of each exchange, which takes into account access fees and rebates, the active-to-passive ratio, and

---

[31] Battalio et al., 'Can brokers have it all?', 2016.

the cost of displayed versus non-displayed executions. Exchange fee schedules are complex and vary by characteristics such as volume, tape, price, and lit versus dark. Generally, most fee schedules are 'tiered', offering varied pricing based on volume thresholds that are unique to a given venue. Tiers typically manifest themselves in higher rebates and/or lower fees for the highest-volume participants.

In order to generalize venue costs, several assumptions are required. First, we use the top tier and basic tier fee schedules to demonstrate the potential spectrum of execution costs. Second, pricing often varies depending on tape and share price (e.g. whether above or below $1). For our estimate of blended cost, we use fees and rebates associated with Tape A symbols whose share price is at least $1 to create the most inclusive dataset, since NYSE trades only Tape A securities as of the first quarter of 2017. Third, another factor in pricing is whether volume is displayed or non-displayed. We use the hidden volume rate[32] to determine the relative weights to apply to the displayed versus the non-displayed fee schedules. Finally, we apply each exchange's midpoint fee schedule to the non-displayed portion of exchange volume. In practice, given that the vast majority of exchange volume is displayed (with the exception of IEX), the impact of midpoint versus other non-displayed pricing is fairly negligible. Furthermore, IEX assesses the same fee for any non-displayed volume,[33] so no distinction is necessary.

Our results are shown in Figure 5.6. Unsurprisingly, 50 per cent is the point at which maker-taker and inverted venues intersect, and one group may become more preferable from an explicit trade execution cost perspective. It is important to note that this analysis assumes that the volume of a given participant is in line with an exchange's overall lit-to-dark liquidity ratios. For example, a midpoint strategy interacting on Arca would receive lower rebates for adding liquidity than a strategy focused on posting displayed quotes. In addition, our blended cost estimate generalizes across all securities; based on the trading characteristics of a given symbol (e.g. price, spread, volatility, volume, among others), venues with certain pricing paradigms as well as fee levels may be more attractive from an economic standpoint. We exclude implicit execution costs here, as these are addressed in the following sections.

---

[32] Since hidden volume is not demarcated on the tape, we must rely on alternate sources of data. The SEC Market Structure website publishes a number of metrics by exchange on a quarterly basis, including the hidden trade rate and the hidden volume percentage. As IEX is not currently included in the SEC's publicly available MIDAS statistics (as of the end of the first quarter of 2017), we apply the SEC Market Activity Report Methodology (SEC, *Market Activity Report Methodology*, 2017) to IEX data. We measure the hidden volume rate on IEX as the volume against hidden orders divided by the total volume; data for other exchanges is from the SEC Market Structure website. See https://www.sec.gov/marketstructure.

[33] See IEX, *Investors Exchange Fee Schedule*, 2017.

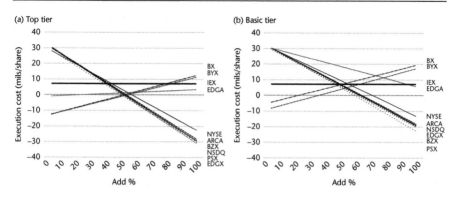

Figure 5.6. Blended cost of execution by exchange and fee schedule tier (top tier and basic tier)

Note: our estimate of blended cost takes into account access fees and rebates, the active-to-passive ratio, and non-displayed trading. We use fees and rebates for Tape A symbols with share price above $1, and midpoint fee schedules in conjunction with the hidden volume rate for each exchange.

Table 5.4. Example of blended cost, expressed in mils per share, based on the active-to-passive ratio and pricing tier reached

		Tier	
		Basic	Top
Active-to-passive ratio (remove %/add %)	75%/25%	14.8	11.0
	25%/75%	−2.6	−9.6

In light of these results, we posit that, given today's exchange economics, a particular venue cannot be considered cheap or expensive without the proper context of 'for whom' and 'under what circumstances'. As an example, Table 5.4 shows a simple matrix of the blended cost a given broker may receive, based on two dimensions: the active-to-passive ratio and the pricing tier reached. In this example, we assume that volume is distributed across exchanges proportional to each venue's market share. A broker removing liquidity 75 per cent of the time and paying the basic-tier rates would pay an average of 14.8 mils per share. Conversely, a broker adding liquidity 75 per cent of the time and receiving top-tier rates would receive a rebate of approximately 10 mils per share. This considerable per-share differential of 25 mils indicates that trading fees alone cannot be the sole determinant of execution cost.

We therefore evaluate execution costs in a number of different ways. We focus on trade markouts, which are effectively equivalent to realized spreads (Section 5.5.1). We also evaluate the likelihood and amount of price improvement (Section 5.5.2), which occurs when a marketable order receives a better price than what is currently quoted. Finally, we compare three additional proxy measures of execution costs: quoted spread, effective spread, and the effective-to-quoted spread ratio (Section 5.5.3).

5.5.1 *Markouts and Realized Spread*

Generally speaking, trading is a zero-sum game in the short term. As a result, it follows that the most straightforward way to measure the quality of an execution strategy would be to simply measure its profitability. Unfortunately, since many trading strategies open positions on one market and close on another, or close much later in time, it is often difficult to directly measure the profitability of a specific trade as an outside observer. Further, if a position is held for a substantial amount of time, the data may be influenced by many variables and thereby may become noisy very quickly.

To address these challenges, we examine *trade markouts* as a measure of execution quality of nonmarketable limit orders. The premise of a trade markout is that for each individual execution, we measure the profitability of that execution had it been closed out at some assumed price after a certain fixed amount of time had elapsed. Depending on the amount of time chosen, as well as the type of close-out price chosen, we can measure the potential profitability of various trading scenarios. As such, markouts are an extremely versatile metric, and we consider them a key statistic in evaluating execution quality.

There are many reasonable and potentially interesting variations of markouts to explore. Reasonable variations, depending on the goal of the analysis, include:

- Using the midpoint of the NBBO as the close-out price.
- Using the midpoint of the NBBO at the time of execution instead of the execution price.
- Using the far price (i.e. NBB for an incoming seller, NBO for an incoming buyer) as the close-out price.
- Incorporating exchange fees into the prices to measure all-in profit or loss.
- Measuring markouts in basis points as opposed to mils.

For the purposes of this study, we compare an execution's trade price to the midpoint of the market at various future points in time, as the NBBO midpoint provides a neutral indicative price at which a trader would reasonably expect to exit a position given the current state of the market. By using the NBBO midpoint we can thus achieve a measure of expected short-term trading gains per share executed.

A positive markout suggests that if the trade were the opening of a position, that position could have been closed out for a profit at this point in the future. Conversely, a negative markout suggests the presence of adverse selection— the trade likely resulted in an effective loss. Informed traders impose adverse selection costs by selling to (buying from) a resting buy (sell) order shortly before prices fall (rise).

We observe that trade markouts, which are widely used in the industry, are equivalent to *realized spreads*, which are commonly reported in the literature. Realized spreads differ solely semantically from markouts in that the side is defined relative to the liquidity taker (e.g. a markout defined for a resting buy order is the same as realized spread defined for a seller-initiated trade). As with markouts, realized spread can be used to measure losses systematically incurred from providing liquidity to better-informed traders.[34] Both trade markouts and realized spreads are only measured from the perspective of the liquidity adder, not the remover, so they primarily reflect the execution costs experienced by liquidity providers.

5.5.1.1 DEFINITIONS

We denote M_t as the NBBO midpoint for a given symbol at time t,

$$M_t = \frac{1}{2}(NBB_t + NBO_t) \tag{1}$$

where NBB is the National Best Bid, or the highest bid price across all exchanges, and NBO is the National Best Offer, or the lowest available offer price across all exchanges. We then define the trade markout (marked to the midpoint) for an execution i at time t as follows:

$$\delta_{markout} = \begin{cases} M_{t+\tau} - p_{i,t} & \text{for buy orders} \\ p_{i,t} - M_{i,t+\tau} & \text{for sell orders} \end{cases} \tag{2}$$

where $p_{i,t}$ is the execution price of trade i, and $\tau > 0$ is some fixed time interval. As we cannot always infer the direction of trades (i.e. whether the liquidity remover was a buyer or seller) happening inside the NBBO, we need to restrict this statistic to executions at the NBB or NBO. In other words, we compute markouts from the perspective of the liquidity adder (i.e. the resting order) for buy orders where $p_{i,t} = NBB_t$ and sell orders where $p_{i,t} = NBO_t$. We volume-weight markouts by the shares executed in the trade.

In order to scale the dollar amounts for better comparison across exchanges, we also compute the relative markout, which is the markout divided by the NBBO midpoint at the time of trade. More formally, we define the relative markout $\delta_{\%markout}$ for a trade i that executed at time t as follows:

$$\delta_{\%markout} = \begin{cases} \dfrac{M_{t+\tau} - p_{i,t}}{M_t} & \text{for buy orders} \\ \dfrac{p_{i,t} - M_{t+\tau}}{M_t} & \text{for sell orders} \end{cases} \tag{3}$$

[34] Bessembinder and Venkataraman, 'Bid-ask spreads', 2010.

Table 5.5. Example of NBBO prices for computing trade markouts

Time	NBB	NBO	NBBO midpoint (M)
t	$10.00	$10.01	$10.005
$t+\tau$	$9.99	$10.00	$9.995

We note that the realized spread of a trade, similar to markouts, is the side-adjusted difference between the execution price and the NBBO midpoint M some time τ after the trade. Unlike markouts, however, it is defined relative to the trade-initiating order. More formally, realized spread δ_{realized} for a given trade i executing at time t can be defined as follows:

$$\delta_{\text{realized}} = \begin{cases} 2\left(M_{t+\tau} - p_{i,t}\right) & \text{for seller-initiated trades} \\ 2\left(p_{i,t} - M_{t+\tau}\right) & \text{for buyer-initiated trades} \end{cases} \tag{4}$$

The trade markout is thus equivalent to the realized half-spread, or $\delta_{\text{markout}} = \frac{1}{2}\delta_{\text{realized}}$.

To illustrate how we measure trade markouts, we use the example NBBO prices in Table 5.5. At time t, we observe an execution at price $p_t = \$10.00$, which is the NBB. This is presumably a resting buy order trading with a spread-crossing sell order; in other words, the trade was initiated by the seller. We compute markouts from the perspective of the resting buy order given the NBBO midpoint some time τ after the trade, or $M_{t+\tau} = \$9.995$:

$$\delta_{\text{markout}} = \$9.995 - \$10.00 = -\$0.005 = -50 \text{ mils}$$

$$\delta_{\%\text{markout}} = \frac{\$9.995 - \$10.00}{\$10.005} = -0.0005 = -5 \text{ basis points}$$

$$\delta_{\text{realized}} = 2(\$9.995 - \$10.00) = -\$0.01$$

5.5.1.2 RESULTS

The SEC's definition of realized spreads, as codified in Rule 605 of Regulation NMS,[35] sets τ to 5 minutes after the time of trade. This assumes that the liquidity provider closes out its position within that time frame, but 5 minutes is an unduly long interval given the high-speed nature of today's trading environment, in which many of the informational advantages that exist are measured in milliseconds. To take into account market participants' varying trading horizons, we compute markouts for $\tau \epsilon \{1\text{ms}, 10\text{ms}, 100\text{ms}, 1\text{s}, 5\text{s}, 10\text{s}, 20\text{s}, 30\text{s}, 1\text{min}, 5\text{min}\}$ after each trade. These time intervals are also in line with previous work.[36]

---

[35] SEC, *Regulation NMS*, 2005.   [36] Conrad et al., 'High-frequency quoting', 2015.

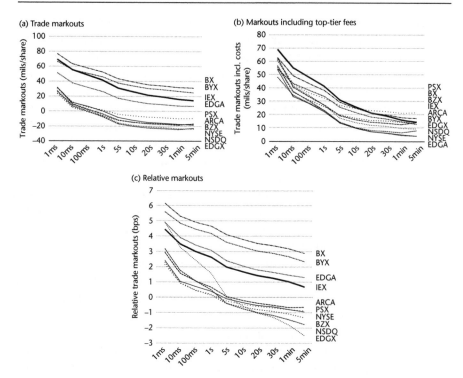

Figure 5.7. Variants of trade markouts, measured from the liquidity adder's perspective as the difference between the trade price and the NBBO midpoint some time post-trade for executions at the NBBO

Note: estimation of fees assessed by exchange is based on top-tier Tape A fees for displayed shares executed at or above $1 (Figure 5.1).

As evidenced in Figure 5.7(a), there is a dramatic difference in markouts across different exchanges. Of particular note, there is a substantial gap between the three exchanges at the top of the chart (IEX, BX, and BYX), and the five exchanges at the bottom of the chart (NYSE, Arca, NASDAQ, BZX, and EDGX). The difference between these two groups of exchanges is on the scale of 40 to 50 mils per share, even just 1ms post-trade. In other words, on average, immediately after receiving an execution on one of the standard maker-taker exchanges, a trader is half a cent worse off per share than they would have been had their order been executed on IEX, BX, or BYX. While this notion may be intuitive and unsurprising to experienced market practitioners, if one takes a step back, it becomes apparent that it represents a major problem with the current market structure. Because NMS considers all exchanges at the NBBO to be equally protected regardless of fee structure, and because explicit trade execution costs on exchanges are typically absorbed by brokers rather than by the end beneficiary of the trade, brokers have a clear economic incentive to route passive order flow to traditional maker-taker exchanges, which provide them with rebates of approximately 20–30 mils per share but lead to an average implicit cost to their customers of as much as 50 mils per share. Yet the significantly longer average queue sizes at the largest maker-taker venues (as discussed in Section 5.4.3) illustrate the degree to which some brokers prioritize rebate accrual over probability of execution—many market participants would rather receive a rebate to join a long line at these maker-taker exchanges than post on a venue with shorter queues.

We can draw similar conclusions from our results for both markouts net of top-tier fees and rebates, as well as relative markouts (Figures 5.7(b) and (c), respectively). Evaluating markouts including fees and rebates allows us to determine whether rebates compensate for inferior execution quality on the high-fee venues. We observe that markouts across exchanges do not fully converge over time, indicating that rebates, even if passed on to the customer, may not provide adequate compensation depending on a market participant's trading horizon.[37] Relative markouts are normalized by the NBBO midpoint, and we observe a similar trend in which trades on the inverted exchanges and IEX offer much higher potential profitability than executions on the maker-taker venues, for nearly all time intervals.

Various symbol characteristics (such as price and volume) may have a significant impact on where and how such symbols trade, thereby affecting performance metrics such as markouts and realized spread. Such characteristics typically manifest themselves in a stock's quoted spread, which is the difference between the NBB and NBO. Therefore, we also measure markouts for symbol clusters as based on spread at the time of trade. Grouping symbols into three categories by spread (1 cent, 2 to 4 cents, and 5+ cents), we observe the same general pattern across the three groups: markouts on the inverted exchanges and IEX tend to be higher than those on NYSE, Arca, NASDAQ, BZX, and EDGX. While the magnitude of the markouts generally increases with spread, the relative order of venues by performance remains fairly consistent. These results persist across the various time intervals used.

5.5.2 Price Improvement

When making the decision to cross the spread with an aggressive order and to trade immediately, a broker can take several factors into account. If the order is large relative to the number of shares available at the inside across the market, most brokers route to multiple trading venues simultaneously in order to capture as much liquidity as possible. If the order is small relative to the

---

[37] Similar to results published by Battalio et al., 'Can brokers have it all?', 2016.

aggregated quote, the broker may decide where to route based on a tiebreaker. Often, the primary determining factor in this equation is simple trade execution economics; in other words, the broker routes to the venue with the lowest removal fee (or highest rebate, in the case of inverted exchanges).

Another common factor is the likelihood of price improvement. Price improvement refers to the situation where an aggressive order is filled at a price strictly better than the inside quote: in the case of an aggressive buy (sell) order, receiving a fill at a price lower (higher) than the NBO (NBB). Price improvement and the effective-to-quoted spread (which we discuss in Section 5.5.3) are often cited by retail brokers as two of the primary statistics used to evaluate execution quality.[38]

Following the definition by Cboe Global Markets,[39] we compute per-share price improvement as the difference between the trade price and the NBO (NBB) for buy (sell) orders:

$$PI = \begin{cases} NBO_t - p_{i,t} & \text{for buy orders} \\ p_{i,t} - NBB_t & \text{for sell orders} \end{cases} \tag{5}$$

To determine aggregate price improvement, we volume-weight the price improvement for a given execution by the trade size. A positive price improvement value indicates the trade occurred at a price better than the far side of the NBBO. Figure 5.8 illustrates the overall per-share price improvement on each exchange, as computed based on the methodology described by Cboe Global Markets.[40] We note that this is based on TAQ data, and as such calculates PI for all volume, as we cannot distinguish spread-crossing orders from those targeting the midpoint. We find that IEX offers the most price improvement—more than double that available on the next highest venue, NASDAQ. This is in no small part due to IEX's rich midpoint liquidity (Section 5.4.2), as midpoint trades also represent a powerful tool for half-spread price improvement.

In a second, complementary approach, we assess price improvement via data from the IEX router,[41] as this allows us to restrict the PI computation to spread-crossing orders only. The router is designed to always send aggressive child orders at the current or prevailing inside of the market, taking into account its previous actions. As such, we measure price improvement in this metric relative to the child order's limit price. Some order routers specifically check markets at the midpoint prior to crossing the spread as a general rule of

---

[38] Scottrade, *Trade Quality & Execution*, 2017; E*TRADE, *Execution Quality*, 2017; TD Ameritrade, *Order Execution Quality*, 2017; Charles Schwab & Co., Inc., *Trade Execution Quality & Routing*, 2017; Fidelity, *Commitment to Execution Quality*, 2017.
[39] Cboe Global Markets, *Execution Quality Definitions*, 2017.
[40] Cboe Global Markets, *Execution Quality Definitions*, 2017.
[41] See https://iextrading.com/trading/router.

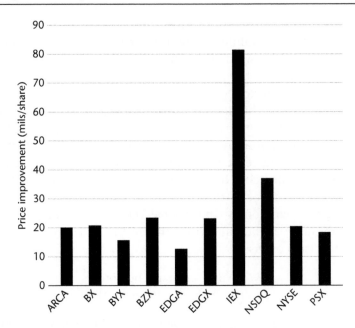

Figure 5.8. Price improvement, as based on the definition by Cboe Global Markets, by exchange

thumb, whereas other routing strategies may prioritize venues where price improvement is more likely. The IEX router interacts with liquidity resting on IEX; it also sweeps all markets displaying protected quotes. Thus we can assess and compare price improvement across venues by analysing orders routed to each exchange from the IEX order router. Table 5.6 summarizes a number of price improvement metrics across the various exchanges. It is important to note that the IEX router exclusively sends spread-crossing orders, so its price improvement can be considered serendipitous: the router was willing to pay the full spread, but it received a better price than it expected. This suggests that optimal routing strategies should consider the hidden liquidity profiles of venues, which might call for order allocation even in the absence of a displayed quote. Not doing so may represent a significant opportunity cost, due to forfeiting the half-spread price improvement possible when executing at the midpoint.

In both analyses, we find a higher potential for price improvement on IEX versus the other venues, but most notably versus the inverted exchanges. This is significant in light of the opportunity to capture rebates when taking liquidity on the inverted venues, as a broker is in effect deciding whether to prioritize its own economics or to seek out an opportunity for price improvement for its client.

Table 5.6. Price improvement metrics by exchange

Exchange	IEX router volume	PI%	PI (mils/share)	Avg. PI (mils/share)
ARCA	402,400,350	4.9	117	5.8
BX	80,081,908	7.1	134	9.5
BYX	154,481,515	6.1	172	10.4
BZX	148,110,990	6.6	114	7.5
EDGA	26,336,597	5.6	140	7.8
EDGX	212,111,276	4.1	118	4.8
IEX	281,051,416	10.9	169	18.4
NSDQ	461,282,320	6.4	151	9.7
NYSE	579,631,179	4.7	103	4.9
PSX	29,169,849	4.4	88	3.9

Notes: IEX router volume is the total volume routed and executed at each venue by the IEX order router. PI% is the percentage of volume receiving positive price improvement. PI is the total price improvement obtained, summed over all price-improved executions, in mils per share. Average PI is the expected price improvement per trade in mils per share, computed as the likelihood of price improvement (PI%) multiplied by the total price improvement obtained (PI).

5.5.3 Quoted and Effective Spread

Quoted spread, defined as the difference between the bid and offer prices, is the simplest measure of execution costs. It reflects the cost of both buying and selling a security, if trades are executed at the quoted prices.[42] More formally, the quoted spread on a given exchange e at time t is defined as follows:

$$\delta_{\text{quoted}} = BO_t^e - BB_t^e \tag{6}$$

where BB_t^e is the best (highest) bid price and BO_t^e is the best (lowest) offer price. Wider quoted spreads may reflect greater adverse selection.[43] We measure quoted spread at the time of trade on each venue, excluding executions for which the quoted spread is not defined (i.e. when a market centre's BBO does not exist).

Another measure of trading costs is *effective spread*, which focuses on the quote midpoint in effect at the time of trade relative to the execution price. The closer the two prices, the narrower the effective spread. Effective spread can be interpreted as the cost paid when an incoming order executes against a resting order, and unlike quoted spread it captures other features of a market centre, such as hidden and midpoint liquidity as well as market depth.[44] Following the definition by Cboe Global Markets,[45] we define the effective spread for a trade i that occurred at time t as:

$$\delta_{\text{effective}} = 2|p_{i,t} - M_t| \tag{7}$$

---

[42] Bessembinder and Venkataraman, 'Bid-ask spreads', 2010.
[43] Glosten and Milgrom, 'Bid, ask and transaction prices', 1985.
[44] Riordan and Storkenmaier, 'Latency, liquidity and price discovery', 2012.
[45] Cboe Global Markets, *Execution Quality Definitions*, 2017.

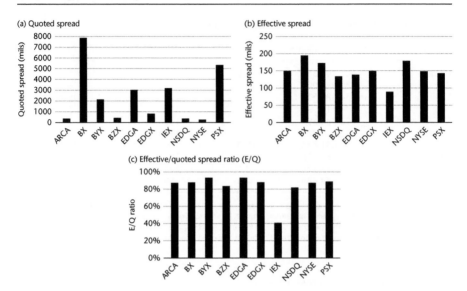

Figure 5.9. Quoted spread, effective spread, and the effective-to-quoted spread ratio (computed as the effective spread divided by the NBBO quoted spread at the time of trade), by exchange

The *effective-to-quoted spread ratio*, or E/Q ratio, is calculated by dividing a market centre's effective spread by the NBBO quoted spread at the time of trade:

$$EQ = \frac{2|p_{i,t} - M_t|}{NBO_t - NBB_t} \tag{8}$$

The E/Q ratio is 1 when an order is executed exactly at the NBBO quote; a lower effective-to-quoted spread ratio reflects executions at prices better than the NBBO. We report the volume-weighted E/Q ratio for each exchange.

Figure 5.9 shows the volume-weighted quoted and effective spreads for each exchange, as well as the effective-to-quoted spread (E/Q) ratio. We observe the narrowest quoted spread on the largest venues (NYSE, Arca, NASDAQ, BZX, and EDGX). We find the widest quoted spread on BX and PSX, followed by IEX, EDGA, and BYX. PSX is an exception due to its low market share (Table 5.1), but otherwise the list of wide-spread venues includes all the inverted exchanges (i.e. BYX, BX, EDGA) and IEX. This result is intuitive, as the economic incentives of access fees mean that brokers are more likely to add liquidity on maker-taker exchanges, thereby narrowing quoted spreads on those venues.

Effective spread is a better measure of the cost of trading than quoted spread,[46] and we can see in Figure 5.9(b) that IEX has the lowest effective spread across all exchanges. Lower effective spread indicates that orders on IEX tend to execute

---

[46] Bessembinder and Venkataraman, 'Bid-ask spreads', 2010.

close to or at the NBBO midpoint at a greater rate than orders on other exchanges. This result is in line with execution quality statistics reported by Cboe Global Markets.[47] We also find that IEX offers the lowest E/Q ratio across all exchanges (Figure 5.9(c)); on average, IEX's effective spread is approximately 40 per cent as wide as the NBBO quoted spread at the time of trade.

5.6 Price Discovery

Price discovery, which is the process by which prices incorporate new information, is a critical function of any market. Given the widespread fragmentation of trading across multiple exchanges and dark pools,[48] it is important to identify the venues that are the largest contributors to the price formation process. We compare exchanges across a number of metrics to assess their potential contribution to price discovery, including time and size at the inside in general (Section 5.6.1) and time at the inside during locked and crossed markets (Section 5.6.2). We do not measure which venues most often set the NBBO, as the speeds with which prices transition make universal agreement on which was 'first' to set the NBBO difficult. Indeed, this observation is often driven by an observer's location relative to select venues. Someone observing a price change in NYSE's Mahwah data centre may conclude that Arca was the first to set the inside. Conversely, an observer in NASDAQ's Carteret data centre might believe that it was, in fact, NASDAQ. Another consideration is that, while the fastest exchange to process an order will set the inside first, very often the delta between the first and nth exchange is inconsequential for the majority of market participants observing a price change.

5.6.1 *Time at Inside*

While we do not directly measure each exchange's contribution to price discovery as based on which venues are establishing the NBBO, as a proxy measure we compare the percentage of time and size at the inside or at the NBBO (i.e. when the exchange is on either the NBB or the NBO, or both) by exchange. The more often an exchange is at the inside, the more likely it is to

---

[47] Cboe maintains an 'Execution Quality' metric that they publicize on their website. Their measure of effective spread compares the execution price against the NBBO midpoint in effect at the millisecond in which the trade occurs. Cboe computes effective spread for each symbol in the S&P 500, reporting the count of symbols for which a given venue is ranked either 1st, 2nd, or 3rd. In their statistics, IEX had the lowest effective spread across all venues in nearly all of the S&P 500 symbols (Cboe Global Markets, *Execution Quality*, 2017).

[48] O'Hara and Ye, 'Market fragmentation', 2011.

have a greater contribution to price discovery across all markets. Therefore, we compute the following metrics:

- the equal-weighted percentage of time an exchange is at the inside,
- the volume-weighted percentage of time an exchange is at the inside,
- the equal-weighted percentage of size an exchange has available at the inside, and
- the volume-weighted percentage of size an exchange has available at the inside.

We measure the total time an exchange is at either the bid or the offer, or both, in a given symbol, and divide by total time in the trading day. To capture how many shares are available at the inside quote on each exchange, we compute each symbol's percentage of size at the inside during the day (similar to the average queue size metric in Section 5.4.3). If volume-weighting, we weight by the symbol's total market-wide volume on that day.

Figures 5.10(a) and (b) show the percentage of time at the inside quote, across all securities, given the two different weighting schemes. Our results indicate that NASDAQ is the exchange most frequently at the inside. PSX and IEX tend to quote at the inside in higher-volume symbols, as their volume-weighted per cent of total time at the inside is more comparable to the other venues. NYSE's lower ranking in this metric is because it trades Tape A securities exclusively, and our metrics are based on all symbols, not just those on a given tape. When we look at the percentage of shares available at the inside quote (Figures 5.10(c) and (d)), we find that NASDAQ, Arca, NYSE, and EDGX tend to quote the largest size at the inside. IEX tends to quote smaller size at the inside, particularly in high-volume symbols, as its percentage of size at the inside relative to other exchanges drops once volume-weighting is applied. Relative time at the inside will naturally reflect relative market share (Table 5.1), but it may also be a second-order effect of current fee structures. We observe that time at the inside appears to be strongly correlated with rebates for liquidity provision, as the exchanges at the inside more often are not only the largest but also those that employ a maker-taker pricing model.

5.6.2 Locked and Crossed Markets

The prevalence of rebates in posting liquidity and the fragmentation of trading across multiple exchanges creates the potential for both a *locked market*, where the bid on one exchange is simultaneously equivalent to the offer on another, and a *crossed market*, where the bid on one exchange exceeds the offer on another. Locked and crossed markets impede price discovery: during such situations the price formation process is essentially frozen, and it is unclear

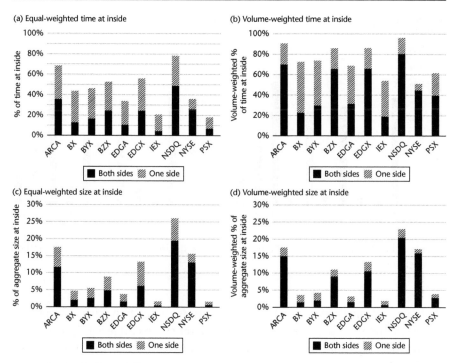

Figure 5.10. Equal-weighted and volume-weighted percentage of time and aggregate size available at the NBBO, by exchange

what the true trading interest in a stock is. The distinct structural and fee characteristics of venues may also mean that certain exchanges contribute to locked and crossed markets more frequently than others, as these situations may not represent a fundamental need to buy or sell. For example, in a situation where a buyer and seller find themselves at the same price on different markets, neither may be willing to access the other's quote since that would result in paying an access fee and forgoing a rebate.

To investigate each exchange's contribution to either locked or crossed markets, we measure the volume-weighted per cent of time in a locked (crossed) market for which an exchange is quoting at the NBBO. Each instance of a locked market is uniquely specified by the locking price and starting time, where $NBB = NBO$; similarly, each instance of a crossed market is uniquely specified by the NBB and NBO, where $NBB > NBO$. We volume-weight each symbol's percentage by the market-wide volume traded in that symbol on that day. Note that multiple venues may be at the bid or offer during a locked market, so these percentages do not sum to exactly 100 per cent.

Figure 5.11(a) illustrates the per cent of time at which each exchange is at the inside during a locked market. IEX is at the bid or offer approximately

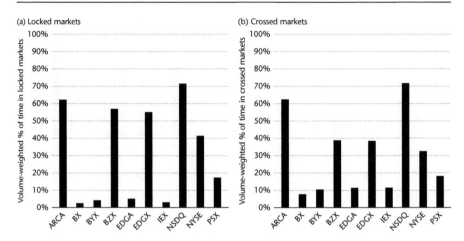

Figure 5.11. Volume-weighted time at the inside during locked and crossed markets, by exchange

3 per cent of the time during locked markets. Contrast that with a venue such as PSX, which has less than 1 per cent market share (Table 5.1) but is on the bid or offer during locked markets 17 per cent of the time, over 5 times as often as IEX. During crossed markets (Figure 5.11(b)), we observe that IEX is at the inside 11 per cent of the time.

In general, our results indicate that the top contributors to both locked and crossed markets are NYSE, NASDAQ, Arca, EDGX, and BZX. These are the top five exchanges by market share, which generally reflects increased quoting and trading activity, and all employ a maker-taker pricing model that rewards liquidity providers via rebates. What is also notable is that PSX, another maker-taker venue, is at the bid or offer during a locked market significantly more often—despite having significantly lower market share—than the inverted venues and IEX. We observe a similar trend with crossed markets, where the maker-taker venues are contributing towards a disproportionately large fraction of crossed markets. This suggests that a venue's contribution towards locked and crossed markets is primarily a reflection of its overall time at the inside, which is in turn influenced by its willingness to pay rebates to providers of liquidity.

5.7 Market Stability

Market stability, which we characterize as the execution of significant volume without excess price fluctuations, is a desirable feature in a market as it both promotes efficient price discovery and reflects a market participant's ability to trade at accessible prices. Hence, another hallmark of superior execution quality on a venue is quote stability, particularly around trades. Market stability also corresponds to some degree to the prevalence of intermarket sweep orders (ISOs). Since ISOs are used specifically to access displayed liquidity across several market centres, a higher prevalence of ISOs on a given exchange may correspond to less quote stability. In our dataset, ISOs represent at least 40 per cent of volume on all exchanges other than IEX, where the ISO volume rate is near 0 per cent. However, the results presented in the following sections still hold when we exclude trades resulting from ISOs. We therefore present results for all trading (inclusive of ISOs) since we are most interested in comparing the full trading experience across venues.

The circumstances under which market participants quote on various venues may also impact stability. Inverted venues may be more likely to receive passive orders if many maker-taker venues are already quoting, as market participants might attempt to obtain a more favourable position in the intermarket queue (due to the rebates that inverted exchanges pay to firms accessing their liquidity). In such circumstances, the quote is likely to be more stable. An equally important driver of this dynamic is the order in which market centres are accessed, and that being the case, the results presented in this section may have important implications for firms determining the optimal venues on which to display resting orders. This determination is partially driven by the likelihood of being a preferred destination for a would-be contraparty. Market stability is a strong proxy for this likelihood, precisely because being among the first venues accessed improves the probability of trading in a stable quote environment.

To evaluate stability, we analyse the post-trade price movement of midpoint executions (Section 5.7.1), as well as the percentage of volume executed during an unstable NBBO (Section 5.7.2).

5.7.1 Post-Trade Midpoint Movement

A relatively unstable NBBO can be unhealthy for markets. Rapid quote changes on the order of milliseconds, for instance, are generally inaccessible without a combination of co-location and direct feeds from exchanges.[49] In addition, instability in the NBBO could lead to executions at adverse prices for orders pegged to the NBBO midpoint.[50] Market stability is partially improved with the presence of displayed quotes (Section 5.6.1). But if many of those quotes are primarily incentivized by a rebate, then in times of market distress,

---

[49] Laughlin et al., 'Information transmission', 2014.
[50] Ding et al., 'How slow is the NBBO?', 2014.

the rebate may not be sufficient compensation for the provision of liquidity, leading to fleeting liquidity during periods of market instability.[51]

Midpoint trades, by nature, have less informational value than trades at the NBBO because the aggressiveness and direction of the liquidity remover cannot be determined by an outside observer. For example, when a buyer crosses the spread to trade at the offer price, the buyer is expressing greater urgency to trade than the resting seller. However, with a midpoint trade, the urgencies of the parties involved are obfuscated. As such, midpoint trades increase market stability by providing liquidity (and price improvement) with less impact on the NBBO than other executions, which is desirable for many large traders and investors.

To examine the effect of each exchange's midpoint liquidity on market stability, we evaluate the percentage of executions occurring at the midpoint of the NBBO, where the midpoint is unchanged at various snapshots after the trade.[52] We consider the best overall outcome to be for the market to remain unchanged at a snapshot following a midpoint execution, which would suggest that neither participant was adversely selected and that information on the trade was minimized with respect to other trades. A high value in this measure would suggest that a given venue has midpoint order flow that minimizes the impact on the NBBO. Figure 5.12 shows our results, with symbols with narrow spreads (under 2 cents) at the time of trade plotted

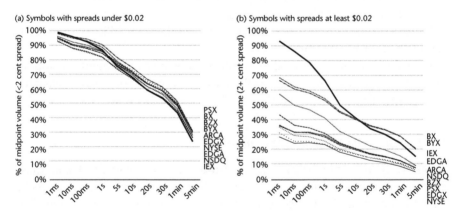

Figure 5.12. Percentage of midpoint volume where the NBBO midpoint is unchanged some time after the trade, by exchange, broken out the symbol's quoted NBBO spread at the time of trade

[51] Easley et al., 'Microstructure of the "flash crash"', 2011.
[52] In line with our markouts computation (Section 5.5.1), this metric only looks at the NBBO midpoint some interval τ after the trade. It is possible that the NBBO midpoint changed during this interval before reverting back to its previous value. See Section 5.7.2 for an analysis of NBBO stability across exchanges.

separately from those with wide spreads (2 cents or greater) at the time of trade. Relative to other exchanges, IEX has a much larger percentage of midpoint volume, with no post-trade price movement within the first 5 seconds in wider-spread symbols.[53] Also note that at longer time intervals after the trade, micro-scale trading dynamics are no longer in play, so these results are more likely to reflect the distribution of the securities traded on the market.

5.7.2 Quote Instability

Traditional market participants consider quote stability a desirable characteristic for a market centre; however, quote *instability* has become a great source of opportunity for speed-based strategies that utilize data and technology purchased directly from exchanges in order to detect price fluctuations ahead of other participants.

To assess quote instability across exchanges, we examine midpoint volume that occurred immediately prior to an NBBO change, or during an unstable NBBO. More specifically, for every midpoint trade on a venue, we classify it based on whether or not it executed in the 2ms window prior to an NBBO quote change.[54] We then compute the midpoint volume executed either within or outside this window, which provides an approximation of the volume executed at imminently stale prices on each exchange.

We find that IEX has the lowest percentage of midpoint volume within the 2ms window prior to an NBBO change (Figure 5.13(a)), and the highest midpoint ADV outside the 2ms window (Figure 5.13(b)). In contrast, over 44 per cent of midpoint volume on NASDAQ and NYSE executed within 2ms of a quote change—in other words, during a soon-to-be-stale NBBO. This indicates that executions on IEX have a stronger tendency to be during times of quote stability in comparison to those on other exchanges, as the vast majority of IEX's executed midpoint volume is during a stable NBBO price. IEX's high rank in this metric is due both to the nature of its rich midpoint liquidity and to the unique features of its market, such as its speed bump and the crumbling quote signal (Section 5.4.2), which work in concert to prevent executions at imminently stale prices.

---

[53] We find that the inclusion of Tick Size Pilot Program securities, whose spreads have been widened to 5 cents as discussed in Section 5.3, does not affect this observation, as the results for symbols with spreads within 2 to 4 cents are nearly identical.

[54] We evaluated volume at a number of different interval lengths (1ms, 2ms, 5ms, and 10ms), and found the general trends to hold, so we only report results for 2ms intervals here. This time length is in line with Hasbrouck and Saar ('Low-latency trading', 2013), who find that the fastest traders respond to market events in about 2–3ms.

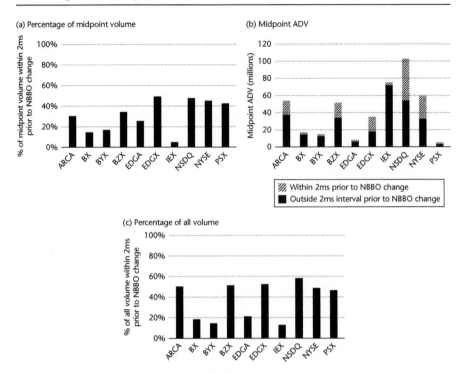

Figure 5.13. Percentage of midpoint volume, average daily midpoint volume, and percentage of all volume for trades executing within the 2ms window immediately prior to an NBBO change

We can apply the same classification scheme described above to all trades in our dataset, and our results are shown in Figure 5.13(c). The connection between market stability and access fees is most clearly visible here, where there is an obvious line of demarcation between the venues that pay rebates to liquidity adders, and those employing an alternative pricing structure (whether inverted or otherwise). We observe that IEX and the inverted exchanges tend to have the lowest percentage of volume executed immediately prior to an NBBO change. We believe this to be due to dynamics driven by the maker-taker pricing paradigm. All things being equal, firms are incentivized to remove liquidity at the cheapest venues (i.e. those that charge the lowest fee or pay a rebate). As such, in situations where a firm needs to execute only a fraction of the displayed liquidity, and that execution could occur anywhere, the firm may seek liquidity at BX or BYX (for which they would be paid rebates). Conversely, if a firm needs to execute a very large order, such as one that exceeds the aggregate amount displayed across all venues, the firm would need to access each exchange with a displayed quote. In these cases, a firm accessing liquidity on a venue charging a high fee is more likely to do so en route to clearing out (or attempting to clear out) an entire price level. Therefore, the proportion of volume executed as part of a market-wide sweep is more likely to be significantly higher on the venues that charge the maximum fee, which contributes to a less stable NBBO on those maximum-fee exchanges. However, as discussed above, venues that charge the maximum access fee generally also provide the largest rebates to adders of liquidity. As such, market participants who route orders to these maximum-fee venues in pursuit of the largest possible rebate are more likely to be adversely selected.

5.8 Conclusions

The recent introduction of Investors Exchange, or IEX, offers the opportunity to evaluate comparative execution quality across the incumbent US stock exchanges and identify potential drivers behind qualitative disparities in performance. In this study, we primarily use publicly available Daily TAQ data in an effort to promote transparency, and we focus on four dimensions of market quality: liquidity provision, execution costs, price discovery, and market stability.

One limitation of this study is that we analyse a non-exhaustive set of execution quality metrics. In addition, market quality across US stock exchanges depends largely on fundamental differences between venues and the variance in usage these differences create. Many differences between exchanges are closely tied to venue design choices or broader market structure dynamics, and execution quality on the level of an individual market partici-pant is a direct byproduct of brokers' venue choices and their interactions with a given market. However, we believe that our use of publicly available TAQ data (instead of venue- or broker-specific data) facilitates further analyses of execution quality across different exchanges. We hope that our study empowers market participants to conduct their own analyses of venue per-formance going forward.

Notably, we observe a wide range of execution quality across venues, and our results suggest a consistent trend in venue stratification by fee structure across a number of performance metrics. For instance, we find that the inverted exchanges and IEX offer the most favourable trade markouts for passive orders, indicating higher potential profit, whereas market participants on maker-taker exchanges are at greater risk of adverse selection. In fact, traders with orders on maker-taker venues tend to be on average half a cent worse off per share immediately after executing, compared with if they had executed on an inverted exchange or IEX. This means that by placing orders on maker-taker venues in order to receive rebates of approximately 20 to 30 mils per share, brokers are implicitly costing their customers as much as

50 mils per share—so these rebates, even if passed on the customer, may not compensate for potentially inferior execution quality.

The inverted exchanges also tend to offer a more stable market than the maker-taker venues: they have a higher percentage of midpoint volume with no post-trade price movement, as well as less volume during an unstable NBBO. This is another byproduct of the dynamics driven by the maker-taker pricing paradigm. A greater portion of the volume on maker-taker venues charging the maximum access fee tends to be from market-wide sweeps, in comparison to the inverted exchanges, simply because taking liquidity on those venues is more expensive. This contributes to a less stable NBBO on those maker-taker venues. However, given that venues charging the maximum fee to take generally also offer the largest rebates to add, market participants who route orders in pursuit of the largest possible rebate are essentially self-selecting into market centres with an unstable NBBO.

In addition, our results demonstrate that average queue sizes tend to be stratified by fee structure, with the shortest queues on the inverted exchanges. Shorter queues reflect less competition at the inside and greater likelihood of execution. Yet the inverted venues and IEX trade less volume than the maker-taker exchanges and have shorter queues. This provides compelling evidence of certain brokers' prioritization of rebates over best execution when making routing decisions.

In aggregate, these results suggest that the disparities in market quality across exchanges are fundamentally an outgrowth of access fees and rebates. Maker-taker and inverted pricing regimes perpetuate economic incentives misaligned with the tenets of best execution, as market participants executing orders on behalf of their customers have to weigh their financial interests against their best execution obligations. Brokers have a clear economic incentive to route passive order flow to traditional maker-taker exchanges over other venues. Therefore, despite greater adverse selection, less stability around executions, significantly longer queues at the inside, and a lower probability of execution, the maker-taker exchanges dominate the US equities trading landscape in market share.

The conclusions we draw herein illustrate the significant impact of market structure on trading outcomes. Structural inefficiencies in today's equity markets have exacerbated conflicts of interest between brokers, investors, and exchanges. Proffering rebates for liquidity provision can incentivize behaviour that is detrimental to market quality, as it promotes the expedient or cost-effective option over the one that is best for the customer. Resolving this conflict will be of paramount importance in achieving fair, orderly markets that promote interactions between natural investors, and that contribute towards price formation and the efficient allocation of capital.

Appendix

Query 1: Core Trades

/

Function which, in conjunction with filterTrades, is meant to provide a standardized base of trade data for use in calculating various trade-based metrics. Retrieves data for all trades on a given date, with an option to filter for a given set of symbols.

The primary fields of interest are the symbol, the time, size, and price of trade, the executing venue, and the prevailing NBBO; others include midpoint and block status, which are used for certain metrics, as well as other metadata used for filtering.

Parameters:
d   Date atom for which to pull data
symList   (Optional) List of symbols to which to limit the data
\

```
getTrades:{[d;symList]
    c:enlist (=;`date;d); if[count symList;c,: (in;`sym;enlist
      symList)];
    tt:?[trade;c;0b;{x!x}` sym`time`size`price`ex`cond`corr`tte];
    tt:tt lj 1!select sym:taqsym,tape,etf:sectype=`ETF,isTestSym
      from.ustaq.getRefDataForDate[d];
    tt:aj[`sym`time;tt;select `p#sym,time,bid,ask from nbbo where
      date=d];
    tt:update midTrade:price=mid from update `long$size,mid:0.5*bid
      +ask from tt;
    tt:update buy:price<=mid,block:(size>=10000)|(price*size)>=2e9
      from tt;
    tt:update ex:"T" from tt where ex="Q";
    tt
    };
```

/

Function which, in conjunction with getTrades, is meant to provide a standardized base of trade data for use in calculating various trade-based metrics. Takes the output of getTrades and filters across various fields to provide a dataset intended to best resemble continuous trading.

The filters are as follows:
Excluding the TRF
Excluding the pre- and post-market sessions
Excluding most last-sale ineligible trades, most notably auctions
Excluding corrections

Excluding symbol BRK.A
Excluding test symbols

Excluding trades in locked, crossed, zero- and one-sided markets
Excluding trade-through exempt trades outside the NBBO
Excluding trades more than 10% outside the NBBO

Parameters:
tt   Table of trades to filter (usually the output of getTrades)

```
\
filterTrades:{[tt]
    // Trade-based filters
    tt:select from tt where ex<>"D";
    tt:select from tt where time within (09:30;16:00);
tt:select from tt where not cond like "*[BCGHLMNOPQRTUVWZ456789]*";
    tt:select from tt where corr like "0[01]";
    tt:select from tt where sym<>`BRK.A;
    tt:select from tt where isTestSym="N";

    // Market data-based filters
    tt:select from tt where bid<ask,bid>0,ask<0W;
    tt:select from tt where not (tte="1")&(price<bid)|price>ask;
    tt:select from tt where price within (bid-0.1*mid;ask+0.1*mid);
    tt
    };
```

Query 2: Midpoint & Block Volume

Function which sums trade volume on a given date by whether it occurred at the prevailing NBBO midpoint and whether it was a block, as well as other categories of interest including executing venue, tape, and whether the symbol was an ETF.

Parameters:
d   Date atom for which to pull data

```
\
getMidBlockVolume:{[d]
    0!select sum size by ex,tape,etf,midTrade,block from filterTrades
      [getTrades[d;()]]
    };
```

```
/
```
Function which aggregates the outputs of getMidBlockVolume run on multiple days.

```
Parameters:
tt        Table of razed getMidBlockVolume outputs
\
aggMidBlockVolume:{[tt]
    0!select sum size by ex,tape,etf,midTrade,block from tt
    };
```

Query 3: Queue Size

```
/
```

Function which calculates the time-weighted average size available at the NBBO inside by executing venue for a given date.

Due to the relative size of NBBO data, this function allows for partitioning the symbol universe and serially running each partition.

```
Parameters:
d         Date atom for which to pull data
n         Number of partitions
\
getQueueSize:{[d;n]
    symList:(select distinct sym from nbbo where date=d)`sym;
    nn:raze {[d;symList]
        nn:select sym,time,bexs,bsizes,asizes,aexs from nbbo where
          date=d,sym in symList;
        nn:update dur:next deltas 09:30|16:00&time by sym from nn;
        nn:update `p#sym from select from nn where dur>0;
        raze {[nn;s]
            nn:select from nn where sym=s;
            bids:ungroup `dur xkey select dur,ex:bexs,bsizes from nn;
            asks:ungroup `dur xkey select dur,ex:aexs,asizes from nn;
            0!(select AvgBidSize:(sum dur*bsizes)%("n"$06:30) by sym:
                s,ex from bids) uj
              (select AvgAskSize:(sum dur*asizes)%("n"$06:30) by sym:
                s,ex from asks)
          }[nn;] each distinct nn`sym
      }[d;] each ((n|1),0N)#symList;
    update date:d from nn lj 1!select sym:taqsym,roundlot from .ustaq.
      getRefDataForDate[d]
    };
```

```
/
```

Function which aggregates the outputs of getQueueSize run on multiple days.

```
Parameters:
nn          Table of razed getQueueSize outputs
\
aggQueueSize:{[nn]
    index:(cross/){?[x;();1b;{x!x}enlist y]}[nn] each `date`sym`ex;
    nn:update 0^AvgBidSize,0^AvgAskSize,100^roundlot from index lj
      `date`sym`ex xkey nn;
    0!select AvgBidAsk:avg 0.5*roundlot*AvgBidSize+AvgAskSize by ex
      from nn
    };
```

Query 4: Hidden Volume

Function which calculates the percentage of trades and volume on IEX on a given date that are against hidden resting orders, meant to replicate methodology used for SEC MIDAS data.

Runs against IEX proprietary data, not TAQ; this is provided for context as IEX data is currently unavailable through MIDAS.

```
Parameters:
d           Date atom for which to pull data
\
getMidasHiddenVolumeStream:{[d]
    sidList:exec SymbolId from getLatestSecurityRefData[d] where
      SecurityType=`CommonStock;
    tt:select SymbolId,SequenceTime,LastSize,LastMarket,TradeLiqui
      dityIndicator from mTrade where date=d;
    tt:select from tt where SymbolId in sidList,LastMarket=`IEXG,
      SequenceTime within (09:35;16:00);
    tt:select Volume:`long$LastSize,Hidden:TradeLiquidityIndicator
      in `I`S from tt;
    tt:select Trades:count i,HiddenTrades:sum Hidden,sum Volume,
      HiddenVolume:sum Volume*Hidden from tt;
    update date:d,HiddenRate:100*HiddenTrades%Trades,HiddenVolumeRate:
      100* HiddenVolume%Volume from tt
    };
```

Query 5: Markouts

```
/
```
Helper function which takes a table of trades and a table of NBBO data, and augments the trade table with markout data at the given time lags.

Markouts are defined for a buy order as the difference between the NBBO midpoint at (trade time + lag, capped at the close) and the trade price, and the reverse for a sell order. In an effort to mitigate the impact of outliers, markouts are nulled if the reference NBBO at the lagged time is too wide. Also provided is the option to calculate markouts in percentage terms by dividing by the NBBO midpoint at the time of trade.

```
Parameters:
tt        Table of trades
nn        Table of NBBO data
lags      List of time lags (long type, representing ms) at which to
             calculate markouts
bPct      Boolean that enables percentage-based calculations
\
addMarkouts:{[tt;nn;lags;bPct]
    nn:select `p#sym,time,mid:?[ask within (bid%3;bid*3);0.5*bid
      +ask;0n] from nn;
    f:{[tt;nn;bPct;lag]
      xx:aj[`sym`time;select sym,(time+lag*1000000)&16:00,buy,
        price,tMid:mid from tt;nn];
      exec ?[buy;1;-1]*(mid-price)%?[bPct;tMid;1] from xx
      };
    tt ,' flip (`$"m" ,/: string lags)!f[tt;nn;bPct] each lags
    };
```

/

Helper function which aggregates markout data by volume weighting across trades. Applies to both the raw output of addMarkouts as well as the output of a previous run of itself.

```
Parameters:
tt        Table of markouts to aggregate
lags      List of time lags (long type, representing ms) to aggregate
aggUnit   List of columns to aggregate by
bInit     Boolean set to true if aggregating raw data, and false if
             re-aggregating previous output
\
aggMarkouts:{[tt;lags;aggUnit;bInit]
    mCols:`$"m" ,/: sLags:string lags;
    sCols:`$"size" ,/: sLags;
    a:$[bInit;`size ,/: mCols;sCols ,' mCols];
    0!?[tt;();{x!x}aggUnit;(`size,sCols,mCols)!(enlist (sum;
      `size)),({sum x where y<>0n};{x wavg y}) cross a]
    };
```

/

*Helper function which aggregates markout data not by a weighted average
but by accumulating trade counts and volume based on the direction of the
markout. Applies to both the raw output of addMarkouts as well as the
output of a previous run of itself.*

Parameters:

tt   Table of markouts to aggregate

lags   List of time lags (long type, representing ms) to aggregate

aggUnit List of columns to aggregate by

*bInit   Boolean set to true if aggregating raw data, and false if re-
           aggregating previous output*

```
\
aggMarkoutDir:{[tt;lags;aggUnit;bInit]
    mCols:`$"m" ,/: sLags:string lags;
    tvns:`$(string (tvn:`trades`size)) cross sLags;
    if[bInit;
      tt:update trades:1j from tt;
      tt:?[tt;();(aggUnit,mCols)!aggUnit,{?[0n=x;-2;signum x]} ,'
        mCols;{x!sum ,' x}tvn];
      tt:raze {[tt;aggUnit;mCols;tvn;tvns;s]
              tt:?[tt;();{x!x}aggUnit;tvns!({[x;y;z] sum x where y=z}
                  [;s;] ,/: tvn) cross mCols];
              update sign:s from 0!tt
              }[tt;aggUnit;mCols;tvn;tvns] each -1 0 1;
      ];
    0!?[tt;();{x!x}aggUnit,`sign;{x!sum ,' x}tvns]
    };
```

*/
Function which calculates three variants of markouts at a given set of
time lags for a given date and aggregates by a given set of columns.
Returns a dictionary containing all three result sets, which can then be
further aggregated if necessary using aggMarkouts/aggMarkoutDir.*

The variants are:

*std   Standard (not percentage-based) markouts for trades at the bid
          or offer*

pct   Percentage-based markouts for trades at the bid or offer

midDir   Directional trade and volume counts for trades at the midpoint

Parameters:

d   Date atom for which to pull data

*lags   List of time lags (long type, representing ms) at which to
          calculate markouts*

aggUnit List of columns to aggregate by

```
\
getMarkoutTypes:{[d;lags;aggUnit]
    tt:filterTrades[getTrades[d;()]];
    tt:update spreadBin:{x xbin y}[0 1 100 200 300 400 500;ask-bid] from tt;
    nn:select `p#sym,time,bid,ask from nbbo where date=d,sym in asc
        distinct tt`sym;
    ttm:addMarkouts[tt;nn;lags;0b];
    ttp:addMarkouts[tt;nn;lags;1b];
    std:aggMarkouts[select from ttm where (price=bid)|price=ask;lags;
        aggUnit;1b];
    pct:aggMarkouts[select from ttp where (price=bid)|price=ask;lags;
        aggUnit;1b];
    midDir:aggMarkoutDir[select from ttm where midTrade;lags;
        aggUnit;1b];
    `std`pct`midDir!(std;pct;midDir)
    };
```

Query 6: Effective Spread & Quoted Spread

```
/
```

Function which calculates the average effective spread and NBBO quoted spread by executing venue on a given date.

Effective spread is defined as twice the absolute difference between the trade price and prevailing NBBO mid at the time of trade. EQ ratio is defined as the ratio between the effective spread and the NBBO quoted spread, which is the width of the prevailing NBBO at the time of trade. Both effective spread and the EQ ratio are aggregated by volume weighting across trades. In an effort to mitigate the impact of outliers, trades are excluded if the reference NBBO at the time of trade is too wide.

Parameters:

d   Date atom for which to pull data

```
\
getEQ:{[d]
    tt:select from filterTrades[getTrades[d;()]] where ask<=3*bid;
    tt:update eq:es%ask-bid from update es:2*abs price-mid from tt;
    0!select sum size,size wavg es,size wavg eq by ex from tt
    };
```

```
/
```

Function which aggregates the outputs of getEQ run on multiple days.

Parameters:

tt   Table of razed getEQ outputs

```
\
```

```
aggEQ:{[tt]
    0!select size wavg es,size wavg eq by ex from tt
    };
```

```
/
```
Function which calculates the average quoted spread by executing venue on a given date.

Quoted spread is defined as the width of the BBO of the executing venue at the time of trade. Quoted spread is aggregated by volume weighting across trades. In an effort to mitigate the impact of outliers, trades are excluded if the reference BBO at the time of trade is too wide.

Parameters:
d   Date atom for which to pull data
```
\
getVenueQS:{[d]
    tt:select from filterTrades[getTrades[d;()]] where ask<=3*bid;
    tt:raze {[d;tt;s]
      tt:select from tt where sym=s;
      qq:`ex`time xasc select ex,time,bid,ask from quote where date=d,
        sym=s;
      tt:aj[`ex`time;tt;qq];
      tt
      } [d;update `p#sym from tt] each distinct tt`sym;
    tt:select from tt where bid<ask,bid>0,ask<0W,ask<=3*bid;
    0!select sum size,venueqs:size wavg ask-bid by ex from tt
    };
```

```
/
```
Function which aggregates the outputs of getVenueQS run on multiple days.

Parameters:
tt   Table of razed getVenueQS outputs
```
\
aggVenueQS:{[tt]
    0!select size wavg venueqs by ex from tt
    };
```

Query 7: Price Improvement

```
/
```
Function which calculates average price improvement per executing venue on a given date.

Price improvement is defined as the difference between the prevailing NBO and the trade price for a buy remover, and the difference between the trade price and the prevailing NBB for a sell remover. Since getTrades signs trades from the perspective of the likely adder, this function needs to reverse the side for the proper price improvement perspective. In an effort to mitigate the impact of outliers, trades are excluded if the reference NBBO at the time of trade is too wide.

Parameters:
d   Date atom for which to pull data
```
\
getPI:{[d]
    tt:select from filterTrades[getTrades[d;()]] where ask<=3*bid;
    tt:update pi:?[not buy;ask-price;price-bid] from tt;
    0!select sum size,size wavg pi by ex,piFlag:pi>0 from tt
    };
```
Function which aggregates the outputs of getPI run on multiple days.

Parameters:
tt   Table of razed getPI outputs
```
\
aggPI:{[tt]
    tt:update piSize:size*piFlag from tt;
    0!select sum size,piPct:(sum piSize)%sum size,piAvg:piSize wavg pi,
      piOverall:size wavg pi by ex from tt
    };
```

```
/
```
Function which calculates price improvement from the perspective of the IEX Router on a given date.

Price improvement here is defined for a buy order as the difference between the child order limit and the trade price, and the reverse for a sell order. This is a reasonable proxy as the IEX Router always prices its aggressive child orders at its understanding of the NBBO inside.

Runs against IEX proprietary data, not TAQ; this is provided to supplement the TAQ version with a data set where it is explicitly known that the remover is trying to cross the spread.

Parameters:
d   Date atom for which to pull data
```
\
getPIStream:{[d]
    c:((=;`date;d);(|;(<>;`LastMarket;enlist `IEXG);(=;`AddRemove
    Flag;enlist `Removed)));
```

```
   a:`SymbolId`SequenceTime`LastSize`LastPrice`LastMarket`Order-
     Side`OrderLimit;
   tt:update `long$LastSize,LastPrice%10000 from ?[FixMessage_Fill-
     From Venue;c;0b;a!a];
   tt:update pi:?[OrderSide=`Buy;1;-1]*OrderLimit-LastPrice from tt;
   tt:tt lj 1!select SymbolId,Symbol,IsTestSymbol from
     getLatestSecurityRefData[d];
   nn:select `p#SymbolId,SequenceTime,bid:BestBidPrice,ask:BestAsk
     Price from NbboUpdate where date=d;
   tt:update mid:0.5*bid+ask from aj[`SymbolId`SequenceTime;tt;nn];

   tt:select from tt where SequenceTime within (09:30;16:00);
   tt:select from tt where Symbol<>`BRK.A;
   tt:select from tt where not IsTestSymbol;

   tt:select from tt where bid<ask,bid>0,ask<0W;
   tt:select from tt where not (LastPrice<bid)|LastPrice>ask;
   tt:select from tt where LastPrice within (bid-0.1*mid;ask+0.1*mid);

   0!select size:sum LastSize,LastSize wavg pi by ex:LastMarket,
 }; piFlag:pi>0 from tt
```

Query 8: Time & Size at Inside

```
/
Function which calculates the time and size-weighted time spent at one
and both sides of the NBBO inside by executing venue for a given date.
Output is partitioned by whether the NBBO was locked, crossed, or nei-
ther; a subset can be used, for example, to calculate a venue's contribu-
tions to just locked markets.

Due to the relative size of NBBO data, this function allows for partition-
ing the symbol universe and serially running each partition.


Parameters:
d          Date atom for which to pull data
n          Number of partitions
\
getTimeAtInside:{[d;n]
    symList:(select distinct sym from nbbo where date=d)`sym;
    raze {[d;symList]
        nn:select `p#sym,time,bexs,bsizes,bid,ask,asizes,aexs from
            nbbo where date=d,sym in symList;
    nn:select from (update dur:next deltas 09:30|16:00&time by sym from
        nn) where dur>0;
```

```
nn:update lctype:`crossed`locked`normal 1+signum ask-bid from nn;
xx:raze { [nn;1]
    f:({first x where y=z} [;;1]');
    nn:update vbsize:0^f [bsizes;bexs] , vasize:0^f [asizes;aexs] from
      nn;
    nn:update sides: (vbsize>0) +vasize>0 from nn;
    0!select sum dur, sDur:sum dur*vbsize+vasize by ex:1,lctype,
      sym,sides from nn
    } [nn;] each "ABCJKMNPTXYZV";
xx:xx lj select sum `long$size by sym from trade where date=d,sym in
  symList,isVolumeEligible;
  update date:d from xx
  } [d;] each ((n|1),0N)#symList
};
```

/
Function which aggregates the outputs of getTimeAtInside run on multiple
days. Aggregates across symbols and dates both by straight average and by
weighting by the symbol volume for each day.

Parameters:
nn   Table of razed getTimeAtInside outputs
\
```
aggTimeAtInside:{ [nn]
    nn:update bOr:sides>0,bAnd:sides=2 from update sDur%sum sDur by
      date,sym from nn;
    nn:select orPct:(sum dur*bOr)%sum dur,andPct:(sum dur*bAnd)%sum
      dur,first size,
    orSPct:(sum sDur*bOr),andSPct:(sum sDur*bAnd) by date,sym,ex from
      nn;
    0!(select avg orPct,avg andPct,avg orSPct,avg andSPct by agg:`avg,
      ex from nn) uj
    (select size wavg orPct,size wavg andPct,size wavg orSPct,size wavg
      andSPct by agg:`volwavg,ex from nn)
    };
```

Query 9: Market Stability

/
Function which calculates what portion of trade volume is followed by a
stable NBBO for each of a given list of time lags by executing venue on a
given date.

141

A trade is considered to have been stable for a given lag if there are no
NBBO price changes in the interval (time of trade;time of trade+lag).

Parameters:

d   *Date atom for which to pull data*
lags   *List of time lags (long type, representing ms) at which to cal-*
          culate stability

```
\
getStableStats:{[d;lags]
    tt:filterTrades[getTrades[d;()]];
    nn:select `p#sym,time from nbbo where date=d,(sym<>prev sym)|
      (bid<>prev bid)|(ask<>prev ask);
    nn:update ntime:next time by sym from nn;
    tt:aj[`sym`time;tt;nn];
    f:{[tt;lag]
      ![tt;();0b;(enlist `$"stable",string lag)!enlist ({not x within
        (y;y+1e6*z)};`ntime;`time;lag)]
      };
    tt:f/[tt;lags];
    cs:`$"stable",/: string lags;
    0!?[tt;();{x!x}`ex`midTrade;(`size,cs)!(enlist (sum;`size)),
      ({sum x where y};`size),/: cs]
    };
```

```
/
```
Function which aggregates the outputs of getStableStats run on multiple
days.
Parameters:
tt   *Table of razed getStableStats outputs*
lags   *List of time lags (long type, representing ms) to aggregate*
```
\
aggStableStats:{[tt;lags]
    cs:`$"stable",/: string lags;
    0!?[tt;();{x!x}`ex`midTrade;{x!sum ,' x}`size,cs]
    };
```

References

Angel, James J., Lawrence E. Harris, and Chester S. Spatt. 'Equity trading in the 21st century'. *Quarterly Journal of Finance* 1, no. 1 (2011): 1–53.

Angel, James J., Lawrence E. Harris, and Chester S. Spatt. 'Equity trading in the 21st century: An update'. *Quarterly Journal of Finance* 5, no. 1 (2015): 1550002.

Battalio, Robert, Shane A. Corwin, and Robert Jennings. 'Can brokers have it all? On the relation between make-take fees and limit order execution quality'. *Journal of Finance* 71, no. 5 (2016): 2193–238.

Bennett, Paul, and Li Wei. 'Market structure, fragmentation, and market quality'. *Journal of Financial Markets* 9, no. 1 (2006): 49–78.

Bessembinder, Henrik. 'Issues in assessing trade execution costs'. *Journal of Financial Markets* 6, no. 1 (2003): 233–57.

Bessembinder, Hendrik, and Herbert M. Kaufman. 'A cross-exchange comparison of execution costs and information flow for NYSE-listed stocks'. *Journal of Financial Economics* 46, no. 3 (1997): 293–319.

Bessembinder, Hendrik, and Kumar Venkataraman. 'Bid-ask spreads: Measuring trade execution costs in financial markets'. *Encyclopedia of Quantitative Finance.* Chichester: John Wiley & Sons, 2010.

Biais, Bruno, and Thierry Foucault. 'HFT and market quality'. *Bankers, Markets and Investors* 128, no. 1 (2014): 5–19.

Boehmer, Ekkehart. 'Dimensions of execution quality: Recent evidence for US equity markets'. *Journal of Financial Economics* 78, no. 3 (2005): 553–82.

Brogaard, Jonathan, Terrence Hendershott, and Ryan Riordan. 'High-frequency trading and price discovery'. *Review of Financial Studies* 27, no. 8 (2014): 2267–306.

Budish, Eric, Peter Cramton, and John Shim. 'The high-frequency trading arms race: Frequent batch auctions as a market design response'. *Quarterly Journal of Economics* 130, no. 4 (2015): 1547–621.

Cardella, Laura, Jia Hao, and Ivalina Kalcheva. 'Liquidity-based trading fees and exchange volume'. Working paper, Texas Tech University, 2017.

Cardella, Laura, Jia Hao, Ivalina Kalcheva, and Yung-Yu Ma. 'Computerization of the equity, foreign exchange, derivatives, and fixed-income markets'. *Financial Review* 49, no. 2 (2014): 231–43.

Cboe Global Markets. *Bats BYX Exchange Fee Schedule.* Available at: https://www.bats. com/us/equities/membership/fee_schedule/byx, 2017.

Cboe Global Markets. *Bats BZX Exchange Fee Schedule.* Available at: https://www.bats. com/us/equities/membership/fee_schedule/bzx, 2017.

Cboe Global Markets. *Bats EDGA Exchange Fee Schedule.* Available at: https://www.bats. com/us/equities/membership/fee_schedule/edga, 2017.

Cboe Global Markets. *Bats EDGX Exchange Fee Schedule.* Available at: https://www.bats. com/us/equities/membership/fee_schedule/edgx, 2017.

Cboe Global Markets. *Execution Quality.* Available at: http://www.bats.com/us/equities/ market_statistics/execution_quality/, 2017.

Cboe Global Markets. *Execution Quality Definitions.* Available at: http://www.bats.com/ us/equities/market_statistics/execution_quality/definitions/, 2017.

Cboe Global Markets. *Historical Market Volume Data.* Available at: http://www.bats. com/us/equities/market_statistics/historical_market_volume/, 2017.

Cboe Global Markets. *Press Release: Bats Announces Fee Overhaul of EDGA Equities Exchange.* Available at: http://cdn.batstrading.com/resources/press_releases/Bats-EDGA-Reprice-FINAL.pdf, 2017.

Charles Schwab & Co., Inc. *Trade Execution Quality & Routing*. Available at: http://www.schwab.com/public/schwab/active_trader/trading_tools/execution_quality, 2017.

Chicago Stock Exchange. *Fee Schedule of the Chicago Stock Exchange, Inc.* Available at: http://www.chx.com/_literature_119763/CHX_Fee_Schedule, 2017.

Conrad, Jennifer, Sunil Wahal, and Jin Xiang. 'High-frequency quoting, trading, and the efficiency of prices'. *Journal of Financial Economics* 116, no. 2 (2015): 271–91.

Ding, Shengwei, John Hanna, and Terrence Hendershott. 'How slow is the NBBO? A comparison with direct exchange feeds'. *Financial Review* 49, no. 2 (2014): 313–32.

Easley, David, Marcos M. López de Prado, and Maureen O'Hara. 'The microstructure of the "flash crash": Flow toxicity, liquidity crashes, and the probability of informed trading'. *Journal of Portfolio Management* 37, no. 2 (2011): 118–28.

E*TRADE. *Execution Quality*. Available at: https://us.etrade.com/trade/execution-quality, 2017.

Fidelity. *Commitment to Execution Quality*. Available at: https://www.fidelity.com/trading/execution-quality/overview, 2017.

FINRA (Financial Industry Regulatory Authority). *Guidance on Best Execution Obligations in Equity, Options, and Fixed Income Markets*. Regulatory Notice 15–46, 2015.

Foucault, Thierry, and Albert J. Menkveld. 'Competition for order flow and smart order routing systems'. *Journal of Finance* 63, no. 1 (2008): 119–58.

Glosten, Lawrence R., and Paul R. Milgrom. 'Bid, ask and transaction prices in a specialist market with heterogeneously informed traders'. *Journal of Financial Economics* 14, no. 1 (1985): 71–100.

Goldstein, Michael A., Pavitra Kumar, and Frank C. Graves. 'Computerized and high-frequency trading'. *Financial Review* 49, no. 2 (2014): 177–202.

Harris, Larry. *Maker-taker Pricing Effects on Market Quotations*. Technical report. USC Marshall School of Business, 2013.

Hasbrouck, Joel, and Gideon Saar. 'Low-latency trading'. *Journal of Financial Markets* 16, no. 4 (2013): 646–79.

Hendershott, Terrence, Charles M. Jones, and Albert J. Menkveld. 'Does algorithmic trading improve liquidity?' *Journal of Finance* 66, no. 1 (2011): 1–33.

Hirschey, Nicholas. 'Do high-frequency traders anticipate buying and selling pressure?' Working paper, London Business School, 2018.

Holden, Craig W., and Stacey Jacobsen. 'Liquidity measurement problems in fast, competitive markets: Expensive and cheap solutions'. *Journal of Finance* 69, no. 4 (2014): 1747–85.

Huang, Roger D., and Hans R. Stoll. 'Dealer versus auction markets: A paired comparison of execution costs on NASDAQ and the NYSE'. *Journal of Financial Economics* 41, no. 3 (1996): 313–57.

IEX Group, Inc. *Investors Exchange Fee Schedule*. Available at: https://www.iextrading.com/trading/#fee-schedule, 2017.

Intercontinental Exchange. *Daily TAQ*. Available at: http://www.nyxdata.com/Data-Products/Daily-TAQ, 2017.

Jain, Pankaj K. 'Institutional design and liquidity at stock exchanges around the world'. Working paper, Indiana University, 2003.

Laughlin, Gregory, Anthony Aguirre, and Joseph Grundfest. 'Information transmission between financial markets in Chicago and New York'. *Financial Review* 49, no. 2 (2014): 283–312.

Malinova, Katya, and Andreas Park. 'Subsidizing liquidity: The impact of make/take fees on market quality'. *Journal of Finance* 70, no. 2 (2015): 509–36.

NASDAQ, Inc. *BX Pricing*. Available at: http://www.nasdaqtrader.com/Trader.aspx?id= bx_pricing, 2017.

NASDAQ, Inc. *Price List—Trading Connectivity*. Available at: http://www.nasdaqtrader. com/Trader.aspx?id=PriceListTrading2, 2017.

NASDAQ, Inc. *PSX Pricing*. Available at: http://www.nasdaqtrader.com/Trader.aspx?id= PSX_Pricing, 2017.

NYSE Group, Inc. *New York Stock Exchange Price List 2017*. Available at: https://www. nyse.com/publicdocs/nyse/markets/nyse/NYSE_Price_List.pdf, 2017.

NYSE Group, Inc. *NYSE MKT Equities Price List*. Available at: https://www.nyse.com/ publicdocs/nyse/markets/nyse-mkt/NYSE_MKT_Equities_Price_List.pdf, 2017.

NYSE Group, Inc. *Schedule of Fees and Charges for Exchange Services*. Available at: https:// www.nyse.com/publicdocs/nyse/markets/nyse-arca/NYSE_Arca_Marketplace_Fees.pdf, 2017.

O'Hara, Maureen, and Mao Ye. 'Is market fragmentation harming market quality?' *Journal of Financial Economics* 100, no. 3 (2011): 459–74.

Peterson, Mark A., and Erik R. Sirri. 'Order preferencing and market quality on US equity exchanges'. *Review of Financial Studies* 16, no. 2 (2003): 385–415.

Popper, Nathaniel. 'Stock exchange prices grow so convoluted even traders are confused, study finds'. *New York Times*. Available at: https://www.nytimes.com/2016/03/ 02/business/dealbook/stock-exchange-prices-grow-so-convoluted-even-traders-are-confused-study-finds.html, 1 March 2016.

Riordan, Ryan, and Andreas Storkenmaier. 'Latency, liquidity and price discovery'. *Journal of Financial Markets* 15, no. 4 (2012): 416–437.

Scottrade. *Trade Quality & Execution*. Available at: https://www.scottrade.com/online-brokerage/trade-quality-execution.html, 2017.

SEC (US Securities and Exchange Commission). *Regulation NMS*. 17 CFR Parts 200, 201, 230, 240, 242, 249, 270, 2005.

SEC. *In the Matter of the Application of Investors' Exchange, LLC for Registration as a National Securities Exchange*. Release No. 34-78101; File No. 10-222, 2016.

SEC. *Maker-Taker Fees on Equities Exchanges Memorandum*, 2015.

SEC. *Market Activity Report Methodology*. Available at: https://www.sec.gov/mar ketstructure/mar_methodology.html#.WMwoFhsrIUE, 2017.

SEC. *Notice of Filing and Immediate Effectiveness of Proposed Rule Change Amending Rule 11.1, Hours of Trading, Interpretations and Policies .01, to Cease Trading on the Exchange's System as of February 1, 2017*. Release No. 34-80018; File No. SR-NSX-2017-04, 2017.

SEC. *Order Approving the National Market System Plan to Implement a Tick Size Pilot Program by BATS Exchange, Inc., BATS Y-Exchange, Inc., Chicago Stock Exchange, Inc., EDGA Exchange, Inc., EDGX Exchange, Inc., Financial Industry Regulatory Authority, Inc., NASDAQ OMX BX, Inc., NASDAQ OMX PHLX LLC, The Nasdaq Stock Market LLC,*

New York Stock Exchange LLC, NYSE MKT LLC, and NYSE Arca, Inc., as Modified by the Commission, For a Two-Year Period. Release No. 34-74892; File No. 4-657, 2015.

TD Ameritrade. *Order Execution Quality.* Available at: https://www.tdameritrade.com/tools-and-platforms/order-execution.page, 2017.

Ye, Mao, and Chen Yao. 'Tick size constraints, market structure, and liquidity'. Working paper, University of Illinois at Urbana-Champaign, 2015.

Zhang, X. Frank. 'The effect of high-frequency trading on stock volatility and price discovery'. Working paper, Yale University, 2010.

6

What has Changed in Four Years?

Are Retail Broker Routing Decisions in 4Q2016 Consistent with the Pursuit of Best Execution?

Robert Battalio

6.1 Introduction

Battalio, Corwin, and Jennings used public order routing disclosures to examine the order routing of several large retail brokerages in 4Q2012.[1] They found that their sample brokerages generally employed one of two order routing strategies: they appeared either to route all customer orders in a given stock to a market maker (wholesaler) or to route marketable orders to wholesalers and nonmarketable orders to exchanges that offered relatively large liquidity rebates.[2] Most, but not all, of the retail brokers examined by Battalio et al. charged fixed commissions and accepted payments from wholesalers for their marketable orders and rebates from exchanges when their standing limit orders executed. Battalio et al. provide empirical evidence suggesting that routing orders in a

---

[1] Battalio et al., 'Can brokers have it all?' 2016. The author would like to thank Haim Bodek, Shane Corwin, Robert Jennings, and Chris Nagy for their comments. Any errors that remain are the author's responsibility.

[2] An order is said to be marketable if it is priced such that it will execute when it arrives at the trading venue with the best posted quote (assuming the posted quote is still valid when the order arrives). An order is nonmarketable if it is priced so that it will not execute against displayed liquidity when it arrives in the marketplace. Nonmarketable orders provide liquidity (e.g. give others the opportunity to trade at a pre-specified price) while marketable orders demand liquidity. Wholesalers are market makers that profit by selectively purchasing and executing marketable retail orders at (or within) the best prices posted in the marketplace. All else equal, venues with aggressively priced (displayed) nonmarketable orders attract more marketable orders (and hence execute more trades). As a result, starting in the 1990s, some exchanges began offering market participants liquidity rebates to attract nonmarketable orders. These rebates are paid when standing orders execute.

manner that maximizes order flow payments can result in diminished execution quality for standing limit orders (e.g. longer times to execution, lower fill rates, and a higher percentage of executions in adverse market conditions). Furthermore, any impact that order flow payments have on commissions does not flow back to investors who miss favourable trading opportunities because of their broker's order routing strategy. Following US Senate hearings on this topic in June 2014, the Financial Industry Regulatory Authority (FINRA) issued a target examination letter to around ten brokers requesting detailed information as to how they route customer orders.[3] The purpose of this chapter is to revisit the economics of order routing in US equity markets and to examine the extent to which retail broker order routing changed between 4Q2012 and 4Q2016.

6.2 The Economics of Order Routing

Regulation, as well as market forces, constrains the routing decisions of retail brokers. In the US, retail brokerages are required to conduct regular and rigorous reviews of execution quality for customer orders 'on a security-by-security, type-of-order basis (e.g. market order, limit order, market on open order)'.[4] US regulators recommend that these reviews be conducted at least four times per year and that they compare, among other things, 'the quality of the executions the member is obtaining via current order routing and execution arrangements (including the internalization of order flow) to the quality of the executions that the member could obtain from competing markets'.[5] Finally, as noted in the following passage taken from FINRA NTM 01-22, brokers should not allow cash inducements to interfere with the pursuit of higher fill rates:

> in evaluating its procedures for handling limit orders, the broker-dealer must take into account any differences in execution quality (e.g. the likelihood of execution) among various markets or market centers to which limit orders may be routed. The traditional non-price factors affecting the cost or efficiency of executions should also continue to be considered; however, broker-dealers must not allow an order routing inducement, such as payment for order flow or the opportunity to trade with that order as principal, to interfere with its duty of best execution.[6]

Soon after the introduction of real-time trade and quote data to equity markets in 1982, market makers (wholesalers) began offering $0.01 to $0.02 per share

---

[3] See http://www.finra.org/industry/order-routing-and-execution-quality-customer-orders.
[4] See http://finra.complinet.com/en/display/display_main.html?rbid=2403&record_id=14301.
[5] See http://finra.complinet.com/en/display/display_main.html?rbid=2403&record_id=14301.
[6] See NASD Notice to Members 01-22, 'Best execution: NASD Regulation reiterates member firm best execution obligations and provides guidance to members concerning compliance'. Available at: http://www.finra.org/sites/default/files/NoticeDocument/p003889.pdf.

to brokers for their market orders securities listed on the New York Stock Exchange (NYSE).[7] The wholesalers guaranteed immediate executions at the National Best Bid or Offer (NBBO). For retail brokers, the alternative at the time was to send their marketable orders to NYSE, where it took upwards of two minutes and cost up to $0.03 per share to get their customer orders executed. As a result, order routing transitioned from a cost centre into a profit centre during the 1980s. As competition for retail orders increased in the late 1980s and early 1990s, per-share order flow payments also increased.[8]

Concerned that some brokers might maximize order flow payments rather than execution quality, the US Securities and Exchange Commission (SEC) passed Rule 11Ac1-5 (now Rule 605) and Rule 11Ac1-6 (now Rule 606) in 2001. Together, these rules were intended to bring sufficient transparency for investors to determine whether their brokers are making optimal order routing decisions. Rule 605 requires exchanges to produce execution quality statistics, mostly for marketable orders, on a monthly basis. Rule 606 requires brokers to reveal on a quarterly basis the destinations to which they route orders and whether they receive compensation for their routing choices. Consistent with the rules' objectives, Boehmer, Jennings, and Wei find that the routing of marketable order flow became more sensitive to cross-venue changes in execution quality after Rule 605 execution quality statistics became available.[9]

Today most equity exchanges operating in the US utilize the make/take or the 'inverted' take/make fee schedule. Exchanges that utilize the make/take fee schedule pay orders that provide (make) liquidity a rebate and charge orders that demand (take) liquidity a fee. Exchanges that utilize the inverted fee schedule assess a fee on orders that provide liquidity and offer a rebate to orders that demand liquidity. These fees and rebates often vary depending upon the amount of volume that a market participant routes to the exchange during a given month and whether or not the broker participates in retail

[7] Bernard L. Madoff Securities first began the practice of payment for order flow. See Chapman, 'Before the fall', 2009 (available at: http://www.tradersmagazine.com/issues/20_292/-103503-1.html).
[8] This practice was introduced into US equity options markets soon after the options listing war of August 1999. See 'SEC Office of Compliance Inspections and Examinations Office of Economic Analysis special study: Payment for order flow and internalization in the options market', available at: https://www.sec.gov/news/studies/ordpay.htm.
[9] Boehmer et al., 'Public disclosure', 2007. In his article 'Who makes money on your stock trades', published in the 28 February edition of *Barron's*, Bill Alpert uses the 605 and 606 reports to investigate the execution quality provided by different retail brokers. Alpert was forced to make several 'heroic' assumptions to conduct this analysis. First, he assumed that the retail broker's orders receive the average execution quality provided by a destination over a three-month period. Second, he assumed that the mix of orders routed by the broker to the venue over the three-month period is the same as the mix of orders executed by that venue over the same period. As brokers can often negotiate to take lower order flow payments in return for higher execution quality, the assumption that each retail broker receives the average is non-trivial. For this reason, many industry participants, including Ameritrade and the BATS stock exchange group, have expressed support for a revision to these rules that requires brokers to report execution quality statistics on a monthly basis.

Table 6.1. Liquidity fees and rebates generated by orders in NASDAQ-listed securities executed on US stock exchanges as of 1 October 2016

Exchange	Take Fees	Liquidity Rebates			
	ITG	ITG	Ameritrade	E*Trade	Fidelity
NYSE ARCA	+$0.0030	−$0.0020	−$0.0030^		
BATS BZX	+$0.0030	−$0.0020			−$0.0030
Nasdaq	+$0.0030	−$0.0020		−$0.0028^	
EDGX	+$0.0029	−$0.0020	−$0.0034^	−$0.0031^	−$0.0030
EDGA	−$0.0002	+$0.0005			
BATS BYZ	−$0.0010	+$0.0018			
Nasdaq BX	−$0.0010	+$0.0020			

Notes: the NYSE did not trade NASDAQ-listed stocks during the fourth quarter of 2016 and is therefore omitted from the table. ^ = payments were as high as the amount reported in this table. Positive take fees and liquidity rebates are costs, while negative take fees and liquidity rebates represent revenue.

Source: the data used to construct Table 6.1 were obtained from the Investment Technology Group, Inc. and from the 4Q2016 Rule 606 order routing reports produced by Ameritrade, E*Trade, and Fidelity.

attribution programmes.[10] Table 6.1 provides a description of the cost associated with demanding and supplying liquidity in NASDAQ-listed stocks on various US stock exchanges as of 1 October 2016. The top four exchanges listed in Table 6.1 utilized the make/take fee schedule in 4Q2016, while the bottom three exchanges used inverted fee schedules.

Data on the liquidity fees and rebates generated by orders routed to the various exchanges as of 1 October 2016 are provided by the agency broker Investment Technology Group (ITG). Where possible, I supplement the liquidity rebate data received from ITG with information on the liquidity rebates obtained by retail brokers as detailed in their 4Q2016 Rule 606 filing. Three venues charge the maximum permissible take fee of $0.0300 per share and two offer liquidity demanding investors a rebate of $0.0010 per share. All else equal, when each of the venues is offering to sell stock at the National Best Bid (NBB), we would expect investors to first consume liquidity at BATS BYX and NASDAQ BX. Why? Because each of these venues offers a payment of $0.0010 per share to those who take liquidity on their exchange. After liquidity is exhausted at those two venues, we would expect investors to next demand liquidity at EDGA, and then move to EDGX.[11] Finally, we would

---

[10] See, for example, 'Notice of filing and immediate effectiveness of a proposed rule change to adopt rule 11.24 to permit members to designate their retail orders to be identified as retail on the exchange's proprietary data feeds', filed on 26 September 2014 and available at: https://www.sec.gov/rules/sro/bats/2014/34-73237.pdf.

[11] Among the things being held constant here are differences in hidden liquidity (and thus, price improvement) across venues and the certainty with which the liquidity displayed at the various venues can actually be accessed.

expect liquidity-demanding investors to route their orders to one of the three venues charging the maximum permissible take fee only if there were no other venues at the NBB.

To understand the impact that differential take fees have on limit order execution quality, consider the following example. Assume, for the sake of illustration, that Pudgy's Chicken is a NASDAQ-listed stock, and that the current NBB for a share of Pudgy's common stock is $10.00 and the current National Best Offer (NBO) is $10.02. Now suppose that Broker A receives a limit order to buy 1000 shares of Pudgy's Chicken at a price of $10.01. Where should Broker A route this order if she wants to maximize the probability that the order executes (ignoring liquidity rebates)? In this situation, since the order will establish a new NBB, it doesn't matter which venue that the order is routed to, as a liquidity demanding-seller will route her order to the venue on which the limit buy order is displayed. There is no other option. In this instance, Broker A can route the order to a venue that charges the maximum permissible take fee in order to fund aggressive liquidity rebates without impacting the probability (or the conditions in which) the order executes. So, let's assume that Broker A routes the order to EDGX, a venue with a take fee of $0.0030 per share. This is a situation where routing standing orders in a manner that maximizes rebates does not adversely impact limit order execution quality.

For actively traded stocks such as Sirius XM and Ford, it is typically the case that investors place limit orders that join (rather than establish) a new NBB or NBO. Returning to the example, assume now that a different broker, Broker B, receives a client order to purchase 1000 shares of Pudgy's Chicken at a price of $10.01. If Broker B's goal is to maximize the probability that the order executes before the market moves away from the client's limit price (e.g. in this example, before prices rise), Broker B needs to place the order on a venue that has a take fee which is lower than the venue on which Broker A's order rests. Although placing the order on a venue with a lower take fee will generally result in a lower liquidity rebate when the order executes, all else equal, it will ensure the order trades before similarly priced orders displayed on venues with higher take fees do. Let's assume that Broker B routes the order to EDGA, the venue with a take fee of −$0.0002 per share. Since the cost of accessing displayed liquidity on EDGA is lower than the cost of accessing displayed liquidity on EDGX, all else equal an investor seeking immediacy would route her marketable sell order to EDGA rather than EDGX. Thus the limit order routed by Broker B would execute *before* the limit order routed by Broker A, despite the fact that it arrived in the marketplace *after* Broker A's order. One can extend this logic to show that all else equal, limit orders displayed on venues with lower take fees will execute before similarly priced limit orders displayed on venues with high take fees. Battalio, Corwin, and

Jennings provide empirical support for the hypothesis that limit order execution quality is decreasing in the relative level of an exchange's take fee.[12]

To be paid for routing a marketable order to an inverted exchange, the exchange must be at the inside quote. So, routing marketable orders to inverted venues (and receiving rebates) is not always an option for retail brokers. Conversely, brokers in possession of retail customer order flow can typically contract to sell their marketable orders to one or more wholesalers who guarantee execution at (or within) the NBBO. Brokers who sell order flow to wholesalers generally have the ability to contract for higher order flow payments and minimal price improvement (e.g. marketable orders execute at the best posted prices). Alternatively, brokers can contract for lower order flow payments in return for executions that are better than the best posted prices (e.g. economically relevant price improvement). Assuming that the market for order flow is competitive and the information content of retail orders is comparable across brokers, one would expect an inverse relation between the level of payments that a broker receives for its marketable orders and the amount of price improvement that those orders receive.[13]

Ignoring differences in the cost of accessing liquidity across venues, brokers who route marketable orders to exchanges may sometimes find that someone else has beaten them to the exchange and consumed the displayed liquidity. Or, they could find that the liquidity vanishes before the order reaches the exchange. In these instances, marketable orders must be rerouted to alternative exchanges where they are often executed at inferior prices. Conversely, as previously noted, wholesalers provide executions at or with the prevailing NBBO.[14] Thus, brokers can reduce the frequency with which their marketable orders execute at prices that are outside of the NBBO by routing them to wholesalers.

In 2013, the Financial Information Forum (FIF) announced a voluntary programme to provide increased disclosure regarding the quality of execution provided by retail brokers and by wholesalers.[15] Charles Schwab, Fidelity,

---

[12] Battalio et al., 'Can brokers have it all?', 2016.

[13] Blain Reinkensmeyer uses this argument to rank retail brokers as to their marketable order execution quality. See Reinkensmeyer's 21 February 2017 post, 'Order execution – 2017 retail investors' guide', available on www.stockbrokers.com. Dave Lauer also made this point in his 14 August 2015 blog post, 'Retail brokers show dramatic routing differences'.

[14] SEC Rule 611 allows trading venues that have not matched a new NBBO to trade at the old NBBO for one second. McInish and Upson provide evidence suggesting that some market participants profit by selectively executing marketable orders at the old NBBO; see McInish and Upson, 'Quote exception rule', 2013. The SEC fined Citadel $22 million for misleading clients regarding which NBBO (the new or the old) was used as a benchmark when internalizing orders: see https://www.sec.gov/news/pressrelease/2017-11.html.

[15] See FIF Retail Execution Quality Program, available at: https://fif.com/fif-working-groups/rule-605-606-disclosure/rule-605-606-overview. Battalio, Shkilko, and Van Ness provide evidence that suggests the monthly execution quality statistics produced on a voluntary basis by options exchanges are often unreliable. See Battalio et al., 'To pay or be paid?', 2016.

Table 6.2. Financial Information Forum Rule 605/606 working group retail execution quality statistics for market orders seeking to trade securities in the S&P500 index for 4Q2012

	Order size (shares)	Avg. order size	Price disimproved (% of shares)	Price improved (% of shares)	Average et improvement (per order)	Average PFOF (per share)
Fidelity	1–99	33	3.48%	95.49%	$0.63	$0.0000
Schwab	1–99	34	0.40%	92.60%	$0.78	≤$0.00095
Fidelity	100–499	190	3.22%	95.49%	$2.84	$0.0000
Schwab	100–499	196	0.60%	95.90%	$3.15	≤$0.00095
Fidelity	500–1999	833	4.11%	93.00%	$11.29	$0.0000
Schwab	500–1999	849	1.60%	95.10%	$10.25	≤$0.00095

Notes: a market order receives price improvement (disimprovement) if its execution price is within (outside of) the NBBO that was prevailing when the order was received by the executing venue. Average net improvement is the net notional dollar value of price improvement (or price disimprovement) per share multiplied by the number of executed shares divided by the total number of executed orders.

Source: data obtained from https://fif.com/tools/retail-execution-quality-statistics.

and Scottrade responded to the FIF's call for brokers to improve access to execution quality statistics for the retail community by posting quarterly data as to the average amount of price improvement received by different sizes of marketable orders. 4Q2016 statistics for Schwab and Fidelity are presented in Table 6.2. During 4Q2016, Schwab was paid up to $0.00095 per share for its marketable order flow while Fidelity did not accept payment for its marketable order flow. Because different sized orders within an order size category may receive different amounts of price improvement, one cannot determine whether Fidelity's marketable orders received larger per-share price improvements than Schwab's marketable orders. This said, it is interesting to note that Fidelity's orders are more likely to receive price disimprovement (e.g. executions outside of the NBBO) given that Fidelity does not accept payment for its marketable order flow while Schwab does.

The ability of wholesalers to interact with purchased order flow is limited by the Manning Rule, which prohibits market makers from trading at prices which are equal or inferior to the prices of limit orders resting in their order books.[16] As many stocks trade in minimum variation markets (e.g. the width of the NBBO equals the minimum tick size), the Manning Rule prevents wholesalers from trading with purchased orders when they have at-the-quote limit orders resting on their limit order books.[17] As a result, wholesalers who discourage or do not accept standing limit orders can pay more for uninformed marketable orders than wholesalers with deep limit order books. This suggests that wholesalers who do not accept nonmarketable limit orders

---

[16] An at-the-quote limit order seeks to purchase (or sell) shares at the NBB (NBO); and see FINRA Regulatory notice 11–24, May 2011.

[17] Parlour and Rajan, 'Payment for order flow', 2003.

Table 6.3. Order flow payments made to retail brokers in 4Q2012

Venue	Ameritrade	E*Trade	Scottrade	Schwab	Fidelity
Citadel	$0.0016	<$0.0010	≤$0.00125	<$0.00095	$0.0000
KCG	$0.0011	<$0.0010	≤$0.00075	<$0.00095	$0.0000
G1X	$0.0016	<$0.0010	≤$0.00105	<$0.00095	$0.0000

Notes: Schwab routes customer orders to wholesalers only, while the four remaining brokers route marketable orders to wholesalers and nonmarketable orders to exchanges.

Source: order flow payments obtained from the 4Q2012 Rule 606 order routing reports produced by each of the brokers.

can pay retail brokers more for their marketable orders than those who accept both marketable and nonmarketable orders.

Table 6.3 contains a summary of the information provided in recent Rule 606 filings regarding the payments that various brokers received from three wholesalers in 4Q2016. As noted earlier, Fidelity did not accept payment for order flow from wholesalers in 2016. While Ameritrade provided a point estimate as to the average payment received from each wholesaler, Charles Schwab, E*Trade, and Scottrade provided upper bound estimates for the inducements they received. Given the inequalities, the only sharp comparison that can be made is between Ameritrade and Schwab. As discussed below, the Rule 606 filings suggest that Ameritrade's routing was much more tilted toward harvesting liquidity rebates than Schwab's was. Ameritrade appears to have routed no standing limit orders to wholesalers, while Schwab routed all of its limit orders to wholesalers. Consistent with the conjecture that brokers who route both market and limit orders to wholesalers will be paid less for their marketable orders, the data in Table 6.3 indicate that each wholesaler paid Ameritrade more for its marketable order flow than it paid Schwab. Of course, the data are also consistent with the hypothesis that Schwab contracted for a higher level of price improvement for its marketable orders than Ameritrade did. Without more detailed data, one cannot distinguish between these two hypotheses.

Why would a broker route nonmarketable limit orders to a wholesaler rather than to an exchange? One reason may be enhanced limit order execution quality.[18] Brokers who route both marketable and nonmarketable orders to

---

[18] Another reason to route nonmarketable limit orders to a wholesaler would be to generate higher liquidity rebates. Some wholesalers have walls that allow them to keep customer limit orders off of their limit order books. These wholesalers typically route nonmarketable orders to venues that offer liquidity rebates. In a conversation with Haim Bodek, he noted that it is rare for a broker to qualify for the highest rebate volume tier on multiple exchanges. Rather than route nonmarketable orders to an exchange on which they do not qualify for the highest rebate, he stated that brokers will route their nonmarketable orders to a wholesaler who does qualify for the highest rebate on that exchange, who will in turn route those orders to that exchange. Haim remarked that it is common practice to share the difference in rebates (the lower rebate that the broker qualifies for and the higher rebate that the wholesaler qualifies for) equally.

wholesalers may do so to give their limit orders the opportunity to interact with both the broker's and the purchaser's marketable orders. Because of this, limit orders resting on a wholesaler's limit order book may execute more frequently and in more favourable market conditions than those resting on exchanges with inverted fee schedules. Battalio, Corwin, and Jennings note that whether this routing strategy is preferable to alternative strategies is a question that cannot be addressed with publicly available equity market data.[19]

Taking advantage of the fact that purchased orders in equity options must be executed on an options exchange, Battalio, Griffith, and Van Ness use the Philadelphia Stock Exchange's 2012 decision to begin migrating option classes from their make/take pricing model to a payment for order flow pricing model to examine how allowing nonmarketable limit orders to interact with purchased order flow impacts limit order execution quality.[20] The authors present evidence suggesting that limit order execution quality improves (e.g. limit orders execute more quickly, more frequently, and in more favourable market conditions) when option classes begin trading in the payment for order flow model on the PHLX. They attribute the improvement in limit order execution quality to the fact that standing limit orders are able to interact with retail marketable orders after the PHLX begins purchasing order flow.

To summarize, one would expect retail brokers to route marketable orders to wholesalers if they can find a wholesaler that is willing to accept their order flow. Brokers with uninformed retail customer order flow should have no problem finding a wholesaler that is willing to purchase their order flow, while brokers with more informed clients may not have this option and may be forced to route marketable customer orders to exchanges, dark pools, or other venues. Brokers who route marketable orders to wholesalers typically face the tradeoff of receiving larger payments for their order flow or receiving increased price improvement for their customer orders. All else equal, wholesalers will pay more for a broker's marketable order flow (or provide larger price improvements) if the broker does not route standing limit orders to that broker.

With regard to standing limit orders, brokers who seek to maximize the per-share payment they receive for each nonmarketable limit order execution are providing suboptimal limit order execution quality relative to brokers who, when market conditions dictate, utilize inverted exchanges as destination for their customer limit orders. Whether or not brokers who route both market and limit orders in a stock to wholesalers provide better limit order execution quality than could be obtained by using a smart router to optimally display limit orders on exchanges utilizing the make/take and the inverted fee schedules is

---

[19] Battalio et al., 'Can brokers have it all?', 2016.   [20] Battalio et al., 'Make-take fees', 2017.

an open empirical question. There must be some reason, however, that some retail brokers currently route both limit and market orders to wholesalers given that doing so reduces the order flow payments that the broker receives and/or the price improvement that the broker's marketable orders receive.

6.3 Analysis of Broker Routing in 4Q2016

6.3.1 Ameritrade—Bifurcated Order Routing

Information regarding Ameritrade's routing of non-directed customer orders in 4Q2016 is provided in Table 6.4. Interestingly, and in contrast to Ameritrade's order routing in the 4Q2012, Ameritrade routes the bulk of its orders to TD Ameritrade Clearing. This makes it more difficult to discern the venues to which Ameritrade's orders are ultimately routed. Based upon their Rule 606 filing, Ameritrade appears to be routing orders only to wholesalers and to Ameritrade Clearing. However, note that Ameritrade is paid $0.0028 per share for limit orders and other orders by Citi Global Markets (Citi), which is nearly twice as much as Citadel pays Ameritrade for market, limit, and other orders. How can Citi pay nearly twice as much as Citadel for Ameritrade's orders? The data suggest that Citadel is paying for marketable orders (and possibly nonmarketable orders) and Citi is simply displaying Ameritrade's nonmarketable limit orders on exchanges with high-liquidity rebates and passing most of the rebate back to Ameritrade. Indeed, E*Trade routes limit orders to Citi in the fourth quarter of 2016 and notes in its 606 filing that Citi Global Markets 'may utilize NYSE ARCA for the display of limit orders'.

To get a better idea as to where Ameritrade's non-directed customer orders are routed, I assume that TD Ameritrade Clearing routes the orders it receives

Table 6.4. Ameritrade's routing of non-directed orders seeking to trade NASDAQ-listed securities during 4Q2016

Venue	Per-share remuneration	Market share	Market orders	Limit orders	Other orders
TD Am. Clearing		68%	72%	61%	71%
Citi Global Markets	+$0.0028	12%	0%	23%	6%
Citadel	+$0.0016	9%	12%	7%	10%
KCG	+$0.0011	7%	9%	6%	9%
Two Sigma	+$0.0012	4%	7%	3%	4%

Notes: of the 99% of total customer orders that are non-directed, 16% are market orders, 42% are limit orders, and 42% are other orders. TD Am. Clearing = TD Ameritrade Clearing. A market order is an order to buy or sell shares of stock at the best market price available, without conditions or limits. A limit order is an order to buy/sell shares of stock at a price that is no higher/lower than a pre-specified limit price. Other orders are orders for which the customer requests special handling, including orders submitted with stop prices, all or none orders, fill or kill orders, not held orders, and orders for other than regular settlement.

Source: data obtained from the 4Q2016 Rule 606 order routing report produced by Ameritrade.

Table 6.5. Ameritrade Clearing's routing of non-directed orders seeking to trade NASDAQ-listed securities during 4Q2016

Venue	Per-share remuneration	Market share	Market orders	Limit orders	Other orders
Citadel	+$0.0016	31%	42%	23%	33%
G1X	+$0.0016	13%	19%	5%	18%
KCG	+$0.0011	13%	19%	6%	18%
Two Sigma	+$0.0012	9%	16%	4%	10%
EDGX	Add: +$0.0034^	20%	0%	39%	12%
NYSE Arca	Add: +$0.0030^	7%	0%	15%	2%

Notes: of the 99% of total customer orders that are non-directed, 17% are market orders, 38% are limit orders, and 45% are other orders. ^ = the per-share liquidity rebate was as high as the number reported in this table. A market order is an order to buy or sell shares of stock at the best market price available, without conditions or limits. A limit order is an order to buy/sell shares of stock at a price that is no higher/lower than a pre-specified limit price. Other orders are orders for which the customer requests special handling, including orders submitted with stop prices, all or none orders, fill or kill orders, not held orders, and orders for other than regular settlement.

Source: data obtained from the 4Q2016 Rule 606 order routing report produced by Ameritrade Clearing.

Table 6.6. TD Ameritrade's implied routing of non-directed orders seeking to trade NASDAQ-listed securities during 4Q2016

Venue	Per-share remuneration	Market orders	Limit orders
Citadel	+$0.0016	42.24%	21.03%
G1X	+$0.0016	13.68%	3.05%
KCG	+$0.0011	22.68%	9.66%
Two Sigma	+$0.0012	18.52%	5.44%
Citi Global Markets	+$0.0028	0.00%	23.00%
EDGX	Add: +$0.0034^	0.00%	23.79%
NYSE Arca	Add: +$0.0030^	0.00%	9.15%

Notes: the percentages of market orders and limit orders routed to each venue are computed under the assumption that the non-directed market and limit orders that TD Ameritrade routes to TD Ameritrade Clearing are routed to venues in same proportions as described in TD Ameritrade Clearing's 4Q2016 Rule 606 filing. ^ = the per-share liquidity rebate was as high as the number reported in this table. A market order is an order to buy or sell shares of stock at the best market price available, without conditions or limits. A limit order is an order to buy/sell shares of stock at a price that is no higher/lower than a pre-specified limit price.

from Ameritrade to executing venues in the same proportion as the averages provided in TD Ameritrade Clearing's orders in 4Q2016. I then combine this information with the routing information in Table 6.4. Information regarding TD Ameritrade Clearing's order routing is provided in Table 6.5, while an estimate of the venues to which Ameritrade's orders were ultimately routed in 4Q2016 is given in Table 6.6.

Battalio, Corwin, and Jennings assume that brokers who choose to sell their market orders to market makers rather than route them to venues with take fees are likely to route marketable limit orders to market makers and standing limit orders to exchanges offering high rebates.[21] In his 2014 senate testimony,

---

[21] Battalio et al., 'Can brokers have it all?', 2016.

Steven Quirk, Ameritrade Senior Vice President, validated this assumption for Ameritrade when he said that his firm routes virtually every order to the market that offered the largest inducement. Based on this statement and data provided in Ameritrade's Rule 606 filing from the fourth quarter of 2012, Ameritrade routed 53 per cent of its limit orders to EDGX, a venue that paid Ameritrade liquidity rebates as high as $0.0035 per share. Mr Quirk's statement suggests these were nonmarketable limit orders. Based on the estimates in Table 6.6, Ameritrade routed 55.94 per cent of its limit orders to venues with high-liquidity rebates (and high take fees) in 4Q2016. If I continue to assume that Ameritrade routes orders to the venue that offers the highest rebate, this implies that 55.94 per cent of Ameritrade's limit orders seeking to trade NASDAQ-listed securities in the fourth quarter of 2016 were nonmarketable.

The evidence presented in Table 6.6 suggests that Ameritrade is continuing to route marketable orders to wholesalers and its nonmarketable limit orders to venues offering high-liquidity rebates. However, while Ameritrade's Rule 606 filing describes where 100 per cent of its limit orders were routed, Ameritrade Clearing's filing describes where it routed only 92 per cent of the customer limit orders that it handled. If Ameritrade Clearing's Rule 606 report is representative as to where Ameritrade's orders were sent, then 4.88 per cent of Ameritrade's limit orders were routed to venues that do not appear on Ameritrade's 4Q2016 Rule 606 filing. How big is 4.88 per cent? In 2016, Credit Suisse reported that 9 per cent of US equity trading volume occurred on the three exchanges that utilized inverted pricing schedules.[22] The frequency with which Ameritrade's customer limit orders would have benefited from being displayed on an inverted venue depends on the frequency with which those orders were placed in actively-traded stocks for which the minimum variation is binding. If these orders accounted for less than 5 per cent of Ameritrade's limit orders and if Ameritrade selectively routed these orders to inverted venues, Ameritrade may have routed limit orders in 4Q2016 in a manner consistent with seeking best execution for customer limit orders. For this assumption to be true, however, the percentage of Ameritrade's limit orders that were nonmarketable would have had to have increased from 53 per cent in 4Q2012 to 60.82 per cent in 4Q2016. If, on the other hand, these limit orders were instead routed to other high-fee venues such as NASDAQ or BATS BZX, one could reasonably conclude that Ameritrade's order routing strategy was more consistent with harvesting order flow payments than with optimizing limit order execution quality. Regardless, it is safe to conclude that it has become more difficult to discern where Ameritrade is routing its customer orders.

---

[22] See Avramovic, 'Credit Suisse U.S. Chartbook', 2017.

6.3.2 E*Trade—Bifurcated Order Routing

In 4Q2012, E*Trade routed 97.12 per cent of its market orders to two wholesalers for payments averaging less than $0.0015 per share and it routed 60.55 per cent of its limit orders to EDGX and Citi in return for liquidity rebates of less than $0.0032 per share. EDGX receive no market orders from E*Trade, while Citi received 1.39 per cent of E*Trade's market orders. As it is unlikely E*Trade would sell almost all of its market orders and pay to have its marketable limit orders executed, I again assume that only marketable limit orders were routed to the wholesalers. This implies that just over 60 per cent of E*Trade's limit orders were nonmarketable in 4Q2012.

Table 6.7 details the venues receiving E*Trade's non-directed customer order flow in 4Q2016. All of E*Trade's market orders were routed to wholesalers and 62.63 per cent of E*Trade's limit orders were routed to venues that offered high-liquidity rebates and charged liquidity demanders $0.0030 per share. Assuming that marketable limit orders were sold to the wholesalers, 62.63 per cent of E*Trade's limit orders were nonmarketable in 4Q2016 compared to 60.55 per cent in 4Q2012. Unlike Ameritrade's Rule 606 filing, which only describes where 95.12 per cent of its limit orders were routed, E*Trade's Rule 606 filing covers 99.97 per cent of its limit orders. Thus, the data in E*Trade's 4Q2016 describes where almost all of its non-directed customer orders were routed during the quarter. This allows one to conclude that, as was the case in 4Q2012, E*Trade continues to route nonmarketable customer limit orders in a manner that generates high-liquidity rebates, possibly at the expense of diminished limit order execution quality.

Table 6.7. E*Trade's routing of non-directed orders seeking to trade NASDAQ-listed securities during 4Q2016

Venue	Per-share remuneration	Market share	Market orders	Limit orders	Other orders
G1X	<+$0.0010	42.74%	53.09%	26.36%	83.71%
Citadel	<+$0.0010	18.46%	33.41%	7.92%	4.32%
KCG	<+$0.0010	7.60%	12.27%	2.76%	11.80%
Wolverine	<+$0.0010	0.65%	1.23%	0.23%	0.14%
EDGX	<+$0.0031	18.31%	0.00%	37.59%	0.00%
NASDAQ	<+$0.0028	12.20%	0.00%	25.04%	0.00%
Citi Global Markets	<+$0.0027	0.03%	0.00%	0.07%	0.00%

Notes: of the 93.51% of total customer orders that are non-directed, 42.58% are market orders, 48.71% are limit orders, and 8.71% are other orders. E*Trade's Rule 606 filing notes that Citi Global Markets 'may utilize NYSE ARCA for the display of limit orders'. A market order is an order to buy or sell shares of stock at the best market price available, without conditions or limits. A limit order is an order to buy/sell shares of stock at a price that is no higher/lower than a pre-specified limit price. Other orders are orders for which the customer requests special handling, including orders submitted with stop prices, all or none orders, fill or kill orders, not held orders, and orders for other than regular settlement.

Source: data are obtained from the 4Q2016 Rule 606 order routing report produced by E*Trade.

Table 6.8. Scottrade's routing of non-directed orders seeking to trade NASDAQ-listed securities during 4Q2016

Venue	Per-share remuneration	Market share	Market orders	Limit orders	Other orders
Citadel	<+$0.00125	25.27%	34.00%	7.52%	29.66%
KCG	<+$0.00075	23.42%	30.93%	5.46%	28.52%
G1X	<+$0.00105	13.20%	22.44%	3.65%	13.37%
Two Sigma	<+$0.00085	7.54%	5.10%	0.87%	11.98%
EDGX	<+$0.00298	13.46%	0.00%	38.54%	7.80%
NASDAQ	<+$0.00298	14.62%	0.00%	42.77%	8.03%

Notes: of the 100% of total customer orders that are non-directed, 24.64% are market orders, 24.68% are limit orders, and 50.69% are other orders. A market order is an order to buy or sell shares of stock at the best market price available, without conditions or limits. A limit order is an order to buy/sell shares of stock at a price that is no higher/lower than a pre-specified limit price. Other orders are orders for which the customer requests special handling, including orders submitted with stop prices, all or none orders, fill or kill orders, not held orders, and orders for other than regular settlement.

Source: data obtained from the 4Q2016 Rule 606 order routing report produced by Scottrade.

6.3.3 Scottrade—Bifurcated Order Routing

As was the case in 4Q2012, the routing data presented in Table 6.8 demonstrates that Scottrade continues to route marketable orders to wholesalers in return for rebates and (presumably) nonmarketable limit orders to exchanges that offer aggressive liquidity rebates (and charge high take fees). Again assuming that a broker seeking to monetize its order flow would not send marketable orders to exchanges with high take fees, I infer that the limit orders routed to EDGX and NASDAQ in 4Q2016 were nonmarketable. This suggests that 81.31 per cent (38.54 per cent + 42.77 per cent) of Scottrade's limit orders were nonmarketable, which compares to 79.25 per cent in 4Q2012. As is the case with E*Trade's Rule 606 filing, Scottrade's Rule 606 filing describes where 98.81 per cent of its customer limit orders were routed. This suggests that no more than 1.09 per cent of Scottrade's limit orders were displayed on one of the three exchanges utilizing inverted pricing schedules. Thus, as was the case in 2012, the routing information in Table 6.8 indicates that Scottrade continues to pursue high-liquidity rebates at the expense of limit order execution quality.

6.3.4 Fidelity—Bifurcated Order Routing

As noted by KOR Group in their 14 August 2015 blog post, 'Retail brokers show dramatic routing differences', Fidelity began requesting increased price improvement in lieu of payments for its marketable order flow toward the end of 2014.[23] The data presented in Table 6.2 suggests that Fidelity's smaller market orders receive larger price improvements than comparable orders placed with a competing retail broker that accepts payment for marketable orders. This said,

---

[23] See http://kortrading.com/blog/.

Table 6.9. Fidelity's routing of non-directed orders seeking to trade NASDAQ-listed securities during 4Q2016

Venue	Per-share remuneration	Market share	Market orders	Limit orders	Other orders
KCG	$0.0000	32.97%	42.19%	19.84%	45.21%
Citadel	$0.0000	32.66%	42.61%	17.71%	49.01%
BATS BZX	Add: +$0.0030	11.57%	0.00%	27.09%	0.01%
EDGX	Add: +$0.0030	9.26%	0.00%	21.66%	0.11%
G1X	$0.0000	3.91%	4.98%	3.72%	0.00%

Notes: of the 96.02% of total customer orders that are non-directed, 46.71% are market orders, 42.69% are limit orders, and 10.60% are other orders. A market order is an order to buy or sell shares of stock at the best market price available, without conditions or limits. A limit order is an order to buy/sell shares of stock at a price that is no higher/lower than a pre-specified limit price. Other orders are orders for which the customer requests special handling, including orders submitted with stop prices, all or none orders, fill or kill orders, not held orders, and orders for other than regular settlement.

Source: data are obtained from the 4Q2016 Rule 606 order routing report produced by Fidelity.

as can be seen in Table 6.9 below, Fidelity continued to bifurcate its order flow during 4Q2016, routing 48.75 per cent of its customer limit orders and no market orders to two venues that paid Fidelity liquidity rebates of $0.0030 per share and routing 89.78 per cent of its market orders to three wholesalers.

In 4Q2012, Fidelity routed 30 per cent of its limit orders in NASDAQ-listed stocks to venues offering aggressive liquidity rebates. In the most recent quarter, Fidelity routed 48.75 per cent of its limit order in NASDAQ-listed stocks to venues charging take fees of $0.0029 per share or higher and earned a liquidity rebate of $0.0030 per share. Fidelity's Rule 606 filing suggests that it only routed nonmarketable limit orders to EDGX and BATS BZX. However, given that Fidelity no longer received payment from the wholesalers for its order flow, it now seems more likely that Fidelity routed nonmarketable limit orders to the wholesalers.

6.3.5 Charles Schwab—Stock by Stock Order Routing?

Statistics from Charles Schwab's fourth-quarter 2016 Rule 606 filing are provided in Table 6.10. Note that each of the venues to which Schwab routed orders during this quarter receives roughly the same percentage of Schwab's market orders, limit orders, and other orders. For example, the wholesaler UBS received 34.3 per cent of Schwab's non-directed customer orders. As can be seen in the first row of Table 6.10, UBS received roughly 34.3 per cent of Schwab's market orders (36.0 per cent), limit orders (32.6 per cent), and other orders (34.8 per cent). The remaining rows in Table 6.10 reveal that the difference between the percentage of all orders and the percentage of each type of order routed by Schwab to the other four wholesalers is relatively small. For this reason, it appears that Schwab is routing orders to wholesalers

Table 6.10. Charles Schwab's routing of non-directed orders seeking to trade NASDAQ-listed securities during 4Q2016

Venue	Per-share remuneration	Market share	Market orders	Limit orders	Other orders
UBS	<+$0.00090	34.3%	36.0%	32.6%	34.8%
Citadel	<+$0.00095	24.5%	24.6%	24.3%	25.0%
KCG	<+$0.00095	22.5%	20.3%	24.7%	20.8%
G1X	<+$0.00095	14.2%	14.6%	13.8%	14.6%
Two Sigma	<+$0.00095	4.3%	4.4%	4.2%	4.4%

Notes: of the 98.7% of total customer orders that are non-directed, 45.9% are market orders, 48.7% are limit orders, and 5.4% are other orders. A market order is an order to buy or sell shares of stock at the best market price available, without conditions or limits. A limit order is an order to buy/sell shares of stock at a price that is no higher/lower than a pre-specified limit price. Other orders are orders for which the customer requests special handling, including orders submitted with stop prices, all or none orders, fill or kill orders, not held orders, and orders for other than regular settlement.

Source: data are obtained from the 4Q2016 Rule 606 order routing report produced by Charles Schwab.

on a stock-by-stock basis. Schwab routed orders in a similar fashion in the fourth quarter of 2012.

I am unaware of any study that empirically examines whether standing limit orders seeking to trade NASDAQ-listed securities are executed faster, more frequently, and in more favourable market conditions when they are routed to a wholesaler rather than to an exchange with an inverted fee schedule. If the wholesaler accepts Manning responsibilities for customer limit orders, it seems reasonable to assume that the wholesaler displays the customer limit orders that it receives on an exchange.[24] If the wholesaler receives a marketable order before the limit order is executed on an exchange, the wholesaler can cancel the displayed limit order and fulfil her Manning obligations by allowing the limit order to trade with the incoming marketable order. In this instance, the wholesaler does not get to interact with the purchased marketable order. If the limit order is executed on an exchange before the wholesaler receives a marketable order in the same stock, the customer order is executed and the wholesaler receives the liquidity rebate.

Given the economics of order routing, it seems unlikely that a wholesaler would route standing limit orders to inverted venues and risk paying a fee when they execute. Whether or not standing limit orders resting on the order books of wholesalers receive better execution quality than standing limit orders displayed on inverted venues is an empirical question that is likely to depend on the nature of the stock being traded and the amount of retail marketable order flow the wholesaler purchases.

[24] As alluded to earlier, a wholesaler can take steps to keep retail limit orders off of its limit order book. See NASD NTM 03-74, 'Limit Order Protection. Guidance Relating to the Application of NASD's Limit Order Protection Rule When Trading Proprietarily Through a Separate MPID', available at: https://www.finra.org/sites/default/files/NoticeDocument/p003061.pdf.

6.4 Concluding Remarks

My co-authors and I first began circulating the initial draft of our paper 'Can brokers have it all?' in October 2013. In this paper, we presented data that suggested that four retail brokers routed orders during the fourth quarter of 2012 in a manner that maximized order flow payments rather than limit order execution quality. The *Wall Street Journal* published an article by Bradley Hope and Scott Patterson based on our paper on 17 December 2013, and on 23 May 2014 I was invited to testify in a hearing held on 10 June 2014 by the US Senate's Permanent Subcommittee on Investigations of the Homeland Security and Government Affairs. The topic of this hearing was conflicts of interest in US equity markets.

The publicity that our work garnered from the senate hearings has increased the impact of our paper. Shortly after the hearing, in July 2014 the Financial Industry Regulatory Authority (FINRA), which operates as an independent, non-governmental regulator for all securities firms doing business with the public in the United States, initiated a review of broker order routing and execution quality.[25] As part of this review, brokerages were asked to explain how order routing decisions are made for customer nonmarketable limit orders and to provide a detailed discussion of how exchange maker-taker fees are considered in the order routing decision. On 13 July 2016, the SEC proposed new rules that would make 'targeted enhancements' to SEC Rule 606 by requiring limit order information to be broken down into marketable and nonmarketable categories, requiring the disclosure of the net aggregate amount of any payment for order flow received, and requiring broker-dealers to describe any terms of payment for order flow arrangements and profit-sharing relationships with certain venues that may influence their order routing decisions. Our paper is cited numerous times in this rule proposal.[26] Finally, in November 2017, FINRA initiated a review concerning the impact that order routing inducements such as payment for order flow and maker-taker rebates have on broker order routing practices and decisions.[27] It will be interesting to see whether the new rules proposed by the SEC become law and whether FINRA's reviews cause brokers to adjust their order routing strategies.

---

[25] See http://www.finra.org/industry/order-routing-and-execution-quality-customer-orders.
[26] See SEC Release No. 34-78309, 'Disclosure of Order Handling Information', available at: https://www.sec.gov/rules/proposed/2016/34-78309.pdf.
[27] See http://www.finra.org/industry/order-routing-conflicts.

References

Alpert, Bill. 'Who makes money on your stock trades'. *Barron's*, 28 February 2015.

Avramovic, Ana. 'Credit Suisse U.S. Chartbook: Market structure review 2016/2017'. Available at: www.hysec.com/f/tsnr/[D2017]/2017-01/TSNR100/12/RR_3003589784.pdf, 10 January 2017.

Battalio, Robert, Shane Corwin, and Robert Jennings. 'Can brokers have it all? On the relation between make-take fees and limit order execution quality'. *Journal of Finance* 71, no. 5 (2016): 2193–238.

Battalio, Robert, Todd Griffith, and Robert Van Ness. 'Make-take fees versus order flow inducements: Evidence from the NASDAQ OMX PHLX Exchange'. University of Notre Dame Working Paper, 2017.

Battalio, Robert, Andriy Shkilko, and Robert Van Ness. 'To pay or be paid? The impact of taker fees and order flow inducements on trading costs in U.S. options markets'. *Journal of Financial and Quantitative Analysis* 51, no. 5 (2016): 1637–62.

Boehmer, Ekkehart, Robert Jennings, and Li Wei. 'Public disclosure and private decisions: Equity market execution quality and order routing'. *Review of Financial Studies* 20, no. 2 (2007): 315–58.

Chapman, Peter. 'Before the fall: Bernard L. Madoff'. *Traders Magazine*, March 2009: 31–2.

FINRA. 'FINRA Regulatory notice 11–24'. Available at: https://www.finra.org/file/regulatory-notice-11-24, May 2011.

McInish, Thomas, and James Upson. 'The quote exception rule: Giving high frequency traders an unintended advantage'. *Financial Management* 42, no. 3 (2013): 481–501.

Parlour, Christine, and Uday Rajan. 'Payment for order flow'. *Journal of Financial Economics* 68, no. 3 (2003): 379–411.

SEC. 'SEC office of compliance inspections and examinations office of economic analysis special study: Payment for order flow and internalization in the options market'. Available at: https://www.sec.gov/news/studies/ordpay.htm, December 2000.

7

Better 'Best Execution'

An Overview and Assessment

Christopher Nagy and Tyler Gellasch

7.1 Introduction

The costs of trading and of investment research have direct and dramatic impacts on returns for investors. Yet, for decades, these costs have been difficult—if not impossible—to quantify. In recent years, asset owners and regulators have begun to aggressively scrutinize these costs. Investment advisers and brokers around the world are all rapidly developing best practices to meet increasingly stringent regulatory and client expectations.

These expectations essentially build upon investment advisers' long-standing fiduciary duty to their customers: the duty of 'best execution'. While the contours of the duty vary significantly across countries, the general theme is the same: advisers are obligated to look out for their customers so that they do not unfairly overpay for securities, trading, and research.

In recent years, regulators, starting in the United Kingdom, have begun to modernize their expectations. European regulators have come to demand that investment advisers take 'sufficient steps' to fulfil their best execution obligations. And they have dramatically expanded both substantive requirements and disclosures related to firms' broker selection, order routing, and execution. In the US, however, the Securities and Exchange Commission (SEC) has essentially taken no significant action to outline investment advisers' best execution obligations[1], nor have they adopted any rules to improve advisers' abilities fulfil their duties.[2]

---

[1] By way of contrast, the Financial Industry Regulatory Authority (FINRA) has recently provided sweeping new guidance on best execution obligations for broker-dealers, including requiring detailed analyses of orders for equities, options, and fixed income.

[2] Amidst a slew of enforcement cases involving Alternative Trading System (ATS) operators and brokers for order routing and execution abuses, the SEC has proposed to modernize Regulation ATS and Rule 606 of Regulation NMS (regarding order routing disclosures).

Nevertheless, global research providers and global investment advisers have been revising their business models and systems to come into compliance with the new European rules. This includes firms based in the US.

In this cloudy environment, investment advisers have developed various strategies to fulfil their duties. These strategies have varied significantly over time, across firms, and even across asset classes and funds within firms. Technological advances in markets and trading operations, and more recently regulators' and asset owners' expectations, have accelerated the evolution of best execution for the 'buy side'.

This chapter draws heavily on a report prepared by the authors for the Healthy Markets Association. Nagy is a founder and Director of Healthy Markets Association. Gellasch serves as the organization's Executive Director. The chapter reviews best execution and new disclosure obligations in relation to investment advisers as well as brokers; it also provides an overview of the strategies they are developing to meet their rapidly changing obligations.

We first outline the analogous best execution obligation for broker-dealers and then explore the contours of the SEC's expectations for investment advisers, including as informed by relevant cases. We then assess the impact of new European best execution obligations and the role of public disclosures in aiding the fulfilment of best execution duties. We conclude by examining various strategies used by investment advisers to fulfil their evolving duties.

7.2 'Best Execution' for US Broker-Dealers

In the US, an investment adviser's best execution obligation is distinct from that of a broker. In particular, a broker's duty is much more clearly defined (and regularly enforced). Nevertheless, because of the similarities of objectives between the two duties, we believe it is useful to first outline US brokers' duty of best execution.

A broker's obligation to obtain best execution 'is based, in part, on the common law agency duty of loyalty, which obligates an agent to act exclusively in the principal's best interest, and also has been incorporated explicitly in FINRA rules'.[3] Broadly speaking, this requires any broker acting as an agent to a customer to 'exercise reasonable care to obtain the most advantageous terms for the customer under the circumstances'.[4]

---

[3] FINRA, *Best Execution: Guidance*, 2015.
[4] Ibid., citing Sec. Exch. Act, 59 FR 55006, 55007 at n.15 (2 November 1994).

Certainly, price is an important consideration. But that is not just the explicit share price.[5] To look at the total price to the customer, a broker must also consider various fees charged throughout the execution chain: e.g. fees charged by exchanges, alternative trading systems (ATSs), liquidity providers or executing brokers.[6]

While a number of FINRA rules touch upon best execution, FINRA Rule 5310 further requires a broker acting as agent to use reasonable diligence to ascertain the best market for the subject security.[7] For a broker to establish that it has fulfilled this obligation, FINRA requires it to consider the character of the market for the security (e.g. price, liquidity, and volatility); the size and type of transaction; the number of markets checked; the accessibility of the quotation; and the terms and conditions of the order.[8]

The subjective nature of these considerations allows a broker to fulfil its best execution obligations even if it uses an execution channel with higher built-in transaction fees, provided that the other facts and circumstances justify it.

In addition, regulators historically have allowed broker-dealers to evaluate execution quality on an aggregated basis pursuant to 'regular and rigorous review' of its routing and execution arrangements, including what it could have received at other markets.[9] In laying out the standards for this 'regular and rigorous review', FINRA has stated that brokers should consider several factors, such as price improvement opportunities (i.e. the difference between the execution price and the best quotes prevailing at the time the order is received by the market); differences in price disimprovement (i.e. situations in which a customer receives a worse price at execution than the best quotes prevailing at the time the order is received by the market); the likelihood of execution of limit orders; the speed of execution; the size of execution; transaction costs; customer needs and expectations; and the existence of internalization or payment for order flow arrangements.[10]

To aid brokers in their pursuit of best execution, and in an effort to provide investors with greater transparency into a broker's routing practices, the Securities and Exchange Commission adopted a basic framework of rules.

---

[5] In this regard, brokers' routing decisions are backstopped by Rule 611 of Regulation NMS, the 'Order Protection Rule'. Rule 611 requires an exchange to implement policies and procedures that are reasonably designed to prevent trade-throughs or orders from executing orders at prices outside the National Best Bid and Offer. Further, Rule 611 protects only the top of the book, and many larger orders will clear multiple levels. Unfortunately, guidelines and practices after the first price level has been cleared are inconsistent.

[6] FINRA, *Best Execution: NASD Regulation*, 2001.

[7] FINRA, *Rule 5310*, 2014. However, several other FINRA rules supplement this 'Best Execution' rule, most notably Rule 2121, which governs commission rates and fees, including markups and markdowns. See FINRA, *Rule 2121*, 2014.

[8] FINRA, *Rule 5310*, 2014.   [9] Ibid., Supplemental Material 0.09 to Rule 5310.

[10] FINRA, *Rule 5310*, 2014.

SEC Rule 605 requires monthly information to be published outlining basic quantitative factors such as price improvement and execution speed. SEC Rule 606 requires brokers to disclose, on a quarterly basis, where they route their orders and under what circumstances the orders are routed. Since their adoption in 2001, the rules, which provide for greater broker routing transparency, have had a favourable impact on routing behaviour. Unfortunately, these disclosures are of very limited utility for institutional investors, and the metrics have become increasingly outdated.

In November 2015, FINRA issued new Guidance on Best Execution Obligations in Equity, Options and Fixed Income Markets.[11] This guidance invites brokers to conduct more order-by-order reviews of execution quality; to perform detailed analysis for fixed income trading and to consider electronic trading platforms; to consider execution quality at venues to which it is not connected and assess whether it should connect to such venues; to take into account market and technology changes that might alter its best execution analysis; to consider material differences in execution quality across order-types; and to use direct feeds to measure execution quality if it has access to them and is otherwise using them to make routing or execution decisions.

Perhaps most importantly, by focusing analysis on an order-by-order basis, FINRA appears to be significantly (albeit indirectly) narrowing the scope of factors that may be relied upon in making order handling decisions.

This may result in focusing more heavily on explicit costs for individual orders (which tend to be a function of just price and fill rates), while potentially having the unintended effect of increasing overall trading costs (which may be heavily influenced by slippage and information leakage). For example, suppose an institutional investor wants to buy one million shares of XYZ stock. This order is the 'parent' order. The investor engages the services of a broker-dealer through the broker's smart order router (SOR). The SOR may then divide the investor's 'parent' order into smaller 'child' orders to be sent out to different market centres. Further, the investor's trading decision itself may actually give rise to multiple orders for the broker. Often, a broker may not know whether it has received all of a client's order, or whether the client investment adviser has already divided the 'parent' order before sending it to the broker.

Should the broker route a 'child' order in a manner that minimizes the total transaction cost for that specific 'child' order, or should the broker route each 'child' order in a way that may minimize the overall transaction costs for executing the entire 'parent' order?

This is important because there is evidence that some venues provide superior execution prices to the first few child orders, but that the cost of executing

---

[11] FINRA, *Best Execution: Guidance*, 2015.

the remaining, unfilled portion of a parent order may increase significantly thereafter.[12]

In this case, the broker may best reduce the overall transaction costs for its customer by considering both trade price and potential information leakage when placing its initial 'child' orders.[13] This may be particularly relevant for routing orders to exchanges or some ATSs that have smaller transaction sizes and participants who are more likely to engage in algorithmic trading strategies that may result in 'toxic' fills.

It is not yet clear how FINRA intends to reconcile its mandate that brokers minimize customers' total costs with this new order-by-order analysis. Given the fact that the majority of the total costs to customers in certain transactions may be the implementation costs (as opposed to commissions), the resolution of this issue will have significant impacts on brokers and, indirectly, investment advisers.

Another key element of FINRA's 2015 guidance was its expectation that brokers engage in detailed analysis for fixed income trading.[14] As described above, best execution analysis has traditionally been far more robust for equities than for other assets, due in large part to the relative transparency of the markets and the relative ability of firms to engage in meaningful analysis. With the increasing automation and transparency of other asset classes, the ability of brokers to engage in similar forms of analysis is increasing rapidly. FINRA's attention on this asset class comes at a critical time, with increasing electronic trading and attention on the disparity in execution costs between equities and fixed income.

The guidance further encourages brokers to consider whether electronic platforms for fixed income trading may improve execution quality and should be incorporated into the broker-dealer's routing decisions. FINRA cited the rise of electronic trading and recent advance in trading technology and communications systems as the rationale underlying these new principles. FINRA's guidance is consistent with SEC's longstanding view that the scope of the duty of best execution must evolve with markets and technology.[15]

Additionally, in late 2016 and early 2017, a pair of regulatory settlements rocked the broker-dealer community. First, in December 2016, Deutsche Bank settled a coordinated set of enforcement actions brought by the New York Attorney General,[16] SEC,[17] and FINRA. From 2012 to mid 2014, the bank was

---

[12] Van Kervel and Menkveld, 'High-frequency trading', 2016.

[13] This phenomenon has been cited by some market participants as justification to reevaluate Rule 611 of Regulation NMS, commonly called the Order Protection Rule. See, e.g., SEC, *Meeting*, 2017 (Statement of Mehmet Kinak).

[14] FINRA, *Best Execution: Guidance*, 2015.   [15] SEC, *Order Execution Obligations*, 1996.

[16] Attorney General of the State of New York—Investor Protection Bureau, *Settlement Agreement*, 2016.

[17] SEC, *Order … in the Matter of Deutsche Bank Securities Inc.*, 2016.

claiming to route orders one way, while really routing them another way. Because the order routing process of the bank's 'black box' was secret, customers were not able to readily evaluate the bank's order routing processes. Deutsche Bank's customers had to trust that its 'black box' was working as advertised. It was not. As history has demonstrated, this problem often arises when clients are unable to evaluate whether their brokers operate as advertised.

Then, in January 2017, Citadel settled with SEC for inadequate disclosures around its execution practices.[18] Citadel paid its broker-dealer clients for access to so-called 'retail' orders. While publicly saying that it was executing these orders at (or within) the best displayed prices, in reality, Citadel was providing executions at the 'best' prices, as measured by the Securities Information Processor (SIP). Citadel knew (because of its faster, direct feeds from execution venues) that better prices were often available. When Citadel's algorithms saw that a better price for the customer was available outside of the SIP, the firm just locked in both sides for an instant profit.

The Deutsche Bank and Citadel cases demonstrate that brokers may route orders in ways that best suit the brokers, not their investor-customers. Following these cases, investment advisers and their lawyers have been left with an array of questions. To date, brokers have not been subject to enforcement actions. Is that coming? If a broker routes orders to some place that consistently provides inferior executions, is it a violation of the broker's best execution obligations? How would a violation be proven? Should the broker be able to outsource its best execution obligations, and if so, what minimum level of due diligence and oversight is required? What can an investor do?

In November 2017, FINRA sent a targeted examination letter to 10 broker-dealers across various business models asking some of these questions.[19] FINRA's letter explored the conflict of interest between those brokers' order routing and their receipt of payments for order flow.[20] Then, in December

---

[18] SEC, *Order...in the Matter of Citadel Securities LLC*, 2017.   [19] FINRA, *Sample Letter*, 2017.
[20] This letter asked just three questions:

1. How does the Firm quantify the benefits, if any, to [FIRM] customers from the Firm's receipt of order routing inducements, such as payment for order flow and maker-taker rebates? Provide analytical or other evidence of such quantified benefits.

2. Describe how [FIRM] fulfills the Firm's duty of best execution and quantifies the benefits, if any, to its customers when routing orders of a particular type to a market center with transaction costs for that order type that are materially higher than the transaction costs for the same order type on other market centers.

3. Describe how [FIRM] manages the conflict of interest that exists between the Firm's duty of best execution to customers and the Firm's own financial interests in situations where the Firm routes customer orders to market centers that pay order routing inducements, such as payment for order flow and maker-taker rebates, or internalizes customer orders (e.g. routing customer orders to an affiliated over-the-counter market maker or alternative trading system in which the Firm has a financial interest).

2017, FINRA released its 2017 Examination Findings Report, which had a whole section dedicated to best execution. In that report, FINRA expressed

concerns regarding the duty of best execution at firms of all sizes that receive, handle, route or execute customer orders in equities, options and fixed income securities. FINRA found that some firms failed to implement and conduct an adequate regular and rigorous review of the quality of the executions of their customers' orders. These deficiencies included:

- failing to compare the quality of the executions firms obtained via their order routing and execution arrangements (including the internalization of order flow) against the quality of the executions they could have obtained from competing markets;

- failing to conduct reviews of certain types of orders (i.e., market, marketable limit and non-marketable limit orders); and

- failing to consider certain factors set forth in FINRA Rule 5310 when conducting a regular and rigorous review, such as speed of execution, price improvement and the likelihood of execution, among others.

As a result of such deficiencies, these firms failed to assure that order flow was directed to markets providing the most beneficial terms for their customers' orders. FINRA notes that conducting a regular and rigorous review of customer execution quality is critical to the supervision of best execution practices, particularly if a firm routes customer orders to an alternative trading system in which the firm has a financial interest or market centers that provide order routing inducements, such as payment for order flow arrangements and order routing rebates.[21]

In FINRA's annual 'Priorities Letter', the regulator further dedicated a whole section to best execution:

Best execution is an important investor protection requirement and remains a FINRA priority. In addition to the concerns identified in the Examination Findings Report, FINRA is expanding our equity best execution surveillance program to assess the degree to which firms provide price improvement when routing customer orders for execution or when executing internalized customer orders. Once the new surveillance pattern is in production, we will review systematically both the frequency of price improvement, as well as the relative amount of price improvement obtained or provided when compared to other routing or execution venues.

In addition, FINRA initiated an examination sweep in November 2017 that focuses on broker-dealers' best execution obligations when they receive order routing inducements, such as payment for order flow and maker-taker rebates, or when they internalize order flow. If a broker-dealer receives an order routing inducement, it must not let that inducement or its proprietary interests interfere with its duty of best execution. FINRA will review how broker-dealers manage the

---

[21] FINRA, *Report*, 2017.

conflict of interest that exists between their duty of best execution and their own financial interests, including whether the broker-dealers' procedures provide for a regular and rigorous evaluation of the execution quality they are likely to obtain from the market centers trading a security.

We will also expand our review of execution quality and fair pricing in fixed income securities. For example, we expect to implement surveillance patterns that focus on fair pricing and best execution in transactions in Treasury securities.[22]

In early 2018, the SEC further released its examination program priorities, which declared that the agency still 'will conduct examinations to assess whether broker-dealers have implemented best execution policies and procedures, consistent with regulatory requirements, for both municipal bond and corporate bond transactions'.[23]

Thus it appears as though, at least for the brokers, regulators in the US are beginning to enhance their best execution expectations. Unfortunately, as will be discussed below, given the current state of disclosures regarding order routing and execution, investment advisers and asset owners in the US still have both a best execution obligation and few tools with which to fulfil that obligation.

7.3 Investment Advisers' Best Execution Obligations

In the United States, courts and the SEC have found that the Investment Advisers Act of 1940 (the 'Advisers Act') imposes a fiduciary duty on advisers to act in the best interests of their clients. The anti-fraud provisions of Section 206 have been interpreted to require an investment adviser to act in utmost good faith in relation to clients, and to provide full and fair disclosure of all material facts, particularly where an adviser's interest may conflict with its client's.[24] The duty to seek best execution for clients' securities transactions flows from these fiduciary duties.

Importantly, it is unclear how investment advisers shall fulfil their best execution obligations. Substantively, the SEC has stated that investment advisers are obligated to 'execute securities transactions for clients in such a

---

[22] FINRA, *Regulatory*, 2018.   [23] SEC, 2018 *2018 National Exam Program*, 2018.

[24] See SEC v. Capital Gains Research Bureau, Inc., *375 U.S. 180*, 1963. In some circumstances, investment advisers are permitted to take actions that might otherwise be viewed as inconsistent with this fiduciary duty, provided that certain conditions are met. For example, 'Section 28(e) provides a safe harbor to money managers who use the commission dollars of their advised accounts to obtain investment research and brokerage services, provided that all of the conditions in the section are met' (SEC, *Interpretive Release*, 1986).

manner that the clients' total cost or proceeds in each transaction is the most favourable under the circumstances'.[25]

This language could mistakenly be read to suggest that the SEC would require an investment adviser to execute each trade at the lowest 'total cost' or best price for the customer. Yet such a results-based approach is simply unworkable, as it would make the investment adviser a guarantor for the actions of brokers to which it may send orders and of other market participants beyond the adviser's control.

The SEC appropriately recognizes this concern, and instead allows investment advisers to meet their obligations by having processes that are designed to obtain best execution for clients' trades, given the timing and circumstances.[26] In developing these processes, the SEC has suggested that investment advisers consider several factors, such as commission rates, brokers' trading expertise and execution capabilities, the value of research provided, and access to markets.[27]

Ultimately, however, the SEC leaves it up to investment advisers to determine how they will consider these factors and what strategies they may use to fulfil their best execution obligations. For example, there is no specific requirement that investment advisers have best execution committees, or engage in any other specific practices to meet their duty.[28]

Many investment advisers' 'best execution' practices arise out of their required disclosures. For example, Item 12 of Form ADV Part 2A requires investment advisers to '[d]escribe the factors that you consider in selecting or recommending broker-dealers for client transactions and determining the reasonableness of their compensation (e.g. commissions)'.[29] Many advisers also disclose their commitment to achieve best execution and the factors they use to select brokers to effectuate the funds' transactions.

In addition, registered investment companies, including mutual funds and closed-end funds, are required to provide statements of additional information (SAI) to supplement the information described in the fund's prospectus.[30]

---

[25] SEC, *General Information*, 2016.

[26] Ibid., citing Exchange Act Release No. 23170 (April 23, 1986).

[27] SEC, *Interpretive Release*, 1986.

[28] But see, Compliance Issues Related to Best Execution by Investment Advisers, Sec. and Exch. Comm'n, July 11, 2018, available at https://www.sec.gov/files/OCIE%20Risk%20Alert%20-%20IA%20Best%20Execution.pdf (detailing 'deficiencies' identified by examination staff) ('2018 OCIE Risk Alert').

[29] SEC, *Uniform Application*, 2017, Part 2A, Item 12.

[30] See, e.g., Selected Funds, *Statement*, 2017: 'With respect to securities transactions for the portfolios, the Adviser determines which broker to use to execute each order, consistent with its duty to seek best execution of the transaction'; see also Westport Funds, *Westport Select Cap*, 2015:

In placing orders for portfolio securities of the Funds, the Adviser is required to give primary consideration to obtaining the most favourable price and efficient execution. Within the framework of this policy, the Adviser will consider the research and investment services provided by brokers or dealers who effect, or are parties to, portfolio transactions of the Funds or the Adviser's

The SAI requires a description of the fund's brokerage allocation and other practices that may impact best execution.[31]

These factors often include price; costs; speed; likelihood of execution and settlement; size; nature; and anything else the firm deems relevant to the execution of an order. They may also include provision of research.

Advisers must also clearly disclose and adequately explain their actual and potential conflicts of interest with respect to their trading practices.[32] Trading conflicts that may impact best execution include the use of an affiliated broker on an agency or principal basis; research and/or brokerage obtained through soft-dollar arrangements; and interest in, or material business relationships with, broker-dealers, including use of brokerage to recognize sales and distribution activities of broker-dealers and their affiliates for products offered advised by the adviser or its affiliates.

While Form ADV and SAIs are typically viewed as appropriate places to make best-execution-related disclosures, these types of disclosures are also often contained in investment advisory agreements, firm brochures, other regulatory filings, firm websites, and marketing materials.[33]

Notably, since 1975, Section 28(e) of the Securities Exchange Act of 1934 has provided a safe harbour wherein, provided certain conditions are met, investment advisers will not be deemed to be acting unlawfully or in breach of their fiduciary duties (of best execution) solely on the basis that they use client commissions to pay brokers for research.[34] Thus, while there is no guidance on what steps investment advisers must take to fulfil their best execution obligations,[35] there is guidance on what does not violate it—reasonable payments for research.

other clients. Such research and investment services are those which brokerage houses customarily provide to institutional investors and include statistical and economic data and research reports on particular companies and industries. Such services are used by the Adviser in connection with all of its investment activities, and some of such services obtained in connection with the execution of transactions for the Funds may be used in managing other investment accounts. Conversely, brokers furnishing such services may be selected for the execution of transactions of such other accounts, and the services furnished by such brokers may be used by the Adviser in providing investment management for the Funds. Commission rates are established pursuant to negotiations with the broker based on the quality and quantity of execution services provided by the broker in light of generally prevailing rates. The Adviser's policy is to pay higher commissions to brokers for particular transactions than might be charged if a different broker had been selected on occasions when, in the Adviser's opinion, this policy furthers the objective of obtaining the most favourable price and execution. In addition, the Adviser is authorized to pay higher commissions on brokerage transactions for the Funds to brokers in order to secure research and investment services described above, subject to review by the Board of Trustees from time to time as to the extent and continuation of the practice. The allocation of orders among brokers and the commission rates paid are reviewed periodically by the Board of Trustees.

[31] SEC, *Registration Form*, 2017.

[32] SEC, *Speech by Lori Richards*, 2006; Centre for Financial Market Integrity, *Trade Management Guidelines*, 2002.

[33] 40 Act Lawyer, *Best Execution*, 2013.

[34] Securities Exchange Act of 1934, as amended, 15 U.S.C., § *78bb(e)*.

[35] But see, Compliance Issues Related to Best Execution by Investment Advisers, Sec. and Exch. Comm'n, July 11, 2018, available at https://www.sec.gov/files/OCIE%20Risk%20Alert%20-%20IA

7.3.1 SEC Enforcement Cases

While the SEC has aggressively pursued other types of actions against investment advisers, enforcement for best execution cases has traditionally been somewhat rare. That said, the few cases that have been brought provide critical insight into how the SEC views investment advisers' best execution responsibilities. Most notably, SEC actions have typically centred on discrepancies between how the adviser (or its fund) asserts that it selects brokers and trades versus how it actually selects them.

For example, in 2008, the SEC brought an enforcement action against Fidelity Management and Research Company ('Fidelity') for violating its best execution obligations.[36] The SEC found that Fidelity 'allowed certain employees' receipt of travel, entertainment and gifts and certain employees' family or romantic relationships to enter into the selection of brokers'.[37] Of course, Fidelity did not disclose these factors in its Form ADV or SAIs. This practice, according to the SEC, resulted in the substantial possibility of higher execution costs for Fidelity's customers, in violation of Section 206 of the Advisers Act.[38]

In 2011, the SEC brought an action against Pegasus Investment Management LLC ('Pegasus') for best execution violations.[39] According to the settlement order, Pegasus entered into an arrangement with a proprietary trading firm whereby trades of that firm were bundled with trades of funds managed by Pegasus in order to obtain reduced commission rates from an executing broker. In exchange for benefiting from the funds' trading volume, the proprietary trading firm allegedly made monthly cash payments to Pegasus. The SEC alleged that the receipt of the advisers' receipt of undisclosed payments constituted fraud. The SEC argued that Pegasus's fraud was receiving benefits that were generated by the use of fund assets and also suggested that the receipt of the rebate made it impossible for Pegasus to satisfy its best execution obligation.

More recently, in 2013, the SEC brought an action against Goelzer Investment Management ('Goelzer') for alleged discrepancies between Goelzer's statements regarding its best execution policies and its actual practices.[40] In particular, Goelzer stated that it considered a list of factors and conducted comparative brokerage firm commission rate analysis in its Form ADV, but when asked by the SEC, Goelzer was unable to provide any evidence of its analysis.

%20Best%20Execution.pdf (detailing 'deficiencies' identified by examination staff) ('2018 OCIE Risk Alert').

[36] SEC, *Order...in the Matter of Fidelity Management and Research Company*, 2008, citing to Investment Advisers Act, Section 206.

[37] Ibid., p.6.   [38] Ibid.

[39] SEC, *Order...in the Matter of Pegasus Investment Management*, 2011.

[40] SEC, *Order...in the Matter of Goelzer Investment Management*, 2013.

Collectively, while the SEC does not appear to be imposing any specific requirements on investment advisers through its enforcement powers, it is still sending a clear message that it expects advisers both to disclose material information and to 'do what you say you do'. This may be changing somewhat as a result of the SEC's examinations team's identification of 'deficiencies' in investment advisers' disclosures and practices.[41]

7.3.2 Impact of European Reforms

Regulators in the United Kingdom and European Union (UK and EU) are now at the forefront of best execution reforms.[42] And it is their work that is now shaping the best execution regulatory environment. After years of study, they have adopted new business conduct rules that are quickly changing business practices around the globe.

More than six and a half years ago, during the course of its examinations, the UK's Financial Services Authority (FSA) found that 'some firms no longer saw conflicts of interest as a key source of potential detriment to their customers' and 'had relaxed controls' below what it had felt were established market norms.[43] It began a comprehensive review, and in November 2012 released a groundbreaking report on conflicts of interests between asset managers and their customers.[44]

That report covered a broad swath of conflicts between asset managers and their customers, as well asset managers' treatment of their different customers.[45] One of the most troubling findings in that report was that the FSA found 'breaches of our detailed rules governing the use of customers' commissions and the fair allocation of trades between customers'.[46] The regulator

> found the majority of investment managers had inadequate controls and oversight
> when acquiring research goods and services from brokers or other third parties in

---

[41] See generally the 2018 OCIE Risk Alert.

[42] While less influential, Canada is developing its own best execution standards that are also worth noting. 'Best Execution' as defined under National Instrument 23-101 requires a dealer acting as agent for a client to 'ensure that the client receives the best execution price', and the NI 23-101 obligation, which applies to dealers and advisers, is to use 'reasonable efforts' to achieve best execution (IIROC, *National Instrument 23-101*, 2001). The Investment Industry Regulatory Organization of Canada (IIROC) regulates dealers. The IIROC's obligation, as set out in Rule 5.1 of the Universal Market Integrity Rules (UMIR), is to 'diligently pursue the execution of each client order on the most advantageous execution terms reasonably available under the circumstances' (IIROC, *Re-Publication*, 2016). Additional guidance is included in the UMIR policies and in Companion Policy 23-101, and UMIR Rule 7.1 requires the adoption of written policies and procedures. In Canada, best execution is subordinated to other rules, including the 'best price' rule and the order protection rule, which are designed to generally seek to ensure the execution of better-priced orders. These obligations apply to all registered dealers and advisers.

[43] FSA, *Conflicts of Interest*, 2012, p.4.   [44] Ibid.   [45] Ibid.   [46] Ibid.

return for client dealing commissions ... [and] were unable to demonstrate ... how items of research met the exemption under our rules and were in the best interests of their customers.[47]

It found that asset managers were passing through the costs of research—including so-called 'corporate access'—on to their customers without sufficiently scrutinizing and minimizing the costs to their customers.

In response to these findings, in May 2014, the Financial Conduct Authority (FCA) revised its rules to 'ensure investment managers seek to control costs passed onto their customers with as much rigour as they pursue investment returns'.[48] In July 2014, the FCA followed up the rules changes with a report on best execution and payment for order flow,[49] as well as a discussion paper on asset managers' use of commissions.[50]

In the meantime, on a parallel track, the European Commission took up and adopted significant reforms as part of the June 2014 Market in Financial Instruments Directive (MiFID) II.[51] MiFID II places a heavy emphasis on improving investor protection by introducing robust controls to avoid conflicts of interest, by encouraging greater transparency both pre- and post-execution, and by significantly reforming the use of commission dollars to pay for research (so-called unbundling).

MiFID II prohibits firms from routing orders based on inappropriate 'inducements' (also known as 'payment for order flow' or 'rebates') and explicitly requires advisers to pay for research using their own assets, specially dedicated Research Payment Accounts (RPA), or some combination of the two.

Previously, European rules required brokers and investment advisers to engage in 'all reasonable steps' to ensure best execution. Under Article 27 of MiFID II, which officially took effect on 3 January 2018, that standard was raised significantly, requiring brokers and advisers to take 'all sufficient steps to obtain ... the best possible result for their clients taking into account price, costs, speed, likelihood of execution and settlement, size, nature or any other consideration relevant to execution'. This change raised the expectation from simply having a reasonable process to having a process that actually achieves a specific result.

The new rules further require firms to have detailed specifications for selecting brokers, routing orders, and paying for research. For example, an adviser may be expected to know not only why it selected a broker, but a particular algorithm. It may also have to monitor for performance and adjust its decisions accordingly. At a minimum, this requires explicitly knowing the dollar amounts for any research that might be paid by the adviser's underlying customers. Further, to improve analysis of firms' compliance with these

---

[47] FCA, *Changes*, 2014, p.6.   [48] Ibid.   [49] FCA, *Best execution*, 2014.
[50] FCA, *Discussion*, 2014.
[51] European Parliament and Council, *Directive 2014/65/EU*, 2014.

standards, the new rules dramatically expand disclosure obligations. For example Regulatory Technical Standard (RTS) 28, which became effective in April 2018, requires firms to disclose the top five firms to which they route orders and provide summaries of the execution quality received. RTS 27, which became effective in June 2018, requires execution venues and market makers to provide quarterly execution quality reports. Collectively, these reports should provide markets participants with significantly more information about where firms route their orders, and how well they do. It should also allow firms to compare performance across firms.

The US regulatory response to the MiFID II reforms has been mixed. The SEC has offered 'clarifications' through a handful of 'no action' letters to SIFMA,[52] SIFMA AMG,[53] and ICI[54] that may be viewed as both facilitating compliance with, but also blunting the impact of, those reforms. Specifically, these 'no action' letters provide that

1. broker-dealers, on a temporary basis, may receive research payments from money managers in hard dollars or from advisory clients' research payment accounts;

2. money managers may continue to aggregate orders for mutual funds and other clients; and

3. money managers may continue to rely on an existing safe harbor when paying broker-dealers for research and brokerage.[55]

The response by market participants has been equally interesting. Some research providers have reportedly begun offering their research services in Europe at very low costs, often a fraction of what they had, until just months earlier, been paid for those same services. This will benefit the firms' investment advisory clients, particularly those who have committed to paying out of their own assets for research. On the other hand, these research providers will still expect payment. As a result, many have speculated that these firms

---

[52] SEC, *Letter from Elizabeth Miller*, 2017, granting, for 30 months, assurances that the SEC staff would not recommend action 'if a broker-dealer provides research services that constitute investment advice under section 202(a)(11) of the Advisers Act to a Manager that is required to pay for the research services by using Research Payments'.

[53] SEC, *Letter from Heather Seidel*, 2017, granting assurances the SEC staff would not recommend action 'against a money manager seeking to operate in reliance on Section 28(e) of the Exchange Act if it pays for research through the use of an RPA, as described in your letter and conforming to the requirements for RPAs in MiFID II, provided that all other applicable conditions of Section 28(e) are met'.

[54] SEC, *Letter from Aaron Gilbride*, 2017, granting assurances that the SEC staff would not recommend action 'against an investment adviser that aggregates orders for the sale or purchase of securities on behalf of its clients in reliance on the position taken in SMC Capital while accommodating the differing arrangements regarding the payment for research that will be required by MiFID II' (citing to SEC, *Letter from Karrie McMillan*, 1995).

[55] SEC, *Press Release*, 2017.

will be paid through receipt of more executions and, more disturbingly, through bundled commissions arising from trading by non-MiFID-covered customers ('cross-subsidization'). In fact, we are aware of at least one global research provider explicitly advising a US-based investment adviser of this 'cross-subsidization' payment option.

While the European regulator with primary jurisdiction, the European Securities and Markets Authority (ESMA), is exploring whether these prices are artificially low or otherwise may constitute a prohibited 'inducement' for trading, the regulator's authority and willingness to address the issue may be limited.

In the United States, following the issuance of the 'no action' relief, the Securities and Exchange Commission is expected to engage in a broad review of best execution obligations for investment advisers and brokers, as well as issues related to payment for research.

In Europe, of course, there are very detailed demands on advisers. And the regulators have already made it clear that they do not think firms operating there have been complying with their rules. In March 2017, the UK's FCA declared that it had found that firms were failing to ensure effective oversight of best execution[56] and failing to meet their expectations on use of commissions.[57] At that time, the powerful regulator explicitly threatened investigations and enforcement cases for non-compliance.

7.3.3 *Key Concerns Regarding Execution Quality for Investment Advisers*

For years, investment advisers and asset owners have worked to identify and reduce their 'execution' costs. In fact, in their quest to fulfil their fiduciary duties and respond to competitive pressures, asset owners and investment advisers are increasingly utilizing sophisticated analytical tools to evaluate trading execution performance and costs.[58] Combined with numerous regulatory and market innovations, institutional investors' explicit execution costs have fallen dramatically over the past several decades.

While numerous regulatory and technological reforms could further reduce investors' explicit trading costs, the majority of the investors are now increasingly focused—at least in US equities—on reducing their implicit trading costs (such as opportunity costs). Explicit execution costs may now be just fractions of these more difficult to quantify implicit trading costs.

To best identify, quantify, and reduce these implicit trading costs, asset owners and investment advisers will need more and better information, including detailed information about how their orders are routed and

---

[56] FCA, *Investment Managers*, 2017.   [57] FCA, *Firms Continue*, 2017.
[58] Healthy Markets Association, *Better Best Execution*, 2017.

executed. In the US, the SEC has proposed to help provide investors with some of this important information,[59] which will further empower investment advisers to fulfil their best execution duties.[60]

But these efforts address only part of the asset owners' overall costs. In fact, while the relative portion of the 'bundled' rate that is attributed to trade execution has fallen, the remaining 'research' portion has increased. Unfortunately, in this area, market forces and regulatory reforms have not kept pace.

While the costs for investment research have historically been borne by the asset owner, there has often been very little to protect them from overpaying for the research. At a very basic level, for example, there is no requirement in the US that the research even benefit the fund whose assets are being used to pay for it.

For example, assume that an investment adviser manages two funds: one small and mid-cap fund and a separate mid-cap fund. The adviser consumes extensive third-party research for its small and mid-cap fund, but does not for its mid-cap fund. However, its small and mid-cap fund does not trade in significant volumes. In this scenario, it would be common for the adviser to pay for that research by sending bundled trades to the broker/research provider for the pure mid-cap fund. In this case, the adviser has made the decision to directly use the assets of the mid-cap fund (i.e. its investors) to pay for expenses incurred to benefit the small and mid-cap fund. These could be entirely different investors.

Similarly, while the payments must be 'reasonable', there is also no regulatory requirement that the amounts of payments be tied to the value of the research provided. For example, assume an investment adviser had a $2 billion fund that traded 50 million shares in 2015. Assume further that the fund received equal research and trading execution services from 10 brokers (i.e. each provided equivalent research and traded 5 million shares). All of the shares were traded at commission rates of 4 cents a share, with half attributed to the executions and half for the research. All of the $2 million in bundled commissions is paid from the fund, with $1 million being paid for the executions and the rest for the research.

Then, in 2016, the firm got a new portfolio manager who decided to trade 100 million shares. The adviser received exactly the same amount of research from the same 10 brokers, and paid exactly the same bundled commission

---

[59] SEC, *Regulation*, 2016.

[60] Not only has Healthy Markets offered comments to improve those proposals, we have also provided market participants with copies of the Healthy Markets ATS Questionnaire™ and the separate Healthy Markets Order Routing Questionnaire, each of which is designed to assist firms with their due diligence efforts. Current versions of these questionnaires are available at https://www.healthymarkets.org/ats-questionnaire2017/ats-questionnaire and https://www.healthymarkets.org/orderrouting-questionnaire/, respectively.

rate of 4 cents per share. Only this time, the fund paid $4 million in bundled commissions, with $2 million attributed to executions and the other $2 million for research. While the increased cost attributed to the increased trading makes sense (brokers should be paid for their work), the increased payment for the research does not. In this case, just because the fund traded more, the brokers got paid $1 million more than they had the year before for the same volume and quality of research. Asset owners are increasingly arguing that they should not bear that arguably inflated cost.

This type of arrangement, where brokers are paid for research in amounts that are dependent upon the volume of trading by the adviser—as opposed to the true value of the actual research provided—has been historically prevalent in the US.[61]

Similarly, commissions in some products (or in securities outside of the United States) may be based on the underlying market value of the underlying trade. In these instances, changes in the market values of those financial products could dramatically impact the commission amounts attributed to trades. For example, as European market prices have risen in 2017, payments for research for some asset owners have risen commensurately. Again, asset owners and regulators may question the appropriateness of having the compensation to research providers change merely because of changes in the value of the underlying transactions.

There are also significant concerns about what is actually categorized as 'research.' For example, in the United States, a broker providing 'access' to corporate executives is considered 'research', while this is not the case in the UK.[62] Assume a US-based investment adviser is introduced to an executive team of a Chinese technology company by a broker-dealer. That adviser could, under existing US rules, 'pay' that broker-dealer for that 'research' by directing trades from a purely US-based fund. Again, the US customers could be subsidizing other customers for the adviser.

At the same time, the bundling of research and execution payments has had a dramatic impact on research providers and investment advisers. Some large research providers have traditionally required investment advisers to pay for that research by sending them orders for execution. This benefits the research providers with increased trading volumes.

---

[61] In many instances, firms will engage in a voting practice wherein traders and portfolio managers will rank and weight brokers for research and execution values based on objective and subjective criteria, and then attempt to 'direct' their overall trading activities (and 'commission wallet') to those brokers in those ratios.

[62] When explicitly denying 'corporate access' as a permissible use of client funds, the Financial Conduct Authority found '[n]one of the investment managers we visited could justify to us how Corporate Access met the evidential criteria for research under our rules to allow them to pay for it with dealing commissions'. See FCA, *Changes*, 2014.

(a) Price improvement percentage

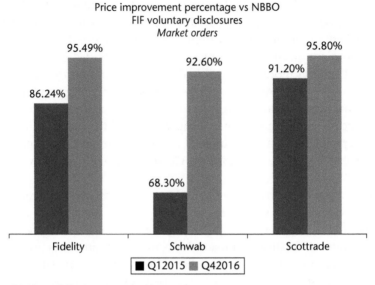

(b) Share dollar improvement

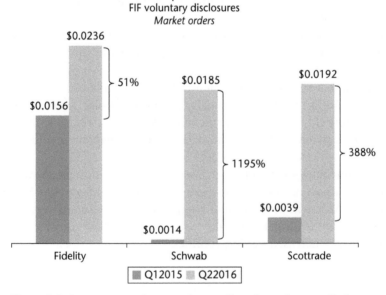

Figure 7.1. Improvement in execution quality after voluntary disclosure

Unfortunately, this insistence forces investment advisers and asset owners to choose between getting the research they need and the ability to shop for likely higher-quality or lower-cost executions. This poses significant challenges to investment advisers seeking to fulfil their best execution obligations.

Not surprisingly, regulators, investors, and some investment advisers have asserted that paying for research with commission dollars could give rise to conflicts of interest and higher costs for investors. Nevertheless, soft dollar payments for research are still a crucial part of many US investment advisers'— and research providers'—businesses. At the same time, with the advent of MiFID II, the practice is rapidly disappearing in Europe.

7.3.4 Self-Help: Importance of Order Routing and Execution Disclosures

Aside from their substantive requirements, regulators on both sides of the Atlantic Ocean have placed a heavy emphasis on improving order routing and execution quality disclosures. In the United States, the SEC and FINRA have been engaged in updating order routing and execution disclosures for brokers and dark pools. And MiFID II will impose dramatically enhanced disclosures as well. Unfortunately, these reforms are not yet fully implemented.

That said, there is reason to believe that these disclosures will be powerfully effective tools for modifying behaviour. For example, in 2015 an industry consortium known as the Financial Information Forum (FIF) pursued a voluntary disclosure programme to help fill the gap of the outdated rule set and aid investors with an apples-to-apples comparison of a broker's routing. Odd lot trades (trades for under 100 shares) were not included in the original SEC Rules, but were adopted by FIF. Several brokers signed up in an effort to promote transparency in their practices, and the results of the voluntary disclosure were quite stunning. As Figures 7.1(a) and (b) show, execution quality improved dramatically among firms for odd lot trades. As measured by the National Best Bid and Offer price for US Stocks, some firms witnessed a 24-basis-point increase in price improvement. Moreover, the actual dollar amount of improvements provided to trades increased substantially, in some cases by more than 1100 per cent. Thus, in the case of transparency and disclosure, positive order-routing behavioural change can occur, reducing the need for overbearing regulation.

7.4 Investment Advisers' Best Execution Strategies

Over the years, investment advisers have developed a multitude of policies, procedures, and practices designed to demonstrate their reasonable efforts to achieve best execution, including establishing and maintaining best execution committees; measuring and regularly reviewing execution quality; regularly evaluating broker performance and selection; quantifying the value of research and reviewing commission-sharing agreements; and periodically reviewing policies, procedures, and practices.

These strategies are evolving rapidly with the advent of the MiFID II reforms, which are causing firms around the world—even those that are not directly affected—to revise their policies, procedures, and practices in fundamental ways. This cross-border impact is being driven by US and European customers who are demanding consistent policies and practices, as well as by global investment advisers looking to simplify compliance regimes for order routing and execution, as well as research provision, valuation, and payment.

7.4.1 *Best Execution Committees*

Investment advisers typically establish best execution committees,[63] which are often the heart of an investment adviser's efforts to satisfy its best execution obligations. These committees are generally staffed by individuals with relevant trading, legal, and compliance backgrounds. Best execution committees assume a variety of tasks. They maintain, and periodically review and revise, the firm's overall trade management policies and procedures (including best execution policies, the development of 'approved' brokers lists, and broker selection guidelines); they assess relevant industry, regulatory, and technological changes that may impact trade execution; they review the firm's broker selection, trading performance, and execution quality; they oversee internal or third-party service providers with analyses of the firm's broker selection, trading performance and execution quality; and they regularly review research payments and usage, as well as other commission sharing relationships.

Most Best Execution Committees appear to meet on at least a quarterly basis, with additional meetings, calls, or reviews conducted throughout the year on specific issues that may arise, such as a regulatory settlement by a broker service provider. When issues arise regarding an investment adviser's compliance with its best execution obligations, the best execution committee's work will likely be a key point in the inquiry. Accordingly, many investment advisers prepare detailed information packets for committee meetings and formal meeting minutes. Effective best execution committees often follow the procedures laid out within Form ADV, and play an active role in evaluating trading performance and broker selection.

---

[63] Centre for Financial Market Integrity, *Trade Management Guidelines*, 2002.

7.4.2 *Measuring and Reviewing Execution Quality*

Investment advisers periodically evaluate the range and quality of brokerage services that they receive from their broker-dealer service providers. In assessing execution quality, advisers typically focus on three often interrelated questions. First, are the full costs incurred by clients (including market impact, opportunity costs, spreads, and commissions), based on post-trade analyses of client order execution, consistent with my duty to seek best execution? Second, are my policies, procedures, and practices sufficient to ensure compliance with my best execution obligations? And, third, are my disclosures regarding my practices for placing orders, selecting brokers, and monitoring trading performance accurate?[64]

An investment adviser may conduct its trade evaluation process in-house or it may outsource some or all of the process to a third-party service provider. The SEC has recognized that advancements in technology and the availability of third-party assistance has the potential to greatly assist advisers in evaluating a broker's execution and in fulfilling their best execution obligation; therefore, investment advisers may have an obligation to pursue such technological or third-party assistance if it would improve their evaluation of execution quality.[65]

Many advisers have determined that in order to fulfil their best execution obligations, they need to engage in increasingly sophisticated transaction cost analysis (TCA). As trading commissions have fallen significantly in recent years,[66] implementation costs for large block trades may dwarf the commissions paid to brokers, as shown in Figure 7.2.[67] As this shift has occurred, so has investment advisers' focus on their true and total costs of trading.

Trade analytics is now a key tool for investment advisers seeking to drive down total trading costs. With the ability to capture orders, messages, and executions down to the millisecond level and compare the market data to an investor's trades also provided at the millisecond level, a new level of

---

[64] See Appendix J—Selected Staff Reports and Other Publications of the SEC, in: Anderson et al., *Investment Advisers*, 2002.

[65] SEC, *Market 2000*, 1994.

[66] Since fixed minimum commissions were prohibited in 1975, commission costs have generally been on a long decline towards zero. This decline accelerated with the advent of competition for executions, the 'unbundling' of commissions and research payments, and increases in technology-driven trading opportunities. See, generally, Dolgopolov, 'Insider trading', 2008.

[67] Meaningful trading analytics is significantly limited by the availability of comprehensive data. This block trading data, obtained from ITG, Inc., is referenced here to be illustrative of the relative weights of commissions versus other costs of trading. One of the greatest contributions regulators and market participants could make to improve fairness and transparency in the market would be to improve the collection and publication of meaningful order and execution statistics.

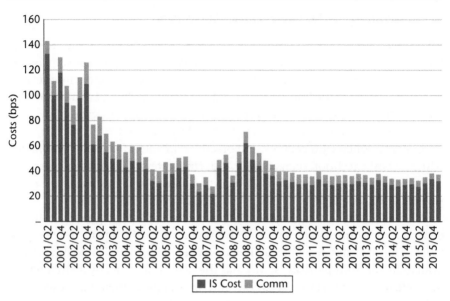

Figure 7.2. Implementation shortfall and commission costs (source: Investment Technology Group)

measurement is now possible. As timelines become more precise, many investment advisers are now increasingly looking to quantitatively evaluate the performance of the brokers they use and the venues where they trade. According to a survey of buy-side trades by Greenwich Associates, a leading research firm, over three-quarters of all equity traders indicated that they used TCA as part of their investment process.[68]

Trade analytics has also evolved to encompass other asset classes such as fixed income, foreign exchange, options, and futures. Each of these asset classes has been subject to regulatory efforts and market evolutions that attempt to improve transparency and visibility into broker behaviour and transaction costs. For example, FINRA and the Municipal Securities Rulemaking Board recently proposed disclosures of markups and markdowns in fixed income trading. And the US Congress and the SEC have been considering these improvements for a few years.[69] Fully automated fixed income trading is now here, as are numerous trading venue options.[70] As these other markets evolve to have greater transparency, we may expect regulators to ratchet up their expectations, as they have with the equities markets.

---

[68] Greenwich Associates, *U.S. Equities*, 2016.

[69] US Congress—Senate—Committee on Banking, Housing, and Urban Affairs, *Bond Transparency Act, 2014*. See also SEC, *Speech by Commissioner Michael S. Piwowar*, 2014.

[70] For example, in September, 2015, Liquidnet began operating an ATS for fixed income trading. See Liquidnet, *Liquidnet Launches*, 2015.

To perform modern TCA, advisers and asset owners look at not just commission rates and other explicit costs, but also implementation costs. Many firms believe that in order to do this effectively, they need details regarding the handling of their own orders, but they also need a comprehensive view of the marketplace within which that order routing occurs.[71]

To obtain some basic quantitative metrics, such as price and commission rates, many advisers request periodic trading reports from their brokers that show such things as commissions charged, transactions executed, and failed trades. However, these reports can also be far more detailed, examining trading performance across brokers and execution venues by effective spread, realized spread (over various timescales to demonstrate toxicity), implementation shortfall, and other cost metrics.[72]

Many investment advisers also use broker-provided tools to analyse trades in an interactive fashion, analysing performance and other metrics cross-sectionally. For example, an investment adviser could use a TCA tool to compare actual executed prices to various benchmarks, including volume-weighted average price, opportunity cost implementation shortfall, performance, open or close price, and other customer benchmarks. The most common metric would typically measure the actual executed transaction price versus the national best bid and offer at the time an order was submitted. They could do this kind of analysis on different security subsets, such as average daily volume, market cap, or sector. Sophisticated TCA tools can also break down commissions per share, market impact of trades, the costs of any delay when the trader placed the trade, and the overall trends in a firm's executions.

A 2016 survey from Greenwich associates found that over 78 per cent of large buy-side firms utilize TCA across asset classes.[73] But the ability to perform TCA varies significantly across asset classes. In equities, TCA is far more advanced than in other asset classes due to the availability of quote, trade,

---

[71] We note that many third-party TCA providers and broker-offered TCA products still rely upon the SIP data feeds for execution quality analysis. Given the known latencies between the private data feeds and the SIP feeds, as well as the known exploitation of those latencies by some market participants, we worry that these tools provide an incomplete, and a potentially misleading, view of a firm's true execution quality.

[72] Modern trade analytics can be traced back as far as 1972, when a landmark study attempted to measure the impact of block trades by comparing the prices after the block print went up (Kraus and Stoll, 'Price impact', 1972). By the end of 1988, the volume weighted average price (VWAP) was being used to show that the total cost of a trade was 23 basis points, even though the commissions were just 18 (Berkowitz et al., 'Total cost', 1988). Over time, investment advisers started to poke holes in the all-day VWAP, questioning its validity as a way to measure their trading costs. The reasoning was simple: a portfolio manager may not have sent the order to their trading desk until 11:00 a.m., so measuring the desk against the full-day VWAP did not seem terribly accurate. With the advent of timestamps, firms began to think of their trading costs against other benchmarks, such as Available VWAP (AVWAP), Interval VWAP (IVWAP), and Implementation Shortfall (IS). See Wagner, *Complete Guide*, 1989.

[73] Greenwich Associates, *U.S. Equities*, 2016.

and depth-of-book-level data, and more specifically microsecond-level resolution. In other asset classes (such as fixed income), the lack of this level of data makes useful TCA exceedingly difficult. Still, with the introduction of mandatory fixed income trade reporting by FINRA,[74] fixed income analysis (excluding treasuries) is becoming more commonplace. Derivatives present different issues unique to their markets, such as when an asset is traded on only a single execution venue. That said, they may allow for the examination of price slippage and implementation shortfall. Foreign exchange lacks virtually any transparency necessary to perform detailed, useful analytics (such as market-wide quote data), although some firms are increasingly offering to provide this type of analysis based on proprietary and limited datasets.[75]

Because of the importance of the information and the lack of standards and consistency in its provision, in July 2016, the SEC proposed additional disclosures by broker-dealers to customers about the routing of their orders.[76] The proposed enhancements aim to modernize many of the quantitative metrics, but also to incorporate broker-dealer institutionally based disclosure of execution quality. In the proposing release, the SEC noted that investment advisers have a compelling interest to monitor the order handling methods of their executing brokers in helping them quantify best execution.[77] If adopted, these reforms would mandate that information be made available to advisers upon request. This information would become an integral tool for advisers seeking to fulfil their best execution obligations.

Similarly, in Europe, MiFID II will be requiring markedly more detailed disclosures regarding order routing practices and policies and procedures for best execution for covered firms. These disclosures will likewise provide significant inputs for firms' best execution analyses, particularly their evaluations of broker performance and selection.

7.4.3 *Regular Evaluation of Broker Performance and Selection*

Investment advisers regularly evaluate brokers and many also evaluate venues to which their orders are routed. Many investment advisers conduct these reviews on at least a quarterly basis, although monthly reviews are also common. Part of this practice is to respond to a disclosure obligation. Item 12 (Brokerage Practices) of form ADV Part 2A requires investment advisers to describe the factors considered in selecting brokers and determining the reasonableness of their commissions. It further requires investment advisers to

---

[74] FINRA obligates broker-dealers to report corporate bond and Treasury transactions using its Trader Reporting and Compliance Engine (TRACE). For more information about TRACE reporting, consult the online resource FINRA, *Trade Reporting*, 2018.
[75] Mercer, *Press Release*, 2015.   [76] SEC, *Disclosure*, 2016.   [77] Ibid.

describe any arrangement in which the investment adviser is paid cash or receives some economic benefit.

To assist in their reviews, investment advisers increasingly utilize interviews and questionnaires with their brokers and/or execution venues.[78] Many investment advisers create scorecards based on various qualitative and quantitative measures. This information is typically evaluated in conjunction with the TCA performed by the firm or the firm's third-party provider. While the exact factors that an adviser will utilize may differ from firm to firm, frequently used elements are

- material differences in execution quality, including such metrics as VWAP, TWAP, price improvement, price disimprovement, implementation shortfall, realized spread, and effective spread;
- pricing feeds utilized (e.g. SIP or market centres' direct feeds);
- speed and average size of execution;
- passive order performance and likelihood of execution;
- explicit transaction and commission costs;
- breadth and depth of reach, including algorithmic routing capabilities, order-type availability, and access to various pools of liquidity;
- the existence of conflicts of interest, such as broker-owned trading desks interacting with broker-owned dark pools;
- venue performance related to system availability and capacity;
- information leakage risks;
- past or current regulatory issues and disciplinary actions;
- transparent operating procedures such as order handling procedures and order execution algorithms;
- performance during strenuous market conditions;
- performance during times of peak trading, such as at the market open and close.

The above list represents some of the basic elements found in scorecards but is not an all-inclusive list. Some firms have developed and even patented their own scorecards for evaluations.[79]

---

[78] Healthy Markets has created the Healthy Markets ATS Questionnaire™ to assist investment advisers and routing brokers with evaluation of Alternative Trading Systems (ATSs). This questionnaire is available on the Healthy Markets website at http://www.healthymarkets.org/ats-questionnaire.

[79] Scottrade for example was issued patent 7,698,200 *Method and system for evaluation of market centers for security trading performance* to scorecard its venues. Credit Suisse also developed the AES Alpha Scorecard to aid the counterparty with its ability to identify venue toxicity and allows clients to determine counterparties based off of the scorecard results.

Increasingly, investment advisers may also review execution venues as well.[80] These reviews often differ according to the type of venue in question. For example, a review of one ATS may differ in nature from a review of an exchange or an ATS with a different trading model. While this venue-level analysis for best execution is required for brokers, this level of analysis by investment advisers is in its early stages.

In particular, recent regulatory enforcement cases against ATSs have prompted many investment advisers and routing brokers to send them comprehensive questionnaires. These questionnaires may cover technology, order flow characteristics, client characteristics, execution quality, relationships with affiliates and third parties, order routing practices, conflicts of interest, and other potentially relevant information.[81] The information gathered from such questionnaires and due diligence is often incorporated into the investment adviser's regular and rigorous review of best execution. And investment advisers are learning from this new analysis. In fact, a 2016 survey of buy-side traders found that 45 per cent of traders who used venue-level analysis had changed their order routing practices based upon their findings.[82]

Even further, investment advisers are increasingly evaluating prospective brokers and venues to whom they do not route orders. While it may impractical to evaluate the universe of brokers and venues available on a monthly or quarterly basis, some investment advisers conduct various levels of due diligence for these unused but potentially usable brokers and venues.[83] Investment advisers appear to be increasingly conducting reviews and scorecarding of current and alternative brokers and venues.

7.4.4 Quantifying the Value of Research and Reviewing Commission Sharing Agreements

Many investment advisers frequently review the value of the research they receive and their payments for research to help ensure that they continue to stay within the safe harbour outlined by Section 28(e). However, qualifying for Section 28(e) is significantly different from what is expected in the UK,

---

[80] Greenwich Associates, *U.S. Equities*, 2016.
[81] Healthy Markets Association has developed and publicly distributes its ATS Questionnaire™ to parties upon request. Please see the Healthy Markets website at http://www.healthymarkets.org/ats-questionnaire.
[82] Greenwich Associates, *U.S. Equities*, 2016.
[83] Notably, brokers are obligated to do so. Evaluating prospective venues is a critical component of a broker's regular and rigorous review, which FINRA recently reaffirmed. See FINRA, *Best Execution: Guidance*, 2015, p.5: 'a firm should regularly consider execution quality at venues to which it is not connected and assess whether it should connect to such venues'.

where regulators demand that asset managers should explicitly quantify the value of research they consume, decouple the amount paid for research from the volume of the trade, and ensure that the fund paying for research is the beneficiary of such research. All of these principles are directly embedded in MiFID II. To date, the SEC has not explicitly required any of these concepts as part of compliance with the Section 28(e) safe harbour.

That said, in efforts to bridge the regulatory gap, many US investment advisers are increasingly engaging in 'best practices' that include identifying and determining the explicit values of executions and research, separately; establishing research payment mechanisms that can comply with both MiFID II and Section 28(e) obligations;[84] creating research payment strategies that decouple the amount paid for research from trading volumes;[85] evaluating trading decisions and adjusting routing decisions based upon increasingly sophisticated analyses; and dramatically revising their disclosures of best execution and order routing practices. While the full impacts are not yet known, we expect that the development of these practices will lead to a convergence of 'best practices' that is remarkably similar to the expectations of MiFID II.

7.5 Conclusion

Over the past several years, investment advisers have received little guidance from the SEC as to what is expected from them for best execution. At the same time, European regulators have dramatically expanded their expectations for investment advisers and both FINRA and the SEC have dramatically expanded best execution obligations for brokers. Given the seriousness of these concerns, we expect regulators on both sides of the Atlantic to continue offering much greater clarity on the expectations for investment advisers over then next few years. The SEC staff's 2018 OCIE Risk Alert and the reported investigations by UK authorities are likely just the first few steps in what could be a long and messy process. Best execution is a process, after all.

---

[84] For example, many large US-based investment advisers declared in the months leading up to the implementation date for MiFID II that they would directly pay for research for their MiFID II-covered customers. See Flood, 'BlackRock', 2017, and also Thompson, 'T Rowe Price', 2017. In Europe, those costs are borne by the investment advisers or the advisers' other customers, while in the US, asset owners will likely continue to absorb those costs directly—in addition to having their advisers being denied the opportunity to shop for better execution quality.

[85] This can be done by setting research budgets in advance, on a portfolio level or customer level, and by using commissions to pay for research, ensuring that executions with the provider thereafter may be at 'execution only' rates or reimbursed by the adviser.

References

40 Act Lawyer. *Best Execution: Legal and Practical Considerations for Investment Advisers and Funds*. Available at: http://www.40actlawyer.com/wp-content/uploads/2017/01/4b-best-ex7-15-13.pdf, 2013.

Anderson, James E., Marianne K. Smythe, and Robert G. Bagnall. *Investment Advisers: Law and Compliance*. 2nd edn. LexisNexis, 2002.

Attorney General of the State of New York—Investor Protection Bureau. *Settlement Agreement in the Matter of Deutsche Bank Securities Inc., Dec. 16*. Available at: https://ag.ny.gov/sites/default/files/2016.12.15_db_settlement_agreement.pdf, 2016.

Berkowitz, Stephen A., Dennis E. Logue, and Eugene A. Noser, Jr. 'The total cost of transactions on the NYSE'. *Journal of Finance* 43, no. 1 (1988): 97–112.

Centre for Financial Market Integrity. *Trade Management Guidelines*. Available at: http://www.cfapubs.org/doi/pdf/10.2469/ccb.v2004.n3.4007, 2002.

Dolgopolov, Stanislov. 'Insider trading, Chinese walls, and brokerage commissions: The origins of modern regulation of information flows in securities markets'. *Journal of Law, Economics and Policy* 4, no. 2 (2008): 311–68.

European Parliament and Council of the European Union. *Directive 2014/65/EU of the European Parliament and of the Council of 15 May 2014 on markets in financial instruments and amending Directive 2002/92/EC and Directive 2011/61/EU Text with EEA relevance*. EU Official Journal. Available at: https://eur-lex.europa.eu/legal-content/EN/TXT/?uri=celex:32014L0065, 2014.

FCA (Financial Conduct Authority). *Best Execution and Payment for Order Flow (TR14/13)*. Available at: https://www.fca.org.uk/publications/thematic-reviews/tr14-13-best-execution-and-payment-order-flow, 2014.

FCA. *Changes to the Use of Dealing Commission Rules: Feedback to CP13/17 and Final Rules (PS14/7)*. Available at: https://www.fca.org.uk/publication/policy/ps14-07.pdf, 2014.

FCA. *Discussion on the Use of Dealing Commission Regime: Feedback on our Thematic Supervisory Review and Policy Debate on the Market for Research (DP14/3)*. Available at: https://www.fca.org.uk/publication/discussion/dp14-03.pdf, 2014.

FCA. *Firms Continue to Fail to Meet our Expectations on their Use of Dealing Commission*. Available at: https://www.fca.org.uk/publications/multi-firm-reviews/firms-fail-meet-expectations-use-dealing-commission, 2017.

FCA. *Investment Managers Still Failing to Ensure Effective Oversight of Best Execution*. Available at: https://www.fca.org.uk/publications/multi-firm-reviews/investment-managers-failing-ensure-effective-oversight, 2017.

FINRA (Financial Industry Regulatory Authority). *Best Execution: Guidance on Best Execution Obligations in Equity, Options, and Fixed Income Markets*. Available at: https://www.finra.org/sites/default/files/notice_doc_file_ref/Notice_Regulatory_15-46.pdf. Regulatory Notice 15-46, 2015.

FINRA. *Best Execution: NASD Regulation Reiterates Member Firm Best Execution Obligations And Provides Guidance To Members Concerning Compliance*. Available at: http://www.finra.org/sites/default/files/NoticeDocument/p003889.pdf. Regulatory Notice 01-22, 2001.

FINRA. *Regulatory and Examination Priorities Letter*. Available at: http://www.finra.org/industry/2018-regulatory-and-examination-priorities-letter, 2018.

FINRA. *Report on FINRA Examination Findings*. Available at: http://www.finra.org/sites/default/files/2017-Report-FINRA-Examination-Findings.pdf, 2017.

FINRA. *Rule 2121: Fair Prices and Commissions*. Available at: http://finra.complinet.com/en/display/display.html?rbid=2403&element_id=11539, 2014.

FINRA. *Rule 5310: Best Execution and Interpositioning*. Available at: http://finra.com plinet.com/en/display/display_main.html?rbid=2403&element_id=10455, 2014.

FINRA. *Sample Letter Regarding Order Routing Conflicts*. Available at: http://www.finra.org/industry/order-routing-conflicts, 2017.

FINRA. *Trade Reporting and Compliance Engine (TRACE)*. Available at: http://www.finra.org/industry/trace, 2018.

Flood, Chris. 'BlackRock to foot bill for external research under Mifid II'. *Financial Times*. Available at: https://www.ft.com/content/fb9e2552-9939-11e7-a652-cde3f882dd7b, 14 September 2017.

FSA (Financial Services Authority). *Conflicts of Interest between Asset Managers and their Customers: Identifying and Mitigating the Risks*. Available at: http://www.fsa.gov.uk/static/pubs/other/conflicts-of-interest.pdf, 2012.

Greenwich Associates. *U.S. Equities: Venue Analysis Drives Next Generation TCA*. Available at: https://www.greenwich.com/equities/us-equities-venue-analysis-drives-next-generation-tca, 2016.

Healthy Markets Association. *Better Best Execution: A Guide for Investment Advisers*. Available at: https://www.healthymarkets.org/better-best-execution-report, 2017.

IIROC (Investment Industry Regulatory Organization of Canada). *National Instrument 23–101, Trading Rules*. Available at: http://www.iiroc.ca/industry/Documents/NationalInstrument23101_en.pdf, 2001.

IIROC. *Re-publication of Proposed Provisions Respecting Best Execution to the Universal Market Integrity Rules (UMIR) and the Dealer Member Rules (DMR)*. Available at: http://www.iiroc.ca/Documents/2016/e7ad75f1-5c59-4924-bfdb-e84ac618b64b_en.pdf, 2016.

Kraus, Alan, and Hans R. Stoll. 'Price impact of block trading on the NYSE'. *Journal of Finance* 27, no. 3 (1972): 569–88.

Liquidnet. *Liquidnet Launches Fixed Income Dark Pool to Centralize Institutional Trading of Corporate Bonds*. Available at: http://www.liquidnet.com/#/news/liquidnet-launches-fixed-income-dark-pool-to-centralize-institutional-tradi/, 2015.

Mercer. *Press Release: Mercer Enhances FX Trading Analytics Capability through Agreement with Abel Noser Solution*. Available at: https://www.uk.mercer.com/newsroom/Mercer-enhances-FX-trading-analytics.html, 2015.

SEC (US Securities and Exchange Commission). *2018 National Exam Program Examination Priorities*. Available at: https://www.sec.gov/about/offices/ocie/national-examination-program-priorities-2018.pdf, 2018.

SEC. *Disclosure of Order Handling Information*. 81 Fed. Reg. 49431. Available at: https://www.federalregister.gov/documents/2016/07/27/2016-16967/disclosure-of-order-handling-information. Release No. 34-78309; File No. S7-14-16, 2016.

SEC. *General Information on the Regulation of Investment Advisers*. Available at: https://www.sec.gov/divisions/investment/iaregulation/memoia.htm, 2016.

SEC. *Interpretive Release Concerning the Scope of Section 28(e) of the Securities Exchange Act of 1934 and Related Matters.* Available at: https://www.sec.gov/rules/interp/34-23170. pdf. Release No. 34-23170, 1986.

SEC. *Letter from Aaron Gilbride, SEC, to Dorothy Donohue, ICI.* Available at: https://www. sec.gov/divisions/investment/noaction/2017/ici-102617-17d1.htm, 26 October 2017.

SEC. *Letter from Elizabeth Miller, SEC, to Steve Stone, Morgan Lewis (on behalf of SIFMA).* Available at: https://www.sec.gov/divisions/investment/noaction/2017/sifma-102617-202a.htm, 26 October 2017.

SEC. *Letter from Heather Seidel, SEC, to Timothy W. Cameron and Lindsey Weber Keljo, SIFMA AMG.* Available at: https://www.sec.gov/divisions/marketreg/mr-noaction/2017/sifma-amg-102617-28e.pdf, 26 October 2017.

SEC. *Letter from Karrie McMillan, SEC, to SMC Capital, Inc.* Available at: https://www.sec.gov/divisions/investment/noaction/smccapital090595.htm, 5 September 1995.

SEC. *Market 2000: An Examination of Current Equity Market Developments, V-3.* Available at: https://www.sec.gov/divisions/marketreg/market2000.pdf. Division of Market Regulation, 1994.

SEC. *Meeting of the Equity Market Structure Advisory Committee to the Securities and Exchange Commission, Apr. 5,* 2017.

SEC. *Order Execution Obligations.* Available at: https://www.sec.gov/news/digest/1996/dig090996.pdf. Release No. 34-37619A, File No. S7-30-95, 1996.

SEC. *Order Instituting Administrative and Cease-and-Desist Proceedings . . . and Imposing Remedial Sanctions and a Cease-and-Desist Order—In the Matter of Citadel Securities LLC.* Available at: https://www.sec.gov/litigation/admin/2017/33-10280.pdf. Securities Act of 1933 Release No. 10280, 2017.

SEC. *Order Instituting Administrative and Cease-and-Desist Proceedings . . . and Imposing Remedial Sanctions and a Cease-and-Desist Order—In the Matter of Deutsche Bank Securities Inc.* Available at: https://www.sec.gov/litigation/admin/2016/33-10272.pdf. Securities Act of 1933 Release No. 10272, 2016.

SEC. *Order Instituting Administrative and Cease-and-Desist Proceedings, Making Findings and Imposing Remedial Sanctions and a Cease-and-Desist Order . . . in the Matter of Fidelity Management and Research Company, and FMR Co., Inc.* Available at: https://www.sec.gov/litigation/admin/2008/ia-2713.pdf. Investment Advisers Act of 1940, Release No. 2713, 2008.

SEC. *Order Instituting Administrative and Cease-and-Desist Proceedings, . . . Making Findings and Imposing Remedial Sanctions and a Cease-and-Desist Order in the Matter of Goelzer Investment Management, Inc. and Gregory W. Goelzer.* Available at: https://www.sec.gov/litigation/admin/2013/34-70083.pdf. Investment Advisers Act of 1934, Release No. 70083, 2013.

SEC. *Order Instituting Administrative and Cease-and-Desist Proceedings, . . . Making Findings and Imposing Remedial Sanctions and Cease-and-Desist Orders in the Matter of Pegasus Investment Management, LLC, Peter Benjamin Bortel, and Douglas Wayne Saksa.* Available at: https://www.sec.gov/litigation/admin/2011/ia-3215.pdf. Investment Advisers Act of 1940, Release No. 3215, 2011.

SEC. *Press Release, SEC Announces Measures to Facilitate Cross-Border Implementation of the European Union's MiFID II's Research Provisions.* Available at: https://www.sec.

gov/divisions/investment/noaction/smccapital090595.htm. https://www.sec.gov/news/press-release/2017-200-0, 2017.

SEC. *Registration Form for Open-End Management Companies—Form N-1A*. Available at: https://www.sec.gov/files/formn-1a.pdf, 2017.

SEC. *Regulation of NMS Stock Alternative Trading Systems*. 80 Fed. Reg. 80998. Available at: https://www.gpo.gov/fdsys/pkg/FR-2015-12-28/pdf/2015-29890.pdf. Release No. 34–76474; File No. S7–23–15, 2015.

SEC. *Speech by Commissioner Michael S. Piwowar: Advancing and Defending the SEC's Core Mission*. Available at: https://www.sec.gov/news/speech/2014-spch012714msp. US Chamber of Commerce, Washington DC 2014.

SEC. *Speech by Lori Richards, Director, Office of Compliance Inspections and Examinations: Fiduciary Duty: Return to First Principles*. Available at: https://www.sec.gov/news/speech/spch022706lar.htm. Eighth Annual Investment Adviser Compliance Summit, 27 February 2006.

SEC. *Uniform Application for Investment Adviser Registration—Form ADV*. Available at: https://www.sec.gov/about/forms/formadv.pdf, 2017.

Securities Exchange Act of 1934, as amended, 15 U.S.C. § *78bb(e)*.

SEC v. Capital Gains Research Bureau, Inc. *375 U.S. 180*. Available at: https://supreme.justia.com/cases/federal/us/375/180/case.html, 1963.

Selected Funds. *Statement of Additional Information—SAI*. Available at: http://selectedfunds.com/downloads/SFSAI.pdf, 2017.

Thompson, Jennifer. 'T Rowe Price to absorb Mifid II research costs'. *Financial Times*. Available at: https://www.ft.com/content/46fff37d-d422-34db-ab41-fb83258f5e4a, 21 August 2017.

US Congress—Senate—Committee on Banking, Housing, and Urban Affairs. *Bond Transparency Act of 2014 (S.2114)*. 113th Cong. 2014.

Van Kervel, Vincent, and Albert Menkveld. 'High-frequency trading around large institutional orders'. Working paper. Available at: https://papers.ssrn.com/sol3/Papers.cfm?abstract_id=2619686, 2016.

Wagner, Wayne. *The Complete Guide to Securities Transactions: Improving Performance and Reducing Costs*. John Wiley & Sons, 1989.

Westport Funds. *Westport Select Cap Fund Statement of Additional Information—SAI*, 2015.

Part 3
Analytical and Regulatory Frameworks

8

Naked Open-Market Manipulation and Its Effects

Merritt B. Fox, Lawrence R. Glosten, and Gabriel V. Rauterberg

8.1 Introduction

References to material in this chapter should cite the full article from which it was adapted: Fox et al. 'Stock market manipulation', 2018.

More than 80 years after US federal law first addressed stock market manipulation, the federal courts remain fractured by disagreement and confusion concerning manipulation law's most foundational issues.[1] There remains, for example, a sharp split among the federal circuits concerning manipulation law's central question: *Whether trading activity alone can ever be considered illegal manipulation under federal law?* Academics have been similarly confused—economists and legal scholars cannot agree on whether manipulation is even possible in principle, let alone on how to properly address it in practice.[2]

This confusion is particularly striking because preventing manipulation was a primary motivation for enacting the US's securities laws. In the midst of the Great Depression, manipulation struck Congress and varied commentators as a principal cause of the 1929 stock market crash and the ensuing economic collapse.[3] As a result, the Securities Exchange Act of 1934 (the 'Exchange Act')

---

[1] For particularly helpful comments, we are grateful to Michael Guttentag, Elizabeth Pollman, Andrew Verstein, Yesha Yedav, and participants at faculty workshops at Columbia Law School, Loyola Law School, Oxford University, and University of Cincinnati.

[2] The literature on manipulation features a chorus of commentators arguing about the definition and usefulness of the concept of manipulation. See, e.g., Fischel and Ross, 'Should the law prohibit "manipulation"?', 1991 (famously arguing that the concept of manipulation should be abandoned); Pirrong, 'Squeezes, corpses', 1994, 54 ('[T]o define just what manipulation means . . . is a more difficult task than one might think, because the term "manipulation" is used very imprecisely and indiscriminately').

[3] See, e.g., Fischel and Ross, 503 ('The drafters of the Securities Act of 1933 and the Securities Exchange Act of 1934 . . . were convinced that there was a direct link between excessive speculation,

expressly prohibits manipulation in its Sections 9 and 10(b).[4] The continued confusion is also striking because if one uses for comparison the rough proxy of enforcement by the US Securities and Exchange Commission (SEC), *the problem of manipulation is of a similar scale to insider trading*. In its statistics for the last five years, the SEC reported bringing a combined total of 237 civil and administrative enforcement actions for insider trading and 229 for market manipulation.[5] Yet while there is a vast legal and economic literature addressing insider trading, efforts to analyse manipulation have been far more limited.

This chapter seeks a way out. We start with some simple constraints on a theory of manipulation and suggest that for a trading strategy to be considered manipulation prohibited by the Exchange Act, four essential questions must be answered in the affirmative. First, is the strategy, purely as a conceptual matter, distinguishable from other, clearly acceptable trading strategies, and does the strategy cause social harm? Second, does the strategy plausibly fit under the broad dictionary meaning of the term 'manipulation'? Third, are there circumstances under which the strategy can yield positive expected profits, and do they occur frequently enough to cause concern? Fourth, are there practical procedures for implementing a ban on the strategy whereby the social gains from its reduction or elimination exceed the social costs of doing so, including deterring socially valuable transactions that might be errone-ously identified as examples of the practice?[6] In essence, this four-question approach begins with some minimal rules of statutory interpretation to define the outer borders of what is plausibly within the reach of the prohibitions of manipulation in Sections 9 and 10(b). It combines this with a normative analysis, based on economic efficiency and fairness, as to which of the strat-egies that would fit within these outer borders should actually be subject to legal sanctions.

Our focus here is on one of the three types of market manipulation that have been the subject of commentary both in the case law and by legal and

the stock market crash of 1929, and the Great Depression of the 1930s'); Roach, 'Hedge fund regulation', 2009, 178 ('The shocking results of the [Congressional] investigation uncovered high levels of market manipulation and led Congress to pass the first federal securities laws, the Securities Act of 1933'). However, there is significant debate as to whether significant manipulation had been in fact occurring in the years preceding the Great Depression. See Mahoney, *Wasting a Crisis*, 2015, 100–18; Jiang, Mahoney, and Mei, 'Market manipulation', 2005, 168–9.

[4] See Securities Exchange Act of 1934, 15 U.S.C. § 78i(a)(2) (2012); 15 U.S.C. § 78j(b) (2012).

[5] Calculations made by the authors and on file with them.

[6] A practice or regulation can lead to a social harm if it reduces economic efficiency in a particular way or systematically leads to unfair results. It can lead to a social gain if it improves economic efficiency or ameliorates some unfairness (see Section 8.3). Thus, the desirability of a regulation that seeks to prohibit a given practice depends on whether, considering on a net basis all the social harms and benefits involved in a comparison between a world with and without the regulation, the world with the regulation is superior to the world without it.

economics scholars—naked open-market manipulation.[7] What has often been missing in the treatments of manipulation, however, is a perspicuous identification of exactly who is harmed and who is helped if the practice is left unregulated and how this would change if the practice instead were legally prohibited. Our framework allows a comparison of the two worlds in terms of economic efficiency and the fairness of the various market participants' resulting wealth positions. We then use that analysis to derive an approach that can enable regulators to deter genuinely socially undesirable activity without unnecessarily deterring similar-appearing, but socially useful, trades. Indeed, while objections to manipulation are often framed in terms of its unfairness, we argue that manipulation is undesirable on straightforward efficiency grounds.

The framework we develop draws on normative and analytical building blocks of microstructure and financial economics. Normatively, we argue that the main social functions of trading markets relate to guiding the efficient allocation of capital among firms and between households and enterprise over time, with the liquidity and price accuracy of a market serving as useful proxies for these ultimate social functions. Analytically, we present an informal model of how the secondary equity market typically functions.

With these foundations in hand, we show that open-market manipulation will typically harm both of a market's central social functions—facilitating liquidity and enhancing price accuracy. Although most commentary focuses on the impact of manipulation on price accuracy, the harm to liquidity can be more important. Whether there is harm to price accuracy as well turns on when the manipulation is corrected by an event (say, a corporate disclosure) that causes a stock's price to revert to its accurate level after a successful manipulation distorted it. Surprisingly, our analysis reveals that the core harm of a manipulation will actually depend on the speed and nature of such price 'correction'. If a correction usually occurs rapidly, then the harm of manipulation due to its effects on price accuracy will typically be trivial. The manipulation's focal harm will be to liquidity.[8] If, on the other hand, a manipulation's effects on price are corrected only slowly, then the harm due to its effects on price accuracy will be significant as well. We discuss conceptually the various possibilities for how correction can occur.

The remainder of this study proceeds as follows. Section 8.2 provides an overview of the forms of manipulation we will analyse. Section 8.3 establishes

---

[7] See, e.g., Putniņš, 'Market manipulation', 2011 (providing a notable survey of various manipulative strategies, although the focus and scope differ from our own).

[8] How the correction precisely occurs, however, will still matter to how a manipulation affects the wealth of various market participants and how dramatically it harms liquidity. See Section 8.5.1.1.b (showing that if the correction occurs due to informed trading, then liquidity providers will lose significantly again, while if it corrects due to a public disclosure, they will not).

our normative framework for assessing whether a potentially manipulative trading strategy is actually socially undesirable and whether the social benefits of prohibiting the strategy outweigh the costs. There we identify the ways in which manipulation and its regulation can affect the efficiency with which the economy operates. We also explain how we evaluate the fairness of a given practice. Section 8.4 briefly explores the basic institutional and economic features of the stock market to provide the tools necessary for understanding complex trading strategies.[9] Section 8.5 considers naked open-market manipulation. We then conclude.

8.2 Overview

8.2.1 *Naked Open-Market Manipulation*

Naked open-market manipulation involves the purchase of a number of shares, with an upward push on prices, and then their resale under circumstances where the corresponding downward push on prices is less severe, thereby resulting in the average sale price exceeding the average purchase price.[10] This strategy yields positive expected profits where, at the time of the purchase, the likelihood of profit from this asymmetric price reaction is sufficiently great to make up for the costs of the trading involved.[11]

As will be developed below, we believe that this asymmetric-price-reaction condition for positive expected profits is met under certain circumstances, but that such circumstances arise relatively infrequently.[12] As a result, we ultimately conclude that such a trader should be subject to legal sanctions, but only where it can be proved that she had, at the time of her purchase, good reason to believe that this condition was met.[13] Imposing sanctions without requiring such proof is likely to deter socially useful purchases followed by sales that look very much the same to an external observer. The most important example is simply fundamental-value informed trading, where a trader buys a stock, based on analysis enabling a more accurate appraisal of its value than is reflected in the then-current price, and resells when the market price catches up with her appraisal.

---

[9] Portions of Sections 8.3 and 8.4 draw significantly on more detailed treatments in our prior work. See Fox et al., 'New stock market', 2015, 217–26; Fox et al., 'Informed trading and its regulation', 2018.

[10] The purchase referred to in the text may consist of just one buy transaction or a series of buy transactions in a relatively short period of time. The concept also covers a sale of a certain number of shares and their repurchase, under circumstances where the difference in the price reaction to the sale versus the repurchase results in the average repurchase price being less than the average sale price.

[11] See Harris, *Trading and Exchanges*, 2003, 158. In their widely cited theoretical paper, Franklin Allen and Douglas Gale term this 'trade-based' manipulation. See Allen and Gale, 'Stock-price manipulation', 1992, 505.

[12] See Section 8.5.2.   [13] See Section 8.3.3.2.

8.2.2 *The Extent and Nature of Manipulation*

The fact is that we know relatively little about the extent of manipulation in the equity markets. Of course, we can count the number of manipulation actions by the SEC, and a couple of papers have done so. Aggarwal and Wu combed the SEC's litigation releases for those announcing the filling of a complaint from 1990 to 2001, identifying 142 cases.[14] Most of the cases involve small illiquid securities and almost half of the sample traded on over-the-counter venues. Prosecuted manipulation cases are relatively rare on the established exchanges. An interesting feature of the cases is that among the cases 48 per cent had an insider defendant, 32 per cent had a large (> 5 per cent) shareholder defendant, and 64 per cent had a broker defendant (obviously, at least some cases involved multiple defendants). The paper also shows that any one manipulation can combine pure trade-related strategies with the propagation of rumour, false news, and broker encouragement. Near the end of Section 8.5 we will provide further evidence of manipulations and plausible examples of when manipulation might be profitable.

8.3 Overview

Assessing the social value of a trading strategy and the desirability of prohibiting it by deeming it illegal manipulation requires reference to the basic functions served by the equity trading market. It also requires recognition that if a particular form of trading takes place and its extent is generally understood, other actors in the system will generally take these facts into account in determining their own actions. Thus, the normative question is how the existence of a form of trading and any attempts to regulate it affect the system's ultimate capacity to further the multiple social goals that equity trading markets are expected to serve and that form the justificatory basis for regulation when these markets fall short.

8.3.1 *Social Goals*

Five basic social goals animate most discussion of secondary equity markets and their regulation: (1) promoting the efficient allocation of capital so that it goes to the most promising new investment projects; (2) promoting the efficient operation of the economy's existing productive capacity; (3) promoting the efficient allocation of resources between current and future periods so as to best satisfy the needs of firms seeking funds for real investments (trading

---

[14] Aggarwal and Wu, 'Stock market manipulations', 2006.

the promise of future dollars to obtain current dollars) and the needs of savers seeking to forgo current consumption in order to enjoy future consumption (trading current dollars to obtain the promise of future dollars); (4) promoting the efficient allocation among investors of the risks associated with holding securities so that their volatility is borne by risk-averse investors with the least disutility; and (5) operating fairly and fostering an overall sense of fairness.[15] In addition, any intelligent discussion of the desirability of manipulation and its regulation must take into account the impact of the trading on the real resources that society devotes to trading in, and operating, the stock market, and to the enforcement and compliance costs associated with its regulation, including the socially useful transactions that any regulation may deter.

8.3.2 *The Use of Ex Post and Ex Ante Analysis*

The impact of an ongoing trading practice on these five basic social goals is most easily understood by starting with a single instance of the practice and seeing the ex post effect of the transaction. From this, we can see the impact of the trade on the wealth position of the various participants involved, which in turn is a guide to the incentives that the availability of the practice generates. Then we can consider, from an ex ante perspective, the impact of the practice as a generally-known ongoing phenomenon occurring over the long run within a competitive environment. This ex ante analysis allows us to see what the efficiency and fairness implications of the practice are. As is relatively standard in the law and economics literature concerning corporate and securities law, we evaluate efficiency in Kaldor-Hicks terms, and consider fairness in terms of a practice's effects on various participants' wealth positions from the ex ante perspective.[16]

The initial four basic values and cost considerations listed above, and even the 'sense of fairness' that we mention with respect to the fifth, all go to the efficiency aspect of the problem. The 'operating fairly' aspect of the fifth value goes to the ultimate underlying fairness. Conceptions of fairness are too many and too multifarious to address generally in depth. However, fairness also plays too prominent a role in public criticism of the securities markets to be entirely ignored. Our strategy here is simply to take as an exemplar one

---

[15] In the primary market, stocks are purchased from the company issuing those stocks, while in the secondary market, traders buy and sell stocks from each other. Stock exchanges are secondary markets.

[16] Hicks, 'Foundations', 1939; Kaldor, 'Welfare propositions', 1939 (together introducing the Kaldor-Hicks conception of efficiency). The Kaldor-Hicks conception of efficiency, with all its limitations, remains the standard welfare criterion in law-and-economics analyses of corporate and securities law. Compare Kraakman et al., *Anatomy of Corporate Law*, 2017, 23 n.87. Other conceptions of fairness are of course possible (and plausible), and to the extent that such views are held, this study simply offers a complementary critique of manipulation.

prominent conception of fairness that frequently appears in commentary on markets.[17] We argue that this conception of fairness is of limited use in assessing trading behaviour and leave things at that. More generally, we think that many of the concerns that the quest for fairness targets, while genuine, can be more perspicuously articulated within an efficiency framework. The choice of the ex ante perspective to assess underlying fairness implies that if a practice does not affect a market participant's *expected* outcomes, it is not unfair. Because the practice is available and another person engages in it, a given transaction entered into by the participant may leave her worse off. But the practice is not unfair to the participant if, on average, she is not worse off entering into such transactions due to the practice. The idea that fairness can be assessed in terms of expected outcomes is bolstered by the fact that most investors engage in many transactions over time, and, like the myriad other risks that investors undertake, the risk of being hurt by the practice can essentially be eliminated by holding a diversified portfolio. To the extent that any of the assumptions in this characterization—repeated transactions or diversification—turn out not to characterize a given trader, then our argument above will not apply.[18] This approach to fairness may also have far less appeal in other arenas of social life. We will see that the kind of manipulation that we examine does not have unfair effects from this ex ante perspective.

8.3.3 *Market Characteristics that Impact on These Goals*

A given form of trading may impact these five social goals in complex ways that are related to a stock market's two most important characteristics: the price accuracy and the liquidity of the stocks trading in it.[19] The social impact of any given form of trading is most easily evaluated through a two-step process: first assessing the effect of the type of trading on each of these two market characteristics and then identifying the effect of the characteristic on the five basic social goals discussed above.

8.3.3.1 PRICE ACCURACY
Price accuracy relates to the accuracy with which the market price of an issuer's shares predicts the issuer's future cash flows. Because the price of

---

[17] See, e.g., Lewis, *Flash Boys*, 2014.

[18] See Davis, 'Investors' gains and losses', 2015 (arguing, *inter alia*, that diversification assumptions are often false).

[19] Foucault, Pagano, and Röell, *Market Liquidity*, 2013, 31 ('The two main roles of a securities market are to provide trading services for investors who wish to alter their portfolios, and to determine prices that can guide the allocation of capital by investors and firms... [A] market is efficient if it enables investors to trade quickly and cheaply (i.e., if it is liquid) and if it incorporates new information quickly and accurately into prices.')

any new share offering by a publicly traded issuer will be determined largely by the price of its already outstanding shares in the stock market, more accurate stock market prices will lead to capital raised by new share issuances being more likely to go to the issuers with the most promising new real investment projects, the first such basic social goal.[20] Share price also influences the availability of new project funding from other outside sources and the willingness of managers to use internal funds for investment, and so greater price accuracy assists the efficient allocation of capital in these other ways as well.[21]

More generally, more accurate share prices help reveal managers who are performing poorly both in terms of their deployment of internal funds for new investment projects (again assisting the efficient allocation of capital) and in terms of their management of the issuer's current assets (assisting the efficient operation of the economy's existing productive capacity, the second basic social goal).[22] They also improve the effectiveness of share price compensation schemes, the threats of hostile takeovers, and activist hedge fund pressures as incentives for better managerial decision-making in terms of promoting these first two basic social goals.[23]

Over time, more accurate share prices also likely lead to a greater sense of fairness on the part of investors, part of the fifth basic social goal, because they will experience fewer negative surprises at some point in time after their purchase or sale.[24]

8.3.3.2 LIQUIDITY

A second characteristic is how liquid the market is. Liquidity is a multi-dimensional concept that relates to the size of a trade, the price at which it is accomplished, and the time it takes to accomplish the trade. Generally, the larger the size of the purchase or sale and the faster one wishes to accomplish it, the less desirable will be the price. The more liquid the market is, however, the less severe these tradeoffs are. For a small retail purchase or sale of stock, the 'bid-ask spread' (the spread between the best available bid and best available offer in the market) is a good measure of liquidity because the trader can effect a buy or sell transaction immediately at those respective prices and, in essence, will be paying half the spread to do so. For larger orders, the volume of

---

[20] See, e.g., Chen et al., 'Price informativeness and investment sensitivity', 2007 (showing that the number of investment decisions tend to increase when a stock's price has just risen).

[21] See Fox, 'Civil liability', 2009, 260–4; Kahan, 'Securities laws', 1992.   [22] Fox, 258–60.

[23] Ibid. There is ample empirical evidence to suggest that accurate price signals do in fact have efficiency-enhancing effects on managerial decisions. See Foucault et al., 361–8 (collecting relevant empirical studies); see, e.g., Bond et al., 'Real effects', 2012.

[24] In an efficient market, the market price is an unbiased predictor of an issuer's future cash flows.

stock available at prices not too inferior to this best bid or offer (the 'depth of the book') is relevant as well.[25]

Liquidity also has an impact on a number of social goals, as follows.

a. More Efficient Allocation of Resources Over Time

To start, the prospect of greater liquidity promotes more efficient allocation of society's scarce resources between uses that support current consumption and uses that support new real investment that in turn allows greater consumption in the future. This relates to the third basic social goal, the efficient allocation of resources with regard to consumption over time. Consider this first in terms of enterprises seeking new capital to devote to real investment projects through the issuance of stock. In essence, they are purchasers of current dollars in return for the promise of future dollars. The more liquid an issuer's shares, the more valuable their shares are to hold for any given level of expected future cash flow. Thus, when an issuer offers shares in the primary market, the more liquid that investors anticipate the shares will be in the future, the higher the price at which the issuer can sell its shares, all else equal. Hence, the lower will be the issuer's cost of capital.[26]

In welfare economics terms, illiquidity, just like a tax, results in a 'wedge' between the value of what the savers (the purchasers of future dollars) expect to receive in the future and the value of what the entrepreneurs or issuers (the suppliers of future dollars in the form of future dividend streams) expect to give up in the future.[27] This wedge prevents certain transactions from occurring that would have occurred if the shares were expected to be more liquid. The fact that, absent this wedge, the issuer and savers would have willingly entered into these transactions means that the transactions prevented by illiquidity are ones that would have made both parties better off on an expected basis. These lost transactions are projects with expected returns that are lower than those of the marginal project that gets funded in a world with a certain degree of illiquidity, but still high enough to make some people feel that, absent liquidity concerns, sacrificing their current dollars for the projects' promises of future ones would be a worthwhile exchange.[28]

In essence, illiquidity harms the efficiency with which society allocates its scarce resources between uses that support current consumption and uses that

---

[25] This concept of the best bid and offer—the prices at which small retail traders can fill, respectively, a market sell order and a market buy order—and the idea of depth of book will be explored further in Section 8.4.

[26] The cost of capital is lower because the prospect of a smaller bid-ask spread results in the issuer's expected future cash flow being discounted to present value at a lower discount rate. See Amihud and Mendelson, 'Asset pricing', 1986; Amihud and Mendelson, 'Liquidity', 1988.

[27] See Foucault et al., 322–5 (analysing how illiquidity functions as a wedge separating transaction prices from assets' fundamental values).

[28] Harris, *Trading and Exchanges*, 214–15.

support consumption in the future. Savers save less, and entrepreneurs and issuers engage in less real investment, than the levels that would be mutually more advantageous but for the savers' concerns about the liquidity of the issuers' shares.

b. More Efficient Allocation of Risk

Greater liquidity also promotes the more efficient allocation of risk, the fourth basic social goal. At any given point in time, each investor has an optimal portfolio in terms of the proportion of his total wealth that is invested in risky securities and the proportion of this risky security portfolio that should be invested in each available risky security. An investor's taste for safety versus risk may stay relatively steady over at least the medium run. However, almost everything else determining what portfolio is optimal for him—for example his personal circumstances, the risk-free rate of interest, the expected returns associated with each available risky asset, and the variances of the returns on each such asset and the co-variances among them—may be subject to frequent change. Thus what constitutes an optimal portfolio is likely to be always shifting. By reducing the transaction costs associated with both the purchase and sale of securities, greater liquidity allows the individual investor to cost-effectively adjust her portfolio over time to keep it closer at each moment to what at that point is optimal for her.

c. Greater Share Price Accuracy

More liquidity also lowers the transaction costs associated with speculative trading based on acquiring a variety of bits of publicly available information and observation of the world and analysing them to make more accurate predictions of an issuer's cash flows, i.e. trading which creates fundamental-value information. Thus, more liquidity stimulates such activity and in the process increases share price accuracy, with the attendant benefits discussed just above in terms of more efficient capital allocation and utilization of existing productive capacity—the first two basic social goals.

8.4 The Workings of the Equity Market

A basic understanding of how the equity market works is a necessary starting point for determining any particular trading strategy's impact on price accuracy and liquidity. Accordingly, this section provides a quick survey of the different types of participants; the nature of trading venues and the types of orders used on them; how liquidity is generated; and the determinants of the prices at which transactions occur. From what follows, the reader will be able to see a baseline description of how the market would work in the absence of naked open-market manipulation, and will have the tools to understand the discussion in Sections 8.5 and 8.6 concerning its impact.

8.4.1 *Market Participants and Their Reasons for Trading*

Traders in the market can be broken down into four categories: informed traders, uninformed traders, noise traders, and anti-noise traders.[29] In addition, the buyers and sellers in the market include professional suppliers of liquidity.

8.4.1.1 INFORMED TRADERS

Informed traders are motivated to buy or sell based on information that allows a more accurate appraisal of the stock's value than what its current market price implies. This information can be one of several kinds. Fundamental-value information is an estimate of the future cash flows to a shareholder discounted to present value. Such information is based on a person gathering bits of publicly available information or observations about the world and analysing what the person has learned in a sophisticated way that allows a superior assessment of these cash flows.[30] Announcement information involves information contained in an announcement by an issuer or other institution with obvious implications as to the issuer's future cash flows. Announcement information remains profitable only during the brief period of time between the announcement and when the information is fully reflected in price. Issuer inside information is information held within an issuer that is relevant to predicting its future cash flows but is not yet public and reflected in price. Non-issuer inside information is information relevant to predicting an issuer's future cash flows that is held within an institution other than an issuer and is not yet public and reflected in price.

As developed below, informed trading, on the one hand, moves share price on average in the direction of greater accuracy, and, on the other hand, reduces liquidity.[31] Thus it is necessary to net out the tradeoff between the positive social impact from improved share price accuracy and the negative social impact from decreased liquidity. We have concluded in another publication that trading on the basis of fundamental-value information is socially desirable, while trading on the basis of announcement information, issuer inside information, and non-issuer inside information (unless

---

[29] While separating traders into informed and uninformed is a basic building block of microstructure economics, our taxonomy owes much in general to Larry Harris's work. See Harris, *Trading and Exchanges*, 194.

[30] Ibid. (discussing the different forms of information on which an informed trader may transact).

[31] See Section 8.4.3.

permitted by the non-issuer institution that generated the information) is socially undesirable.[32]

8.4.1.2 UNINFORMED TRADERS

Uninformed traders buy and sell shares without possession of information that allows a more accurate appraisal of the stock's value than the assessment of value of the stock implied by current market prices. A trade by an uninformed person can be motivated by one of several reasons. For example, a purchase of a share is a way of deferring until a later period the consumption in the current period that the cash the trader possesses would otherwise permit. In the later period when the purchaser wishes to consume, she sells the share. The expected return at the time of purchase will simply be the expected return on the market as a whole adjusted to reflect the risk characteristics of the particular firm's shares.[33] Thus neither the purchase nor the sale of the share is motivated by information not yet reflected in share price at the time of the transaction.

A purchase or sale of a share of stock may also be motivated by a change in what constitutes an investor's optimal portfolio—the mix of securities that achieves the best tradeoff of risk for return and that best suits the investor's tastes in terms of how risk averse she is and her particular circumstances—and thus again is not motivated by information yet to be reflected in share price at the time of the transaction. As noted in Section 8.2, facilitating trades associated with consumption deferral and portfolio risk adjustment is one of the social benefits that a well-functioning stock market can provide. The market can also be a source of entertainment for traders who do not believe they have any special information, but buy and sell because they enjoy gambling.

8.4.1.3 NOISE TRADERS

Noise traders believe they have information not reflected in a stock's price that permits a more accurate appraisal of an issuer's future cash flows. What distinguishes them from fundamental-value traders is that, in fact, the information either already is reflected in price or is irrelevant to making a more accurate appraisal. To the extent that idiosyncratic beliefs drive noise traders, their buy and sell trades will tend to cancel each other out and have no effect on price. To the extent that a widespread fad or fashion drives noise traders, however, their trades will push a stock's price in the direction suggested by the fad or fashion. Such trading would thus drive price away from being the best estimate of an issuer's future cash flows given all publicly available information.

---

[32] See Fox et al., 'Informed trading'.   [33] Brealey et al., *Principles*, 2013, 302–8, 689.

8.4.1.4 ANTI-NOISE TRADERS

Anti-noise trading is a particular form of informed trading. A trader engaging in anti-noise trading actively searches for new information about an issuer's future cash flows and is prepared to transact in the opposite direction when she sees prices move at a time when her search suggests there is no new information. Thus, when fad-driven noise traders push price in one direction and anti-noise traders become reasonably confident that there is no new information to justify this price move, anti-noise traders will trade in the opposite direction. Before the anti-noise traders reach this level of confidence that there is no news to justify an observed price change, time may elapse as they engage in a search to see whether there is in fact is such news. So, there may be a delay in their countertrading, leaving prices for a time at unjustified levels.

Because of the synergies of engaging in fundamental-value informed trading and the information search that is the basis of anti-noise trading, the same person or entity often engages in both types of trading.

Anti-noise traders play a special role in our story about naked open-market manipulation discussed below in Section 8.5 because, as with fad-driven noise trading, the price changes caused by the manipulator are also not based on new information that would help predict an issuer's future cash flows. Such manipulation involves a person with no belief that the current price is incorrect trading in one direction, then reversing and trading in the opposite direction, and profiting because the price reaction to the first set of trades is greater than the price reaction to the reverse trades. On the one hand, the ability of the manipulator to push price in the first direction represents a situation where the anti-nose traders did not identify in time that there was no information driving the price change. On the other hand, the price at the end of the manipulator's trading is not back to the price that would have prevailed absent the manipulation. Anti-noise traders can be the force that ultimately brings the price back to this level as, over time, they become sufficiently confident that no new information drove the changes in price caused by the manipulator.

8.4.1.5 PROFESSIONAL LIQUIDITY SUPPLIERS

The professional supplier of liquidity in an issuer's shares engages in both their frequent purchase and frequent sale, making a business out of standing ready to buy and sell these shares up to stated amounts at quoted prices (respectively a 'bid' and an 'offer' or 'ask'). Today, this is typically a high frequency trader (HFT). An HFT uses high-speed communications to constantly update its information concerning transactions and the quotes of others occurring in each stock that it regularly trades and changes its own quotes accordingly, rather than using information about the issuer itself to determine these quotes.

Thus the professional liquidity supplier is not 'informed' in the sense that we use the term here. Indeed, because of its unique intermediary market-making role, unlike all other buyers and sellers of securities in the market, we will not refer to it as a 'trader'.

8.4.2 *Trading Venues and Orders*

Any given stock is potentially traded in each of a number of competing venues. Almost all these venues are *electronic limit order books*, where a liquidity supplier or a trader can post, as a *limit order*, its firm commitment, until cancelled, to buy or sell up to a specified number of shares at a quoted price. A computer (the venue's *matching engine*) matches these posted limit orders with incoming buy and sell *market orders*, which are orders from traders willing to trade immediately and unconditionally at whatever is the best available price in the market. HFTs, acting as professional liquidity suppliers, post a significant portion of the limit orders that are matched in this fashion and that result in executed trades.[34] The law further requires that orders transact at the best prices displayed at any stock exchange.[35] The lowest offer displayed at any exchange is known as the national best offer (NBO) and the highest bid displayed at any exchange is known as the national best bid (NBB).[36]

8.4.3 *The Economics of Liquidity Provision*

What follows provides a baseline of how securities markets would work if there were no naked open-market manipulation. With this baseline set, the sections that follow will consider the impact of this type of trading. Throughout, we will assume that, for expository simplicity, all limit orders posted on trading venues are from HFT professional liquidity suppliers and all traders use market orders.

8.4.3.1 THE LIQUIDITY SUPPLY BUSINESS

The professional liquidity supplier makes money if on average it sells the shares that it buys for more than the price paid. Doing so is not as easy as it might seem, even though at any one point in time the liquidity supplier's offer is always higher than its bid. The problem begins with the fact that the stock

---

[34] See Brogaard et al., 'High-frequency trading', 2014 (finding that HFTs supply liquidity for 42 per cent of all trades and provide the market quotes 42 per cent of the time).

[35] See 17 C.F.R. § 242.611(a)(1) (2015) (establishing the rule); ibid. § 242.600(b) (defining relevant terms).

[36] See Fox et al., 'New stock market', 207–16 (providing a detailed exposition of the mechanics of stock market trading).

market is largely anonymous. Thus, the person with whom a liquidity supplier transacts generally does not reveal her identity and, what, if anything, she knows. So there is always the possibility that she is an informed trader. Liquidity suppliers, as will be demonstrated immediately below, lose money on average when they transact with informed traders.

8.4.3.2 TRANSACTING WITH INFORMED VERSUS UNINFORMED TRADERS

An informed trader will buy from the liquidity supplier only when her superior assessment of the stock's value suggests that the value is above the liquidity provider's offer. And she will sell to the liquidity supplier only when her superior assessment suggests that the value is below the liquidity provider's bid. Thus, in transactions with an informed trader, the liquidity supplier sells at prices that the informed trader's information suggests is below the value of the stock, and buys at prices that the informed trader's information suggests is above the value of the stock. These transactions on average will be losing transactions for the liquidity supplier. In essence, the liquidity supplier faces a classic adverse selection situation.[37]

Fortunately for the liquidity supplier, the rest of its transactions are with uninformed traders. On average, these transactions should be profitable. The assessment of value of the stock implied by current market prices is the midpoint between the NBO and NBB. Because the uninformed trader has no private information, there is no reason to think that on average this market assessment is wrong. So when a liquidity supplier purchases from an uninformed trader at the NBB and sells to an uninformed trader at the NBO, each of these transactions on average yields an expected profit equal to half the spread between the two quotes, with the liquidity supplier on average buying for a little less than value and selling for a little more than value.

In sum, whatever the source of an informed trader's private information, the liquidity provider will be subject to adverse selection and will on average lose money when it buys at the bid from informed sellers or sells at the offer to informed buyers. The liquidity provider can still break even, however, as long as there are enough uninformed traders willing to suffer the inevitable expected trading losses of buying at the offer and selling at the bid. There simply needs to be a large enough spread between the bid and offer that the losses accrued by transacting with informed traders are offset by the profits accrued from transacting with uninformed investors.

---

[37] See generally Akerlof, 'Market for "lemons," ' 1970 (analysing how informational asymmetries can drive declines in the quality of goods traded in a market until only 'lemons' are left). Liquidity suppliers face the constant threat that they are trading under conditions of information asymmetry and are thus only transacting when the trade is adverse to their interests.

8.4.3.3 HOW LIQUIDITY SUPPLIERS SET THEIR BIDS AND OFFERS

A liquidity supplier operates in a competitive market. To survive, it must set its quotes aggressively enough to attract business, but not so aggressively that the money it makes by buying from, and selling to, uninformed traders is less than what it loses by engaging in such transactions with informed traders. Thus, in a world where a liquidity supplier rationally expects a higher level of informed trading, it will need to set its offers higher and bids lower to break even and survive in a competitive market.[38]

A liquidity supplier knows that there is a certain possibility that the next marketable order that arrives to execute against one of its quotes will be from an informed trader. The liquidity supplier knows that if the next marketable order to arrive is a buy, there is a certain chance that it is motivated by positive private information and no chance it is motivated by negative private information. Similarly, if the next order to arrive is a sell, there is a certain chance that it is motivated by negative private information and no chance it is motivated by positive private information. Thus, the liquidity supplier knows that whichever kind of order arrives next, it will alter the liquidity supplier's estimate of the stock's value: up if the order is a buy, and down if it is a sell order. The offer and the bid are set in advance of knowing which it will be, but with the offer being contingent on the next arriving order being a buy and the bid on it being a sell. Thus, when a liquidity supplier is deciding on its offer price, it knows that an informed trader will only transact against this price if the information possessed by the informed trader is positive and thus that the arrival of a buy order will cause the liquidity supplier to revise its estimate upward. So, for a transaction with a buy order to be regret-free, the liquidity supplier must, in advance of the arrival of the order, set its offer quote, based on the information it then knows, to reflect this upward revision of estimated value that will inevitably accompany the buy order's arrival. The same logic applies for setting the bid: to be regret-free it must reflect the downward revision that would inevitably accompany the arrival of a sell order. Once one kind of order or the other arrives, the liquidity supplier has new information and the process starts over again. Thus, in a world where the liquidity supplier rationally expects a higher level of informed trading, these upward and downward revisions will be larger and so, again, it will need its offers higher and bids lower.[39]

---

[38] A more complete model of how the bid-ask spread is set would include a consideration of the costs of operations, compensation for the utility decreasing risks to its principals of having a not fully diversified portfolio concentrated in particular securities, and the need for capital. Breaking even in the long run requires covering these costs and a normal market return on capital.

[39] See Glosten and Milgrom, 'Bid, ask', 1985 (providing a model of trading behaviour under information asymmetries in securities markets).

8.4.3.4 THE PATTERN OF TRANSACTION PRICES IN THE PRESENCE OF INFORMED TRADING

This description of how liquidity suppliers set their quotes highlights an important byproduct of rational liquidity provision in a market with informed traders. Liquidity suppliers will be constantly updating valuations in response to transactions. With a sufficient number of trades, the market price will come to reflect the informed trader's information. The behaviour of rational liquidity providers thus reflects a kind of 'invisible hand': simply as a result of their efforts to avoid losses to informed traders, liquidity providers are repeatedly revising their quotes so that, with time, they come to fully reflect informed traders' information.

For example, suppose that there were one or more informed traders possessing a particular piece of positive information. During their period of trading, there would of course also be buying and selling by uninformed traders. So both marketable buy and marketable sell orders will arrive at trading venues, but there will be more buys than sells. As a result, although there will be ups and downs in the offers and bids as the liquidity-supplier estimates of value move up and down with the arrival of each buy and sell order, the ups will predominate and the mid-point between the bid and offer will trend upward until the offer gets high enough that it equals or exceeds the informed traders' estimate of the share's value. Empirical evidence strongly supports the results from these adverse selection models. Analyses of intraday changes in quotes and in the prices of executed transactions consistently show that they respond to the pattern of buy and sell orders at the time.[40] Simulations suggest that the adjustment in price described here often completes itself quite quickly.

8.5 Naked Open-Market Manipulation

Naked open-market manipulation involves the purchase of a number of shares, with its upward push on prices, and then their resale under circumstances where the corresponding downward push on prices is less severe, thereby resulting in the average sale price exceeding the average purchase price. The manipulator is not an informed trader in terms of knowing anything special about the issuer's future cash flows. Rather, his profits come purely from the trading profits yielded by this asymmetric price response.

---

[40] See Chan et al., 'Intraday behavior', 1995 (suggesting that adverse selection is an important determinant of the intraday behaviour of bid-ask spreads); Glosten and Harris, 'Estimating', 1988 (estimating a model in which the bid-ask spread is divided into an adverse selection component and a transitory component due to inventory costs, clearing costs, and other factors).

The analysis below suggests that naked open-market manipulation is a trading strategy that gives rise to an affirmative answer to each of the four foundational questions posed at the beginning, and hence is an appropriate target of a ban under the Exchange Act. It is socially harmful in a way that makes it distinguishable as a conceptual matter from other trading strategies. It also fits under a broad dictionary meaning of the word 'manipulation'.[41] There are circumstances under which the strategy can yield positive expected profits. And there are situations where it will be provable that a trader has reason to know of the existence of these circumstances, meaning that if legal sanctions are imposed only when such a situation can be proved to have existed, not many socially valuable transactions—ones not driven by this strategy—will be deterred.

8.5.1 *Wealth Transfers: Fairness and Efficiency*

Understanding the wealth transfer implications of naked open-market manipulation is most easily understood by starting with an example and seeing the ex post effect of the trade. Then we can consider, from an ex ante perspective, what the impact of the practice is as a generally known ongoing phenomenon occurring over the longer run within a competitive environment. From this, we can make conclusions both about the efficiency implications of the practice in terms of liquidity and share price accuracy and the fairness of its impact on different members of society.

8.5.1.1 EX POST PERSPECTIVE

Mani is a skilled manipulator who wishes to manipulate the price of NetSuite's stock by taking advantage of his rational assessment that it is probable that there will be an asymmetric price reaction to his purchases versus his later sales. For simplicity, assume that during the period of Mani's purchases and subsequent sales, although liquidity suppliers are unsure of whether there is any new information that has emerges or been developed about NetSuite, in fact none has. So Mani's trading is the exclusive cause of the initial upward trend and the following downward trend in NetSuite prices.

a. The Actual Manipulation

Mani uses a large number of market orders, averaging 5000 shares per hour, to purchase 10,000 NetSuite shares over two hours. Prior to Mani's purchases, the national best bid (NBB) for NetSuite was $10.00 and the national best offer (NBO) was $10.10. The order flow arriving at trading

---

[41] In its definition of 'manipulate', the Merriam-Webster dictionary includes 'to change by artful or unfair means so as to serve one's purpose'. *Merriam-Webster*, 2009, 'Manipulate'.

venues from uninformed traders during this period involves an essentially even number of buys and sells because neither new information nor price changes motivate their trades. Thus Mani's buy orders will leave liquidity suppliers facing each hour an excess of 5000 buy orders over sell orders. Because the liquidity suppliers fear that the excess might be due to informed trading based on positive information, assume that each 5000 shares of excess buy orders pushes their bids and offers up by $0.10. Therefore at the end two hours, NetSuite's NBB is $11.00 and its NBO $11.10. Had Mani not traded, NetSuite's NBB and NBO would have remained roughly at $10.00 and $10.10.

Mani now turns around and begins to sell his inventory of 10,000 NetSuite shares, this time selling 5000 shares per hour for two hours. This means that liquidity suppliers now face each hour an order imbalance of 5000 more shares sold than bought. Mani's expectation that the price response will be asymmetric proves correct: each 1000 shares of excess buy orders pushes their bids and offers down by only $0.25. Thus, at the end of his ten days of selling, the NBB and NBO are, respectively, $10.50 and $10.60.

Buying at the offer as the NBO rises, Mani accumulates 10,000 NetSuite shares for an average price of $10.55. Selling at the bid as the NBB falls, Mani sells these 10,000 shares at an average price of $10.75. Mani thus achieves a profit of $10,000 \times \$0.20 = \$2000$.

The distributive question is who has benefited from these trades and who has been harmed. Because secondary market trading in pursuit of profits is a zero-sum game, gains and losses by different market participants are mirror images of each other and must sum to zero.[42] In the example, Mani makes profits of $2000. The liquidity suppliers, who sold him his shares for an average of $10.55 and repurchased them for an average of $10.75, have suffered a corresponding loss of $2000. In aggregate, uninformed traders experience the change in stock price as a wash, with sellers being better off than if Mani had not traded and buyers being reciprocally worse off.

b. The Price Correction After the Manipulation

Even though the liquidity suppliers are back in balance, having purchased from Mani as many shares as they originally sold to him, this is not the end of the story. When Mani finishes his sequence of trades, the NBB and NBO are, respectively, $10.50 and $10.60, not down to $10.00 and $10.10, the prices that would have prevailed absent the manipulation. To be successful, the open-market manipulator has caused the stock price to deviate from what represented the market consensus of its value. The dynamics of when, if ever, the stock price's distortion is 'corrected', with the manipulation's impact

---

[42] See Harris, *Trading and Electronic Markets*, 2015, 22 (suggesting that '[t]rading is a zero-sum game when gains and losses are measured relative to the market index').

having been eliminated, are crucially important to the welfare effects of manipulation. We see four plausible possibilities: three different ways in which the price can be corrected, and then the stark possibility that correction never occurs.

The first two possibilities involve the price going back down to $10.00/$10.10, both of which involve further losses to the liquidity suppliers. One way is that NetSuite credibly announces that there is no undisclosed information within its possession that could explain the rise to $11.00/$11.10 and then the fall (partway) back to $10.50/$10.60. It would then be clear to the market that there was no reason the price should not be back at $10.00/$10.10. Announcement traders would be briefly able to profit at the expense of liquidity suppliers as the price quickly adjusted down to $10.00/$10.10.

Absent such an announcement, a second way that the price could adjust back to its original level is through the action of anti-noise traders. This may take considerably longer and involve considerably larger additional losses to the liquidity suppliers. The searches of the anti-noise traders to see whether there was new information justifying the price changes took too much time for them to have had the confidence to engage in trades that would have counteracted the price increases caused by Mani's purchases or accentuated the price decreases caused by Mani's sales. Eventually, however, an increasing number of anti-noise traders will become convinced that there is no new information that can justify the $10.50/$10.60 price level and will start to sell. As they do, they are, as noted earlier, engaging in a special kind of informed trading in the sense that they have good reason to believe that there is no such price-justifying information when others do not know this. Just like sales by a regular informed trader in possession of negative information, the sales of the anti-noise traders create an order imbalance that causes liquidity suppliers to acquire shares at a price above what the anti-noise trader correctly believes is their value and so leads to additional liquidity-supplier losses. And just like sales by a regular informed trader in possession of negative information, the continuing order imbalance will prompt the liquidity suppliers to gradually lower their bids and offers until they reach the neighborhood of $10.00/$10.10, at which point the trades of the anti-noise traders will stop.

Anti-noise trading cannot be assured to occur with every naked open-market manipulation, however, because the potential anti-noise traders may not be sufficiently confident that there is no new information to justify the elevated price after the manipulation is completed.

A third way that price can return to its proper level is simply the materialization, at some later date, of what, immediately prior to the manipulation, were the future cash flows being predicted by the pre-manipulation price. For example, if the share price immediately prior to the manipulation suggested that expected future cash flows would remain steady in perpetuity, but the elevated price after the manipulation was completed suggested an increase in expected future cash flows, the price would return to its original, pre-manipulation level (barring any other news) once subsequent earnings reports showed that in fact cash flows had not increased. Obviously, this final process could take considerable time, leaving prices inaccurate for a significant period.

8.5.1.2 EX ANTE PERSPECTIVE

Now assume, not unrealistically, that all the players have unbiased (though not necessarily accurate) expectations concerning the prevalence of successful naked open-market manipulation, and that all the players operate within a competitive environment. We want to compare what the longer-run equilibrium would look like in a world where such a trading strategy is occurring freely with what it would look like in a world where it is somehow blocked. The object is to see how the availability of the practice affects the wealth positions of the various participants and the implications of these effects in terms of fairness and, through the incentives they create, on efficiency.

a. Manipulators

Naked open-market manipulation will generate positive trading profits on an expected basis to the extent that its practitioners can accurately predict when asymmetric price responses will occur. The resources necessary to conduct a business in such trading are a combination of ordinary and specialized inputs. The ordinary inputs are physical, organizational, and financial assets that could equally usefully be deployed elsewhere in the economy. The specialized inputs are the efforts of key persons who possess abilities and skills uniquely useful for predicting such situations and acting on them. All of these inputs will be drawn into this business up to the point where, at the margin, the expected profits from successfully predicting and acting on such situations equals the costs of paying for the inputs. This activity occurs in an openly competitive environment and so the suppliers of the ordinary inputs will be paid a market return comparable to what they would earn if the resources they supplied were deployed instead another way. Thus, whether naked open-market manipulation occurs freely or not has no effect on their wealth positions. The persons with uniquely useful abilities and skills will be paid greater rents than they would be paid if they had to work in a different business because naked open-market manipulation was somehow blocked. Thus their wealth positions will be enhanced if such manipulation is allowed to occur freely.

b. Liquidity Suppliers

As we have seen from the example, ex post, liquidity suppliers will lose in their transactions with a successful naked open-market manipulator because the reversing purchases from the manipulators are on average at higher prices than the initial sales to them. The liquidity suppliers lose a second time in their transactions with the announcement or anti-noise traders that bring the price back to the level it would have been without the manipulation.

From the ex ante perspective, however, all these losses are passed on by the liquidity suppliers to the other traders in the market. This is because, as discussed in Section 8.4, liquidity suppliers gain in their transactions with uninformed traders, making half the spread with each sale to the uninformed trader and half from each purchase from an uninformed trader. To survive in a competitive market, a liquidity supplier must set its bids and offers so that these losses and gains balance out (plus, if we add some real-world flavour to the description, the gains must cover the returns paid to its personnel, a market return on the capital needed for real estate and equipment and for engaging in the trading itself, and compensation for the undiversified nature of the portfolio that the business will be holding most of the time). If its spreads are wider than this, it will not attract orders because they will be undercut by other liquidity suppliers. If they are narrower than this, at least some of its inputs will be receiving less than a market return, and thus the business will not be able to survive in the longer run.[43]

Notwithstanding the passing on by liquidity traders of these losses, the existence of naked open-market manipulations will still have a negative effect on the wealth positions of certain persons associated with the liquidity supply business, but only indirectly. As we have seen, the ex post trading losses are passed on through a wider spread between the bid and offer. This wider spread increases the cost of trading, which means that less trading occurs. Less trading means that less of both their ordinary and specialized inputs will be pulled into the business. Suppliers of the ordinary inputs will earn the same ordinary market return whatever the level of liquidity supply activity. For persons with abilities and skills uniquely useful for liquidity supply, however, they will be paid less in rents and so their wealth positions would be negatively affected by the prospect of successful manipulation of this type.

c. Uninformed Traders
The expected cost to uninformed traders from naked open-market manipulation is the need, in the cycle over time of a purchase and sale, to pay the increase in spread because this kind of manipulation is occurring: they will purchase at the offer but only be able to sell at the bid. Calculating the

---

[43] The description in this paragraph is a bit of an oversimplification, because, unlike in the example here involving Mani, the market will include informed traders as well. Given the prospect of losses as the result of naked open-market manipulation, the spread, which is the same for all traders, will be wider for informed traders as well, and so some of the losses are passed on to them. See Section 8.5.1.2.d.

ultimate incidence of this cost on uninformed traders is a bit complicated, however. When an issuer's entrepreneurs and initial investors engage in an initial public offering, the shares they are offering will be discounted to reflect the prospect that the spread must be paid with each subsequent sale and purchase in the secondary market as well as the prospect that any future equity offerings by the issuer over time will be similarly discounted. So, the entrepreneurs and early investors receive less than if there were no impact on the spread by this kind of manipulation. This discount continues at the same level for as long as the firm appears to have a long-run future. For uninformed investors who buy and sell less frequently than average, this discount makes the purchase a bargain and so they are gainers from naked open-market manipulation. Those who buy and sell more frequently than average are hurt by repeatedly paying the spread more than they are helped by the discount, and so they are losers from the practice.[44]

d. *Informed Traders*

Informed traders of each kind pay the same increased spread due to the presence of naked open-market manipulation that uninformed traders do. This increase in their cost of doing business has a depressing effect on the level of each of the kinds of informed activity. This decreases the level of resources going into each of these activities, with a negative wealth impact on the suppliers of the specialized inputs. The level of fundamental-value informed trading will be most sensitive to this increase in cost. This is because fundamental-value informed traders create, at a cost to them, the information on which they trade. A wider spread means their trading will be less profitable and so they have less incentive to create information. In contrast, the level of issuer insider and non-issuer insider informed trading and trading based on the tips of such insiders depends mostly on the opportunities that the insiders encounter in their employment.

The decrease in the level of fundamental-value informed trading is unfortunate because the social gain from its contribution to long-run price accuracy exceeds the social costs of the activity.[45] Thus, the social disadvantage from a lower level of fundamental-value informed trading is likely to dominate the advantage from the likely smaller decrease in the other, socially undesirable, forms of informed trading.

e. *Anti-Noise Traders*

The prospect of naked open-market manipulation will draw resources into the business of anti-noise trading, which increases the level of resources going

---

[44] Barber and Odean, 'Behavior', 2013, 1534 ('Many apparently uninformed investors trade actively, speculatively, and to their detriment.')
[45] See Fox et al., 'Informed trading'.

into this activity. This produces a positive wealth impact on the suppliers of the specialized inputs.

8.5.1.3 FAIRNESS CONSIDERATIONS

Based on the survey above, we can see that freely occurring naked open-market manipulation will not affect the wealth position of uninformed traders from an ex ante point of view because they are as likely to benefit as to be hurt when the price at which they buy or sell is influenced by such a manipulation. It may add to the riskiness of their trading, but this is a risk that can typically be eliminated by holding a diversified portfolio. They will face an increase in the bid-ask spread, but on average this will be compensated by the lower cost of buying shares that earn a given expected payoff.

The wider bid-ask spread will result in fewer resources being drawn into the businesses of liquidity supply and fundamental-value informed trading, thereby decreasing the wealth positions of their specialized input suppliers. The prospect of profits will draw resources into the business of manipulation and the business of anti-noise trading, thereby increasing the wealth positions of their respective specialized input providers. A prospective flow of rents is not an entitlement, however. In a market economy, the offer of rents to prompt the suppliers of specialized inputs to come forward is simply the mechanism by which these resources get directed to the activity for which they are most particularly suited. The effects on the rents being paid in the case of the four businesses being considered here do not raise any greater fairness issues than do the rents paid persons with special abilities and skills across the whole market-based part of our economy. The bottom line is that the more serious normative question concerning naked open-market manipulation is whether its effect on the allocation of resources enhances or decreases efficiency.

8.5.1.4 EFFICIENCY CONSIDERATIONS

From an efficiency point of view, naked open-market manipulation has no redeeming virtues. It consumes resources that could be usefully employed elsewhere in the economy and has a negative impact on both price accuracy and liquidity.

a. Price Accuracy

As our discussion of the workings of the market shows, in the absence of manipulation, market prices have the remarkable quality of reflecting a large amount of information relevant to predicting an issuer's future cash flows. Naked open-market manipulation moves price away from where it otherwise would be, at least temporarily and sometimes for longer, hence reducing price accuracy. In essence, it acts as a kind of informational pollutant, making stock prices noisier signals of actual value. Interestingly, however, while most commentators and jurists focus on the price distortion effects of the practice, reduced price accuracy may be in most cases the less important of its negative social consequences, at least unless an issuer's shares were subject to such manipulation very frequently. This is because the period over which such a manipulation distorts price is typically quite short, a matter of days at most, at which point the issuer may credibly announce that there is no undisclosed information within its possession that could explain the price rise and only partial fallback, or because anti-noise traders quickly gain confidence that there exists no such information and trade accordingly.[46]

Recall that the ways that accurate prices benefit the economy is by helping to allocate the economy's scarce capital to the most promising potential real investment projects and by improving the utilization of the economy's existing productive capacity through optimizing the signals provided to management about investment decisions and the signals given to boards and shareholders about the quality of management decisions.[47] Very short-run distortions in price of the kind that will typically occur with naked open-market manipulation will not seriously undermine the role that share prices play in guiding the real economy in these ways. However, if neither of these corrective forces comes into play, then the price can remain significantly inaccurate for a substantial period of time.[48] In this event, the manipulation would result in both inefficiencies arising from longer-term price inaccuracies and negative efficiency related to liquidity, which we will now discuss.

b. Liquidity

The prospect of freely occurring naked open-market manipulation has a clear long-term, ongoing negative impact on the liquidity of an issuer's shares because liquidity suppliers will defend themselves against the possibility of losing to such manipulators, and losing again in the price correction process, by widening their bid-ask spreads and decreasing their depth of book. As we have seen, less liquidity reduces social welfare because of the resulting misallocation of resources over time and misallocation of risk: socially beneficial transactions fail to occur, leaving investors with suboptimal, riskier portfolios, and driving up the cost of capital for firms.[49] By raising the costs of fundamental-value informed trading and thereby lessening the incentives to search out and trade on new information, less liquidity also reduces longer-run share price accuracy.[50]

---

[46] See Section 8.5.1.1.b.   [47] See Section 8.3.3.1.   [48] See Section 8.5.1.1.b.
[49] See Section 8.3.3.2.   [50] See Section 8.3.3.2.

c. Resource Misallocation

The prospect of naked open-market manipulation also pulls additional resources into the anti-noise trading business. While these traders perform the socially useful function of correcting prices from their distorted level at the end of a manipulation, their efforts would not be needed in the first place absent the manipulation. Without the prospect of manipulation, these extra resources would be used elsewhere in the economy, positively contributing to the production of goods and services.

d. Market Confidence

There is one additional, more nebulous efficiency consideration: market confidence. This relates to a sense among investors that the market is fair, part of the fifth basic social goal discussed above. Even if naked open-market manipulation does not in fact decrease the wealth position of ordinary investors, and the additional risk created by it can be diversified away, public awareness that it occurs may hurt everyday investors' 'confidence' in the stock market. Such manipulations may strike the public as unfair and improper in some way that is harmful to them. As a result, to the detriment of both them and others, they may participate in the stock market to a lesser degree.[51] Typically, the best response to public misunderstanding is to resolve it through education, but where a perception may be especially difficult to eradicate and it is causing damage, then that perception may provide an independent policy ground for prohibiting the relevant conduct.

8.5.2 Are There Expected Profits?

The example of Mani above suggests that there can be expected profits associated with naked open-market manipulation. This is in sharp contrast with the conclusions of Daniel Fischel and David Ross's seminal article, in which they argue that manipulation should not be legally prohibited.[52] One of their two principal reasons for reaching this conclusion is that open-market manipulation cannot have expected profits associated with it. Thus, it need not be made illegal because it is self-deterring.

8.5.2.1 THE FISCHEL AND ROSS ARGUMENTS

Fischel and Ross make two arguments as to why profitable manipulation is not possible.[53] First, they say, most securities markets, and especially the stock of large public firms, are highly elastic and liquid.[54] Because of this, they reason,

---

[51] See Saad, 'U.S. stock', 8 May 2013. Michael Lewis attributes this drop, which occurred in the face of a sharply rising market over the previous five years, to a sense that the market is unfair. See Lewis, 200–1; see also Editorial Board, 'Hidden cost', 2014.
[52] Fischel and Ross, 506.   [53] Ibid., 517–18.   [54] Ibid., 517.

trading will typically have no effect on price, as holders of a security will simply sell it to a willing purchaser and substitute into a different security with a similar cash-flow profile. This argument, though, ignores the basic lesson of microstructure economics that, to a liquidity supplier in an anonymous market, all trade in a stock is potentially informed and thus will in fact will generally move price at least to some extent.[55]

Fischel and Ross's second line of argument at least recognizes the possibility that a trade could be interpreted as indicating someone has information not yet reflected in price. Here, they say that bids and offers may move up if a trader putting in purchase orders is perceived to be informed by the market, in which case quoting behaviour will adjust to reflect the information thought to be motivating a transaction, but the trader will also be thought to be informed when she sells as well, thereby on average driving bid and ask back down to where they were.[56] Moreover, the would-be manipulator will buy at the offer on the way up and sell at the bid on the way down. So on average, she will actually suffer a net loss. Given this, in the long run would-be manipulators will certainly lose, and so Fischel and Ross conclude that market manipulation is self-deterring. Anyone foolish enough to be a would-be manipulator will eventually learn her lesson and stop trying.

The problem with this second argument is that it fails to recognize the possibility of an *asymmetric price response*.[57] Empirically we observe that the price response to new orders relating to any stock can, in fact, vary over time.[58]

8.5.2.2 CAN AN ASYMMETRIC PRICE RESPONSE EVER BE ANTICIPATED?

The mere fact that the price response to new orders varies over time does not by itself prove that naked open-market manipulation can generate expected profits. It is also necessary that circumstances arise under which an asymmetric response has some degree of predictability. Note that in the Mani example set out above, we posit that Mani rationally assesses that it is probable that his purchases will push price up by more than his subsequent sales will push them down, but we do not discuss his basis for this expectation.

---

[55] See Section 8.4.3.   [56] Fischel and Ross, 518.

[57] Since Fischel and Ross's work, many other commentators have recognized this flaw in their argument, often in different respects. See Harris, *Trading and Exchanges*, 2003, 259, 265–8 (developing the possibility of asymmetric price response); Allen and Gale, 'Stock-price manipulation', 1992; Thel, '$850,000 in six minutes', 1994, 240–7 (discussing how a manipulator may profit by trading so as to alter others' expectations); see also Allen and Gorton, 'Stock price manipulation', 1992; Jarrow, 'Market manipulation', 1992.

[58] See Section 8.4.3; see also Easley et al., 'Flow toxicity', 2012, 1478; Easley et al., 'Time-varying', 2008, 198 (arguing that trading dynamically reacts to the perception of information-based trading).

Thus, a key question is whether there are in fact circumstances under which it is more likely than not that there will be an asymmetric price response in a particular direction. The answer is that there are. Below, we give examples of a few such circumstances.

a. A Period of Unusual Uncertainty

One such circumstance is where it is predictable that there will be more fear of informed trading before a certain moment in time than after. For example: an issuer is expected to announce its earnings on a certain date and there is uncertainty as to what will be announced, with the possibility that it might be either above or below some mean expectation.[59] In the run-up to the announcement, a liquidity supplier finds an order imbalance in either direction to have heightened significance because of the greater-than-usual likelihood that an issuer insider, or her tippee, is trading. Thus, if the manipulator put in orders creating such an imbalance during this period of extra uncertainty, it would prompt a greater than usual adjustment in the liquidity supplier's bid and offer. Once the announcement is made, the fear of issuer insider trading would diminish and the liquidity suppliers' bid and ask adjustments in response to order imbalances would diminish along with it. Thus, the manipulator can reverse her transactions with less impact on price and end up with a profit.

We should note, however, that while this kind of circumstance may arise quite often, it may not prompt very much manipulation. A manipulator trying to take advantage of such a circumstance will put herself in an unusually risky situation. The very reasons that make the liquidity supplier so sensitive to order imbalances mean that there is a heightened chance that informed trading is in fact going on. If it is, there is a 50–50 chance that the informed trader or traders are trading in the opposite direction from the manipulator, who is uninformed and hence has no idea which way they are trading. In such a case, the manipulator would need to transact in a very large number of shares for the price to move significantly because her orders would be just cancelling out the imbalance created by the informed trader or traders. At the end, the manipulator would be stuck with a huge inventory of shares at the time of the announcement, which, as predicted by the informed traders, moves the price in the wrong direction from what the manipulator wants.

---

[59] See Easley et al., 'Time-varying', 197–9 (showing how the probability of informed trading varies around the days of earnings announcements: 'the proportion of informed trades increases as the announcement date approaches and declines after the announcement').

b. Shopping for Stops

Another circumstance, sometimes referred to as 'shopping for stops', would be where there are an unusually large number of stop loss orders existing at the moment.[60] On the offer side, a stop-loss order is an order to buy if the price goes above a certain level. It would typically be placed by someone who is in a short position. He does so in order to place a ceiling on his potential losses if the share price goes above a certain point. If there are an usually large number of stop-loss orders on the offer side, the manipulator's purchases on the way up will have a super-charged effect on price because, as his orders drive the price up, the stop-loss orders are tripped, thereby triggering more buying orders. When the manipulator turns around to sell, the prices in the market, as they go down, will on average be well above the bid side stop-loss orders (typically put in by someone in a long position seeking a ceiling on her losses). So, prices do not decline as fast in reaction to the manipulator's sales because none of the bid stop-loss orders are tripped. The tricky part of this game, though, is that stop-loss orders that are posted with exchanges are not revealed. Also they may just be resting with a broker who is directed to submit them if the price reaches a certain level. Still, with aggressive trading to test the state of the market, a manipulator might be able to detect a situation with an usually large number of stop-loss orders, though it could be expensive to do so.

c. Book Fragility

Adam Clark-Joseph provides fascinating indirect evidence of manipulative behaviour in the E-Mini S&P 500 futures contract market that appears to involve instances of naked open-market manipulation.[61] Clark-Joseph offers the following facts. There are, in the Commodity Futures Trading Commission data, eight high frequency traders (HFTs) who regularly lose money on a series of small marketable orders. These same traders also make considerable money at times from a sequence of large marketable orders.

Clark-Joseph argues that the small marketable orders are exploratory, designed to determine whether the order book is 'fragile' on one side or the other. A fragile order book on a given side is one where the quantity of shares available at prices near the best quote is relatively small and does not refill immediately as marketable orders execute against the visible quotes that are there. In such a situation, a large marketable order executing against these quotes will move price significantly. If the exploratory trades reveal that the book is fragile on the offer side, then the HFT will be able to move the price with

---

[60] Harris, *Trading and Electronic Markets*, 2015, 14 (discussing the triggering of stop-loss orders as a market manipulation strategy).

[61] Clark-Joseph, 'Exploratory trading', 2013 (documenting the existence of a kind of price decoding high frequency trader in the futures market).

large, aggressive buy orders. If the HFT also forecasts that there will be a large number of marketable buy orders coming in (something that is often predictable), then it will be able to quickly unload the shares that it just purchased without a similarly strong downward pressure on price. Putting the position on has a large price impact because the book is fragile; taking off the position is expected to have a small price impact because it involves transacting with the anticipated marketable orders.

8.5.3 *The Appropriateness of Legal Sanctions*

The other principal reason that Fischel and Ross oppose the legal prohibition of manipulation is that no observable conduct separates manipulative trading from trading for other purposes. Determining the purpose of the transaction is highly speculative. Thus, they argue, making open-market manipulation illegal will deter many worthwhile transactions as well. This is because persons contemplating these worthwhile transactions will fear that their transactions will be mistaken for manipulative ones. We agree with their concern but take issue with their assumption that there is never observable conduct to distinguish manipulative transactions from socially useful ones.

Consider the three circumstances we discussed in Section 8.5.2.2 where it may be possible for a manipulator to assess that an asymmetric price response is more probable than not. In the case of the first circumstance—unusual uncertainty that will be resolved soon—there is indeed no observable conduct that would separate the manipulator from an investor who simply buys based on hard work analysing the future of the issuer, and then sells when his best guess turns out to be correct when the issuer's price increases. Thus, while, at least as a conceptual matter, there may be times in such a situation where naked open-market speculation will have positive expected profits, we see no way of intelligently imposing legal sanctions except where there is direct evidence, such as an email, as to the trader's purpose.

In contrast, in the other two circumstances, shopping for stops and book fragility, a manipulative trader would need to engage in observable market conduct to enjoy expected profits: she would need to test the market to see what the stop loss or book fragility situation is. We thus advocate a rule that imposes legal sanctions for a series of purchases followed by a series of sales (or vice versa) that yield a profit where the first set of transactions was preceded by this kind of testing of the market. This kind of conduct would strongly suggest that the trader was entering into these transactions at least in part to profit from the socially negative practice of naked open-market manipulation, and quite possibly this was the only motivation. In other words, there is a low risk that the rule would deter transactions solely motivated by some other socially worthwhile purpose. There is nothing wrong with deterring transactions that are motivated both by a desire to profit from such manipulation and by some other socially worthwhile purpose. This is because something affirmative and observable—the testing of the market—was necessary for the socially negative manipulation motive to be included. So imposing legal sanctions should deter undertaking the affirmative conduct, which is the vehicle for acting on the manipulative motive, but not transactions based on a socially worthwhile purpose.

8.6 Conclusion

Preventing the manipulation of securities has long preoccupied the popular and political imaginations. Yet, much of the scholarly literature has remained suspicious of manipulation as a coherent and useful concept. This chapter considered a particular form of manipulation, attempted to identify who was harmed from the perspective of microstructure economics, and assessed the economic welfare effects of these harms. It should thus offer counsel to both governmental enforcement agents and defense lawyers alike by developing a more precise approach to the evidentiary burdens regulators should impose in optimally prosecuting manipulation, while avoiding the deterrence of desirable trades.

References

Aggarwal, Rajesh K., and Guojun Wu. 'Stock market manipulations'. *Journal of Business* 79, no. 4 (2006): 1915–53.

Akerlof, George A. 'The market for "lemons": Quality uncertainty and the market mechanism'. *Quarterly Journal of Economics* 84, no. 3 (1970): 488–500.

Allen, Franklin, and Douglas Gale. 'Stock-price manipulation'. *Review of Financial Studies* 5, no. 3 (1 July 1992): 503–29.

Allen, Franklin, and Gary Gorton. 'Stock price manipulation, market microstructure and asymmetric information'. *European Economic Review* 36, no. 2 (1992): 624–30.

Amihud, Yakov, and Haim Mendelson. 'Asset pricing and the bid-ask spread'. *Journal of Financial Economics* 17, no. 2 (1986): 223–49.

Amihud, Yakov, and Haim Mendelson. 'Liquidity and asset prices: Financial management implications'. *Financial Management* 17, no. 1 (1988): 5–15.

Barber, Brad M., and Terrance Odean. 'The behavior of individual investors'. In *Handbook of the Economics of Finance*, ed. George M. Constantinides, Milton Harris, and René M. Stulz, 2nd edn, 1533–70, Amsterdam: Elsevier Publishing, 2013.

Bond, Philip, Alex Edmans, and Itay Goldstein. 'The real effects of financial markets'. *Annual Review of Financial Economics* 4, no. 1 (1 October 2012): 339–60.

Brealey, Richard, Stewart Myers, and Franklin Allen. *Principles of Corporate Finance*, 11th edn. New York: McGraw-Hill, 2013.

Brogaard, Jonathan, Terrence Hendershott, and Ryan Riordan. 'High-frequency trading and price discovery'. *Review of Financial Studies* 27, no. 8 (2014): 2267–306.

Chan, Kalok, Y. Peter Chung, and Herb Johnson. 'The intraday behavior of bid-ask spreads for NYSE stocks and CBOE options'. *Journal of Financial and Quantitative Analysis* 30, no. 3 (1995): 329–46.

Chen, Qi, Itay Goldstein, and Wei Jiang. 'Price informativeness and investment sensitivity to stock price'. *Review of Financial Studies* 20, no. 3 (2007): 619–50.

Clark-Joseph, Adam D. 'Exploratory trading', 2013. Available at: http://www.nanex.net/aqck2/4136/exploratorytrading.pdf.

Davis, Alicia J. 'Are investors' gains and losses from securities fraud equal over time? Theory and evidence'. University of Michigan Law and Economics, Olin Working Paper, 2015.

Easley, David, Robert F. Engle, Maureen O'Hara, and Liuren Wu. 'Time-varying arrival rates of informed and uninformed trades'. *Journal of Financial Econometrics* 6, no. 2 (2008): 171–207.

Easley, David, Marcos M. López de Prado, and Maureen O'Hara. 'Flow toxicity and liquidity in a high-frequency world'. *Review of Financial Studies* 25, no. 5 (2012): 1457–93.

Editorial Board. 'The hidden cost of trading stocks'. *New York Times*, 22 June 2014. https://www.nytimes.com/2014/06/23/opinion/best-execution-and-rebates-for-brokers.html.

Fischel, Daniel R., and David J. Ross. 'Should the law prohibit "manipulation" in financial markets?' *Harvard Law Review* 105, no. 2 (1991): 503–53.

Foucault, Thierry, Marco Pagano, and Ailsa Röell. *Market Liquidity: Theory, Evidence, and Policy*. Oxford University Press, 2013.

Fox, Merritt B. 'Civil liability and mandatory disclosure'. *Columbia Law Review* 109, no. 2 (2009): 237–308.

Fox, Merritt B., Lawrence R. Glosten, and Gabriel V. Rauterberg. 'The new stock market: Sense and nonsense'. *Duke Law Journal* 65, no. 2 (2015): 191–277.

Fox, Merritt B., Lawrence R. Glosten, and Gabriel V. Rauterberg. 'Informed trading and its regulation'. *Journal of Corporation Law* 43 (2018).

Fox, Merritt B., Lawrence R. Glosten, and Gabriel V. Rauterberg. 'Stock market manipulation and its regulation'. *Yale Journal on Regulation* 35 (2018).

Glosten, Lawrence R., and Lawrence E. Harris. 'Estimating the components of the bid-ask spread'. *Journal of Financial Economics* 21, no. 1 (1988): 123–42.

Glosten, Lawrence R., and Paul R. Milgrom. 'Bid, ask and transaction prices in a specialist market with heterogeneously informed traders'. *Journal of Financial Economics* 14, no. 1 (1985): 71–100.

Harris, Larry. *Trading and Exchanges: Market Microstructure for Practitioners*. Oxford University Press, 2003.

Harris, Larry. *Trading and Electronic Markets: What Investment Professionals Need to Know*. CFA Institute Research Foundation, 2015.

Hicks, J. R. 'The foundations of welfare economics'. *Economic Journal* 49, no. 196 (1939): 696–712.

Jarrow, Robert A. 'Market manipulation, bubbles, corners, and short squeezes'. *Journal of Financial and Quantitative Analysis* 27, no. 3 (1992): 311–36.

Jiang, Guolin, Paul G. Mahoney, and Jianping Mei. 'Market manipulation: A comprehensive study of stock pools'. *Journal of Financial Economics* 77, no. 1 (1 July 2005): 147–70.

Kahan, Marcel. 'Securities laws and the social costs of inaccurate stock prices'. *Duke Law Journal* 41 (1992): 977–1044.

Kaldor, Nicholas. 'Welfare propositions of economics and interpersonal comparisons of utility'. *Economic Journal* 49, no. 195 (1939): 549–52.

Kraakman, Reinier, John Armour, Paul Davies, Luca Enriques, Henry Hansmann, Gerard Hertig, Klaus Hopt, Hideki Kanda, Mariana Pargendler, Wolf-Georg Ringe, and Edward Rock. *The Anatomy of Corporate Law: A Comparative and Functional Approach*, 3rd edn. Oxford: Oxford University Press, 2017.

Lewis, Michael. *Flash Boys*. New York: W.W. Norton & Company, 2014.

Mahoney, Paul G. *Wasting a Crisis: Why Securities Regulation Fails*. Chicago: University of Chicago Press, 2015.

Merriam-Webster's Collegiate Dictionary, 11th edn. Springfield, MA: Merriam-Webster, 2009.

Pirrong, Craig. 'Squeezes, corpses, and the anti-manipulation provisions of the Commodity Exchange Act'. *Regulation* 17, no. 4 (1994): 52–63.

Putniņš, Tālis J. 'Market manipulation: A survey'. *Journal of Economic Surveys* 26, no. 5 (2011): 952–67.

Roach, William A., Jr. 'Hedge fund regulation: "What side of the hedges are you on?"' *University of Memphis Law Review* 40 (2009): 165–214.

Saad, Lydia. 'U.S. stock ownership stays at record low'. *Gallup*, 8 May 2013. http://news.gallup.com/poll/162353/stock-ownership-stays-record-low.aspx.

Thel, Steve. '$850,000 in six minutes: The mechanics of securities manipulation'. *Cornell Law Review* 79 (1994): 219–98.

9

Algorithmic Trading and Market Regulation

Yesha Yadav

9.1 Introduction

This chapter examines the impact of algorithmic trading on anchoring concepts in market regulation and governance. Recent years have witnessed expansive growth in the use of algorithms—pre-set computerized processes—to guide virtually all aspects of the trading process. Using algorithms, tasks such as order submission, routing, matching, and trade settlement can be entirely automated in their operation.[1] Through sophisticated programming, algorithms can accomplish these tasks without need for real-time human intervention or for trade-by-trade decision-making. Advances in programming, artificial intelligence, data mining, and communication technologies have enabled algorithms to harness speed, volume, and quantitative power to deliver rapid-fire trading across multiple trading platforms and types of security.[2]

Policy-makers have offered a partial response to the challenges raised by automated market mechanics. A number of important initiatives have sought to make trading infrastructure more resilient to operational risks, such as those stemming from suboptimal technology, monitoring, and systems security.[3] For example, the US Securities and Exchange Commission (SEC) has implemented Regulation Systems, Compliance and Integrity (Reg SCI) to address vulnerabilities in the design of equity trading platforms. Reg SCI mandates

---

[1] Cormen et al., *Introduction to Algorithms*, 2009, 5–6. ('Informally, an algorithm is any well-defined computational procedure that takes some value, or set of values, as input and produces some value, or set of values, as output. An algorithm is thus a sequence of computational steps that transform the input into the output.')

[2] Foresight, 'Future of computer trading', 2012, 20–50; MacIntosh, 'High frequency traders', 2013, 3–5. See also Brummer, 'Disruptive technology', 2015.

[3] SEC, Regulation Systems Compliance and Integrity, 2015. The CFTC has proposed Regulation Automated Trading designed to bolster systems integrity of algorithmic traders utilizing derivatives exchanges. CFTC, Regulation Automated Trading, 2015.

that trading venues perform testing, foster resiliency in systems design, and maintain tools to control the spread of disruptions and operational risks.[4] The US Commodity Futures Trading Commission's (CFTC) proposed Regulation Automated Trading (Reg AT). Though a work in progress, the CFTC's initial proposal sought to require derivatives trading algorithms to include built-in pre-trade risk controls (e.g. testing, limits on order size) and damage limitation mechanisms (e.g. to rapidly cancel existing orders and shut down trading in case of fallout) as part of their programming.[5]

Policy-makers, however, have given little attention to the interaction between automated markets and fundamental, foundational legal concepts underlying market regulation. Beyond simply raising concerns at the level of operational systems design, algorithmic trading challenges conventional applications of entrenched legal concepts governing the imposition and enforcement of civil and criminal liability.

This chapter provides an overview of some of these core concepts. It surveys eight framework notions critical to regulation and examines how these might apply in an automated marketplace. It addresses the following: (1) reasonableness; (2) strict liability; (3) foreseeability; (4) contribution; (5) scienter; (6) damage and harm; (7) evidence and proof; and (8) disclosure and information dissemination. In foregrounding its analysis, the chapter summarizes key features of algorithmic trading and how these distinguish modern market structure from past iterations. By highlighting the unique features of current market structure, this chapter offers an initial analysis of how deeply-held assumptions guiding regulation have come to sit uneasily in innovative, evolving markets. This analysis provides an overview of the interaction between established laws and evolving markets. Its aim is to motivate a more thoroughgoing examination of the impact of algorithmic trading on law and regulation. The discussion in this chapter is based on arguments and research advanced in a series of recent articles on the impact of algorithmic trading on foundational concepts in securities market regulation and market design.[6]

9.2 Algorithmic Trading and Market Design

9.2.1 *Key Features of Algorithmic Trading*

Algorithmic trading depends on the workings of pre-programmed computerized instructions—algorithms—to buy and sell securities. With the aid of

---

[4] SEC, Regulation Systems Compliance and Integrity.   [5] Ibid., 78,937–9.

[6] The discussions underpinning this note are based on a series of articles examining the interaction of core notions in securities regulation with automated, particularly high frequency, trading. See, in particular, Yadav, 'Failure of liability', 2015; Yadav, 'Insider trading', 2016; Yadav, 'How Algorithmic Trading', 2015.

precisely crafted programming, algorithms help to automate the various stages of a securities transaction. From submitting an order to purchase or dispose of a security, routing this order to an exchange, and matching buy with sell orders to finally settling a trade, algorithms have become essential to the mechanisms of market structure. For a basic trade, programming must enable algorithms to collect data, to mine it for information, and to ascribe a value to this information in the form of an order to buy and sell a security at a certain volume and price point.[7]

Automation allows transactions to turn over at speed, using vast quantities of data, complex financial modeling, and sophisticated trading strategies.[8] High frequency trading (HFT)—a strategy that harnesses algorithms to trade in milliseconds and microseconds—showcases the capacity of algorithms to transact at speeds that far exceed the bounds of traditional, human-guided trading. As a result, HFT necessarily depends on algorithms and automation at almost every step of the trading process. HFT has become central to the marketplace, driving around 50–70 per cent of all equity trading by volume, 60 per cent in the futures market, and almost 50 per cent in US Treasuries.[9] But even at (relatively) slower speeds, automation has become the norm. According to a 2013 study by the Australian Securities and Investments Commission (ASIC), 99.6 per cent of all trading messages in Australian equity markets were sourced from an automated trading program. Indeed, the study observed that all types of market participants used algorithmic trading, not just high frequency traders. And many of those that claimed to be slower were, in fact, only marginally less fast than specialist speed traders.[10]

Automation offers numerous benefits for market quality. First, the capacity for algorithms to gather and process enormous quantities of data can make markets stronger at reflecting information about a security or an asset (e.g. commodities, interest rates, or credit risk). Speed should mean that this news is processed rapidly, emerging faster and more fully than ever before into the prices at which securities trade. If prices reveal a wider breadth of information about a particular security or asset, investors have a sharper window into what these claims are really worth. A number of commentators have noted that automated markets, characterized by HFT, have made markets

---

[7] Bates, 'Algorithmic trading', 2010, 27–8. ('An algorithm is a sequence of steps to achieve a goal' and the general case of algorithmic trading is 'using a computer to automate a trading strategy').

[8] IOSCO, 'Regulatory issues', 2011, 10. ('In its simplest guise, algorithmic trading may just involve the use of a basic algorithm ... to feed portions of an order into the market at pre-set intervals to minimise market impact cost. At its most complex, it may entail many algorithms that are able to assimilate information from multiple markets ... in fractions of a second.')

[9] Foresight, 20–50; MacIntosh, 3–5; Osipovich, 'Algorithmic trading', 10 January 2012; Stafford et al., 'Nasdaq sets stage', 4 April 2013.

[10] ASIC, 'Dark liquidity', 2013.

markedly more efficient and better at reflecting information in prices, at least in the very short term.[11]

Second, automation and HFT can be beneficial for investors by lowering the transaction costs that they face. Specifically, HFT can make markets better at executing trades more cheaply and on desirable terms for investors. High frequency (HF) traders can provide a readily available contract party for those wishing to enter the market. By transacting at speed and at volume, HF traders can make small incremental gains from each deal and a steady profit over time. In its initial public offering filing, the HFT firm Virtu Financial reported that this market-making activity had yielded reliable profit over time, with Virtu experiencing only a single unprofitable day in around four years of business.[12]

These private gains for HFT firms can bring public benefit. High-speed market making can help investors to gain access to the market rapidly, receiving ready execution and facing less uncertainty about whether they will lose out on a trade. Moreover, HFT firms face limited exposure to market uncertainties in providing this market-making function. HF traders enter and exit at speed and thus hold risks on their books for tiny amounts of time. Many are under no obligation to trade unless they actually wish to do so, such that they do not need to remain on the exchange in times of trouble, as traditional market makers have had to do in the past.[13] Cheaper market making can result in lower costs to investors, with one study estimating that HFT market makers reduced spreads on one exchange by as much as 50 per cent.[14] Indeed, these reduced costs have proven important to investors. Attempts to regulate HFT on the Toronto Stock Exchange, for example (through a higher fee affecting passive HFT market makers), prompted an increase in effective spreads and caused retail investors to suffer meaningful intra-day losses.[15]

Markets are heavily dependent on algorithmic trading and the structure that supports their operation. This reliance is made abundantly clear in those instances when algorithmic traders have reduced or retreated from the market in response to some anomalous event. On 6 May 2010, for example, an abnormally stressed trading environment led to the sudden, short-lived collapse of the stock market, with the Dow Jones index losing almost 1000 points in a few minutes before rebounding. In the initial CFTC/SEC's inquest into the

---

[11] See notably, Brogaard et al., 'High frequency trading and price discovery', 2013 (on higher market efficiency in high frequency markets); Brogaard et al., 'High frequency trading and extreme price movements', 2014; Martinez and Rosu, 'High frequency traders', 2013.
[12] Laughlin, 'Insights', 2014, 2–4.   [13] Glosten, 'Insider trading', 1989.
[14] Menkveld, 'High frequency trading', 2013; Dolgopolov, 'Regulating merchants', 2016 (offering an overview of the history of market making and the rise of HFT).
[15] Malinova et al., 'Do retail traders suffer?', 2013 (this study examined an increased fee on message traffic that affected passive HFT as market making can require high volumes of messages to succeed; there was less impact on institutional investors).

event, the sharp plunge seen during this 'flash crash' could be attributed, in part, to HFT market makers that quickly left the market in response to the difficult environment: exiting HF traders stopped providing liquidity and made it impossible to transact on reasonable terms.[16] Relatedly, in October 2014, the US Treasury market—where about 50 per cent of all trading volume is driven by HFT—experienced its own abnormal (and still unexplained) trading event. On that day, HFT traders did not leave the market—as they had done in the case of the May 2010 flash crash. Rather, they continued trading. However, they did change how they provided liquidity, with the official inquiry into this crash noting that informal market maker HFTs showed the largest reduction in the depth of order book relative to traditional dealers.[17]

This importance of algorithmic trading for market function means that disruptions in these markets can extract a heavy and unpredictable price. Seen through this lens, the role of the legal system in policing the conduct of automated traders takes on significant economic importance. Where the legal system cannot adequately deter or punish instances of mistake, misconduct, or manipulation in algorithmic markets, the impact can potentially result in systemic uncertainty and risk. In the absence of oversight tailored to today's faster, automated, and more interconnected markets, even small mishaps can assume outsize significance. When markets are too prone to regular disruptions—causing algorithmic traders to react in unpredictable ways—capital allocation can suffer. Investors might seek out ways to protect themselves by discounting the capital they place at risk in the market or by seeking out ways to limit their participation in it, for example, by moving to off-exchange venues.[18]

9.2.2 Risks of Algorithmic Trading

Algorithmic trading—and HFT in particular—presents two key sources of risk: (1) operational risks caused by poor technology, suboptimal monitoring, and misfiring infrastructure; and (2) the endemic risk of error caused by the need for pre-set programming to guide the real-time workings of high speed algorithms. Regulation has been formulated to try and deal with the former. However, regulatory policy has not yet fully accounted for the implications of the latter.

---

[16] CFTC and SEC, 'Findings', 2010, 45. See also Kirilenko et al., 'Flash crash', 2014. But see United States v. Sarao, Criminal Complaint U.S. District Court Northern District of Illinois, Case Number 15 CR 75., 11 February 2015. See also Meyer and Stafford, 'Flash crash trader', 2018.

[17] US Treasury Department et al., 'Joint staff report', 2015, 3, 5–6 (referred to as 'Principal Trading Firms' in report).

[18] The sections below rely, in part, on research undertaken and arguments set out in Yadav, 'Failure of liability'.

9.2.2.1 OPERATIONAL RISKS

Operational risks are ever-present in the workings of automated trading and algorithmic markets. With deep reliance on computer processing, communications technology, data availability and mining, and inter-operability between trading venues, the chance that any one of these processes might fall short and disrupt the system is pervasive. Recent regulatory efforts have focused on standardizing investment in technology, improving monitoring, and putting in place mechanisms to deal with the fallout from disruptive events.

The CFTC proposed Reg AT focused, in large part, on developing a range of tools to handle operational risks. Reg AT sought to standardize pre-trade and post-trade risk controls for algorithmic traders; introduce mandatory registration; build a more searching reporting regime through regular performance reports. Pre-trade risk controls required, for example, that traders put in place systems to control the size and number of orders entering the market.[19] Firms were also required to set such limits as needed to reasonably safeguard against a disruptive event.[20] From the post-trade perspective, firms had to be equipped to cancel orders resting in the market, to prevent new orders from entering, and to provide a form of 'kill switch' for their trading system—all measures that could control the spread of a disruptive event.

These steps complement those taken by the SEC in its Reg SCI that seek to bolster the operational health of major trading venues. Reg SCI requires trading systems to put in place policies that are designed to reasonably maintain the safety and soundness of the market. In addition, the SEC's Market Access Rule mandates that broker-dealers implement procedures that reasonably assure compliance with securities laws and operational requirements. This Rule makes broker-dealers de facto gatekeepers entrusted to protect markets from investors that use the broker-dealer's trading infrastructure to enter the marketplace.[21]

9.2.2.2 RISKS OF INHERENT ERROR

Current regulation fails, however, to account for a fundamental risk in algorithmic markets, particularly for HFT. Put simply, the risk of error is endemic to the operation of complex algorithms, especially those designed to transact at high speeds.[22] In order to enable transactions to take place in microseconds and milliseconds, algorithms need to be pre-programmed in advance of

---

[19] CFTC, Regulation Automated Trading, Proposed § 1.80(a)(1)(i).
[20] Ibid. § 1.80(a)(2). Regulation § 1.83 of the proposal requires compliance reports to be provided.
[21] SEC, Exchange Act Rule 15c3-5, 2010, 17 C.F.R. 240.15c3-5.
[22] Yadav, 'How algorithmic trading'.

trading. Because human beings cannot take trade-by-trade decisions and cannot intervene in real time to address errors or malfunctions, algorithms must be exactly and predictively instructed about how to independently trade over periods in the day. This means that programmers and traders must estimate how the market is likely to behave and then craft their algorithms in anticipation of these future conditions before the algorithms can begin trading. Their instructions must include steps for collecting data, interpreting this data for useful information, and ascribing a value to this news in the form of an order for the sale or purchase of securities. Additionally, algorithms must route these orders to the best venue, determine whether a trade has been successfully consummated, and take steps to adaptively react to the impact of this trading for the next set of transactions. Algorithmic programming needs to establish processes for the algorithm to react dynamically to the trading of other market participants and to modify its reactions accordingly.[23] It also needs to include instructions on what an algorithm should do if market conditions become unpredictable and indicative of more risk than traders can tolerate.

The challenge of precisely predicting the future means that algorithms are susceptible to the risks of random, endemic error. In the absence of certain knowledge about future market conditions, programmers can make understandable mistakes in anticipating how the markets might behave. Errors, imprecision, and potentially disruptive trading in algorithmic markets might arise for any number of reasons.

- Traders can fail to anticipate market conditions accurately. For instance, programming may use models that are not suited to a particular trading environment. A model might base its assumptions on trading being rational and in accordance with historic norms. External events, however, may be unusual. On 24 August 2015, for example, turmoil in China prompted chaotic, volatile trading in US markets, with almost 14 billion shares traded on a single day and $630 billion changing hands. As the Dow Jones fell more than 1000 points and then rebounded, the market suffered 1278 separate trading halts in 471 different stocks. Algorithms transacted erratically, with market-making operations and cross-market arbitrage unable to function smoothly as HFT operations shut down on account of the difficult conditions.[24] As scholars observe, unpredictable events and crises create 'preference uncertainty' for traders, meaning that traders must choose between various possible options in reacting to

---

[23] Kearns and Nevmyvaka, 'Machine learning', 2013.
[24] Pisani, 'What happened', 25 September 2015; Blackrock, 'US equity market structure', 2015; SEC, 'Research Note', 2015, 2–6.

unusual events.[25] Pre-set programming, however, is ill-suited to dealing with such preference uncertainty where instructions must be precisely and fairly rigidly set in advance. It is to be expected that traders may not be able to correctly predict future market conditions or how others may trade in response to the algorithm. Imprecise or erroneous responses should be expected.

- In reacting in milli- and microseconds to new information, algorithmic reactions may be immediate and only gradually become more refined as fuller information emerges. Also, incoming data may not be checked for its veracity and accuracy. A study by *Nature* magazine, examining 18,500 ultra-fast mini-flash-crashes between 2006 and 2011, explained these events as reflecting a process of reacting to and refining responses to new information.[26] This process of reaction, refining, and competing to do so in microsecond intervals may generate volatility and disruption.

- Certain kinds of information may be difficult for algorithms to analyse. Scholars note that 'soft', more contextual information, in contrast to hard data, can be especially challenging for algorithms to interpret.[27] While algorithms may be adept at reacting to news focused on data and hard indicators, they may be less precise in dealing with predictions, forward-looking statements, clarifications to data (e.g. through footnotes), and opinions.[28] Artificial intelligence in language processing is making steady gains. However, it remains early days in understanding its empirical effectiveness for processing softer, unstructured information.

- Algorithmic programs may respond in a correlated manner to similar data and outside input. With traders all looking to profit rapidly, perhaps using similar strategies such as market-making or cross-market arbitrage, programming may be similar across a large swath of traders. This might result in stronger-than-expected reactions to new information as automated traders respond similarly to emerging input. One study, for example, observed trading in the foreign exchange market to be correlated to news events.[29]

- Additionally, systems may simply malfunction. Despite regulations such as Reg SCI, or the Market Access Rule, errors may occur through software glitches, erroneous source code, or disruptions in connectivity. Even source code that is workable may react disruptively when confronted by

---

[25] Biais et al., 'Equilibrium pricing', 2014, 1402–3.

[26] Johnson et al., 'Abrupt rise', 2013; Dugast and Foucault, 'False news', 2014; Biais et al., 'Equilibrium', 2014 (noting the privately inefficient overinvestment in high-speed trading technology by traders); Wigglesworth, 'AI decodes', 25 October 2017.

[27] Zhang and Riordan, 'Technology', 2011.   [28] Yadav, 'How algorithmic trading'.

[29] Chaboud et al., 'Rise of the machines', 2013 (higher efficiencies in foreign exchange markets).

malfunctions in technology or (as discussed above) in unusual market conditions. Technological errors have become quite routine. The collapse of Knight Capital—when the firm sent out around 4 million orders instead of 212, resulting in $460 million of losses in 45 minutes—is illustrative. The damage arose as a result of a misfiring router—an unfortunate but nevertheless fairly foreseeable type of error in a hi-tech market.[30]

9.2.2.3 INTERCONNECTION

Modern markets also represent a collection of fragmented venues connected to one another through strong informational and transactional links.[31] This feature is not special to automated markets. However, automated HF traders are well placed to take advantage of fragmentation and the close linkages that connect platforms to one another.

Fragmentation is pervasive within US equity markets, where Regulation National Market System and Regulation Alternative Trading Systems have fostered the creation of 13 exchanges and around 40 dark pools.[32] By contrast, exchange-traded derivatives represent more consolidated markets, with trading concentrated within a single venue or a handful of venues. Despite these differences between equity and derivatives markets, however, algorithmic trading has thickened interconnections across venues and asset classes. Algorithmic traders can transact across multiple platforms, for example, to engage in arbitrage-related strategies or to make markets in both equity and exchange-traded derivatives. In response to news, HFTs might trade rapidly across different asset classes on various exchanges and off-exchange venues. Anecdotally, the impact of these informational and transactional linkages is becoming increasingly evident. As seen in the May 2010 flash crash, trades in the E-Mini S&P stock index futures markets rapidly bled into the broader equity markets. Similarly, the volatility in the US Treasury Market in October 2014 triggered turbulence across other asset classes. From the scholarly standpoint, commentators have observed heightened efficiency across the marketplace, with information traveling at speed across the fragmented, interlinked markets. At the same time, errors also propagate. Their effects can move from one venue to the next at speed, resulting in a cascade of systemic magnitude as algorithms respond to each other automatically and rapidly before humans can begin to intervene in real time.[33]

---

[30] SEC, 'SEC charges Knight Capital', 2013.
[31] Gerig, 'High-frequency trading', 2015; Yadav, 'Oversight failure', 2018.
[32] Mamudi and Massa, 'Dark pools', 23 August 2015. See Yadav, 'Oversight failure'.
[33] Gerig, 'High-frequency trading'; US Treasury Department et al., 'Joint staff report', 3, 5–6; CFTC and SEC, 'Findings'.

9.3 Algorithmic Trading in Law and Regulation

The inherent risk of unpredictable errors in algorithmic markets—combined with their interconnectedness—challenges established legal paradigms designed to control and discipline market participants.[34] This section sets out a summary of how key legal concepts strain in their ability to capture the new risks of the automated high-speed marketplace.

9.3.1 Reasonableness

The concept of reasonableness sets the essential standard of behaviour expected from market participants. Across the spectrum of regulation, the reasonableness standard is pervasive and establishes the minimum cost that any participant must contend with when transacting in securities markets. In proposed Reg AT, for example, traders are required to establish such risk controls as are needed to reasonably preclude a disruptive event, as defined by the CFTC. Further, the SEC's Reg SCI and Market Access Rule mandate that participants put in place such systems as are reasonably needed to control operational, regulatory, and financial risks. By formalizing 'reasonable' behaviour as the controlling standard in many and varying contexts, regulators place heavy reliance on this standard as a basis for grounding market quality.

The reasonableness standard is based in tort law and anchored in a vast reserve of legal and economic analysis.[35] Examined from first principles, the reasonableness standard does not expect that market participants behave perfectly all the time. Rather, the standard requires that participants behave reasonably—in that they invest in taking cost-effective steps to prevent larger harms from arising. Actors do not need to take all steps to prevent all harm from arising—but only those that do not exceed the cost of the harm. If an actor must bear higher costs than the costs of the actual harm itself, then this demand may be considered unreasonably wasteful. In short, an actor is allowed to take some risks so long as these are reasonable—an objective standard that looks to cues such as industry best practice for fleshing out what it means in practice.

The reasonableness standard, however, sits uneasily in algorithmic markets. First, even small-scale, 'reasonable' risk-taking can result in far greater harms than contemplated by a single actor. As complex algorithms require to be pre-programmed and thus need to be predictive regarding future market states, errors and imprecision are realistically to be expected. Traders can, of course,

---

[34] Bratton and Wachter, 'Political economy', 2011 (on the traditional goals of enforcement policy in securities regulation, focusing here on the class action).

[35] Calabresi, *Cost of Accidents*, 1970, 26–7; Goldberg, 'Twentieth-century tort', 2003, 514–30; Rabin, 'Historical development', 1981; Shavell, *Economic Analysis*, 2002, Chapters 2, 4, 5; Polinsky and Shavell, 'Economic analysis', 2005, 8–13.

take steps to minimize these risks. As contemplated by Reg AT, for instance, traders are required to examine their risk controls and to ensure that source codes are well checked and tested to a degree designed to reasonably control disruptive events. Despite these controls, however, errors can persist. Traders may reasonably use models that are wrong or unsuited to market conditions. Their algorithms may reasonably fail to estimate how other traders will respond to their behaviour. As discussed earlier, risk of such errors is built in to the design of HFT: automated programs react immediately to new information and refine their responses only over time as more information is internalized.

Second, interconnection in the marketplace can amplify the effect of even a small, reasonable error. Seemingly non-serious mishaps may breed widespread disruptions owing to the risk that these may travel across multiple venues and asset classes. Algorithmic traders might also react similarly to the same information, deepening the effects of even reasonable errors, imprecisions, or inaccurate programming. Anecdotally, the Knight Capital collapse is illustrative. In that incident, stale code on a misfiring router resulted in around 4 million unwanted orders and around $460 million in losses to the firm. In addition to this direct loss, commentators noted that the collapse of the firm also created a more systemic impact. In the 30 minutes during which the erroneous orders were transmitting, the NYSE and Arca saw around $11 billion more in trading than the previous day, whereas the NASDAQ saw a drop in activity.[36] In a separate set of incidents, the NYSE and the NASDAQ both suffered notable shutdowns in the course of installing routine upgrades for their infrastructure, prompting spillover effects across trading venues.[37]

In automated, interconnected markets, reasonable mishaps can have wide-ranging, damaging consequences. This cost might point to the need to tighten the reasonableness standard and to require actors to be more careful owing to the propensity for potentially serious harm.

However, even a stricter reading of reasonableness does not deal with the fact that complex algorithms and HFT are inherently susceptible to random, unpredictable risks. To the extent that the reasonableness standard leaves some room for manoeuvre, as it is designed to do, errors are to be expected. Interconnection and correlated trading behaviours mean that even small-scale errors can have a disproportionately large impact.

9.3.2 *Strict Liability*

For large-scale losses, the law routinely looks to strict liability to make actors aware of the need to take great care in their actions. For example, strict liability

---

[36] Nanex, 'Knightmare on Wall Street', 2012.
[37] Popper, 'Stock market bell', 8 July 2015; SEC, 'SEC charges NASDAQ', 2013.

is common in environmental regulation and consumer products liability, to motivate actors to ensure that their operations are safe and do not result in large social harms. Using strict liability, an actor can become liable for all harms arising from a bad act. Further, under strict liability, regulators need to show only the fact of harm and do not have to demonstrate that the reasonableness standard has been breached. In securities regulation, by contrast, strict liability is applied to more formalistic, technical violations, such as a failure to file a report, rather than to account for large-scale financial losses in securities markets.[38]

From the economic standpoint, strict liability forces actors to make careful provision to control harms. Because the scale of potential liability can be enormous, often without a dollar ceiling, actors need to build strong systems in advance of acting. This involves recognizing the risks, predicting the likelihood that they materialize, and constructing robust systems to spot and eliminate them. An example may be helpful. A toy-maker knows that 10 out of every 10,000 toys can be faulty and make children sick. The toy company can tailor its monitoring systems and supply lines to seek out these 10 problem toys and to take them out of circulation. Importantly, because the toy company knows roughly how many toys are likely to be faulty based on its past experience, it can predict the vector of harms that might arise: that 10 children might fall sick for every 10,000 toys bought, the seriousness of the damage, and the likely costs of compensating and making whole on this harm.

The examples of large-scale flash crashes in the securities market and sudden collapses such as those affecting Knight Capital might—at first—resemble the notional bad toy that generates large-scale welfare harms. With extensive and visible disruptions, a strict liability standard would appear to offer an obvious tool to force traders to take intensive precautions to avoid damage and to absorb the full costs of their failures.

However, a strict liability standard is problematic in automated markets. For one, risk of random error is endemic to HFT algorithms, especially those designed to transact predictively in real time. While risk is also inherent in manufacturing toys, risks in automated markets appear impossible to predict with any degree of accuracy and thus to provision for in a reliable way. As noted, errors might arise because an asset-valuation model breaks down in unusual market conditions, skewing the orders that are submitted. An algorithm, while exhibiting a trustworthy source code, might still react erratically to incoming inaccurate data or unusually stressed market conditions. For example, the CFTC partially attributed the May 2010 flash crash to consequences

---

[38] Scopino, 'Do automated trading systems', 2015, 253–4.

flowing from the actions of a single foreign trader trying to fool other algorithms into buying and selling at artificial prices ('spoofing'). It seems fair to say that traders could not have predicted how algorithms would react to this single spoofer or guessed at the scale of the chaotic panic that he could cause.[39] The inherent risk of random, unpredictable error suggests that a strict liability standard is unlikely to be workable. Provisioning costs for the many variables and risks are likely to be far too high and still not offer any reliable safety—short of motivating traders to withdraw from the market altogether.

9.3.3 *Foreseeability*

In examining whether conduct is acceptable and how harmful risk taking is likely to be, the law generally demands that actors consider the reasonably foreseeable consequences of their actions. If a trader's actions are likely to create large losses with a sufficient degree of predictability (i.e. that these costly harms are reasonably foreseeable), then conduct will generally fall outside the perimeter of lawful behaviour. The law leans on determinations of what is foreseeable to establish causality as well as for fixing the scope of damages. Losses that can be reasonably predicted in advance are more likely to be caused by a set of bad actions. Similarly, where an actor is found to have acted negligently, she is expected to pay for the reasonably foreseeable consequences of a disruptive action.[40] Foreseeability grounds an important principle. It forces negligent actors to contemplate the expected results of their actions. If a trader might make more money than the foreseeable losses of an action, then she might be motivated to take the risk. Alternatively, by reflecting on these foreseeable consequences, a trader might think twice before entering the market, particularly if the gains from a deal may be uncertain. For regulators seeking to fix a quantum of damages, or to establish a basis for settlement, reasonable foreseeability provides a guidepost in this context.

Foreseeability becomes a more unreliable notion in automated markets. To start with, determining the foreseeable trading behaviour of a smart, sophisticated algorithm in a fast-moving market can be difficult for both traders and regulators. The fuller consequences arising out of a misfiring algorithm may be affected by a multiplicity of factors. For one, even a routine, well-functioning algorithm can estimate market conditions incorrectly or imprecisely (e.g. the May 2010 flash crash). Where an algorithm is programmed without due care

---

[39] Criminal Complaint, United States v. Sarao, No. 15-CR-75 (N.D. Ill. Feb. 11, 2015.); but see Pirrong, 'Did spoofing cause', 22 April 2015.

[40] See, e.g., Overseas Tankship (UK) Ltd v Morts Dock and Engineering Co Ltd or Wagon Mound (No. 1) [1961] UKPC 2, [1961] AC 388, [1961] 1 All ER 404.

(e.g. if it is has not been as thoroughly tested to deal with abnormal markets), then interconnected high-speed markets can amplify the consequences of such an error (e.g. Knight Capital). Alternatively, in other cases of careless programming, the damage may be end up being far less dramatic and minimal (e.g. if an exchange activates its circuit breakers to control a spiral). If similarly risky actions may generate different outcomes based on the responses of other participants and trading venues, reliance on foreseeability as a controlling concept in liability can make for patchy, inconsistent enforcement.

One possible response, here, may be to impose an objective measure in hindsight of what should have been the foreseeable cost of damage in auto-mated markets. For example, looking back at an event, a regulator may make a determination after the fact as to what a trader should have expected the costs of damages to be. This might involve discounting apparently extreme reactions (e.g. a flash crash) and setting out a more modulated version of events as the reasonably foreseeable version of events. In the case of the Knight Capital fiasco, the SEC eventually fined the firm $12 million for its breach of the Market Access Rule, though the impact of the error extended broadly across the market.[41]

The downside of this approach rests in its artifice. Regulators have to work out what constitutes a reasonable set of consequences of a bad algorithm in automated markets. With the relatively short time over which high-speed automated markets have thrived, there is little by way of historical empirical data to reliably map out probable, foreseeable responses to certain types of risk. Additionally, if regulators systematically discount extreme consequences, the market is forced to internalize the leftover costs of careless behaviour.

9.3.4 Contribution

For civil wrongs, the law generally permits a wrongdoer to reduce liability by trying to blame another for contributing to the losses. This concept works uneasily in automated markets.

A wrongdoer can seek to reduce her liability by ascribing some of the blame to another actor that also contributed to the losses. In an automated market, traders that add to the escalation of a cascade of losses might, on this basis, be held liable to contribute to any penalty imposed by regulators for the harm caused. To the extent that strict liability or negligence give rise to high-dollar liabilities, contribution can help cover losses that cannot be paid out by a single trader.

High-speed traders relying on pre-set algorithms face a problematic set of choices in this context. On the one hand, high-speed traders that detect

---

[41] Stevenson, 'Knight Capital', 16 October 2013, B9.

unexpected or abnormal trading might reduce or stop trading until such time as their programmers can figure out what is going on. At first glance, this approach makes a lot of sense. By limiting their trading, they can reduce losses they face from another trader's misfiring algorithm. Also, their programming may be more vulnerable to misjudging troubled market conditions, making it more likely that losses accrue systemically and that possible liability for contribution is triggered. Limiting participation and withdrawing might help stop the interconnected transmission of risk across the market. Seen from the perspective of contributory liability, such an approach might seem the proper one to take to preclude any chances of being held liable alongside a careless trader.

However, in practice, traders that suddenly withdraw or limit their participation in markets can also exacerbate losses; they may, in fact, be as problematic—if not more so—than those that remain and continue trading. HF traders have become essential suppliers of liquidity, with price discovery, information dissemination, and investor participation heavily reliant on their workings. A rapid withdrawal of HF traders can set the stage for a massive loss of liquidity—which can, in turn, deepen the scale of emerging crises. Even a small number of traders withdrawing may signal trouble to others, with diminishing liquidity fueling further distress and encouraging more HF traders to exit. This kind of mass flight was evident in the May 2010 flash crash and, to a more limited extent, in the October 2014 Treasury flash crash, when HF traders reduced the depth of their order book in response to the abnormal trading. On 24 August 2015, as the market panicked in response to problems in China, HF traders periodically stopped trading during the day, prompting mini flash crashes and triggering circuit breakers as they did so.

In short, a theory of contributory liability works imperfectly in automated markets, where interconnected HF traders can spread error by trading as much as they can cause liquidity shocks by withdrawing from the market. This leaves a wrongdoer potentially at risk of paying out higher damages if others deepen the magnitude of the original error. To the extent that a wrongdoer should not or cannot pay, the rest of the market is left to bear the costs of the fallout.

9.3.5 Scienter/Intention

For serious offenses involving deception, manipulation, and deliberate disruption, the law requires that a wrongdoer act with intent or gross recklessness.[42] Under Section 10b of the Exchange Act, Rule 10b-5, and related rulemaking, a showing of intent is essential to the offense, underscoring its

[42] Santa Fe v. Green 430 U.S. 462 (1977); 425 U.S. 185 (1976); Ernst & Ernst v. Hochfelder, 425 U.S. 185 (1976).

seriousness within the taxonomy of wrongs punished by securities regulation. The kinds of behaviour covered by Rule 10b-5 reflect the different ways in which traders can intentionally distort market function. Lying to spread misinformation, manipulating prices, and unfairly blocking others from trading (e.g. via quote stuffing) might all fall within the remit of impermissible conduct punishable under Rule 10b-5 and related regulation. Most recently, the Dodd-Frank Act codifies the offense of spoofing: intentionally submitting non-*bona-fide* orders with the intention of cancelling them.[43] It has become a powerful tool for regulators in overseeing automated markets, with a handful of recent high-profile actions brought to punish spoofing behaviour in derivatives markets.[44]

Still, the need to show intention for harmful offenses poses a conceptual challenge in automated markets. Particularly for algorithms that are pre-programmed to trade independently at speeds that preclude human interaction in real time, the need to show intention presents a dilemma.[45] Can programmers be held liable for algorithms that engage in deliberate misconduct in their operation? On its surface, such a scenario seems far-fetched. Algorithms are governed by their programming and will not act in ways that fall outside of their code. It makes sense, then, to hold their programmers fully accountable for any intentionally disruptive behaviour. Indeed, evidence of intention and recklessness should be much easier to prove by a simple examination of the programming and source code underlying the algorithm.

However, this analysis fails to account for the central tension that underlies the operation of smart, responsive algorithms. Namely, though algorithms are programmed to execute a given strategy, this strategy must be designed to let algorithms take decisions within the parameters set by programming.[46] For example, an algorithm may be instructed to sell a large block of shares quickly without alerting the market. To do this, the algorithm will need to receive data from multiple markets, to divide up the trade into small blocks and to take steps to transact each of these blocks discretely. However, as part of its strategy, it may be rational for an algorithm to be intentionally disruptive. For example, it might gain by 'distracting' other traders. It might send out dummy orders that are designed to stuff the system and prevent others from trading, to distort prices, or to figure out how others might transact through problematic tactics (e.g. aggressive pinging). Within the parameters of artificially intelligent programming, then,

---

[43] US Congress, Dodd-Frank, 2010, Section 747.

[44] See, e.g., Indictment, United States v. Coscia, No. 14-CR-00551 (N.D. Ill. Oct. 1, 2014), available at http://www.justice.gov/sites/default/files/usao-ndil/legacy/2015/06/11/pr1002_01a.pdf; McNamara, 'United States v. Coscia as a Case of First Impression', 6 January 2016; United States v. Sarao, Criminal Complaint U.S. District Court Northern District of Illinois, Case Number 15 CR 75., 11 February 2015.

[45] Scopino, 264–70.   [46] Nevmyvaka et al., 'Electronic trading', 2005.

it might be rational for an algorithm to act in a way that is disruptive, deceptive, and manipulative when viewed through a conventional 'human' lens. From the point of view of a sophisticated algorithm, however, disruptive actions may constitute an efficient, effective execution strategy.

An argument can be made that programmers should be mindful of such dangers and program their algorithms to avoid them. While this argument might appear valid in broad strokes, it creates practical challenges in its application. While programming offers the promise of certainty, the law in this area is far from certain and thus difficult to program into an algorithm as a logistical matter. In the USA, circuit courts differ in their interpretation of what level of intention is necessary to make an action deceptive or deliberately manipulative.[47] The divergence between the DC Circuit and the Second Circuit is illustrative. Whereas straightforward intention is satisfactory to evidence manipulation in the DC Circuit, the Second Circuit is a great deal more exacting. As seen in the case of *SEC v Masri*, manipulative intent must be the sole motive driving the bad act. If an actor might also have investment intent alongside a manipulative one, then this is unlikely to be sufficient to ground manipulation.[48] Within these shifting doctrinal parameters, regulators may struggle to make a case for all but the most obvious types of manipulation. Where algorithms execute a strategy that includes deliberately disruptive behaviour as part of a legitimate investment plan, the case against the trader may end up eroded by complex and blurry jurisprudential lines.

Automated markets raise serious questions about whether certain disruptive practices prevalent in automated markets *ought* to be unlawful as a matter of market policy. In other words, does automated trading create special and unique categories of disruptive practice that are not easily punished under current interpretations of Rule 10b-5? For example, algorithmic trading has elicited concerns about such practices as quote stuffing, rapid order cancellation, marking the close at high speed, or momentum-trading, where traders transact heavily in one direction to move prices.[49] While it might be considered desirable from the policy standpoint, constraining such behaviours

---

[47] Levens, 'Too fast?', 2015, 1515–16; ATSI Communications, Inc v Shaar Fund, Ltd, 493 F3d 87, 101 (2d Cir 2007).

[48] Markowski v SEC, 274 F.3d 525 (D.C. Cir. 2001); SEC v. Masri, 523 F.Supp.2d at 370. For further discussion of intent and automated trading, see Scopino, 264–70. See also City of Providence et al. v. BATS Global Markets et al., No. 15–3057 (2d. Cir.) (Dec. 19, 2017). In this case, the plaintiffs argued that leading exchanges systematically gave HFT traders better trading opportunities than other types of trader and investor in violation of Rule 10b-5. According to the complaint, exchanges accorded preferential access to data, for example, and misled plaintiff investors about trading opportunities on venues.

[49] Easley et al., 'Volume clock', 2012 (describing certain predatory behaviours in high-speed automated trading); Scopino, 264–70.

through current fraud/manipulation actions appears practically difficult under current laws that look for a deliberate intent to deceive without an accompanying or incidental investment motivation.

9.3.6 Damages and Harm

Complex, high-speed algorithms are inherently subject to random error, imprecision, and uncertainty in their operations.[50] Because such algorithms must be pre-programmed, coding can fail to correctly base its instructions on a sound reading of future market conditions. Further, algorithms must make rapid, blunt judgements about incoming data, such that their reactions are subject to raw, immediate readings that need refining over time. Perhaps unsurprisingly, the market has become vulnerable to flash crashes, both large and small, affecting entire markets as well as the securities of single companies such as Apple Inc. or Google.[51]

This predilection towards random error and its uncertain spread across an interconnected market challenges regulators to determine the overall cost of a bad act and how much of it a wrongdoer should pay. In extreme cases—such as the May 2010 or October 2014 flash crashes—the costs can be prohibitively large. Even in incidents like those affecting Knight Capital, the impact can be sufficiently widespread as to raise the possibility of extensive damages for a single or even multiple institutions. Calibrating a correct quantum of damages presents a difficult dilemma for regulators in assigning which losses ought to be regarded as reasonably foreseeable and which fall outside of this objective perimeter.

However, this problem touches upon a more fundamental principle. That is, the task of fixing the proper quantum of damages seeks to achieve two basic policy purposes: (1) to deter actors from carrying out harmful actions; and (2) to make whole those that suffer the consequences of this damage.[52] If damages are under-compensatory, a bad actor has extra incentive to continue committing harms knowing that she might make more money than she has to pay out in compensation. In turn, investors that are left holding the can must pay extra to participate in the marketplace. This can translate into investors reducing what they put into the market, discounting their capital in response to the added costs of a risky trading environment. Alternatively, regulators face difficulties if the quantum of damages ends up being overly punitive, covering (as in strict liability, for instance) the full costs of

---

[50] Yadav, 'How algorithmic trading'.
[51] Elmer-Dewitt, 'Snapshot', 11 February 2011; Bowley, 'Flash crash', 8 November 2010, B1.
[52] Rose, 'Multienforcer approach', 2010.

the harms triggered by a bad act. In the case of interconnected markets, the risk of large-scale damages is especially live. Here, an actor may not have enough money to cover the full scale of the damage. This raises the danger that the risk of extensive damages fosters a predilection towards taking even greater risks than an actor otherwise might. If a trader knows that she will be wiped out, she might be minded to go for broke from time to time. The risk might generate a large reward. The costs of failure, however, will not be fully absorbed if the actor goes bust. If the quantum of damages is not realistic, then the security it provides breeds a false sense of safety. If the reliability of damages is doubtful, markets may have to price in this risk through discounts applied to invested capital.

A major question for determining damages in complex, high-speed markets lies in also deciding what constitutes an actionable harm. Specifically, such incidents as flash crashes might seem relatively innocuous at first sight: prices fall and then rise again, suggesting that any losses are remedied by the rapid market correction. Looked at more deeply, however, a number of harms may still be identified.

First and most obviously, some traders do lose. Those that transact as the market falls and sell within this dip can face steep losses. In the May 2010 flash crash, for example, top-flight blue-chip shares ended up trading for pennies as the market plunged (though, in that case, these transactions were reversed).[53] The market cannot afford to cancel erroneous trades in every flash event owing to the overriding need to promise settlement finality to market participants—that executed trades will be treated as final to avoid uncertainty and to facilitate onward transactions.

Second, the market can suffer more profound damage. Even though some traders might consider periodic losses owing to flash crashes and other disruptions as a cost of doing business, this might not uniformly be the case. The persistent experience of disruptions in the market can dissuade investors from entering and instead motivate them to take their capital elsewhere. Anecdotally, equity markets have seen heavy fragmentation, with well-known institutional investors developing their own trading platforms free of high-speed traders. Derivatives markets are less susceptible to the risks of such ad hoc fragmentation. However, their users span a wide cross-section of actors, from end users to financial firms, many of which may not be well placed to navigate the risk of flash events and random disruptions or to invest in the technology that may help them to do so. How this more nebulous set of risks to capital allocation and market quality should be analysed is a subject ripe for further reflection.

---

[53] CFTC and SEC, 'Findings'.

9.3.7 *Evidence and Proof*

Regulators face heavy costs in enforcing the law and holding market participants accountable for bad behaviour. Where enforcement is costly and regulators struggle with resource pressures, patchy and suboptimal oversight leaves markets vulnerable to risk-taking. If public and private regulators cannot enforce the law on the books effectively, investors may not wish to jeopardize their capital or may apply a discount to reflect the need to police their investments by themselves. Whereas strict liability offenses present the lowest-cost enforcement option, those involving fraud and manipulation are much more challenging from the evidentiary perspective. Despite the heavy toll that deliberate disruption can take on markets, these cases create tradeoffs for enforcers in balancing the costs of investigation versus the likely success of the case.

Automated markets have the potential to radically ease the enforcement burden. Rather than force regulators to glean information about possible mischief from face-to-face backroom deals, where interactions may leave little by way of hard evidence, automation presents a quite opposite proposition. With algorithmic trading generating vast reserves of data and algorithms underpinned by verifiable source code, the task of enforcement should become much easier. Regulators can examine transaction audit trails for evidence of bad acts and can decipher the intent of programmers by analysing the instructions guiding the algorithm. As seen in the spate of recent spoofing cases, patterns of suspicious orders detected through data suggested that traders were trying to fool markets.[54] Rather than forcing a decision on whether to invest in enforcement, data should reduce the investigative burden and thus make it cheaper to bring cases against a wider swath of wrongdoing. Furthermore, with added bite, market participants may take steps to be more careful in their dealings given the greater likelihood of being caught out.

While big data and the availability of source code have the potential to bring great gains for enforcement, they are far from a panacea. A couple of factors bear consideration. First, modern markets generate an enormous amount of data and analysing it can be a complex and expensive task.[55] Actions that are obviously malicious might generate a telling pattern of trading that can be easily spotted and punished. However, more complex wrongdoing may still necessitate significant regulatory resources for interpretation. The case of Knight Capital—though high-impact—required around 14 months of case development, with evidence of violations emerging only after a whistleblower

---

[54] Criminal Complaint, United States v. Sarao, No. 15-CR-75 (N.D. Ill. 11 Feb. 2015).
[55] Brownlees and Gallo, 'Financial econometric analysis', 2006.

helped.[56] Moreover, market interconnections and the ability of algorithms to react automatically to each other's behaviour can vastly complicate the task of teasing out conclusions. Investigations into the May 2010 flash crash, the October 2014 US Treasury flash crash and the August 2015 volatility yielded no firm conclusions about causes. This suggests that determinations about who caused what and when are all likely to require time and effort to resolve and even then may not be enough to establish a firm case.

Second, the ability of data to be helpful also depends on how well the underlying offenses map onto automated HF markets. As noted above, high-speed algorithms are designed to function with a degree of independence in real time. More fundamentally, where algorithms are endemically prone to random errors, the data may only be weakly informative about an underlying offense. Mistakes will happen. These errors may proliferate across the system. Automated programs may react unexpectedly in stressed market conditions. Where strict liability, negligence, and intent-based offenses offer only a partial fit, the data/source code requires analysis and interpretation to fill the gaps in any theory of the case—and may not always do so effectively.

9.3.8 Disclosure and Information Dissemination

Information flows are central to derivatives and equity markets. Information enters the markets through any number of channels including, for example, (1) periodic, mandatory disclosures supplied by listed companies as well as regular reports by regulators (e.g. US Labor Department reports on employment statistics); (2) news events released through dedicated feeds, including those specifically tailored to communicate with HFT and other automated servers; or (3) research and analysis that infuses markets through the transactional behaviour of informed institutional investors and others, ultimately reflected in the prices at which securities trade.

The mechanics through which information enters the markets has undergone transformational change to match the increasing sophistication of algorithms in consuming and capturing data in prices. In order to transact in milli- or microseconds, automated systems must receive data directly from the computer servers of exchanges, news agencies, social media, and government agencies. This information might be pre-coded to reflect sentiment and analysis (e.g. negative sentiment coded for a bankruptcy or bad earnings) or it may also be raw information that is transmitted rapidly without the delay needed to pre-code it.[57] It is commonplace for information flows to be mediated entirely through automated processes, without human traders intervening in real time

---

[56] Stevenson, B9.   [57] Philips, 'How many', 25 April 2013.

to determine their accuracy, significance, or possible correlations. Conversely, this absence of human involvement means that trading can incorporate insights from vast reserves of complex data quickly, far surpassing human abilities in this regard.

These new dynamics governing the flow of information can impact the effectiveness of regulation underpinning mandatory disclosure, information accuracy, and price formation.[58] Public companies, large traders, and providers of trading services must provide regular, detailed reports about their activities. Failure to provide full and frank disclosure can create liability risks for these market participants as well as raise broader concerns about their internal governance, future performance, or competitiveness. Based on the longstanding theory that information eventually percolates into the prices at which securities trade, some abnormal shift in prices can provide a first indication that something deeper is amiss. In Rule 10b-5 on anti-fraud class actions against publicly listed companies, a sudden price drop is often the major trigger for investigation and litigation.[59] These surprise falls can suggest that a company's disclosures are not entirely truthful. Or unusual price behaviour might point to an attempt to distort or manipulate markets on the part of traders, where price formation is out-of-sync with what has been disclosed by a company. In short, disclosures and the mechanisms by which the market reflects this information in prices carry heavy regulatory implications across multiple fronts.

Automated trading and the essential role of HFTs in price formation raise questions about the continued relevance of traditional ways of thinking about how prices reflect information, its accuracy, and liability. As noted earlier, HFTs must be programmed in advance of trading to respond to future market conditions, incoming information, and price data. The anticipatory dynamic and the propensity towards error, imprecision, correlated responses across HFTs, and the basic react-and-refine process endemic to rapid-fire trading can affect how the market processes information. Where errors can spread from one marketplace to another across an interconnected system of trading venues, it is possible that price reactions may exaggerate the reactive impact of news. Additionally, because HFTs have to react to new information in microseconds, sometimes based on pre-coded metrics for data, sentiment, and seriousness, they cannot immediately check the accuracy of information or its fuller import. Relatedly, to the extent that HF traders might look to short-term market movements to make their gains, their algorithms may focus more on certain kinds of information than on others. In other words, HFTs may pay

---

[58] Yadav, 'How algorithmic trading'.
[59] Basic v Levinson, 85 U.S. 224 (1988); Amgen Inc. v. Ct. Ret. Plans and Trust Funds, 133 S.Ct. 1184, 1191 (2013); Cooter, 'Prices and sanctions', 1984; Levens, 'Too fast'.

more attention to the near-term, news-focused data likely to drive immediate price movements, rather than also incorporating data on more fundamental insights in disclosures. To the extent that deeper information may emerge more slowly or patchily, prices in automated markets may be more sensitive to certain types of disclosures than to others.

Consideration of these dynamics raises questions about whether and how regulatory disclosure practices ought to be re-thought to offer a closer match to the dynamics of automated trading. For example, should disclosures be more regular in order to reveal a broader range of data and to make it cheaper for investors to acquire this information, helping to balance and broaden the short-term focus of HFT markets? If market actors must reveal more, does this affect the liability burden to which they will be subject? Should disclosures be formatted to be more carefully interpreted and coded in accordance with the stipulations of those that are liable? In other words, should those that reveal information have greater say in how their information is translated into code and transmitted across the market? Finally, how should courts, regulators, and experts parse through disclosures to 'discount' for the potential errors, over-reactions, biases, and unusual price behaviours that are increasingly a part of automated markets? Where prices closely intersect with and impact regulation, it follows that further thought is needed to better align the response of regulators to the transformation underway in market structure.[60]

9.4 Summary and Conclusions

Algorithmic trading and HFT comprise two unique features that impact foundational concepts underpinning regulation: (1) complex algorithms must be programmed in advance of trading, making random, unpredictable error all but inevitable; (2) deeply interconnected markets can amplify the impact of even small events, as errors can travel across the system of trading venues.

These two features create serious concerns for our understanding of core concepts in law and regulation. Most importantly, the reasonableness

---

[60] For a discussion, see Yadav, 'How algorithmic trading'. For example, recognizing the impact of disclosure mechanisms on how automated traders respond to new information, the US Department of Agriculture is changing how it releases its crop and livestock reports. The department will seek to release its reports online publically to all players at the same time, rather than giving an early look to media sources that would transmit them to HFT traders and give HFT traders a head start in trading. Some argue that this practice will not make much difference in practice as HFT traders will always achieve faster access to exchanges. However, it does show recognition by policy-makers regarding the link between disclosure practices and its impact on automated trading markets. See Osipovich, 'US tries to rein in', 2018.

standard—essential to market regulation—maps poorly onto modern markets. Even reasonable risk taking can create high costs. Not only is error a part of complex automation but interconnection means that small, reasonable mistakes can result in high-impact harms. Strict liability also makes for a poor deterrent, where random, unpredictable error is a core feature of operations. Even if traders take intensive precautions, damage might still happen (e.g. if algorithms poorly predict market conditions). Finally, the law may struggle to punish intentional disruption, if such conduct represents a way for an algorithm to rationally realize an otherwise legitimate investment strategy.

Algorithmic markets also create tensions for the law's ability to compensate investors for large-scale fallouts. For one thing, damage is hard to measure. What kinds of foreseeable harms should concern market participants and regulators? With error unpredictable and its trajectory across the market seemingly unique to each new crisis, an objective understanding of foreseeable harms appears tenuous. Given that such markets have a short history and are constantly evolving forward, empiricists also lack the bank of historical data needed to provide firmer maps of how errors can travel across the market. More fundamentally, how should harm be defined in automated markets? Seen from the perspective of market quality and capital allocation, how should the law measure the costs that investors internalize to protect themselves or the loss of their fullest participation? Second, allocating damages can be especially problematic. Because of interconnection and the potential for large-scale losses from small harms (e.g. Knight Capital), single actors may incur far larger liability than they can realistically bear. Allocating liability through contribution also presents a challenge where automated actors can amplify problems by continuing to trade as well as by retiring suddenly from the market.

The implications for enforcement present opportunities as well as costs. On the one hand, regulators should have a lighter burden where data is readily available and enforcers may look to source code to provide insights into intent. However, challenges persist. Automated markets generate enormous volumes of data whose interpretation needs expertise, resources, and time. Even then, the data may be unclear. Especially for market-wide phenomena such as flash crashes, the multiplicity of actors, variables, venues, and strategies can make drawing firm conclusions about blame and liability elusive. In the case of the May 2010 flash crash, for example, two differing accounts of possible trigger events have been put forward, and disagreement continues as to which is right. The US Treasury flash crash has yet to be explained, despite extensive inquiry into its causes. More fundamentally, where the underlying legal causes of action are a poor fit, the data is unlikely to be of much help in filling the enforcement gap.

References

ASIC. 'Dark liquidity and high-frequency trading (Report 331)'. Sydney. Available at: http://download.asic.gov.au/media/1344182/rep331-published-18-March-2013.pdf, 2013.

Bates, John. 'Algorithmic trading and high frequency trading: Experiences from the market and thoughts on regulatory requirements'. In *Technological Trading in the Markets*. Washington, DC: US Commodity Futures Trading Commission. Available at: https://www.cftc.gov/sites/default/files/idc/groups/public/@newsroom/documents/file/tac_071410_binder.pdf, 2010.

Biais, Bruno, Thierry Foucault, and Sophie Moinas. 'Equilibrium fast trading'. Available at: https://papers.ssrn.com/sol3/papers.cfm?abstract_id=2024360, 2014.

Biais, Bruno, Johan Hombert, and Pierre-Olivier Weill. 'Equilibrium pricing and trading volume under preference uncertainty'. *Review of Economic Studies* 81, no. 4 (1 October 2014): 1401–37.

Blackrock. 'US equity market structure: Lessons from August 24'. Available at: https://www.blackrock.com/corporate/literature/whitepaper/viewpoint-us-equity-market-structure-october-2015.pdf, 2015.

Bowley, Graham. 'The flash crash, in miniature'. *New York Times*. Available at: https://www.nytimes.com/2010/11/09/business/09flash.html?mtrref=www.google.co.uk&gwh=76861C3D5507451D54CFC145018C7077&gwt=pay, 8 November 2010.

Bratton, William W., and Michael L. Wachter. 'The political economy of fraud on the market'. *University of Pennsylvania Law Review* 160 (2011): 69–168.

Brogaard, Jonathan, Allen Carrion, Thibaut Moyaert, Ryan Riordan, Andriy Shkilko, and Konstantin Sokolov. 'High frequency trading and extreme price movements'. Available at: https://papers.ssrn.com/sol3/papers.cfm?abstract_id=25311222017.

Brogaard, Jonathan, Terrence Hendershott, and Ryan Riordan. 'High frequency trading and price discovery'. ECB Lamfalussy Fellowship Programme. Frankfurt. Available at: https://www.ecb.europa.eu/pub/pdf/scpwps/ecbwp1602.pdf, 2013.

Brownlees, Christian T., and Giampiero M. Gallo. 'Financial econometric analysis at ultra-high frequency: Data handling concerns'. Available at: http://papers.ssrn.com/abstract=886204, 2006.

Brummer, Chris. 'Disruptive technology and securities regulation'. *Fordham Law Review* 84, no. 3 (2015): 977–1052.

Calabresi, Guido. *The Cost of Accidents: A Legal and Economic Analysis*. New Haven, CT: Yale University Press, 1970.

CFTC. Regulation Automated Trading, 80 Federal Register § (2015). Available at: https://www.gpo.gov/fdsys/pkg/FR-2015-12-17/pdf/2015-30533.pdf, 2015.

CFTC and SEC. 'Findings regarding the market events of May 6, 2010'. Washington, DC. Available at: https://www.sec.gov/news/studies/2010/marketevents-report.pdf, 2010.

Chaboud, Alain P., Benjamin Chiquoine, Erik Hjalmarsson, and Clara Vega. 'Rise of the machines: Algorithmic trading in the foreign exchange market'. *Journal of Finance* 69, no. 5 (2014): 2045–84.

Cooter, Robert. 'Prices and sanctions'. *Columbia Law Review* 84 (1984): 1523–60.

Cormen, Thomas H., Charles E. Leiserson, Ronald L. Rivest, and Clifford Stein. *Introduction to Algorithms*, 3rd edn. Cambridge, MA: MIT Press, 2009.

Dolgopolov, Stanislav. 'Regulating merchants of liquidity: Market making from crowded floors to high-frequency trading'. *University of Pennsylvania Journal of Business Law* 18, no. 3 (2016): 651–732.

Dugast, Jérôme, and Thierry Foucault. 'False news, informational efficiency, and price reversals'. Available at: https://publications.banque-france.fr/sites/default/files/medias/documents/working-paper_513_2014.pdf, 2014.

Easley, David, Marcos M. López de Prado, and Maureen O'Hara. 'The volume clock: Insights into the high-frequency paradigm'. *Journal of Portfolio Management* 39, no. 1 (2012): 19–29.

Elmer-Dewitt, Philip. 'Snapshot of an Apple flash crash'. *Fortune*. Available at: http://fortune.com/2011/02/10/snapshot-of-an-apple-flash-crash/, 11 February 2011.

Foresight. 'The future of computer trading in financial markets: An international perspective'. London. Available at: https://www.gov.uk/government/uploads/system/uploads/attachment_data/file/289431/12-1086-future-of-computer-trading-in-financial-markets-report.pdf, 2012.

Gerig, Austin. 'High-frequency trading synchronizes prices in financial markets'. Available at: https://arxiv.org/pdf/1211.1919.pdf, 2015.

Glosten, Lawrence R. 'Insider trading, liquidity, and the role of the monopolist specialist'. *Journal of Business* 62, no. 2 (1989): 211–35.

Goldberg, John C. P. 'Twentieth-century tort theory'. *Georgetown Law Journal* 91 (2003): 513–84.

IOSCO. 'Regulatory issues raised by the impact of technological changes on market integrity and efficiency'. Madrid. Available at: http://www.iosco.org/library/pubdocs/pdf/IOSCOPD354.pdf, 2011.

Johnson, Neil, Guannan Zhao, Eric Hunsader, Hong Qi, Nicholas Johnson, Jing Meng, and Brian Tivnan. 'Abrupt rise of new machine ecology beyond human response time'. *Scientific Reports* 3 (2013).

Kearns, Michael, and Yuriy Nevmyvaka. 'Machine learning for market microstructure and high frequency trading'. In *High-Frequency Trading—New Realities for Traders, Markets and Regulators*, ed. David Easley, Marcos López de Prado, and Maureen O'Hara. London: Risk Books, 2013.

Kirilenko, Andrei, Albert S. Kyle, Mehrdad Samadi, and Tugkan Tuzun. 'The flash crash: High-frequency trading in an electronic market'. *Journal of Finance* 72, no. 3 (2017): 967–98.

Laughlin, Gregory. 'Insights into high frequency trading from the Virtu initial public offering'. Available at: https://sniperinmahwah.files.wordpress.com/2014/12/virtuoverview.pdf, 2014.

Levens, Tara E. 'Too fast, too frequent? High-frequency trading and securities class actions'. *University of Chicago Law Review* 82 (2015): 1511–57.

MacIntosh, Jeffrey G. 'High frequency traders: Angels or devils?' Toronto. Available at: https://www.cdhowe.org/sites/default/files/attachments/research_papers/mixed/Commentary_391_0.pdf, 2013.

Malinova, Katya, Andreas Park, and Ryan Riordan. 'Do retail traders suffer from high frequency traders?' Available at: http://qed.econ.queensu.ca/pub/faculty/milne/322/IIROC_FeeChange_submission_KM_AP3.pdf, 2013.

Mamudi, Sam, and Annie Massa. 'Dark pools'. *Bloomberg*. Available at: https://www.bloomberg.com/quicktake/dark-pools, 21 July 2017.

Martinez, Victor Hugo, and Ioanid Rosu. 'High frequency traders, news and volatility – Invited talk'. Available at: https://www.researchgate.net/publication/228261375_High_Frequency_Traders_News_and_Volatility_-_Invited_Talk', 2013.

McNamara, Steven. 'United States v. Coscia as a case of first impression'. *CLS Blue Sky Blog*. Available at: http://clsbluesky.law.columbia.edu/2016/01/06/united-states-v-coscia-as-a-case-of-first-impression/, 6 January 2016.

Menkveld, Albert J. 'High frequency trading and the new market makers'. *Journal of Financial Markets* 16 (2013): 712–40.

Meyer, Gregory, and Phillip Stafford. 'Flash crash trader helps U.S. in fight against market abuse'. *Financial Times*, 30 January 2018.

Nanex. 'Nanex – 01-Aug-2012 – Knightmare on Wall Street'. Available at: http://www.nanex.net/aqck2/3522.html, 2012.

Nevmyvaka, Yuriy, Michael Kearns, Amy Papandreou, and Katia Sycara. 'Electronic trading in order-driven markets: Efficient execution'. *Proceedings—Seventh IEEE International Conference on E-Commerce Technology, CEC 2005*. Available at: http://www.cis.upenn.edu/~mkearns/papers/optexec.pdf, 2005.

Osipovich, Alexander. 'Algorithmic trading in energy markets'. *Risk.net*. Available at: https://www.risk.net/risk-management/2136141/algorithmic-trading-energy-markets, 10 January 2012.

Osipovich, Alexander. 'U.S. tries to rein in high-speed trading in farm patch'. *Wall Street Journal*, 15 July 2018.

Philips, Matthew. 'How many HFT firms actually use Twitter to trade?' *Bloomberg*. Available at: https://www.bloomberg.com/news/articles/2013-04-24/how-many-hft-firms-actually-use-twitter-to-trade, 25 April 2013.

Pirrong, Craig. 'Did spoofing cause the flash crash? Not so fast!' *Streetwise Professor*. Available at: http://streetwiseprofessor.com/did-spoofing-cause-the-flash-crash-not-so-fast/, 2015.

Pisani, Bob. 'What happened during the Aug 24 "flash crash"'. *CNBC*. Available at: https://www.cnbc.com/2015/09/25/what-happened-during-the-aug-24-flash-crash.html, 25 September 2015.

Polinsky, A. Mitchell, and Steven Shavell. 'Economic analysis of law'. John M. Olin Center for Law, Economics, and Business. Available at: http://ssrn.com/abstract=859406, 2005.

Popper, Nathaniel. 'The stock market bell rings, computers fail, Wall Street cringes'. *New York Times*. Available at: https://www.nytimes.com/2015/07/09/business/dealbook/new-york-stock-exchange-suspends-trading.html?mtrref=www.google.co.uk&gwh=89A55774BD8C3D7234914DD76D99D6AF&gwt=pay, 8 July 2015.

Rabin, Robert L. 'The historical development of the fault principle: A reinterpretation'. *Georgia Law Review* 15 (1981): 925–61.

Rose, Amanda M. 'The multienforcer approach to securities fraud deterrence: A critical analysis'. *University of Pennsylvania Law Review* 158 (2010): 2173–231.

Scopino, Gregory. 'Do automated trading systems dream of manipulating the price of futures contracts? Policing markets for improper trading practices by algorithmic robots'. *Florida Law Review* 67, no. 1 (2016): 222–93.

SEC (US Securities and Exchange Commission). Exchange Act Rule 15c3-5: Risk management controls for brokers or dealers with market access. Available at: https://www.law.cornell.edu/cfr/text/17/240.15c3-5, 2010.

SEC. Regulation Systems Compliance and Integrity, Pub. L. No. 34–73639. Available at: https://www.sec.gov/rules/final/2014/34-73639.pdf, 2015.

SEC. 'Research note: Equity market volatility on August 24, 2015'. Washington, DC. Available at: https://www.sec.gov/marketstructure/research/equity_market_volatility.pdf, 2015.

SEC. 'SEC charges Knight Capital with violations of market access rule'. Washington, DC. Available at: https://www.sec.gov/news/press-release/2013-222#.VDDV7PldWSo, 2013.

SEC. 'SEC charges NASDAQ for failures during Facebook IPO'. Available at: https://www.sec.gov/news/press-release/2013-2013-95htm#.VDDpgPldWSo, 2013.

Shavell, Steven. *Economic Analysis of Accident Law*. Cambridge, MA: Harvard University Press, 1987.

Stafford, Philip, Arash Massoudi, and Michael Mackenzie. 'Nasdaq sets stage for HFT in treasuries'. *Financial Times*. Available at: https://www.ft.com/content/6e0ac4de-9d08-11e2-a8db-00144feabdc0, 4 April 2013.

Stevenson, Alexandra. 'Knight Capital to pay $12 million fine on trading violations'. *New York Times*. Available at: https://dealbook.nytimes.com/2013/10/16/knight-capital-to-pay-12-million-fine-on-trading-violations/?mtrref=www.google.co.uk&gwh=D3EC5FEA3995851A29D486A5328FDF12&gwt=pay, 16 October 2013.

US Congress. Dodd-Frank Wall Street Reform and Consumer Protection Act, Pub. L. No. 124 Stat. 1376 (2010).

US Treasury Department, Board of Governors of the Federal Reserve System, Federal Reserve Bank of New York, SEC, and CFTC. 'Joint staff report: The US Treasury Market on October 15, 2014'. Available at: https://www.treasury.gov/press-center/press-releases/Documents/Joint_Staff_Report_Treasury_10-15-2015.pdf, 2015.

Wigglesworth, Robin. 'AI decodes trading signals hidden in jargon'. *Financial Times*. Available at: https://www.ft.com/content/23ae43d4-b3ec-11e7-a398-73d59db9e399, 26 October 2017.

Yadav, Yesha. 'Oversight failure in securities markets'. *Cornell Law Review*. Available at: https://papers.ssrn.com/sol3/papers.cfm?abstract_id=2754786, 2018 (forthcoming).

Yadav, Yesha. 'The failure of liability in modern markets'. Available at: https://papers.ssrn.com/sol3/papers.cfm?abstract_id=2652893, 28 August 2015.

Yadav, Yesha. 'How algorithmic trading undermines efficiency in capital markets'. *Vanderbilt Law Review* 68, no. 6 (2015): 1607–71.

Yadav, Yesha. 'Insider trading and market structure'. *UCLA Law Review* 63 (2016): 968–1033.

Zhang, Sarah, and Ryan Riordan. 'Technology and market quality: The case of high frequency trading'. ECIS 2011 Proceedings. Available at: http://aisel.aisnet.org/ecis2011, 2011.

10

Legal Liability for Fraud in the Evolving Architecture of Securities Markets

From Marketplaces to Traders

Stanislav Dolgopolov[1]

10.1 Introduction

The transformation of the architecture of securities markets—often referred to as 'market structure'—has been shaped by disruptive technological strides, but this process is also a regulatory and legal phenomenon in its origins and future path. For one thing, rapid changes in the modern electronic marketplace have stimulated heated public policy debates, whether prolonged battles over key regulatory decisions impacting various stakeholders or exposés in popular books provoking panic-like demands for a broad-sweeping scrutiny. However, some balance between public policy, whether framed in terms of market reforms or regulatory inertia, and legal liability is inevitable. The applicable liability regime provides both constraints and drivers of change in securities markets, and, likewise, market reforms could suffocate some practices that are already illegal. In some sense, the focus on public policy may serve as a distraction from liability based on prior conduct, and, for some industry circles, it probably is a welcome distraction. Importantly, the current market structure crisis in the US securities markets, a phenomenon being replayed in varying degrees in other countries, has led to numerous lawsuits and

[1] The author thanks Haim Bodek, Vladislav Dolgopolov, Luca Enriques, Walter Mattli, Shayna Gordon, and an anonymous reviewer for their help, comments, and expertise and assumes sole responsibility for all errors. This study summarizes and heavily draws on the author's other publications, especially the forthcoming article in the *William & Mary Business Law Review*. The author's work has involved some of the issues and legal actions discussed in this study.

enforcement actions. One needs to be mindful of various technicalities of securities law specific to the United States, such as the definition of securities fraud, the boundaries of market manipulation, the reach of the insider trading doctrine, the availability of a private right of action, and the distinction between primary and secondary violators. On the other hand, some key issues illuminated by the market structure crisis in the United Sates are very much relevant for other jurisdictions.

Of course, any discussion of legal liability needs to address the sheer complexity of the modern regulatory framework governing securities markets and the very existence of the administrative state. One must account for numerous layers of rules set by governmental authorities, in particular specialized agencies, and self-regulatory organizations (SROs), such as trading venues and industry-wide associations. One pivotal area is represented by the doctrine of securities fraud, which is based on several provisions with different legal thresholds in the federal securities statutes and is typically available to both government and private litigants. This doctrine is a potent weapon to address a wide range of abuses essentially amounting to *deception* of specific market participants or the market as a whole, with notable examples being false and misleading disclosure, express and implied misrepresentations, insider trading, and market manipulation. On the other hand, the doctrine of securities fraud does not cover all forms of wrongful or problematic conduct, such as those connected to negligence, numerous categories of technical violations, or corporate malfeasance. Likewise, specific categories of market players subject to liability may need to be singled out, and two important categories are represented by (1) marketplaces, meaning a gamut of trading venues, such as securities exchanges as traditional yet highly automated entities, much-discussed 'dark pools' as destinations for undisplayed liquidity, and off-exchange market makers as stand-alone liquidity providers; and (2) proprietary traders, notably high frequency traders (HFTs) known for their use of sophisticated algorithms, computing power, and market structure 'ins' and 'outs'. Importantly, trading venues have often been a target for legal actions relating to the realities of the modern electronic marketplace, especially in light of the enforcement program of the US Securities and Exchange Commission (SEC), while the focus is yet to shift from marketplaces to traders.

The phenomenon of high frequency trading (HFT), one of the pivotal ingredients of the current market structure crisis, is indeed a key piece of the legal liability puzzle. However, HFTs have been largely absent from the ranks of parties held liable for securities fraud, despite being referenced in some prominent enforcement actions against other parties. Moreover, some major class action lawsuits even backed away from suing HFTs for securities fraud, perhaps anticipating serious difficulties with mounting an attack on this category of market participants or seeing direct charges as a distraction, although still finger-pointing at HFTs as unnamed violators. If anything, the ability to 'catch' HFTs is critical for several reasons. For instance, securities exchanges, an important category of gatekeepers, typically have broadly worded liability disclaimers and are often sheltered from private, but not governmental, lawsuits alleging securities fraud as SROs by the rather expansive—but now apparently contracting—doctrine of regulatory immunity.

A starting point is that many forms of HFT are in no way illegal, as they represent, in addition to specialization and expertise of these market participants, the modern iteration of time, place, and information advantages in a fragmented architecture of securities markets. More generally, an adverse effect of certain trading strategies on other market participants in the zero-sum game of short-term trading does not automatically equate to fraudulent conduct. Moreover, it is often asserted that HFTs have no clients and hence cannot abuse the latter's orders. On the other hand, the principal-only model does not apply to every firm in this segment, as several key players perform an agency function by the virtue of being off-exchange market makers that *handle* other broker-dealers' order flow, in the process explicitly or implicitly assuming responsibility for best execution.

However, the advantages of time, place, and information, which may be called unavoidable, are only one part of the real story relevant for the purposes of identifying securities fraud. The phenomenon of 'plumbing' has to be considered as well, and it has included nontransparent market structure short-cuts often directly connected to regulatory issues, as contrasted to true quantitative models. The gamut of such shortcuts, which has often involved selective disclosure of information by trading venues to preferred market participants, is indeed broad:

> Features under the umbrella of plumbing may rely on tiered fees and rebates under the maker-taker pricing model, special order type advantages, fragmentation exploitation (e.g., jockeying for top-of-queue in order to trade or collect a rebate), market structure arbitrage, and de facto side-stepping the ban on locked and crossed markets and the trade-through rule established by Regulation NMS. Overall, the existing regulatory framework, notably Regulation NMS, has been gamed by some HFTs and trading venues by: (i) exploiting regulatory loopholes and clever work-arounds, (ii) exploiting rule contradictions and unintended consequences, (iii) exploiting weakness in regulatory constraints resulting from implementation and / or latency, (iv) exploiting liberal interpretation of grey areas and / or utilizing exceptions for purposes other than the original intent, (v) exploiting undocumented or unanticipated features, and (vi) exploiting exchange membership status with regard to regulatory liability and eligibility for regulatory exceptions.[2]

---

[2] Bodek and Dolgopolov, *Market Structure Crisis*, 2015, 54–5.

But perhaps it should not be surprising that bad actors in the HFT segment are hard to catch—at least through the means of private lawsuits. In light of trading venues' inadequate disclosure and concomitant questionable trading practices, the role played by HFTs may appear to be secondary from a doctrinal viewpoint. More generally, HFTs may look like—and, in many instances, objectively are—just skilful beneficiaries courted by trading venues in a cut-throat environment created by the modern electronic marketplace. Moreover, another important scenario of frictions and imperfections in trading venues' protocols does not involve collusion, but is rather based on utilizing 'glitches', which makes such HFTs look even less culpable. These potential obstacles bring out the need to conceptualize the underlying harm and its mechanics in the quest to expand the reach of liability from marketplaces to traders.

Overall, this study analyses the reach of legal liability for securities fraud, as illustrated by a range of abuses shaping the market structure crisis in the United States and often connected to the phenomenon of high frequency trading. The focus of this study is on two categories of market players, which occasionally overlap: marketplaces, meaning a gamut of trading venues, and proprietary traders. The importance of advanced functionalities provided by trading venues is analysed from the standpoint of informational asymmetries in securities markets, with the order type controversy serving as a pivotal example. Moreover, in the modern electronic marketplace, trading venues have been repeatedly exposed to liability, while sometimes being protected by the shield of regulatory immunity, but the issue of liability of proprietary traders is a murkier field. Accordingly, this study addresses potential approaches to the reach of liability to traders and discusses mechanics and proper characterization of the underlying harm. The approaches to liability of traders examined here are represented by secret arrangements between trading venues and preferred market participants, trading glitches, overlaps between marketplaces and traders, and market manipulation. This study concludes by emphasizing the relevance, as well as constraints, of the doctrine of securities fraud in the modern electronic marketplace with its numerous informational asymmetries.

10.2 Advanced Functionalities, the Order Type Controversy, and Informational Asymmetries

Trading protocols govern the interaction of orders, such as setting matching procedures, types of commands submitted by market participants, queue priority, price anchors and other indicators, rebate-fee structures, and order visibility. While there is a hierarchy of rules, starting with the Securities Exchange Act of 1934 itself and various SEC regulations, the specifics of the trading process are largely determined by individual trading venues. The dominance of advanced functionalities characterizes the ever-increasing complexity of trading protocols offered by the evolving gamut of 'lit' and 'dark' venues, with some features merely replicating the pre-electronic environment and others going far beyond it. The process of automation—accompanied by the rise of advanced functionalities—has not unambiguously simplified the marketplace of yesterday, dominated as it was by manual procedures with their uncertainty about human interaction. Concerns about complexity are on the forefront in light of the multitude of order matching rules, modes of interaction between various market participants, and a wide range of execution destinations. The problem of complexity is compounded by the very process of describing trading rules to regulatory agencies—for instance, in the process of regulatory review and approval—and market participants themselves. Indeed, the very existence of such grey areas creates some room for both unintended and deliberate informational advantages.

With these developments in mind, the so-called order type controversy is symptomatic of many advantages occurring in the modern market structure in connection with informational asymmetries in advanced functionalities, which may range from merely undocumented grey areas to discrepancies with formal documentation that constitute direct contradictions. The basic taxonomy of order-type-related abuses has been described as follows:

- unfair order handling practices that permit HFTs to step ahead of investor orders in violation of price-time priority;

- unfair rebooking and repositioning of investor orders that permit HFTs to flip out of toxic trades;

- unfair conversion of investor orders eligible for maker rebates into unfavourable executions incurring taker fees (under the maker-taker pricing model);

- unfair insertion of HFT intermediaries in between legitimate customer-to-customer matching;

- unfair and discriminatory order handling of investor orders during sudden price movements.[3]

However, 'unfair' does not necessarily translate to 'illegal'. In fact, the defining feature of the order type controversy lies in the existence of informational asymmetries combined with selective disclosure by trading venues to preferred market participants, as opposed to just disparities in market participants' respective abilities to utilize certain order types. HFTs have not been just 'better' at communicating with trading venues in a manner available to

---

[3] Bodek, *Problem of HFT*, 2013, 11–12.

every interested party and at investing time and effort to study the relevant documentation. In fact, individual firms have played a direct role in crafting specific order types. In other words, the ability 'to figure out the implications of structural changes [such as new exchange rules and order types] faster than our competitors'[4] certainly plays a role, but, in some instances, there is no level playing field.

Sometimes, the issue of order types has received more attention in litigation relative to other features offered by trading venues from the standpoint of transparency and selective disclosure practices. For instance, in a leading class action lawsuit, the court acknowledged the allegations that 'the Exchanges either did not disclose many of these order types to ordinary investors or marketed them exclusively to HFT firms, so that the ordinary investors were unaware of their existence'.[5] At the same time, the court maintained that the 'Plaintiffs fail[ed] to allege that the Exchanges misrepresented or failed to disclose material information regarding either the proprietary data feeds or co-location services'.[6]

Ultimately, the order type controversy is exemplified by the much-anticipated settlement with Direct Edge's two exchanges, which went to the heart of the matter:

> Complete and accurate disclosure of an exchange's order types and order handling procedures is necessary to promote a fair, orderly, and free and open market . . . When an exchange fails to completely and accurately describe its order types in its rules, it creates a significant risk that the manner in which those order types operate will not be understood by all market participants, thereby compromising the integrity and fairness of trading on that exchange. This risk is compounded when the exchange discloses information regarding the operation of those order types to some but not all of its members.[7]

As discussed in the settlement, 'Instead of a single price sliding process as described in their rules, the Exchanges accepted three different price sliding order types, called "Single Re-Price," "Price Adjust," and "Hide Not Slide."'[8] Importantly, this enforcement action referenced the existence of two HFT firms actively involved with requesting, if not designing, specific queue-position-related functionalities, and one of them even 'advised Direct Edge that implementation of [the requested] order type would likely cause it to increase the order flow that it sent to Direct Edge from 4–5 million orders per day to 12–15 million orders per day'.[9] In any instance, 'although the

---

[4] Cummings, *Make the Trade*, 2016, 76.
[5] *In re* Barclays Liquidity Cross & High Frequency Trading Litig., 126 F. Supp. 3d 342 (S.D.N.Y. 2015), *rev'd sub nom*, 354.
[6] Ibid., 361.   [7] SEC, In the Matter of EDGA EXCHANGE, INC., 2015, 2.   [8] Ibid., 3.
[9] Ibid., 7.

Exchanges provided some information about priority and other characteristics of HNS [Hide Not Slide] in technical specifications made available to members, the technical specifications did not contain complete and accurate information regarding the operation of HNS'.[10] Importantly, while the settlement itself was not based on any charges of securities fraud, the essence of the underlying violations points to the existence of false and misleading disclosures that could have been caught by this legal tool.

Another enforcement action, which also precisely addressed the essence of the order type controversy, was directed against a dark pool, a type of non-exchange alternative trading system (ATS), run by UBS.[11] Once again, inadequate disclosure was involved:

> UBS...fail[ed] to disclose [the] PPP [order type] to all UBS ATS subscribers. Although it was eventually disclosed to most subscribers, PPP was pitched almost exclusively to market makers and / or high frequency trading firms, which UBS expected to be the primary users of the order type.[12]

The hidden subpenny functionality associated with this order type, which provided the ability to interact with other market participants by utilizing a finer pricing grid, 'allowed one subscriber to gain execution priority over another in the order queue by offering to pay an economically insignificant sub-penny more per share [in violation of Rule 612 of Regulation NMS]'.[13] Moreover, the impact of this order type extended beyond the dark pool itself, which highlights the nature of symbiotic relationships between trading venues and preferred traders:

> [B]ecause UBS ATS allowed its subscribers to place orders at prices that were unavailable at ATSs and exchanges that complied with Rule 612 of Regulation [NMS], UBS ATS obtained an unfair competitive advantage over those venues in its efforts to attract and execute orders from market participants.[14]

These enforcement actions need to be considered in conjunction with the process of review and reassessment of order type practices by trading venues themselves, especially equities exchanges. The cleanup of order type practices by trading venues, whether seen as a voluntary or forced initiative, had started around 2012, intensifying rather dramatically two years later. One may point to 'the phenomenon of comprehensive order type-focused rule filings by equities exchanges, which purport to enhance disclosure and provide more clarity, while often maintaining that no or little substantive change is being proposed'.[15] Furthermore, securities exchanges are not the only ones providing additional disclosure relating to their order type practices. Amidst repeated

---

[10] Ibid., 3.   [11] SEC, In the Matter of UBS SECURITIES LLC, 2015.   [12] Ibid., 3.
[13] Ibid., 6.   [14] Ibid.   [15] Bodek and Dolgopolov, 57–8.

calls to apply the same logic to ATSs, the trend of enhanced disclosure by such entities, often manifested in releasing updated mandatory filings and making them publicly available, is plainly visible. This trend is also reinforced by the SEC's proposal that would, among other things, require operators of ATSs 'to provide detailed information about the manner of operations' of these trading venues to the SEC and to make such filings public.[16]

Overall, the order type controversy has exposed trading venues to liability, sometimes solely for not following proper rulemaking procedures, but in some other cases also for securities fraud directly tied to false and misleading disclosures, which amounted to deliberate informational asymmetries in the modern electronic marketplace. While securities exchanges as SROs had been able to deflect private lawsuits to a large degree based on the doctrine of regulatory immunity in the past, the most recent appellate decision maintained that the provision of co-location services, private data feeds, and complex order types 'are wholly divorced from the exchanges' role as regulators'.[17] Moreover, the sheer volume of cleanup by trading venues gives some idea about the prior state of opacity, potential trading profits, and opportunities for selective disclosure as a tool for courting and retaining preferred traders. Also, it is an encouraging sign that some regulatory changes and reform proposals in the market structure space have been viewed through the order type lens. At the same time, the nature and extent of potential liability of market participants themselves, such as HFTs, tend to remain a more tangential issue, perhaps being obscured by the focus on trading venues.

10.3 Secret Arrangements Between Trading Venues and Preferred Traders

The phenomenon of secret arrangements between trading venues and preferred traders relating to the nature of certain functionalities, as illustrated by the order type controversy, puts limitations on the articulated strengths of electronic order matching engines that are said to 'enforce the exchange's trading order precedence and pricing rules without error or exception, and they never favor friends or confederates'.[18] Of course, if complicit with the trading venue in question, HFTs themselves could *at least* be held liable as aiding and abetting securities fraud for a false or misleading disclosure released by that trading venue. On the other hand, classifying these market participants as primary, i.e. direct, violators, as opposed to parties merely assisting in

---

[16] SEC, Regulation of NMS Stock Alternative Trading Systems, 28 December 2015, 80,998.
[17] City of Providence v. BATS Global Mkts., Inc., 878 F.3d (2d Cir. 2017), 48.
[18] Harris, *Trading and Electronic Markets*, 2015, 37.

the underlying fraud, is no easy task. For instance, by analogy to a leading precedent (Janus Capital Grp., Inc. v. First Derivative Traders 2011), HFTs are likely to be outside the definition of primary violators as *makers* of false and misleading statements made by trading venues even if such market participants had offered a hand in designing functionalities and crafting corresponding disclosures.[19] From the standpoint of potential defenses, an even more important consideration is that HFTs may simply be recipients of selectively disclosed information without prior involvement of any kind. Likewise, information about the very mechanics of the trading process, as opposed to direct disclosure of information about specific orders, is arguably different from true inside/price-moving information about securities and underlying companies and thus outside the reach of the insider trading doctrine.

For considering scenarios of liability of users of certain order types as primary violators, the following taxonomy may be employed: (1) an order type has merely undocumented features; (2) an order type has undocumented features that violate some regulatory norm under federal securities law, such as Regulation NMS or another SEC rule; and (3) the actual functioning of an order type contradicts its formal documentation available to the general public or users, such as SRO filings, rulebook/trading procedure disclosures, and technical manuals. Furthermore, one important consideration is that trading venues often *duplicate* or *implement*—sometimes directly regulating their own market participants—regulatory norms under federal securities law. In other words, one may contrast a market participant committing an actual violation of an SEC rule and a market participant taking advantage of some trading-venue-provided functionality that is contrary to an SEC rule, with the second scenario probably being more common. Finally, it is important to remember that a violation of a regulatory norm under federal securities law or a rule of an individual trading venue do not automatically qualify as securities fraud.

Probably the most promising approach to attaching liability to market participants, such as HFTs, lies in breaking rules of trading venues by employing certain functionalities *because* their features are in fact contrary to their publicly disclosed documentation, such as SRO rules. Conceptually—and guided by a sizable body of case law and supporting analysis—it is possible to base a securities fraud claim on violations of SRO rules, as opposed to treating such violations as independent causes of action under federal securities law. While SRO rules approved by the SEC are not the only source of trading rules, this category is an important illustration. Ultimately, the relevant distinction is between universally available trading rules—be they an

---

[19] Janus Capital Grp., Inc. v. First Derivative Traders, 131 U.S. 2296 (2011).

exchange's publicly disclosed rulebook with the regulators' stamp of approval or an ATS's technical manual distributed to all subscribers—and selectively disclosed trading rules.

To condense, a viable approach to attaching primary liability to HFTs as market participants in connection with securities fraud is likely to lay in *violations* of the applicable trading protocol, chiefly meaning rules of individual trading venues, in connection with selective disclosure. Yet it becomes essential to define the nature of the underlying violation, especially because such market participants typically need not take discretionary affirmative action to break the rule in question. It is not about merely using a certain functionality after having received detailed selective disclosure about its features, let alone an imprecise tip or a possibly distorted industry rumour. The crux is in *an intention to use specific and certain discrepancies* between documented and actual features, which, once again, needs to be compared to a less questionable hypothetical of merely undocumented, but not contradictory, features. An important qualification is that some features that appear to be merely undocumented may unambiguously contradict more general rules, such as those relating to the applicable pricing grid or order matching procedures. More generally, if the very purpose of using a certain functionality is to circumvent—and operate contrary to—the existing formal documentation in order to obtain a trading advantage, that logically suggests the existence of securities fraud.

Actual knowledge as a prerequisite for intent is all but guaranteed to be present. After all, a firm requesting or designing a certain functionality would surely scrutinize the applicable formal documentation once this functionality is adopted by the trading venue in question, and, more generally, a market participant is likely to be aware of any discrepancy simply on the basis of selective disclosure. Moreover, such practices may be invisible and thus repetitive, resulting in stealth transfers of wealth likely to be diffused among numerous market participants, which could even be hardly traced and reconstructed in market data and thus be virtually undetectable to an outside observer. This stealthiness is a critical feature of many HFT practices in question, which also points in the direction of their fraudulent nature. Once again, the difference between SRO and non-SRO trading venues should not matter with respect to liability of market participants utilizing discrepancies between the official documentation and the actual functionality.

A helpful analogy is offered is by the fraud-on-the-market doctrine, which serves as a means for plaintiffs to prove their losses from affirmative misrepresentations and, in some instances, omissions without demonstrating specific reliance but instead presuming 'the integrity of the market price'.[20]

---

[20] Basic, Inc. v. Levinson, 485 U.S. 224 (1988), 247.

A comparison proposed by the author is the concept of the *integrity of the trading process*, defined as the compliance with the applicable trading protocol by all market participants combined with the accuracy and transparency of that protocol, which would preclude systematic informational advantages being exploited by any group. Arguably, it may be said that the marketplace as a whole relies on the integrity of the trading process, as a prerequisite for a proper *interaction* of orders. This concept has relevance for the existence of investor harm just as does the integrity of the market price, a concept divorced from the realities of the applicable trading protocol. Both of these approaches address the mechanism of price formation, but neither one requires an idealized informational parity with respect to securities themselves. Likewise, both of these approaches could fit into *Basic*'s rhetorical question about 'roll[ing] the dice in a crooked crap game'.[21] Moreover, the link between the wrongdoers' trading gains and other market participants' losses is much stronger in the case of the concept of the integrity of the market process compared to its counterpart.

Importantly, the phenomenon of secret arrangements is not confined to the order type controversy. Other layers of rules of individual trading venues, albeit sometimes less precise ones, may be affected. One illustration is a settlement between the SEC and Credit Suisse focused on Light Pool, the latter's electronic communication system, as it was

> represented to clients and existing and prospective subscribers that all Light Pool participants, including HFTs, would be classified pursuant to an objective formula and those 'participants,' 'traders,' or 'clients' who were classified as opportunistic would 'lose access to' or be 'kicked out.'[22]

In reality, the relevant Alpha Formula was 'applied . . . separately to the order flow submitted under each system ID of a subscriber', thus allowing such a subscriber to retain direct access.[23] Furthermore, '[s]ubscribers could request different connections to Light Pool, for example, to designate different trading strategies that they may employ for trading in Light Pool'.[24] Similarly, Credit Suisse 'gave direct subscribers—including some HFTs—the opportunity to improve their trading to avoid being labeled "opportunistic." '[25] Overall, this settlement paints a picture of inaccurate representations of certain functionalities and selective disclosure practices, although the sole liable party was a trading venue. Once again, given a varying specificity, if not vagueness, of applicable representations, the path to attaching liability is likely to depend on the existence of clear discrepancies with the disclosed trading protocol and the intent of preferred market participants to use such discrepancies.

---

[21] Ibid., 247 (quoting Schlanger v. Four-Phase Sys. Inc., 555 F. Supp. 535 (S.D.N.Y. 1982), 538).
[22] SEC, In the Matter of Credit Suisse Securities (USA) LLC, 2016, 6.   [23] Ibid.
[24] Ibid.   [25] Ibid.

10.4 Glitches and Gaming

Another type of questionable practices comes under the umbrella of 'gaming', which is often understood as the exploitation of 'glitches' in the applicable trading protocol on the level of individual trading venues. The term 'gaming'—in some instances more accurately described as 'reverse engineering'—does not need to overlap with secret handshakes, as a trading venue's deliberate involvement is typically nonexistent. In this scenario, there is no collusion between a trading venue and preferred market participants, and such discrepancies may arise merely because of that trading venue's negligence or, in some instances, even randomness, with such bugs being discovered fortuitously, searched for systematically, or, quite importantly, revealed by inside sources. Furthermore, it is natural to expect unintended consequences created by the very indeterminacy of complex rules frequently combined with inadequacy of disclosure. As observed in the context of the order matching process, 'The highly intertwined matching logic of a venue makes it difficult to ensure that one component of a trading system does not "overrule" another component resulting in unintended behaviours of the system.'[26] Furthermore, some discovered 'glitches' could actually be a result of a trading venue's selective disclosure of hidden features to *other* market participants rather than unintended consequences.

To the extent that 'gaming' captures the exploitation of unintended consequences or the very nature of complexity, including the phenomenon of conflicting rules disclosed in the same fashion, it is very problematic to outlaw this conduct ex ante. A mere opportunistic exploration, which could be described as 'testing the limits' or, in some instances, 'regulatory arbitrage', is inevitable. The issue of loopholes, generally speaking, is not a new one. As described by one court in an area far removed from securities regulation, 'Taking advantage of loopholes in laws is a time-honored American tradition. It is not a deceitful or unfair means to an end.'[27] Likewise, merely taking advantage of loopholes in rules of trading venues suggests the same outcome. Accordingly, the use of certain undocumented features in the absence of any discrepancies with formal documentation would be a very difficult case for liability.

On the other hand, there is one scenario suggesting the exposure to liability in connection with securities fraud. More specifically, some industry rumours point to HFTs 'figuring out' order matching engines' inner workings in order to exploit undocumented features that are *contrary* to the applicable rulebook, technical specifications, and other disclosures. While there could be some form

---

[26] Ignatovich and Passmore, 'Transparent order priority', 2015, 11.
[27] Buffalo S. R.R. Inc. v. Vill. of Croton-on Hudson, 434 F. Supp. 2d 241 (S.D.N.Y. 2006), 254.

of liability for unauthorized access, no true 'hacking' is necessarily required for such practices. Indeed, there is some awareness within the industry that 'buggy' or 'buggier' trading venues may serve as a source of trading profits. Likewise, there have been rumours of former exchange employees leaving for HFT firms and bringing the applicable order matching engine's source code with them in order to identify any exploitable glitches. Once again, the very feasibility of turning any discrepancies to one's own advantage in the trading process could be a powerful competitive tool. Moreover, the scenario of glitches somewhat resembles the order type controversy in the sense that specific order types or their modifiers are likely be involved. Likewise, this type of conduct may be associated with inadequate disclosure practices of trading venues.

Thus, overall, the nature of the underlying violations lies in an intention to use discrepancies between documented and actual features, which could trigger liability for securities fraud. In other words, from the standpoint of liability, the difference between an HFT taking advantage of selective disclosure and an HFT independently aware of the discrepancy in question may not be meaningful under certain circumstances. Once again, the concept of the integrity of the trading process is a useful paradigm. There would be serious disruptive implications if the multitude of market participants is expected not to rely on the integrity of the applicable trading protocol, as properly disclosed rules of the game, and identify glitches capturing discrepancies between documented and actual features on a self-help basis. Even if any such discrepancy could have been discovered by other market participants, that does not make this piece of information *accessible* to the general public, given the uncertainty of another discovery and potential costs associated with a deliberate search. While using security- or issuer-specific information under otherwise similar circumstances would have been legitimate, taking advantage of *discrepancies* with the general rules governing the trading process itself is much more problematic.

10.5 Overlaps Between Marketplaces and Traders

The distinction between marketplaces and traders is not necessarily clear-cut, and, in practice, there could be overlaps between these two categories, although not necessarily in plain view. More generally, the multiplicity of roles played by some firms in the securities industry is nothing new, just like the traditional need to manage conflicts of interests though disclosure and other means. The existence of any informational asymmetries in the applicable trading protocol is a potential profit-making tool for trading activities, as well as additional evidence indicating false and misleading disclosure.

One example of such overlaps relates to undisclosed/secret trading desks within some dark pools, which exposed some problematic business activities of these trading venues' sponsors. The extent of this phenomenon is hard to estimate, but several enforcement actions by the SEC provide an illustration of the relevant mechanics. One of such actions against Pipeline, which involved a securities fraud charge, portrays an undisclosed trading desk maintained by an affiliate entity:

> Its advertising and other public statements repeatedly claimed that the trading opportunities on the ATS were 'natural,' that the ATS would not reveal the side (*i.e.*, whether an order was to buy or to sell) or price of a customer order before a trade was completed, that the ATS denied 'arbitrageurs' and 'high-frequency traders' information needed to 'front run,' that it provided a refuge from 'predators,' and that it prevented 'pre-trade information leakage.'...These claims were false and misleading in that the Affiliate was on the other side of the vast majority of trades executed on the ATS. The Affiliate sought to predict the side and price of Pipeline customers' orders and then trade on the same side as those orders in other trading venues before filling them on the ATS.[28]

Moreover, the very existence of this trading desk was combined with other advantages, such as the leakage of, 'after the trades were consummated, order and trade data of other customers' and 'certain access and information that improved the Affiliate's ability to trade advantageously, including certain electronic connectivity to the ATS'.[29] Not surprisingly, the trading desk's advantageous position was reflected in its bottom line.[30]

A very similar enforcement action was directed against ITG in connection with the functioning of POSIT, its dark pool. ITG was sanctioned for 'its operation of an undisclosed proprietary trading desk known within ITG as "Project Omega."'[31] The relevant

> trading strategies were based on engaging in high frequency algorithmic buying and selling of NMS stocks at or within the National Best Bid and Offer...in order to make small profits or 'spreads' between the purchase and sale price within extremely short time frames.[32]

While this project was active,

> ITG continued to market and promote itself publicly, as well as to customers and prospective customers, as an 'agency-only' broker that did not engage in proprietary trading. ITG also promoted its products and services as 'reducing market impact' and protecting against 'information leakage' and 'gaming' of customer orders.[33]

---

[28] SEC, In the Matter of Pipeline Trading Systems LLC, 2011, 2.
[29] Ibid.   [30] Ibid., 12.   [31] SEC, In the Matter of ITG INC, 2015, 2.   [32] Ibid., 8.
[33] Ibid., 14.

In fact, Project Omega had access to

> real-time information regarding 'parent' orders routed through virtually all of ITG's algorithms, including: (a) client identifier, (b) symbol, (c) side, (d) quantity of shares, (e) filled shares, (d) target price, (e) the ITG algorithm in which the order was located, and (f) time parameters.[34]

Yet another strain of overlaps between marketplaces and traders is illustrated by the business model of off-exchange market making, in which such a firm acts as a stand-alone trading venue with its own trading protocol and corresponding disclosures. In a key enforcement action against Citadel Securities, the SEC targeted high-speed algorithms that opportunistically used different market data benchmarks and involved undisclosed order handling mechanics.[35] The settlement focused on two algorithms, which were run by Citadel's whole-sale marketmaking unit. Both algorithms were triggered by price discrepancies between the consolidated and private data feeds, i.e. the 'official' market data and more detailed and inherently faster market data products offered by exchanges themselves. Moreover, one of these algorithms went beyond a simple data feed arbitrage, and, as one might speculate, it probably involved additional predictive number-crunching and HFT-style market structure short-cuts. In any instance, the enforcement action against Citadel was based on the existence of affirmative misrepresentations made by the firm as a de facto stand-alone trading venue. As noted in the settlement,

> During the relevant period, CES [Citadel Execution Services] provided a written disclosure to certain retail broker-dealer clients that described a market order as an '[o]rder to buy (sell) at the best offer (bid) price currently available in the market-place,' and made other, similar representations to its clients [which] suggested that CES would either internalize the marketable order at, or seek to obtain through routing, the best bid or offer from the various market data feeds CES referenced.[36]

Going beyond the legal details of the Citadel settlement, it is important to emphasize that the marketplace-trader duality could also be combined with another role, which in turns raises the issue of interaction of different regulatory frameworks governing such functions. For instance, off-exchange market makers are not just proprietary traders functioning as de facto trading venues, as they typically play the role of agents handling order flow routed to them by other broker-dealers. Accordingly, these market makers are subject to the duty of best execution, which is fiduciary in nature and involves a multitude of dimensions. Yet another wrinkle arises because this principal-agent combination is also mixed with the 'trading centre' status under Regulation NMS, which essentially covers all trading venues and also reaches to on-exchange

---

[34] Ibid.   [35] SEC, In the Matter of Citadel Securities LLC, 2017.   [36] Ibid., 10.

and off-exchange market makers. While the duty of best execution is separate from the requirements of the trade-through rule for trading centres established by Regulation NMS, with the latter often seen as a 'backstopper' for the former, complying with one set of requirements does not necessarily satisfy the other set. Indeed, one issue is whether various exemptions of the trade-through rule are abused to the point of constituting breaches of the duty of best execution, which could in turn trigger charges of securities fraud.

10.6 Defining Market Manipulation

The doctrine of market manipulation is not necessarily easy to apply to new practices, although some modern iterations of manipulative trading certainly fit the traditional pattern. For instance, the much-discussed practices of 'spoofing' and 'layering' have been classified as manipulative in legal actions with at least *some* connection to HFT, but such instances seem to be confined to the futures and commodities space. In securities markets, it remains to be seen whether larger players in the HFT space have been involved in manipulative schemes, such as spoofing and layering, and how common such practices are. Yet, overall, a more pressing question is whether a host of HFT practices could even be properly classified as market manipulation. In fact, some practices, such as those based on speed, are problematic to fit into the definition of market manipulation. As remarked in a key judicial opinion, the plaintiffs 'fail to explain how merely enabling a party to react more quickly to information can constitute a manipulative act, at least where the services at issue are publicly known and available to any customer willing to pay'.[37] On the other hand, the appellate decision for this lawsuit concluded that allegations relating to the provision by securities exchanges of co-location services, private data feeds, and complex order types did state a valid legal claim of market manipulation in terms of raising a factual dispute whether such practices 'artificially affect[ed] market activity'.[38] Yet another HFT practice difficult to fit into any truly manipulative category is 'exploratory trading', which has been described as

a form of costly information acquisition [which] does not generate information that relates directly to the traded asset's fundamental value, but that pertains rather to unobservable aspects of market conditions that could eventually become public, ex-post, through ordinary market interactions.[39]

---

[37] *In re* Barclays Liquidity Cross 2015, 362.
[38] City of Providence v. BATS Global Mkts., Inc. 2017, 48–50.
[39] Clark-Joseph, 'Exploratory trading', 2014, 48–9.

Accordingly, it becomes critical to identify the scope of market manipulation as such. As summarized by a leading commentator, 'The essence of the fraud in a Section 10(b) manipulation case is the creation of an artificial price.'[40] Logically interpreted, the term 'artificial price' means, with some inevitable vagueness, pushing the market price in the 'wrong' direction or delaying a move in the 'correct' direction. Not being satisfied by this restriction, one court engaged in doctrinal struggles in its dictum pronouncement in order to bring additional practices under the umbrella of market manipulation: 'There is nothing in the text of Section 10(b) that limits manipulation (a concept which, thanks to the boundless creativity of capitalism, can include many kinds of conduct) to *price* manipulation.'[41] However, the appellate decision for this lawsuit maintained that a claim for market manipulation must allege activities 'for the purpose of artificially depressing or inflating the price of the security'.[42] More generally, the weight of the existing case law, without any significant deviations, points to the necessity of an artificial impact on a security's price, and taking this factor out of the equation would dissolve the existing concept of market manipulation. The courts have also recognized that a mere price impact is not by itself evidence of market manipulation, given that virtually every transaction has some potential marginal impact on the price formation process.

However, stretching the doctrine of market manipulation is not even necessary, even if the underlying practices look manipulation-like in terms of boosting trading volume, which might suggest an element of false appearances/deception. Recognizing that a security's price is not the only dimension of loss, the regulators have been on the path of finding fraudulent conduct even in the absence of any price impact when certain rules of trading venues are flouted or abused—not directly broken—in order to secure/reallocate an economic benefit that otherwise would not have accrued and likely at the expense of others. Of course, drawing a line between mere 'gaming' and 'abuse', short of unambiguous direct violations, is a concern, but the ultimate goals of the rule in question may provide some guidance in a case-by-case analysis. For instance, the SEC characterized as securities fraud the offsetting of transactions designed to obtain market data revenues paid out by the Consolidated Tape Association and shared by NASDAQ with member firms.[43] Likewise, the SEC applied the same characterization to mismarking 'professional' and 'customer' designations that resulted in distorted determination by

---

[40] Markham, *Law Enforcement*, 2014, 392.
[41] Rabin v. NASDAQ OMX PHLX LLC, 182 F. Supp. 3d 220 (E.D. Pa. 2016), *aff'd*, 712 Fed. App'x 188 (3d Cir. 2017), 244.
[42] Ibid., 193.
[43] SEC, 2006. Irfan Mohammed Amanat, Exchange Act Release No. 54,708, 89 SEC Docket 714 (3 Nov. 2006), *aff'd*, 269 Fed. App'x 217 (3d Cir. 2008).

securities exchanges of 'which orders received priority of execution and the amounts of all related transaction credits and debits, including liquidity rebates, "take" fees, transaction costs, and cancellation fees', which deprived these securities exchanges of certain fees, and 'unfairly disadvantaged other professional market participants over whom the Respondents' "customer" orders wrongly received priority of execution for orders at the same price'.[44] Importantly, these examples do not even involve informational asymmetries pertaining to specific functionalities, and the existence of such asymmetries would have further strengthened the case for characterizing underlying practices as securities fraud.

Finally, going back to the practices relevant to the current market structure crisis, including the order type controversy, the reach of market manipulation as such is not essential:

> [T]he scope of securities fraud is much wider than market manipulation. Consider that *riding price changes* with the assistance of inadequately documented functionalities is different from *creating artificial price patterns* in order to profit from them, which is the essence of market manipulation.[45]

In fact, no radical—and potentially problematic—doctrinal restructuring would be required, although the bar for stating a claim for market manipulation appears to be lower. Moreover, even as a mere prediction, any shift to non-price-based market manipulation is unlikely to materialize in the foreseeable future. At the same time, novel methods of market manipulation, which may or may not be based on market-structure-embedded informational asymmetries, still need to be monitored for. In fact, having a market structure perspective on short-term/small-scale price variations, which may appear different from more traditional examples of market manipulation, is indeed warranted for gatekeepers.

10.7 Conclusion

The trajectory of the modern electronic marketplace has been influenced by informational asymmetries offering nontransparent advantages to certain groups of market participants, a factor overlapping and interacting with numerous technological changes, the level of complexity, and the phenomenon of regulatory arbitrage. In fact, a gamut of informational asymmetries, both deliberate and accidental, has been deeply rooted in the evolving market structure and resulted in substantial stealth wealth transfers. A non-trivial point is that informational asymmetries—often as a manifestation of secret

---

[44] SEC, In the Matter of Behruz Afshar, 2016, 11–12, 17.   [45] Bodek and Dolgopolov, 125.

arrangements between trading venues and favoured traders—relate to the trading process itself rather than the underlying securities and companies, as illustrated by more traditional concerns about insider trading. Given the sophistication of the architecture of securities markets, one should not expect a fish bowl, but deliberate informational asymmetries—or, worded in a more legal way, false and misleading disclosures—are a phenomenon of concern, which also form the principal basis of legal liability for securities fraud to reach both marketplaces and traders.

Corruption of self-regulation is hardly a novel theme. However, the traditional scenario of mere lax enforcement of exchange rules should be contrasted to the implementation of highly complex rules, as special products offered by both SRO and non-SRO trading venues, combined with selective disclosure to preferred market participants. As stated by a leading figure in the securities industry, 'With a computerized matching engine, everything is fair. All customers play by the same rules.'[46] Yet this claim is too broad in light of recent legal developments, which can in no way be described as conspiracy theories. In addition to the legal liability dimension, an important issue is how disclosure obligations of trading venues could be reformed, perhaps even in the form of releasing some portions of the underlying code.

While certain HFT practices have been lubricated by secret arrangements with trading venues, some others do not depend on collusion. While there are bits and pieces of evidence about the existence of a wider range of practices, such as an exploitation of bugs, more remains to be explored or disproven. Abusive trading techniques, including market manipulation, certainly survive in the modern electronic marketplace, and an important question is to what extent they are rooted in the HFT space, as opposed to manual or semi-manual traders who are frequently on the regulators' radar and in the news. A more general question is why HFTs have not become an important target in litigation centred on securities fraud. A potential answer lies in difficulties with demonstrating the state of mind, intent, tit-for-tat/conspiracy-like arrangements with trading venues, and knowledge of the inadequacy of formal disclosure, including specific communications that amount to a smoking gun. Furthermore, many practices in question are solely conduct-based and do not involve specific public statements. Similarly, a bird's-eye view of the SEC's recent enforcement program indicates that the regulators have often preferred identifying technical violations, as opposed to asserting the existence of deliberate wrongdoing in the form of securities fraud, and employed a cautionary approach of targeting trading venues alone instead of specific market participants.

---

[46] Cummings, 39.

References

Bodek, Haim. *The Problem of HFT: Collected Writings on High Frequency Trading and Stock Market Structure Reform*. New York: Decimus Capital Markets, 2013.

Bodek, Haim, and Stanislav Dolgopolov. *The Market Structure Crisis*. New York: Decimus Capital Markets, 2015.

Clark-Joseph, Adam D. 'Exploratory trading'. Available at: https://www.aeaweb.org/conference/2015/retrieve.php?pdfid=1133, 2014.

Cummings, Dave. *Make the Trade: A Kansas City Entrepreneur Takes On Wall Street*. Self-published, 2016.

Harris, Larry. *Trading and Electronic Markets: What Investment Professionals Need to Know*. CFA Institute Research Foundation. Available at: https://www.cfapubs.org/doi/pdf/10.2470/rf.v2015.n4.1, 2015.

Ignatovich, Denis A., and Grant O. Passmore. 'Transparent order priority and pricing'. Available at: http://www.mondovisione.com/_assets/files/ai-wp1502.pdf, 2015.

Markham, Jerry. *Law Enforcement and the History of Financial Market Manipulation*. Armonk, NY: M.E. Sharpe, 2014.

SEC (US Securities and Exchange Commission). In the Matter of Behruz Afshar, Shahryar Afshar, Richard F. Kenny, IV, Fineline Trading Group LLC, and Makino Capital LLC. Securities Act of 1933 Release No. 10094, Securities Exchange Act 1934 Release No. 78043, Investment Company Act of 1940 Release No. 32144 (2016). Available at: https://www.sec.gov/litigation/admin/2016/33-10094.pdf, 2016.

SEC. In the Matter of Citadel Securities LLC. Securities Act of 1933 Release No. 10280, Securities Exchange Act of 1934 Release No. 79790 (2017). Available at: https://www.sec.gov/litigation/admin/2017/33-10280.pdf, 2017.

SEC. In the Matter of Credit Suisse Securities (USA) LLC. Securities Act of 1933 Release No. 10014, Securities Exchange Act of 1934 Release No. 77003 (2016). Available at: https://www.sec.gov/litigation/admin/2016/33-10014.pdf, 2016.

SEC. In the Matter of EDGA EXCHANGE, INC., and EDGX EXCHANGE, INC. Securities Exchange Act of 1934 Release No. 74032 (2015). Available at: https://www.sec.gov/litigation/admin/2015/34-74032.pdf, 2015.

SEC. In the Matter of ITG INC. and ALTERNET SECURITIES, INC. Securities Act of 1933 Release No. 9887, Securities Exchange Act of 1934 Release No. 75672 (2015). Available at: https://www.sec.gov/litigation/admin/2015/33-9887.pdf, 2015.

SEC. In the Matter of Pipeline Trading Systems LLC, Fred J. Federspiel, and Alfred R. Berkeley III. Securities Act of 1933 Release No. 9271, Securities Exchange Act of 1934 Release No. 65609 (2011). Available at: https://www.sec.gov/litigation/admin/2011/33-9271.pdf, 2011.

SEC. In the Matter of UBS SECURITIES LLC. Securities Act of 1933 Release No. 9697, Securities Exchange Act of 1934 Release No. 74060 (2015). Available at: https://www.sec.gov/litigation/admin/2015/33-9697.pdf, 2015.

SEC. Regulation of NMS Stock Alternative Trading Systems, Securities Exchange Act of 1934 Release No. 76474, 80 Federal Register 80998 (2015). Available at: https://www.gpo.gov/fdsys/pkg/FR-2015-12-28/pdf/2015-29890.pdf, 2015.

Part 4

Regulatory Agencies and Market Structure Regulation

11

Regulating High Frequency Trading and Dark Liquidity in Australia

Greg Medcraft

11.1 Introduction

Capital markets help fund economic growth and build Australia's real economy. The Australian Securities and Investments Commission (ASIC), Australia's corporate, markets, and financial services regulator, contributes to this through its regulatory objectives—promoting investor and consumer trust and confidence, and ensuring that markets are fair and efficient. Any erosion of trust and confidence in markets leads to lower investor participation and results in higher funding costs.

These regulatory objectives underpin the many roles ASIC plays in Australia's financial sector. The broad scope of ASIC's jurisdiction is unique; it covers the regulation of the provision of financial services and consumer credit, as well as Australia's markets and corporations.

ASIC has adopted a 'detect, understand, and respond' approach to identifying and addressing risks. As part of this approach, ASIC uses a number of regulatory tools, including promoting compliance with and enforcing the law, assisting and providing guidance to stakeholders, facilitating business, and promoting financial literacy.

As technological developments continue to increase in financial markets, ASIC has recognized digital disruption and cyber resilience in financial services and markets as long-term challenges. These developments and innovations are important for competition and efficiency but, from a regulatory perspective, need to be balanced by the protection of investor and consumer trust and confidence. To ensure this balance is right, ASIC has developed an approach to regulating financial innovation that is flexible and adaptable, with a focus on understanding developments before responding.

Technological change, increasing competition, regulatory change, and glo-balization mean that financial markets are changing more rapidly than ever before. While these changes have driven substantial growth in markets and productivity improvements, they also create new challenges for regulators.

This is particularly clear in exchange markets. Trading in exchange market products is now highly automated, with the vast majority of orders generated and executed by computer algorithms. This is largely the case for the full spectrum of market users, from firms that trade their own capital (including high frequency traders) through to market participants who trade on behalf of clients.

These innovations and advances in technology are delivering lower costs and more efficient processes for investors. Information is also more accessible, which can facilitate better consumer decisions. However, alongside these positive changes—and as we see future developments unfold—there is a need for continued testing, monitoring, and accountability.

Competition between trading venues has fragmented liquidity and created additional complexity for investors. The development of dark venues, in part a reaction to these changes, has itself created difficulties. Developments in technology and automation have allowed high frequency traders to earn rent profits from this system's remnant inefficiencies. Investors navigating a landscape of dynamic liquidity have focused on high frequency trading and dark pools as potential sources of toxicity.

This chapter provides some background on Australia's markets and ASIC's role as market conduct regulator. It outlines ASIC's broad regulatory approach and ASIC's specific approach to regulating innovative financial technology. It explains how ASIC's regulatory approach has informed the response to the challenges to investor trust and confidence presented by high frequency trading and dark liquidity. Detailing the structure of the Australian markets based on 2012 and 2015 reviews, the chapter discusses the ASIC responses to both the real and perceived problems in the market, as well as the changes stimulated by ASIC actions.[1]

11.2 Financial Markets in Australia

Australia has sophisticated, highly developed financial markets and is a major centre of capital market activity in the Asian region.

---

[1] ASIC, Report 331, 2013; and ASIC, Report 452, 2015.

In 2017, Australia's financial market comprised

- 18 licensed financial markets (e.g. ASX, ASX 24, and Chi-X Australia), including 6 foreign financial markets (e.g. Ice Futures and the London Metal Exchange);
- 6 licensed clearing and settlement facilities;
- 2 licensed and six prescribed derivative trade repositories;
- 17 participant crossing systems (dark pools);
- 26 professional trading platforms in over-the-counter (OTC) products;
- numerous market, clearing and/or settlement intermediaries; and
- around 2300 listed companies plus numerous other entities that quote their products (e.g. options, warrants, exchange traded funds) on licensed financial markets.

Listings are dominated by the ASX Group, which accounts for 96.2 per cent of all listed entities by number and 99.9 per cent by value. The total market capitalization of ASX-listed stocks was A$1.79 trillion as at end August 2017, corresponding to a total of 2237 stocks.

In October 2011, Australia introduced competition in trading. Chi-X Australia entered the market as a competing exchange and now accounts for 14 per cent of all on-market trading (see Figure 11.1).

An additional form of trading where liquidity is matched away from the visible order book has always been possible in the Australian market. Traditionally this 'dark trading' consisted of block, or special, size transactions and a form of

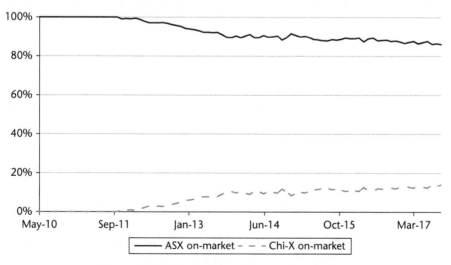

Figure 11.1. Relative share of on-market trading

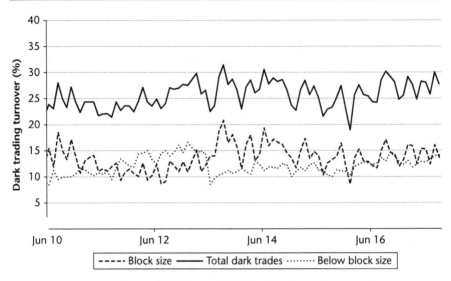

Figure 11.2. Share of dark trading by value

internalization that allowed participants to prioritize their own matching orders at the bid or offer. This has developed into a more formal process where orders remain hidden but transactions are reported immediately to market. Participant-operated venues are known as 'crossing systems'—or colloquially as 'dark pools'—while exchanges have developed their own dark markets to operate in parallel with their lit order-books.

Dark trading constitutes approximately 28 per cent of all turnover (see Figure 11.2), with approximately half of this occurring within the dark electronic venues.

11.2.1 *Changes to Market Structures*

Financial markets, globally and in Australia, are undergoing a period of rapid change. The change is occurring across the entire market, from capital raising through to post-trade services such as clearing and settlement. The reasons for this change include

- proliferation of alternative market venues, particularly in OTC markets and products—for example,
  - some offer services once exclusively provided by exchanges (e.g. capital raising), and
  - others provide the commercial efficiencies of organized trading for an increasing range of non-exchange products, including OTC derivatives, spot foreign exchange (FX), fixed income, and other products (see Figure 11.3);

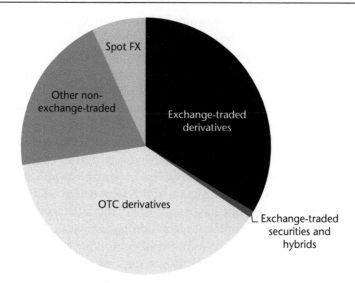

Figure 11.3. Exchange-traded and non-exchange-traded financial products in Australia

- increased complexity in the technology used by market venues;
- use of social media or other technologies to create new forms of market-venue-like platforms;
- globalization and cross-border market venue access;
- exchange group consolidation; and
- the domestic impact of global regulation.

These changes affect the way investors—predominantly professional but increasingly retail—use market venues to meet their investing, capital raising, and risk mitigation objectives.

11.2.2 *Structural Change and Risks Affecting Financial Markets*

Structural change is also altering the shape of Australia's financial markets. Notably, there is a shift to market-based financing, driven in Australia by growth in the superannuation (pension) sector and increased banking regulation. This makes effective securities regulation even more vital. Australia's managed funds industry (including superannuation) is the fourth largest in the world, growing 8.8 per cent ($231.6 billion) over the year to the March 2017 quarter to reach $2.9 trillion in total funds under management. These structural changes amplify many of the risks affecting financial markets in Australia, including digital disruption, cyber-resilience, and globalization.

Digital disruption—technology-enabled new business models threatening incumbents—has brought considerable benefits to consumers of financial services over the last two decades by providing more choice and facilitating new entrants to the markets. However, technological developments also raise challenges and risks for financial stability and regulation. Key among these is the risk of increasing complexity and fragmentation in financial markets and the increased cyber risks.

Technology allows markets to manage cyber incidents effectively and ensure the well-functioning market infrastructure that is critical to the integrity and reputation of financial markets. Nevertheless, cyber threats remain a key risk and cyber-resilience remains a focus for regulators such as ASIC. Australia's financial markets are more integrated with international markets than at any other time in history. International regulation has grown in response to the globalization of markets, both as a means of controlling the risks associated with those markets and as a way of facilitating cross-border activity. At the same time, the increased breadth and strength of international standard-setting has meant that ASIC (and Australia more generally) has needed to introduce, or at least consider introducing, regulation for areas that were not previously regulated.

11.3 ASIC's Role

ASIC is Australia's corporate, financial services, markets, and consumer credit regulator. The commission that leads ASIC comprises a chair, a deputy chair and between one and six other full-time commissioners. ASIC's purpose is to contribute to Australia's economic reputation and wellbeing by ensuring that Australia's financial markets are fair and efficient, supported by confident and informed investors and consumers. The agency is constituted under the Australian Securities and Investments Commission Act 2001.

As financial services regulator, ASIC is responsible for investor and consumer protection in financial services. ASIC administers the Australian financial services licensing regime and monitors financial services businesses to ensure they operate efficiently, honestly, and fairly. These businesses typically deal in superannuation, managed funds, deposit and payment products, shares and company securities, derivatives, and insurance.

As consumer credit regulator, ASIC licences and regulates people and businesses engaging in consumer credit activities (including banks, credit unions, finance companies, and mortgage and finance brokers). This includes ensuring that credit licensees meet the standards—including their responsibilities to consumers—that are set out in the National Consumer Credit Protection Act 2009.

As corporate regulator, ASIC ensures that companies, schemes, and related entities meet their obligations under the Corporations Act 2001. This includes registering and regulating companies from their incorporation through to their winding up, and ensuring that company officers comply with their responsibilities. ASIC registers and, where necessary, takes disciplinary action against company auditors and liquidators. ASIC also monitors public companies' financial reporting and disclosure and fundraising activities.

Finally, as market regulator, ASIC assesses how effectively financial markets are complying with their legal obligations to operate fair and efficient markets. ASIC is responsible for the supervision of trading on Australia's domestic licensed equity, derivatives, and futures markets and advises the Australian government on the authorization of new markets.

ASIC has approximately 1700 full-time equivalent staff positions and in 2017–18 its budget was A\$387.7 million, which includes a departmental appropriation (of A\$340.2 million), revenue from independent sources (such as fees from operating the company register), and capital funding. This budget will fall by around 11.2 per cent to \$344.4 million by 2020–21.

On 15 June 2017, a law was passed to introduce an industry funding model for ASIC from 1 July 2017. Under this model, regulated entities will be levied to recover most of ASIC's regulatory costs. The industry funding model will provide ASIC with greater stability and certainty of funding. However, the amount of ASIC's funding will still be determined by the government as part of its federal budget process. From 1 August 2010 until 30 June 2017, there was a separate Market Supervision Cost Recovery framework which recovered the funding the government provided ASIC for market supervision activities, by imposing fees on market participants. This Market Supervision Cost Recovery regime has been incorporated into the broader ASIC industry funding model from 2017–18 onwards.

11.3.1 *ASIC's Approach to Financial Regulation*

ASIC's regulatory objectives are to promote investor and consumer trust and confidence, and to ensure fair and efficient financial markets. ASIC adopts a risk-based approach to ensure actions are targeted and proportionate using a 'detect, understand, and respond' approach.

ASIC 'detects' misconduct by undertaking surveillances that target areas posing the greatest risk to investors, consumers, and the markets, using the information from gatekeeper breach reports, industry whistleblowers, complaints and reports from the public, and market and industry monitoring. ASIC also uses stakeholder engagement to better understand the markets and industry, and collaborates with academics, industry bodies, consumer groups, and other agencies, both domestic and international, to assess industry, market, and regulatory developments.

ASIC 'understands' by analysing intelligence to assess risks early and respond quickly, gathering insights using technology systems, data management and analytics capabilities, and behavioural insights and research capabilities.

ASIC 'responds' in various ways, including by taking enforcement and other regulatory action to hold gatekeepers accountable, and by providing guidance and engaging with individual firms and industry to drive behavioural change. ASIC responds to misconduct and problems in the market by acting to improve financial capability, engaging with domestic and international stakeholders, and participating in global standard-setting. ASIC also provides policy advice to government and supports the implementation of law reforms.

11.3.2 *Regulating Innovative Financial Technology*

ASIC's approach to regulating innovative financial technology is to understand and respond in a way that encourages innovation while also ensuring that investors can have trust and confidence in markets and that those markets are fair and efficient. Underlying the approach to financial technology are four principles.

The first principle is to be responsive to the speed and nature of change. In 2015, ASIC established a dedicated Innovation Hub to help businesses understand the regulatory framework. The Innovation Hub's informal assistance programme focuses on responding to challenges faced by start-ups, and it is a centre of excellence within ASIC for considering novel approaches from start-up businesses and other participants, as well as for regulation within ASIC. An example of such regulatory innovation is the 'regulatory sandbox', which provides relief from licensing requirements to an entire class of financial service providers, enabling new businesses to test innovative concepts without the need for a financial services licence.

The second principle is to resist the temptation to act without properly understanding the development. This is particularly relevant to ASIC's work on high frequency trading and dark liquidity. In this area, ASIC worked to understand the market by identifying the extent and nature of high frequency trading and dark liquidity in Australia and to identify problems and make changes where necessary. ASIC findings suggested that misinformation had fuelled media interest and investor concern.

Another element within this principle is ensuring that ASIC regularly engages with international regulators. Given the differences in regulatory remit around the world, international engagement facilitates a wider understanding of the many different applications that a particular technological development may have. ASIC monitors developments in the field and engages with international regulators to enrich the domestic perspective.

The third principle is ensuring that regulatory responses are 'technology neutral'. For example, all brokers, whether offline or online, are subject to the same regulatory requirements. While the obligations are the same, the use of different channels may create different risks: for example, in the case of online service providers, technology-related issues such as cyber security, privacy, and data protection present a heightened risk. Depending on the channel used, the way service providers meet their obligations may differ.

The fourth principle is ensuring that ASIC has the necessary skills and expertise to be an effective regulator. This means making data-driven and evidence-based regulatory decisions. ASIC is focused on managing and using the currently accessible range of data, identifying datasets necessary to remain effective into the future, and building a strong data analytics and technology capability.

In 2016–17, ASIC created a specialist data analytics team, recruited staff with expertise in data management and analytics to various areas of the organization, and defined a strategy for data governance to optimize how ASIC collects, stores, and shares data. In addition to existing datasets, ASIC has created a register of desirable datasets that could support supervisory and enforcement objectives, and contribute—ultimately—to a master data repository.

11.3.2.1 FINANCIAL MARKET INFRASTRUCTURE

ASIC seeks to ensure that the standards set for market operators and participants support resilient, reliable, and effective price discovery and post-trade systems.

In 2016, Australia's largest equity market operator, ASX, suffered an outage. ASIC undertook a detailed whole-of-market review and found that despite advances in technology that have underpinned market developments, ASX's trading systems are a single point of failure in the Australian equities markets. From this review, ASIC identified areas of ASX's business that could be enhanced to manage technology risks going forward, including

- business continuity and IT disaster recovery;
- comprehensive and robust technology status monitoring; and
- key enterprise architecture documentation.

ASIC is also focused on improving compliance standards of market participants. Market participants are important gatekeepers to financial markets and must have effective risk management and internal supervision.

Anyone who provides direct market access to clients should maintain appropriate controls to ensure that trading messages do not interfere with the integrity of the market. These controls include appropriate filters and a robust trade monitoring framework. ASIC has imposed additional licence conditions on Australian financial services licensees where there have been concerns about their ability to identify and prevent market misconduct.

11.3.2.2 SUPERVISORY TECHNOLOGY

ASIC has recently increased investment in more sophisticated surveillance systems to undertake effective market supervision and keep pace with technological developments in the market.

(a) Markets Analysis and Intelligence

In 2013, ASIC introduced the Markets Analysis and Intelligence (MAI) surveillance system. Using MAI, the time taken to conduct searches of trading activity was reduced from months or weeks to minutes in some instances. ASIC developed and uses MAI to stay on top of technological developments in financial markets. MAI is built around algorithmic trading technology and gives ASIC the ability to analyse trade data for patterns and relationships. MAI provides sophisticated data analytics capability to identify suspicious trading in real time and across markets, as well as greater levels of detection of insider trading. This enables ASIC to better detect, investigate, and prosecute trading breaches.

MAI is purpose-built and designed to handle the dynamism of financial markets (i.e. to handle increases in high frequency trading and algorithmic trading). This allows ASIC to interrogate very large datasets and monitor market activity, consistent with the increased use of technology in day-to-day trading. MAI is web-based and is hosted by the system provider.

Since the launch of MAI in September 2012, daily trades have fluctuated between 1.3 million and 1.8 million trades. This suggests that overall activity on the market has been generally trending at approximately 1.5 million trades per day, over the five years to September 2017, with no significant growth other than normal fluctuations due to market volatility. From 1 July 2013 to 1 November 2017, there have been just over 170,000 'alerts' triggered by, for example, an unusual trading pattern. This equates to an average of approximately 154.8 alerts, or 0.0086 per cent of trades. Once an alert has been triggered, ASIC seeks to review all real-time alerts within 20 minutes. If the alert is readily explainable, it will be marked as 'explained' with an assessment outlining why the relevant threshold was triggered. If the alert is not readily explainable, ASIC will place it on 'watch' and continue to review and monitor the alert over the course of the day, with the potential for further consideration the following day if there is no resolution. Alternatively, ASIC may place the alert on 'review listed' and open a surveillance on the matter, generally involving the use of compulsory powers to obtain further information from brokers and other market participants.

In determining the correct setting for an alert, there are a number of resources ASIC may use, including

- customized MAI Reports;
- third party information sources, such as IRESS or Bloomberg;
- ASIC's regulatory data repositories;
- media search systems, such as FACTIVA; and
- social media, chat room, or forum searches.

Since implementing MAI, ASIC has introduced several new features, including the incorporation of enhanced regulatory data. From July 2014, participants have been required to provide specific data on orders to market operators, who must record and provide to ASIC all regulatory data they receive. This includes information on the broker and unique client references (client IDs). However, ASIC must still use compulsory information gathering powers to confirm the identity of the traders under these client IDs.

With the enhanced data, ASIC has built in-house surveillance tools, including an account tracker. The account tracker allows ASIC to quickly profile an individual account across all stocks on the market, over a specific period of time, including a record of size, frequency, and type of securities traded. This allows ASIC to quickly identify anomalous trading patterns which need further investigation.

These features enabled ASIC to reduce the number of market inquiry notices issued under legislation to market participants by almost half between 2011 and 2017. Notices are typically issued to seek substantiation of concerns about potential insider or manipulative trades. Not only is the number of notices issued lower (and continuing to fall), the notices issued are more specific and targeted. Participants require approximately 30 per cent less time to respond to these notices.

(b) Analytics

ASIC has also been investing in data analytics capabilities, in terms of both staff and technology. In April 2016, the Australian government announced that it would provide ASIC with an additional A$61.1 million to enhance ASIC's data analytics and surveillance capabilities as well as improving ASIC's information management systems. This followed a 'Capability Review' of ASIC, conducted in 2015, which highlighted the critical role that sophisticated analytics and risk assessment processes can play in identifying and mitigating conduct risk.[2]

---

[2] Australian Government, The Treasury, 'Turnbull Government', 20 April 2016.

Recent technology initiatives include implementing new third-party software for use in investigation and enforcement matters in the Enhanced Investigative Analytics system. This new software allows pattern matching across evidence databases using algorithms that help map target relationships and create chronologies beyond word-search-based capabilities.

In 2017, ASIC conducted a number of trials to explore the use of advanced data analytics, including

- exploring how machine-based learning and pattern recognition can be used to better locate relevant documents for investigations; and

- piloting the use of social media analytics to monitor potential risks in the system.

The social media analytics tool seeks to identify misleading marketing material in a particular sub-sector, while the web-crawling software examines statements hosted on the internet.

ASIC's also has a surveillance focus on predatory trading that manipulates the market. ASIC examines instances of conduct in high frequency trading and dark liquidity that may breach the law. For example, ASIC is experimenting with the use of a natural language processing supervised learning algorithm to read, understand, and classify market announcements for further analysis. ASIC is also developing supervised statistical machine learning procedures—support vector machines—to read MAI data and detect previously unidentified and future new accounts used by fund managers to disguise how they are trading.[3]

11.4 ASIC'S Approach to High Frequency Trading and Dark Liquidity

Over the last decade, there has been significant media interest and investor concern about high frequency trading and the use of dark pools, creating calls for further regulation or regulatory action. ASIC's response to this reflected an important aspect of its regulatory approach: after identifying a potential issue, to first ensure that it is properly understood. To this end, ASIC undertook a review of the Australian market to identify and assess the problems in that market.

After analysing the information gathered by the review, ASIC publicly reported the findings, including problematic and, importantly, *non-problematic* areas in Australian markets. Sharing the findings and publicly identifying

---

[3] More information about ASIC's approach to regtech can be found on our website: http://asic. gov.au/for-business/your-business/innovation-hub/regtech/.

problems was an important part of the response and discouraged some participants from engaging in problematic behaviours.[4] The public report sent an important message to investors about certain perceived problems for which no evidence was found in Australian markets. ASIC also communicated directly with some participants about concerning behaviour.

Following the first review, various regulatory changes were made (discussed below).[5] ASIC then undertook a second, broader review (covering equity markets and futures in equity indices and bonds) and also made the findings of that review public.[6]

Following publication of the findings, communication with participants, and implementation of changes to the rules, ASIC has conducted ongoing monitoring of developments in the market. ASIC is continually improving its ability to understand the operation of high frequency traders and dark liquidity in the Australian market.

11.4.1 *High Frequency Trading in Australia*

Australian markets are now overwhelmingly automated. ASIC estimates that at least 99.6 per cent of all trading messages submitted to equity markets are sourced from an automated order processing system. While those who invest on business fundamentals have different motivations, and behave differently from, short-term traders, many of the execution tools and algorithms used by short-term traders are also used by large fundamental investors.

High frequency trading as a subset of algorithmic trading has been defined in various ways. ASIC uses the International Organization of Securities Commissions (IOSCO) definition, which lists a number of common characteristics of high frequency trading, including

- the use of sophisticated technological tools for pursuing a number of different strategies, ranging from market making to arbitrage;
- a highly quantitative tool that employs algorithms along the whole investment chain (i.e. analysis of market data, deployment of appropriate trading strategies, minimization of trading costs, and execution of trades);
- a high daily portfolio turnover and order-to-trade ratio;
- flat or near flat positions at the end of the trading day, meaning that little or no risk is carried overnight (with positions often held for as little as seconds or even fractions of a second);

---

[4] ASIC, Report 331, 2013.   [5] ASIC, Consultation Paper 202, 2013.
[6] ASIC, Report 452, 2015.

- use mostly by proprietary trading firms or desks; and
- latency sensitivity—successful high frequency trading strategies depend on the ability to be faster than competitors, lower latency meaning faster speeds.[7]

High frequency trading makes up one end of the technical trading spectrum; it has the shortest holding time, the smallest positions, and the greatest frequency. In addition to high frequency trading, there is significant volume of other forms of technical trading.[8] ASIC estimates that 45 per cent of all equity turnover is conducted by traders (professional or otherwise) engaged in some form of day-only trading. Much of this may involve hedging because risks are actively managed through the market process. However, a significant proportion is derived from short-term, and speculative, profit-driven strategies.

High frequency traders are a diverse group. Many operate directly as participants, but others seek anonymity within the client base of larger brokers. For some time, proprietary traders within the large international institutional brokers have formed a large component of the high frequency trading population. However, the regulatory framework enacted through Dodd-Frank has pressured some client-focused participants to withdraw from this activity.

High frequency trading is not restricted to equity markets. Increasingly traders within the futures market have taken high frequency strategies. While 'local' day-trading has always been a large part of the Australian futures market, many of these traders have retained a manual or technology-assisted style of trading. Their behaviour may resemble high frequency trading in intensity and size, but they cannot match the reactive speed of algorithms.

In Australia, the number of high frequency traders operating in both the cash equity and futures markets is small. Within the equities market we have noted that the 20 largest high frequency traders account for 95 per cent of all high frequency turnover and a trend towards greater concentration over time has been readily apparent in the data. In general these traders specialize in either cash or futures products. The lack of cross-over is somewhat surprising given the penetration that ASIC has observed by global high frequency firms into alternative markets such as FX.

11.4.1.1 LEVEL OF HIGH FREQUENCY TRADING IN AUSTRALIAN MARKETS

ASIC's initial review conducted in 2012 showed that high frequency trading levels in Australian markets were comparable to those in the United States and

---

[7] IOSCO, Technical Committee, 'Regulatory issues', 2011.

[8] That is, short-term trading unrelated to fundamental valuation signals. This may include trades generated for the purpose of risk management, facilitation, and trades involving speculative and public supply–demand signals.

Table 11.1. High frequency trading in Australian markets, March quarter 2015

Measure	Equities	SPI futures[1]	Bond futures[2]
Trading accounts	<1%	2%	4%
Turnover	27%	21%	14%
Number of trades	31%	25%	24%
Number of orders	47%	30%	40%

[1] ASX SPI (Share Price Index) 200 Futures contract.
[2] ASX 3 and 10 Year Treasury Bonds Futures contract.

the United Kingdom. Analysis indicated that high frequency trading in Australian equity markets remained reasonably steady at 27 per cent of total equity market turnover from 2012 to 2015, with marginal increases from high frequency traders moving their trading into smaller capitalized securities. This is comparable to levels in Canada, the European Union, and Japan at the time.

Participation rates for the most heavily traded stocks were unchanged, but the lower capitalized end of the market saw considerable growth, rising from a low of 10 per cent in 2012 to 18 per cent in 2015. The headline rate of 27 per cent increased only marginally, as this figure is dominated by activity in the top end of the market.

For futures, there was rapid growth in high frequency trading (starting from a low base). It more than doubled during 2015 to 21 per cent of turnover in the equity index futures market and 14 per cent of bond futures (see Table 11.1). While these levels are not concerning, ASIC closely monitors the growth of high frequency trading.

High frequency traders have a substantial presence in Australian markets but the actual number of individuals engaged in this activity has waned, falling by 30 per cent, to fewer than 50, between 2012 and 2015. Regulatory and environmental pressures weighed on the industry, and client-focused institutional brokers reduced their participation in this activity. While trader numbers have fallen, the remaining competitors have expanded their market share.

Certain features of Australian markets differentiate them from some overseas markets and may temper the growth of high frequency trading in Australia. For example:

- Australian exchanges do not offer pricing models that effectively pay participants for their orders (e.g. maker-taker pricing).[9] ASIC has said publicly that it does not support practices of offering more than a 100 per cent rebate of trading fees because it may distort trading behaviour and exacerbate the risk of conflicts of interest where trading decisions are influenced by fee incentives.

[9] Chi-X Australia has a variation of the maker-taker pricing model, which does not involve it paying a rebate but involves price makers paying a lower trade fee than price takers.

- There has not been a proliferation of preferential order types. ASIC has said that it is unlikely to support models that unduly favour some users over others.[10]

11.4.1.2 CONCERNS WITH HIGH FREQUENCY TRADING

The key question ASIC considered in its reviews was how high frequency trading affected market quality and outcomes for market investors.

Anonymous markets, portrayal by popular media, reports of mass manipulation and the (at times) low accuracy timestamping that marks the public tape have led the broader public, and even some market professionals, to reach conclusions that are not necessarily supported by the data.[11]

There are a number of commonly held negative perceptions about high frequency trading, in particular that:

- orders are small and fleeting;
- high frequency traders are predatory;
- high frequency traders earn excessive revenue; and
- high frequency trading increases transaction costs.

Using order and trade data from the ASX, Chi-X, and ASX 24 markets ASIC identified the nature, extent, and effect of high frequency trading in Australian equity markets and in the highest traded futures contracts on ASX 24: the S&P/ASX 200 Index Futures Contract (SPI) and Three Year and Ten Year Commonwealth Treasury Bond Futures Contracts (bond futures).

(a) Concern that Orders are Small and Fleeting

There has been a perception that traders only hold their positions for a matter of seconds and that they place and cancel orders excessively. However, in the March quarter 2015 ASIC found that:

- traders held their positions for 52 minutes (equities), 31 minutes (SPI), and 39 minutes (bond futures) on average; and
- there were relatively few small and fleeting orders (i.e. orders that do not rest in the market for any meaningful period of time):[12] less than 1 per cent of all equity and bond futures orders were small and fleeting. This was more prevalent in the SPI, with 5 per cent of all orders being small and fleeting, of which high frequency traders accounted for 48 per cent.

---

[10] ASIC, Consultation Paper 202, 2013; and ASIC, Report 452, 2015.

[11] ASIC's Market Competition rule book does speak to exchange timestamping. However, the 10ms accuracy to which the rules speak is well outside the reactivity time of the fastest traders. Consequently order-book sequencing on the public record can be incorrect over closely timed events between markets.

[12] Fleeting orders are orders of less than $500 (equities) and one contract (futures) in value and removed from the market in less than half a second.

(b) Concern that High Frequency Traders are Predatory

Where trading is undertaken to exploit or unfairly induce others to trade, it is often referred to as 'predatory'. Based on ASIC's market surveillance, predatory trading is not widespread in Australian markets but ASIC does actively investigate any possible breach of law.

For example, ASIC has identified and addressed several instances of predatory trading.

- There was a persistent 'pinging' strategy in a highly-traded security on the ASX market. Subsequent inquiries by ASIC led to this behaviour ceasing.[13]

- 'Latency arbitrage', which relies on a speed advantage to detect differences between lit (pre-trade transparent) markets and dark venues, can result in investors' dark orders executing at worse prices than on lit markets. ASIC estimated that revenue generated by traders relating to latency was very low, at most A$1,100 per day. Participants running slow (and at times overloaded) crossing systems were identified and directly contacted. Latencies within the public dark venues were complicated by further considerations because only a small number of traders appeared to participate in this activity and the potential 'latency trades' represented a very small part of their overall trading. ASIC's final assessment was that these transactions were an artefact of discrepancies with timestamping of orders and trades rather than a deliberate strategy.

- A 'crowding' strategy was designed to dominate the futures roll book with excessive order placement. Other users of the futures market were relegated to poorer execution outcomes by a small clique of traders gaming the market's micro-structure over the expiry period. ASIC concerns were heightened by the potential for correlated stops to increase volatility. ASIC staff engaged directly with the market operator and traders on issues of fairness and market quality, resulting in a reduction in the operational and connectivity asymmetries employed by these traders.

ASIC has also observed that institutional investors are increasingly managing their own order flow and execution decisions in order to limit interaction with predatory traders and improve their trading outcomes.

(c) Concern that High Frequency Traders Earn Excessive Revenue

ASIC estimated the gross trading revenue of high frequency traders in Australian equity markets. Over the 12 months to 31 March 2015, analysis indicated that trading revenue was approximately A$110–180 million in aggregate.

---

[13] Pinging is the practice of using the placement of very small orders in dark venues to test if there are other orders.

Table 11.2. Estimated high frequency trading costs

Trading cost	Metric	Dollar amount
Exchange fees	0.12 basis points	A$7,968,621
Clearing fees	0.25 basis points	A$16,601,294
Cost recovery	# trading messages	A$5,770,200
Nominal brokerage	0.5 basis points	A$33,202,589
Total trading fees		A$63,542,704

These figures should be taken in context. Over 2015, turnover on Australian markets was approximately A$2.5 trillion dollars. A 27 per cent market share translates to A$664 billion of high frequency turnover. A simple estimate of basic trading costs suggests that a large percentage of this will be absorbed through fees (see Table 11.2). For example, this activity generates fees of A$8 million in exchange transactions and A$17 million in clearing costs and derives an allocation of A$6 million for the Australian government's market surveillance cost recovery programme. Nominal brokerage costs at around half a basis point would amount to A$33 million. These basic costs tally at A$64 million dollars. Of course, additional investments in staff and systems would be expected in order to operate such businesses.

From the perspective of investors, the intermediation of high frequency traders (on an all things equal basis) translates to an additional cost of 0.7 to 1.1 basis points to other users of the market. This is material but substantially less than other components of trading costs and must be weighed against the liquidity added by high frequency in terms of the narrowing of the bid-offer spread.

(d) Concern that High Frequency Trading Increases Transaction Costs
ASIC analysed all market transactions over a period of four years to understand how high frequency trading affected institutional transaction costs, in order to test the hypothesis that high frequency trading acted to increase transaction costs.

Institutional transaction costs have fallen markedly in Australian equity markets over the past three decades. Estimates of 54 basis points in the late 1990s contrast dramatically with ASIC's 2015 estimate of 7 basis points—indicating that developments in technology, competition, and market structure have reduced transaction costs.[14]

ASIC's analysis did indicate some meaningful association between transaction costs and high frequency trading. However, it did not identify high frequency trading as a dominant factor in those costs. Competition between large,

[14] Elkins/McSherry Co. Inc., 'Trade Execution Report', 1998; and ASIC, Report 452, 2015.

unidirectional order flows—identified as competing institutional entities—arose as the single largest factor. Costs are reduced by higher volume and lower volatility markets.

High frequency traders did not appear to be the root cause of poor execution outcomes. In particular, ASIC found no evidence of systematic scalping. While there is some suggestion of higher execution costs associated with high frequency turnover within mid-tier securities, their direct contribution to costs within the upper end of the market is negligible. A stronger association with lower costs is evident towards the lower end of the market.

11.4.1.3 RESPONSES AND OUTCOMES

During the course of its 2012 review, ASIC worked with participants and market operators to change behaviour and raise awareness (e.g. alerting participants to clients with high volumes of orders and cancellations). This was substantially successful in reducing noise and ASIC continues to monitor this carefully.

ASIC also enhanced the manipulative trading market integrity rules to broaden the range of circumstances that participants must consider (e.g. including the frequency of order placement, order volume, and the extent of cancellations). Those rules were also applied to the futures market at that time.

Following the 2012 review, ASIC observed that negative sentiment towards high frequency trading had tapered off. Institutional investors also suggested that the industry was generally less concerned in 2015 about high frequency trading in Australian markets compared to at the time of the 2012 review.

Market users are now better informed and, increasingly, better equipped to operate within an electronic and high-speed environment. However, there are some concerns about practices overseas being imported into Australian markets, particularly in relation to the profiling and segmentation of liquidity. Furthermore, some investors remain disconcerted by an activity they do not fully understand.

11.4.2 Dark Liquidity

The venues on which trading occurs have changed significantly in recent years. Exchange markets have expanded their dark trading facilities while market participant-operated crossing systems have evolved. There are many reasons why a trader may elect to trade through a dark trading facility; concern about high frequency trader practices is just one reason.

Dark liquidity refers to buy and sell orders that are not visible to the rest of the market, although the trades that result from those orders are typically published immediately after execution. Dark trades can occur on dark venues operated by exchanges (e.g. in Australia, ASX's Centre Point and Chi-X's hidden orders, which are offered by these operators in addition to their 'lit' order books). They can also occur away from exchange markets, where they are accessible only to a subset of the market (e.g. often limited to a market participant and its clients). A crossing system is a dark venue which is operated away from an exchange, typically by a market participant.

11.4.2.1 LEVEL OF DARK LIQUIDITY IN THE AUSTRALIAN MARKET

Dark liquidity has remained reasonably constant in recent years at around 25–30 per cent of total equity market turnover. However, its composition continues to change.

Trading on exchange dark venues (i.e. ASX Centre Point and Chi-X hidden orders) accounted in 2015 for around twice the total dark trading compared to 2012, at 27.6 per cent. ASX Centre Point has been particularly successful in capturing order flow. ASIC's stakeholder feedback indicates that some institutional investors have opted out of using crossing systems after experiencing poor price outcomes and information leakage. Others have taken control of their own order routing and execution.

High frequency traders are active on exchange dark venues, at 14 per cent and 28 per cent of turnover on ASX Centre Point and Chi-X hidden orders respectively. High frequency traders appear to be achieving a better price than other users of these venues around 85 per cent of the time (on trades where one party achieves a better price outcome).

In part, as a result of Australian rule changes as set out below, there has been a shift back to using dark liquidity for large block trades (i.e. the original purpose of dark liquidity). As of March 2015, this accounted for 56.9 per cent of total dark turnover (see Figure 11.4).[15] At the same time, there were fewer small dark trades and in 2015 trades were fairer than in 2012, with any improvement to prices (compared to lit exchange markets) needing to be more equitably shared between counterparties, which was also required by the trade with price improvement ASIC market integrity rule.[16]

There are currently 16 crossing systems operated by 16 market participants in Australia, which accounted for 9 per cent of total equity dark turnover in the March quarter of 2015 (see Figure 11.4), almost half of the level in 2012. Across the Australian futures market, one participant operates a crossing system for wholesale energy contracts. Rules within the futures market only allow for off-market transaction in block size. Despite this restriction, participants are still exploring opportunities for the use of crossing systems in other futures products.

---

[15] 'Block size' refers to trades executed under the pre-trade transparency exceptions in Rules 4.2.1 and 4.2.2 of the ASIC 'Market integrity rules', 2011—typically of $1 million ($200,000 for some issuers' shares since May 2013) or more.

[16] See ASIC, 'Market integrity rules', 2011. Rule 4.1.1 permits crossings at price levels within the prevailing best bid and offer.

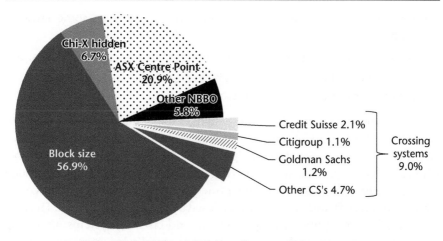

Figure 11.4. Share of dark liquidity, March quarter 2015

High frequency traders (according to ASIC's measure) are active in 11 crossing systems and account for around 2 per cent of total crossing system turnover.[17] On average across all crossing systems, all users are achieving comparable price outcomes (i.e. high frequency traders and the crossing system operator were not achieving better outcomes).

11.4.2.2 CONCERNS WITH DARK LIQUIDITY
ASIC's 2012 review of dark liquidity found that

- dark liquidity was having an impact on market quality for a number of securities, with fundamental investors contributing less to prices;
- lower tick sizes in crossing systems were driving trading activity into the dark;
- there was limited transparency and disclosure in crossing systems;
- there was limited monitoring for misconduct in crossing systems;
- there was a range of potentially concerning conduct, including misleading statements about crossing systems, failure to make disclosures to clients, representations about the regulation of crossing systems, conflicts of interest not adequately being managed, and omissions/errors in crossing system regulatory reports to ASIC;

---

[17] For a small number of these, the crossing system operator has indicated to clients and ASIC that high frequency traders were absent from their venue. It is possible that their definition of high frequency trading differs from ours.

- there was preferential treatment for certain clients in some crossing systems;

- there were limitations for clients to opt out of using crossing systems; and

- there were conflicts of interest when dealing as principal and early signs of payment for order flow models emerging.

To address these concerns, ASIC made changes to the market integrity rules to broaden the framework for crossing systems. These included rules to enhance disclosure to clients about their operations. In addition, the rules enable wholesale clients to request that participants disclose when they have traded with their clients as principal. This principle helps to manage participants' conflicts of interest and has been widely used by institutional clients. The new rules also improve public transparency around crossing systems, including transaction level data with a three-day delay and disclosure about crossing system operations.

There are also new rules to ensure fair treatment, such as standardized tick sizes across exchange markets and crossing systems, a requirement on crossing system operators for a common set of procedures which do not unfairly discriminate between users, and allowing clients to opt out of using a crossing system. The new rules also require crossing system operators to monitor for, and report instances of, suspicious activity.

Rules were also introduced to enhance conflict of interest obligations for participants dealing off-exchange (e.g. to protect confidential client information and prevent participants from receiving negative commissions—also known as payment for order flow).[18]

As a result of the changes to the rules, and buy-side clients demanding improved standards from their brokers or service providers, there has been considerable improvement in disclosure and transparency. This has contributed to investors regaining confidence and trust in crossing system operators. Investors are now able to make more informed choices about where and how their orders are managed, and listed entities are more informed about where their securities are being traded.

However, ASIC continues to have concerns with some practices, as outlined below.

(a) Liquidity Segmentation and Preferencing in Equity Markets
Liquidity segmentation occurs where an exchange market or crossing system operator enables differentiated order execution priority (or other treatment) based on the user or type of user. Market operators may seek to segment liquidity in this way in response to

---

[18] See ASIC, Report 331, 2013; and ASIC, Media Release 13–213, 2013.

- investor concerns about high frequency trading—by enabling investors to avoid interacting with high frequency traders;
- investor distrust of market participants—by enabling investors to avoid interacting with the market participant's own principal orders; and
- competition between exchange market operators and market participant-operated crossing systems.

There have been two phases of liquidity segmentation in Australia. The first was 'broker preferencing' on equity exchange markets, which currently exists to a limited extent on exchange dark order books. This enables market participants to trade with their own or their clients' orders ahead of others' orders at the same price, regardless of their place in the queue.

The second phase involves 'liquidity profiling' and 'liquidity categories'. This is where the operator of an exchange market or crossing system profiles clients or market users and groups them into categories (e.g. high frequency traders, retail investors, and institutional investors) or provides the capacity for market participants to profile their clients. Once clients are grouped into categories, the operator can apply different treatment to the categories. For example, the priority in which orders are matched may favour one or more categories over another, or may enable market users to nominate the categories or individuals they want to interact with or avoid.

These developments could undermine fair, open, and non-discriminatory secondary trading and may be inconsistent with operators' obligations under the Corporations Act 2001 and ASIC market integrity rules. As already noted, ASIC has stated publicly that it is not likely to support any form of liquidity segmentation on an exchange market or crossing system that 'unduly favours some users over others, unfairly limits access to the facilities or otherwise results in the unfair treatment of orders or users'.[19]

(b) Principal Trading and Facilitation
ASIC identified problems in the way some market participants managed conflicts of interest when trading on their own behalf against their clients (either principal trading desks or to facilitate client orders). ASIC made it clear to market participants that

- participants should avoid situations where staff are responsible for the participant's own trading while having access to unexecuted client order information; and

---

[19] ASIC, Report 452, 2015.

- participants should have additional controls (e.g. physical separation of some functions) to manage the conflicts and conduct risk that might arise.[20]

11.5 Looking Forward

ASIC's priority is to ensure all investors have trust and confidence in Australian financial markets. Understanding the market, and using innovative tools to identify and assess conduct, is a key part of ASIC's strategy to ensure that high frequency trading and dark liquidity do not undermine trust and confidence in the market. This approach has enabled the dispelling of some myths about the problems associated with high frequency trading and dark liquidity, as well as identifying and addressing some activities that were of concern.

As of November 2017, ASIC is reviewing the purpose of markets and their fundamental role in an environment of rapid change. While high frequency trading and dark liquidity bring clear benefits to markets, ASIC work seeks to ensure these benefits are not outweighed by the costs. ASIC continues to monitor automated, high frequency, and dark pool trading in Australia's equity and futures markets by focusing on the following existing and emerging risks.

- *Firm culture and conduct risk*: conduct risk can be caused by deliberate actions, or by inadequacies in a participant's practices, frameworks, or staff. ASIC uses cultural indicators in its risk-based surveillances to better understand how culture drives conduct.

- *Handling confidential information and conflicts of interest*: ASIC will publish guidance on sell-side research conflicts, setting out expectations of how financial intermediaries should handle material, non-public information and manage conflicts of interest in the provision of research.

- *Technology risk and cyber resilience*: ASIC will review the technological and operational risk management of market participants, focusing on critical infrastructure providers.

- *Market innovation*: ASIC is focused on building the resilience of markets' systems and controls to ensure that technological developments take place in an environment that supports investor trust and confidence. ASIC is using big data tools to aggregate, unify, process, and analyse disparate and ever growing datasets. ASIC is also trialling artificial intelligence to analyse and identify potential misconduct within the regulated community.

---

[20] Ibid.

References

ASIC (Australian Securities & Investments Commission). Consultation Paper 202, 'Dark liquidity and high-frequency trading: Proposals'. Available at: http://asic.gov.au/regulatory-resources/find-a-document/consultation-papers/cp-202-dark-liquidity-and-high-frequency-trading-proposals/, 2013.

ASIC. 'Market integrity rules (competition in exchange markets)'. Available at: http://asic.gov.au/regulatory-resources/markets/market-integrity-rules/, 2011.

ASIC. Media Release 13-213, 'ASIC makes rules on dark liquidity, high-frequency trading'. Available at: http://asic.gov.au/about-asic/media-centre/find-a-media-release/2013-releases/13-213mr-asic-makes-rules-on-dark-liquidity-high-frequency-trading/, 2013.

ASIC. Report 331, 'Dark liquidity and high-frequency trading'. Available at: http://asic.gov.au/about-asic/media-centre/find-a-media-release/2014-releases/14-105mr-asic-reports-on-dark-liquidity-rules/, 2013.

ASIC. Report 452, 'Review of high-frequency trading and dark liquidity'. Available at: http://asic.gov.au/regulatory-resources/find-a-document/reports/rep-452-review-of-high-frequency-trading-and-dark-liquidity/, 2015.

Australian Government, The Treasury. 'Turnbull Government bolsters ASIC to protect Australian consumers'. Media release. Available at: http://sjm.ministers.treasury.gov.au/media-release/042-2016/, 20 April 2016.

Elkins/McSherry Co. Inc. 'Trade Execution Report', 1998.

IOSCO, Technical Committee. 'Regulatory issues raised by the impact of technological changes on market integrity and efficiency'. Available at: http://www.iosco.org/library/pubdocs/pdf/IOSCOPD354.pdf, 2011.

12

High Frequency Trading and Circuit Breakers in the EU

Recent Findings and Regulatory Activities

Steffen Kern and Giuseppe Loiacono

12.1 Introduction

Over the last decade, securities trading landscapes have undergone significant change. Technological innovation and growing competition have increased the opportunities to employ innovative infrastructures and trading practices.[1]

The emergence of high frequency trading (HFT) is one of the most important technological developments in the trading environment in recent years. At the same time, the EU has made landmark legislative advances with the aim of increasing investor protection, market order, and financial stability, and of containing risks in those areas. Importantly, these include the reforms of the securities and derivatives trading frameworks through the Markets in Financial Instruments Directive II (MiFID II) and Markets in Financial Instruments Regulation (MiFIR) and of market abuse rules (Market Abuse Regulation), and the establishment of rules for short selling activities (Short Selling Regulation).

This chapter reviews the fundamental workings of the EU regulatory framework and its implications for HFT, recent findings on trading practices in the EU, and the European Securities and Markets Authority's (ESMA) regulatory response.

[1] This chapter was prepared as a discussion paper for the conference 'HFT, Dark Pools & Algo Trading: Assessing Regulatory Approaches and Unintended Consequences', 20–2 April 2017, St John's College, Oxford. All views expressed are those of the authors and may not represent those of ESMA. The authors thank Georgios Konstantopoulos and Federico Ramella for valuable research assistance.

12.2 The EU Securities Trading Landscape

The EU single financial market is home to one of the largest securities markets in the world. It comprises[2] 252 trading venues,[3] including 95 regulated markets across all member states of the EU, and 157 multilateral trading facilities (MTFs).[4] This trading infrastructure is complemented by 12 systematic internalizers,[5] 19 central counterparties (CCPs),[6] and 7 derivatives trade repositories.[7]

The market capitalization of EU listed stocks amounts to €12 trillion,[8] with about 9700 companies listed.[9] The UK, France, and Germany make up almost two-thirds of the market, accounting for 27 per cent, 19 per cent, and 15 per cent of total EU market capitalization respectively.[10] The average monthly equity trading volume amounted to €1.4 trillion in 2017. While significantly smaller than the US equity market, with a market capitalization of €27 trillion and a monthly turnover of €4.5trillion, the EU single market stands second in size by international comparison, ahead of China (€8 trillion of market capitalization) and Japan (€5 trillion).[11]

The EU market is also among the most modern and innovative securities trading spaces, where 83 per cent of trading is highly transparent and based on electronic order books,[12] only 15 per cent off-electronic order books, and 2 per cent through dark pool trading, a share expected to be further reduced through the imposition of the MiFID II Double Volume Cap from

---

[2] All data as of November 2017. Data subject to change over time as ESMA registers are updated on a continuous basis.

[3] Information available on the ESMA Registers portal (www.esma.europa.eu).

[4] According to Article 4(1)(22) of MiFID II, an MTF is a multilateral system, operated by an investment firm or a market operator, which brings together multiple third-party buying and selling interests in financial instruments.

[5] According to Article 4(1)(20) of MiFID II, a systematic internalizer is an investment firm which, on an organized, frequent, systematic, and substantial basis, deals on own account when executing client orders outside a regulated market, an MTF, or an OTF without operating a multilateral system.

[6] According to Article 2(1) of the European Market Infrastructure Regulation (2012), a CCP is a legal person that interposes itself between the counterparties to the contracts traded on one or more financial markets, becoming the buyer to every seller and the seller to every buyer.

[7] According to Article 2(2) of the European Market Infrastructure Regulation (2012), a trade repository is a legal person that centrally collects and maintains the records of derivatives.

[8] ESMA calculation based on data from the World Federation of Exchanges, FESE, and ECB, as of end October 2017. Data for CZ, BG, and SK as of end December 2016.

[9] ESMA calculation based on data from the World Federation of Exchanges, FESE, and ECB. Data for CZ, BG, and SK as of end December 2016.

[10] ESMA calculation based on ECB data as of end December 2016.

[11] ESMA calculation based on data from World Bank database, ECB, and World Federation of Exchanges.

[12] This includes reporting transactions (trades reported through a Trade Reporting Facility when only one counterparty provides information on the trade and offers dissemination services at the request of the reporting trader). FESE Statistics Methodology, June 2017.

January 2018 onwards.[13] Innovations in trading and information technology, especially starting with electronic trading and more recently HFT, have transformed the European trading landscape. As well as providing faster transactions and lower marginal costs, these developments have also altered the nature of liquidity provision on financial markets. In practice, traditional intermediaries have been complemented or even replaced by HFTs as a new set of liquidity providers. The securities trading landscape in the presence of HFT practices is characterized by more intense competition for order flows, faster connections between buy- and sell-side firms and the exchanges, cooperation between high frequency traders and exchanges, and the emergence of a rich system of technology providers.

12.3 Strong HFT Activity in EU Markets

Among the most dominant developments in market practices has been the emergence of HFTs. HFT and its implications for market order and stability have been discussed widely, both conceptually and empirically, in a number of jurisdictions.

There is a large body of literature analysing the activity, behaviour, and impact of HFT firms.[14] So far, the literature has employed a number of approaches to identify HFT activity and its effects on market quality. The methodologies employed measure HFT activities indirectly, which leads to differing accounts of HFT presence in the market.

Based on various market quality metrics, there is mixed evidence on the question of whether HFT activity has been beneficial to financial markets. Most notably, HFT is associated with tighter bid-ask spreads and more efficient price formation.[15] However, this may not hold under all market conditions: Breckenfelder finds that in situations where HFTs compete for trades, liquidity decreases and short-term volatility rises.[16] Most publications on this subject cover a single trading venue either in the US, Canada, or in a single country within the EU. Results based on data from one particular trading venue may not necessarily hold on other venues or when a cross-venue analysis is carried out.

---

[13] ESMA calculation based on FESE, European Equity Market Report, data from 1 January 2017 to 31 October 2017. The off-electronic-order-book trading accounted for 32 per cent of total trading in US, 0.5 per cent in China, and 12.5per cent in Japan (ESMA calculation based on data from ECB and World Federation of Exchanges).

[14] For an extensive review of the literature on HFT, see SEC, *Equity Market Structure Literature Review*, 2014.

[15] See Hendershott et al., 'Does algorithmic trading improve?' 2011; Malinova et al., 'Do retail traders suffer?' 2013; and Brogaard et al., 'High-frequency trading', 2014.

[16] Breckenfelder, 'Competition', 2013.

Table 12.1. HFT activity: overall results for the HFT flag and lifetime of orders approaches

	HFT flag	Lifetime of orders	
	Total	Total	Thereof investment banks
Value traded	24	43	22
Number of trades	30	49	23
Number of orders	58	76	19

Note: Figures are weighted by value of trades (value traded), number of trades, and number of orders, in %.
Source: ESMA.

ESMA has contributed to filling this gap in two research papers,[17] exploring HFT activity in EU equity markets[18] and order duplication and liquidity measurement in EU equity markets.[19]

The findings on EU market practices leave no doubt that HFT, in combination with algorithmic trading, has become a significant and in parts dominant trading practice in EU equity markets. HFT activity in the EU represents between 24 per cent and 43 per cent of value traded, between 30 per cent and 49 per cent of the number of trades, and between 58 per cent and 76 per cent of orders in the sample (Table 12.1).

Across all venues, the share of HFTs by value traded was smaller than the share by number of trades, which in turn was lower than the HFT share by number of orders. This indicates, first, that the size of HFT trades is on average smaller than the size of non-HFT trades. Moreover, it shows that the order-to-trade ratio in HFT is on average higher than the order-to-trade ratio in conventional trading.

The findings are based on a dual approach adopted by ESMA to deal with the absence of a universally accepted definition and estimation method.[20] The study provides a lower bound (direct approach based on the primary business of firms) and an upper bound (indirect approach based on the lifetime of orders) for HFT activity.[21]

---

[17] Both ESMA studies discussed here are based on a unique dataset collected by ESMA, covering a sample of 100 stocks on 12 trading venues in nine EU countries for May 2013. Our data allow us to identify market participant activities across different venues. We complement the literature as most of the HFT studies published so far focus either on the US or on a single country within Europe, and few of them analyse the behaviour of market participants across trading venues.

[18] ESMA, 'High-frequency trading', 2014.   [19] ESMA, 'Order duplication', 2016.

[20] Various approaches for estimating HFT activity exist, the application of which can lead to diverging findings. Two main approaches have been used in the literature: (1) a direct approach based on the identification of HFT firms according to their primary business or the types of algorithms they use, and (2) an indirect approach based on statistics such as lifetime of orders or the order-to-trade ratio.

[21] The difference in the results is mainly explained by the HFT activities of investment banks, which are captured under a lifetime of orders approach, but not under an HFT direct approach. Another reason is the overestimation bias of the indirect approach, which may unduly capture slow trading activity in groups classified as HFT firms.

HFT activity varies significantly between trading venues. In terms of value traded, HFT activity ranges from 8 per cent to 40 per cent (average 24 per cent) for the direct HFT identification approach and from 19 per cent to 63 per cent (average 43 per cent) for the lifetime of orders approach. For number of trades, HFT activity ranges between 9 per cent and 44 per cent (average 30 per cent) for the direct HFT identification approach and between 18 per cent and 65 per cent (average 49 per cent) for the lifetime of orders approach. For number of orders the range for HFT activity is between 31 per cent and 76 per cent (average 58 per cent) for the direct HFT identification approach and between 34 per cent and 87 per cent (average 76 per cent) for the lifetime of orders approach.

Our findings for the EU further suggest that

- daily HFT activity is relatively stable, with the median share in daily trading ranging between 21 per cent and 30 per cent, the lowest values being observed at the beginning and at the end of the month in line with conventional trading;
- the weight of HFT differs widely between individual stocks, with HFT shares rising with the liquidity of the market segment;
- the HFT share generally declines sharply at the end of the trading day, indicating that HFT firms tend to avoid auctions; and
- HFT firms are members of more trading platforms than other types of market participants, which, amongst other reasons, may indicate that they are more likely to perform cross-venue arbitrage.

In the context of increased competition among trading venues and growing trading fragmentation, the inequality in terms of speed and technology between conventional and high frequency traders has become quite significant. Using fast trading technology helps financial institutions to cope with market fragmentation, as HFT users can and do trade highly efficiently on a multitude of trading venues concurrently. At the same time, recent events of short-term liquidity shortages and sudden spikes of volatility across market segments have triggered questions relating to the impact of HFT on volatility, liquidity, and, more generally, market quality.

In our study on order duplication and liquidity management, we address these critical questions. With competition among trading venues, traders do not always know on which venue they will eventually execute their transaction. They may advertise their intention to trade by posting similar orders on more than one trading venue at the same time (duplicated orders). Typically, traders may immediately cancel unmatched duplicated orders on other venues after one of their duplicated orders has been filled.

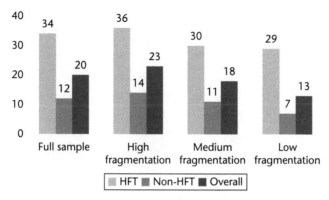

Figure 12.1. Duplicated orders by degree of market fragmentation (source: ESMA)

Note: proportion of duplicated orders by trading fragmentation for the sample stocks, displayed for HFTs, for non-HFTs, and total. In %.

One would expect that market fragmentation would attract HFTs, as they are able to implement cross-venue arbitrage strategies. This is confirmed by the empirics.

- As expected, market fragmentation is positively correlated with order duplication.[22] In fragmented markets, duplicated orders range from 14 per cent for non-HFTs to 36 per cent for HFTs. When fragmentation is low, the proportion of duplicated orders is 7 per cent and 29 per cent, respectively (Figure 12.1).

- In the overall sample, duplicated orders account for around 20 per cent of all orders. The share of duplicated orders varies significantly between HFT firms and non-HFT firms (Figure 12.2); for HFTs, duplicated orders account for around 34 per cent of all their orders compared to 12 per cent for non-HFTs.

- Taking into account the different categories of market capitalization (large caps, mid caps, and small caps), duplicated orders seem to be more relevant for large caps (22 per cent compared to 12 per cent for small caps), consistent with the evidence showing that HFTs are more active in this market segment.[23]

- The incidence of duplicated orders is lower for the shares with higher price volatility (16 per cent for high-volatility stocks compared to 22 per cent for low-volatility stocks).

---

[22] These results are in line with findings by Van Kervel and Menkveld, 'High-frequency trading', 2016.

[23] See Brogaard et al., 'High-frequency trading', 2014.

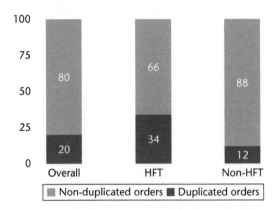

Figure 12.2. Duplicated orders, HFT vs non-HFT across sample (source: ESMA)
Note: duplicated orders, in %, for HFTs, for non-HFTs, and overall.

- In around a quarter of the cases, the trader immediately cancels unmatched duplicated orders. This proportion is higher for HFTs (28 per cent), for large cap stocks (27 per cent), and where trading is more fragmented (31 per cent).

We also look at two different measures of liquidity before and after the conclusion of trades: gross liquidity, the aggregated volume of displayed orders across multiple markets, and net liquidity, which deducts duplicated orders from the gross liquidity measure. We compare these two measures to establish whether order duplication should be taken into account when measuring liquidity in fragmented markets. A stronger fall of the gross liquidity measure after trades compared to the net liquidity measure is an additional indication that a proportion of duplicated orders is indeed immediately cancelled after trades and thus not available to the market.

We test this by looking at gross and net liquidity in specific non-overlapping windows, 100 milliseconds (ms) and 500ms after each trade. Our results show that across different samples the reduction in gross liquidity is always higher than the reduction in net liquidity for both 100ms and 500ms windows (Figures 12.3 and 12.4).[24] In particular, we observe that the biggest decrease of available liquidity occurs in the first 10ms after the trade. This reaction is explained by the trade effect itself and by the existence of duplicated orders. In about 24 per cent of trades, the trader immediately cancels his

---

[24] Gross and net liquidity are computed in discrete data points corresponding to the end of 10ms periods. We have order book snapshots at 10ms intervals, meaning that the trades take place at some point in the interval −10ms to 0ms.

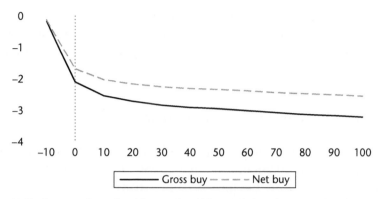

Figure 12.3. Gross and net liquidity in the 100ms window (source: ESMA)

Note: the y-axis depicts the variation over time of available liquidity levels, gross measures, and net measures, divided by the size of each trade. Given data constraints, available liquidity is computed only in equally-spaced and discrete points in time (each 10 ms). The x-axis represents time in ms; the trade takes place in the interval between −10ms and 0ms.

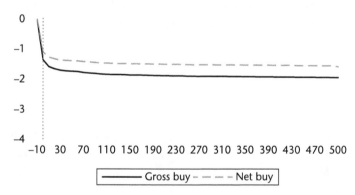

Figure 12.4. Gross and net liquidity in the 500ms window (source: ESMA)

Note: the y-axis depicts the variation over time of available liquidity levels, gross measures, and net measures, divided by the size of each trade. Given data constraints, available liquidity is computed only in equally-spaced and discrete points in time (each 10 ms). The x-axis represents time in ms; the trade takes place in the interval between −10ms and 0ms.

unmatched duplicated orders or updates them at a price far from the trade price, which explains the stronger fall in the gross liquidity measure.

Our findings on order duplication and cancellation suggest that these trading patterns have become part of the strategy to ensure execution in fragmented markets, e.g. for market makers or where institutional investors are searching for liquidity. Their impact on liquidity is negative. To avoid overestimating the available liquidity, duplicated orders should be taken into account when measuring liquidity in fragmented markets, for example by using a net liquidity measure.

In other words, our findings document the profound change in the EU trading landscape in recent years. HFTs have become potent players in markets across the EU, but their contribution to liquidity is less significant than may be expected.

12.4 More Volatile and Vulnerable Markets

Beyond their structural impact on market liquidity, HFT and algorithmic trading have attracted additional attention for their potential role in flash crashes, whose incidence has increased in recent years.[25]

Flash crashes deserve regulatory and supervisory attention as they are incidences of sudden, unexpected, and significant price drops in one or more instruments, followed by a swift (partial or full) reversion of the price (see Figure 12.5). Price movements in these cases are not primarily related to changes in economic fundamentals. This being the case, flash crashes are sources of market uncertainty, heightened volatility, and potential systemic knock-on effects. Recent technological advances considerably sped up

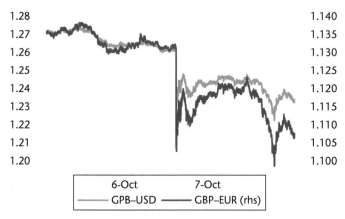

Figure 12.5. GBP flash crash: loss of 6 per cent in less than 10 minutes (sources: Thomson Reuters Eikon, ESMA)

Note: GBP exchange rates on 6 and 7 October 2016, 30-minute data.

---

[25] Since 2010, various flash crash events have been registered globally, including the May 2010 Dow Jones drop (Dow Jones fell nearly 1000 points within minutes), the 18 May 2010 Facebook IPO incident (30,000 orders stuck in the system for more than two hours), the 1 August 2012 Knight Capital incident (losses of $420 million in 30 minutes), the 22 August 2013 NASDAQ flash freeze (NASDAQ-listed securities went offline for 3 hours 11 minutes), the 15 October 2014 Treasuries flash rally (yield on ten-year US Treasury notes fell about 30 basis points), the 24 August 2015 'Black Monday' in Asia (equity selloff in Asia, large price movements in US and European stock futures), and the GBP exchange rate flash crash on 7 October 2016 (GBP depreciated by more than 6 per cent versus the USD in early Asian trading within a few minutes).

economic decision-making and shortened the interval in which market runs could unfold, making flash crashes a more frequently recurring and in some instances drastic phenomenon in mature equity markets.

Flash crashes may be initiated by malfunctioning algorithms or be reinforced by algorithmic trading and HFT, in which case speed and interconnectivity fuel market instability. Particularly during times of market stress, market-making algorithms may provide less liquidity than human traders tasked with maintaining a certain level of market liquidity, with the result that there is less liquidity when risk aversion spikes occur. This may give rise to order imbalances and sudden price drops.

Although algorithmic trading has not yet created significant disruptions in EU markets, a number of events at international level have emphasized the necessity of better understanding the forces at work.[26] The extent to which high frequency and algorithmic trading play a role in such market events—as a cause of the disruption or as an amplifying mechanism—varies across individual incidences.

A study authorized by the US Commodity Futures Trading Commission (CFTC) regarding the flash crash of 6 May 2010 concluded that even though 'high frequency traders did not cause the flash crash, they contributed to it by demanding immediacy ahead of other market participants'.[27] Along the same line, the joint report issued by the US Securities and Exchange Commission (SEC) and the CFTC regarding the flash crash of 6 May 2010 provided a detailed description of what led to the flash crash. One conclusion made was that

> [u]nder stressed market conditions, the automated execution of a large sell order can trigger extreme price movements, especially if the automated execution algorithm does not take prices into account. Moreover, the interaction between automated execution programs and algorithmic trading strategies can quickly erode liquidity and result in disorderly markets.[28]

Unsurprisingly, high frequency and algorithmic trading have become regarded by market participants and analysts alike as a significant potential source of fragility in electronic markets. As O'Hara observes, without the appropriate policy measures current markets are highly exposed to potential flash crash episodes.[29]

Trading venues and regulators have set in place—in many cases already before the advent of today's complex trading strategies—a variety of safeguard mechanisms with the aim of preventing or limiting the occurrence of technically induced market disturbances. In particular, mechanisms to interrupt trading in situations of excessive price movements and volatility have become the main tool to tackle critical market situations.

---

[26] For more details, see ESMA, 'Report on trends', 2017.
[27] Kirilenko et al., 'The flash crash', 2017.   [28] CFTC and SEC, 'Findings', 2010.
[29] O'Hara, 'High-frequency trading', 2014.

12.5 Circuit Breakers Help Limit Excessive Price Movements

Circuit breakers are mechanisms set in place by trading venues to temporarily halt or constrain trading if there is a significant price movement in a financial instrument.

Theory suggests that circuit breakers can be particularly effective if they address transitory volatility, defined as the tendency for prices to fluctuate around their fundamental values. In contrast, the effectiveness of circuit breakers may be more limited if intended to address fundamental volatility. In this case, a trading halt prevents prices from reflecting the new information on fundamental values.

In particular, the functioning of trading halts (Figure 12.6) in idiosyncratic market situations needs to be better understood. Circuit breakers may provide investors with important resting time to re-assess their positions in situations of sudden and large price changes. Optimally, such calming-down periods

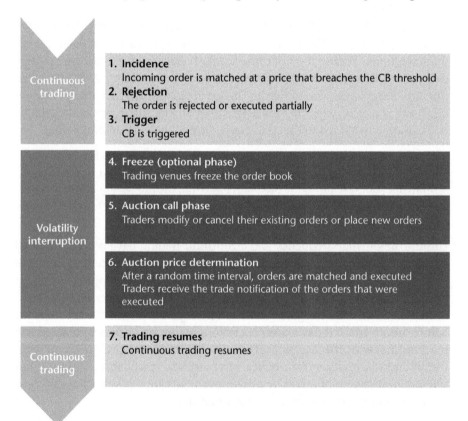

Figure 12.6. Sequencing of circuit breaker mechanism (source: ESMA)

Note: Schematic representation. Details may differ in practice.

enhance the price discovery and help prevent further deteriorations in flash crash situations. At the same time, it is a concern that circuit breakers could be counter-productive if they were to lead to or enhance liquidity drains and diminish market depth, which in turn could create additional uncertainty and, in a worst case, incentivize additional selling. In addition, the greater role that regulators and supervisors are playing in the calibration of trading halts implies that they take a specific interest in a full understanding of their functioning. Again, empirical evidence at EU level has been sparse. In response, ESMA is investigating the EU landscape of trading halts and their effectiveness.[30]

Statistics show that circuit breaker occurrences vary widely depending on market conditions. On average, we find that in our sample circuit breakers have been triggered 44 times per day. However, we observe a multiple of this during times of market stress. In our sample period, this was analysed around four events: the UK referendum on leaving the EU, the publication of the EBA banking stress test results, the US presidential election, and the Italian constitutional referendum (Figure 12.7). In all of these cases, large-cap stocks were

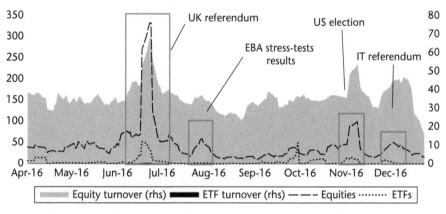

Figure 12.7. Number of circuit breaker trigger events: spikes following market events (sources: Morningstar Real Time, ESMA)

Note: number of circuit breaker trigger events by type of financial instrument in the period from 1 April to 31 December 2016, weekly average. Equity turnover of the EU trading venues under analysis on secondary axis, EUR bn.

---

[30] Guillaumie et al., 'Market impacts', 2018 (forthcoming). Using a unique database of circuit breakers, which were triggered between 1 April 2016 and 31 December 2016 on a sample of 10,000 financial instruments traded on EU trading venues, we analyse the impact of circuit breakers on markets. We find that the price discovery process is not negatively affected by the circuit breaker. We also conclude that price volatility, measured by the normalized standard deviation of mid-prices, declines in both halted and cross-listed stocks at different time intervals (ten, five, and two minutes after the circuit breaker). However, calmer trading conditions come at the cost of higher spreads; the relative bid-ask spreads increase after the halt, and the increase is even more pronounced for stocks cross-listed compared to the halted instruments.

relatively more affected by circuit breakers compared to mid- and small-cap stocks. Heterogeneity of circuit breaker calibration across trading venues is reflected in wide variations of the average duration of trading halts across venues, from less than a minute to 50 minutes. Throughout a trading day, circuit breaker incidents are mostly concentrated in the first 15 minutes of trading and around the opening of US markets, when new information flows need to be incorporated quickly in the prices.

In particular, we address three questions empirically. First, we investigate whether circuit breakers help to improve market conditions such as volatility and liquidity. Results show that during the period of analysis circuit breakers were on average efficient in setting calmer trading conditions in the ten-minute window following the halt, although at the cost of higher spreads which significantly increase after the halt (Figures 12.8 and 12.9). There is also a statistically significant positive difference between post- and pre-circuit-breaker bid-ask spread in the two-minute and in the five-minute windows, although at lower levels, revealing an adoption of the overall market premium after the circuit breaker.[31] It is particularly interesting to observe that the spread increase is larger in the first minutes after the circuit breaker, and decreases as the time interval increases. This could be explained by a decline in trading activity and large price uncertainty in the immediate post-circuit-breaker trading. Circuit breaker impacts also vary with the degree of trading fragmentation. Highly fragmented stocks registered a higher reduction of standard deviation

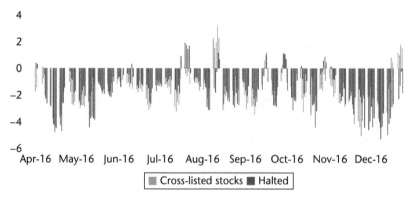

Figure 12.8. Circuit breaker impact: reduced volatility after the circuit breaker incidents (sources: Morningstar Real Time, ESMA)

Note: one-week moving average of the difference of volatility after (10 minutes) and volatility before (10 minutes) the circuit breaker occurrences for the halted instruments and correlated ones. The top and bottom 5% outliers have been removed. Volatility computed as the standard deviation of mid-prices divided by the average mid-price. Data in basis points.

[31] These results are in line with Gomber et al., 'Effect of single-stock circuit breakers', 2013.

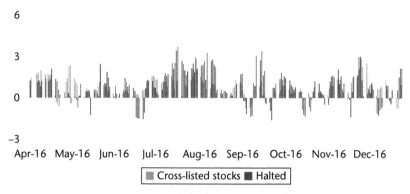

Figure 12.9. Circuit breaker impact: higher spreads after the circuit breaker incidents (sources: Morningstar Real Time, ESMA)

Note: one-week moving average of the difference of bid-ask spread after (10 minutes) and bid-ask spread before (10 minutes) the circuit breaker occurrences for the halted instruments (large caps) and correlated ones. The top and bottom 5% outliers have been removed. Bid-ask spread computed as $(Ask - Bid) / (Bid + Ask) \times 2$. Data in basis points.

compared to less fragmented stocks. In the same way, the widening effect on bid-ask spread is stronger for highly fragmented stocks.

Second, we study the impact of circuit breakers on the price discovery process for the instruments concerned. We find that the price discovery process is not negatively affected by the circuit breaker. On the contrary, results suggest that circuit breaker auction prices provide incremental information for participants, helping a return to orderly trading. In particular, for large cap stocks, where price dissonances around a circuit breaker event are found to be larger, circuit breaker auction prices contributed to a reduction of about 30 per cent in price uncertainty.

Finally, taking advantage of the cross-venue character of the data, we analyse cross-venue impacts of circuit breakers and thus contribute to the discussion on cross-venue circuit breaker coordination. For the purpose of the analysis we differentiate between what we suggest to call reference and satellite markets, where the reference market is the one on which the majority of trading is undertaken, and where satellite markets are generally characterized by lower liquidity levels compared to the reference market. Price discovery processes on the satellite market replicate those on the reference market while on halt. Although satellite markets offer the possibility to engage in continuous trading while the reference market is on halt, investors largely refrain from trading (high order cancellation rates), waiting for the reference market to end the halting period and set the new price. We observe more than twice the number of order cancellations compared to new orders on the satellite market, combined with lower messaging activity on the satellite market (Figures 12.10 and 12.11).

In practice, this means that halting the reference market does not divert traffic to satellite markets but, on the contrary, slows it down in these markets

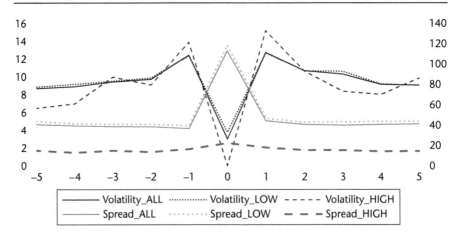

Figure 12.10. Spike in bid-ask spread and sharp fall of volatility during the reference market halt (sources: Morningstar Real Time, ESMA)

Note: median mid-prices standard deviation and bid-ask spread registered on stocks traded on a satellite market when the reference market is halted from 5 buckets before to 5 buckets after the circuit breaker event. Each bucket corresponds to a time interval of the exact same duration as the circuit breaker event. Measures presented for the whole sample of stocks (ALL), for low fragmented stocks (LOW), and for high fragmented stocks (HIGH). Data in bps. Bid-ask spread measures on secondary axis.

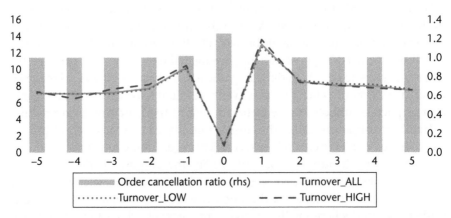

Figure 12.11. Increase in orders cancelled during the reference market halt (sources: Morningstar Real Time, ESMA)

Note: median trading activity share (%) registered on stocks traded on a satellite market when the reference market is halted from 5 buckets before to 5 buckets after the circuit breaker event. Each bucket corresponds to a time interval of the exact same duration as the circuit breaker event. Cancellation ratio on secondary axis computed as order cancelled over new orders submitted. Turnover as the average share of trading period going from −5 to +5 time buckets.

too. In this sense, price uncertainty in satellite markets closely follows price uncertainty in reference markets, and the additional contribution to the price discovery process brought by the satellite markets' continuous trading opportunities is very low.

The latter empirical observation suggests that under the market circumstances observed, in particular with the existence of one dominant reference and at least one less liquid satellite market, a coordination of circuit breakers may de facto not yield materially different outcomes. Further analysis will be needed to establish whether this conclusion also holds for trading landscapes where trading venues of similar size and liquidity compete.

12.6 The Regulatory Approach in the EU

With the rapid growth of EU securities markets and the fast pace of innovative trading technology, maintaining a state-of-the-art regulatory and supervisory framework for securities trading has been a core policy priority in the past decades.

Most importantly, the regulatory framework is harmonized for the entire EU and all member states, based on legislative frameworks adopted by the European Council and Parliament, and detailed implementing measures devised by the European Commission.

ESMA, as the EU authority for securities markets, plays a central role in the regulatory and supervisory process. First, ESMA advises the European Commission before adopting any implementing measures. And second, it coordinates the work on converging supervisory practices among the national authorities in the EU member states, which are in charge of the oversight of trading venues and other infrastructures.

The EU's rules for securities trading represent one of the most important areas of harmonized conditions in the single financial market.

12.6.1 *Harmonized Conditions for HFT in EU Markets*

The cornerstone of the EU's regulation of financial markets was the entry into force of MiFID, which provides a framework of rules for EU financial services. The Directive was seeking to ensure enhanced investor's protection and to boost the competitiveness of EU financial markets by creating a single market for investment services and activities.

Until just over a decade ago, regulated markets and OTC trading covered all market activity; transactions were channeled in a linear way, going from investors to intermediaries to the trading platforms. Dark pools had a negligible market share, their main users being institutions wanting to trade large blocks without revealing their intentions in order to avoid front-running.[32]

---

[32] Lehalle and Laruelle, *Market Microstructure*, 2014, 94–7.

MiFID entered into force in 2007, just about the time when the new market practices based on algorithmic trading were gaining momentum. Since then, a number of technology-driven developments have intensified, such as HFT. MiFID expanded organizational requirements for investment firms, including HFT firms.[33] In particular, there were concerns about HFTs not being contractually required to provide liquidity during stressed market conditions, unlike more traditional liquidity providers, and therefore having the ability to withdraw their liquidity at any time.

In 2009, the Committee of European Securities Regulators (CESR), the EU-level committee preceding the creation of ESMA in 2011, conducted a first evaluation[34] of the working of the new regulatory framework and its impact on market structure in equity markets. CESR issued a call for evidence on micro-structural issues of the European equity markets[35] with the objective of seeking information on various topics including HFT. It emerged that market participants felt that the dynamics of trading were changing, and so was the level playing field. In addition, the repeated occurrence of so-called flash incidents around the world strengthened the case for a revision of the MiFID framework. The issues raised at that stage were addressed in the subsequent MiFID II and MiFIR legislative package,[36] which was adopted in 2014 and entered into force on 3 January 2018.

The new legislative framework takes into account developments in the trading environment since the implementation of MiFID and, in light of the financial crisis, reshapes financial markets with the aim of making them more efficient, resilient, and transparent. According to the impact assessment of the European Commission, accompanying the MiFID II/MiFIR proposals, HFT in the EU in 2011 accounted for 13 to 40 per cent of total share trading taking place in the EU. In particular, it emphasized that

> [t]he most significant new risk arising from automated trading is the threat it can pose to the orderly functioning of markets in certain circumstances. Such threats can arise from rogue algorithms, from algorithms overreacting to market events or from the increased pressure on trading venue systems to cope with the large numbers of orders generated by automated trading.[37]

MiFID II subjects the use of HFT and algorithmic trading to a new set of harmonized EU-wide rules. Under MiFID II, HFT is a specific subset of

---

[33] Article 13, MiFID, 2004.   [34] CESR, 'Impact of MiFID', 2009.

[35] CESR, 'Microstructural issues', 2010.

[36] While the MiFID II/MiFIR package was in negotiation among the EU Institutions, ESMA issued Guidelines in February 2012 aimed at ensuring a common, uniform, and consistent application of MiFID on trading platforms and investment firms in an automated trading environment.

[37] European Commission, 'Impact assessment', 2011.

algorithmic trading. Article 4(1) (40) of MiFID II defines the HFT technique as an algorithmic trading technique characterized by three attributes:

- infrastructure intended to minimize network and other types of latencies, including at least one of the following facilities for algorithmic order entry: co-location, proximity hosting, or high-speed direct electronic access;
- system determination of order initiation, generation, routing, or execution without human intervention for individual trades or orders; and
- high message intraday rates which constitute orders, quotes, or cancellations.[38]

Under MiFID II, persons that apply an HFT technique have to be authorized as investment firms. Furthermore, MiFID II imposes measures and risk controls to overcome the potential threats to orderly markets arising from new technologies. Such measures are targeted both at the firm level (for those players that use algorithmic trading techniques) and at the trading venue level (in particular trading venues that allow or enable algorithmic trading and in particular where order submission and order matching is facilitated by electronic means).

Measures at the level of trading venues include the requirement to implement systems, procedures, and arrangements to make sure that the trading systems are resilient, have sufficient capacity, and are able to ensure orderly trading under conditions of severe market stress. Moreover, trading venues are required to provide co-location services on a non-discriminatory, fair, and transparent basis. Article 48 of MiFID II explores in detail all the requirements for trading venues in order to ensure smooth and orderly market functioning.

Measures at the level of investment firm require algorithmic traders to have effective systems and risk controls in place to ensure their trading systems are resilient and have enough capacity. Such systems should also be subject to appropriate trading thresholds and limits in order to prevent the sending of erroneous orders. Algorithmic traders who carry out market-making activities are required to do so continuously during a specified number of hours while a trading venue is open to ensure continuity in liquidity provision. In order to achieve this objective, algorithmic traders who base their trading strategy on market making will be required to enter into written agreements with relevant trading venues.[39] Furthermore, ESMA has developed Regulatory Technical

---

[38] According to Article 19 of the Commission Delegated Regulation (EU) 2017/565 of 25 April 2016, a high message intraday rate shall consist of the submission on average of any of the following: (1) at least 2 messages per second with respect to any single financial instrument traded on a trading venue; (2) at least 4 messages per second with respect to all financial instruments traded on a trading venue.

[39] A market-making strategy is found where, during half the trading days in a one-month period, the trader posts firm, simultaneous two-way quotes at competitive prices and deals on

Standards to specify the details of organizational requirements imposed to investment firms engaged in algorithmic trading and HFTs.[40]

MiFID II and MiFIR also enlarge the regulatory scope for financial instruments and activities to include non-equity instruments, i.e. bonds, structured finance products, emission allowances, and derivatives.

Through MiFID II, the reforms provide harmonization across the EU member states for trading in financial instruments, mainly by ensuring that an increasing part of such trading takes place on regulated venues. To this end, a new category of trading venue has been introduced with respect to non-equity instruments, the Organised Trading Facility, where multiple third-party buying and selling interests in bonds, structured finance products, emission allowances, or derivatives are able to interact. MiFID II also improves the transparency and oversight of financial markets (including derivatives markets) and addresses some shortcomings in commodity derivative trading. Finally, it enhances investor protection by strengthening the conduct of business rules as well as conditions for competition in the trading and clearing of financial instruments.

In parallel, MiFIR ensures fully harmonized rules across the EU by requiring disclosure of pre- and post-trade information on trading activity to the public, and of transaction data to regulators and supervisors.

In implementing MiFID II and MiFIR, ESMA, from 2018 onwards, provides markets with key transparency and reference data, publishing it on its website (e.g. reference data and, with respect to equity instruments, volumes of trading executed on EU trading venues—including volumes executed under certain waivers—for the purpose of the double volume cap mechanism).

12.6.2 *ESMA Harmonizes Circuit Breaker Parameters*

MiFID II also tackles the issue of repeated crash incidents. Article 48(5) specifies that trading venues must be required to have in place systems to halt trading in periods of volatility. With the view that trading halt parameters should be appropriately calibrated, taking into account liquidity conditions, MiFID II has mandated ESMA to develop guidelines on the appropriate calibration of trading halts.

---

its own account for at least 50 per cent of the daily trading hours, excluding the opening and closing auctions.

[40] Commission Delegated Regulation (EU) 2017/589 of 19 July 2016 supplementing Directive 2014/65/EU of the European Parliament and of the Council with regard to regulatory technical standards specifying the organizational requirements of investment firms engaged in algorithmic trading.

The ESMA Guidelines, published on 6 April 2017, bring for the first time a harmonized approach to trading halts in the EU.[41] Importantly, the new rules provide for a common definition and conceptual delineation of circuit breakers. In addition, ESMA made proposals regarding the dissemination of information about the activation of mechanisms to manage volatility on a specific trading venue, and the procedure and format to submit the reports on parameters relating to trading halts from national authorities to ESMA.

The guidelines define circuit breakers as 'mechanisms to be set in place by trading venues in accordance with Article 48(5) of MiFID to temporarily halt or constrain trading if there is a significant price movement in a financial instrument' and therefore include both 'pure' trading halt mechanisms and other mechanisms used to constrain trading, such as price collars. Trading halts include mechanisms that interrupt continuous trading (mechanisms whereby trading stops on a certain security for a certain time period, during which no trades are executed and no new prices are determined, as well as mechanisms whereby trading switches from continuous trading to a call auction) and mechanisms that extend the period of scheduled or unscheduled call auctions in cases of price divergence with respect to a pre-defined reference price at the end of the auction. In substantive terms, the guidelines provide common directions for the calibration of volatility parameters. Trading venues should calibrate their circuit breakers according to a pre-defined, statistically supported methodology.[42]

12.7 Outlook: Dynamic Effects on Watch Going Forward

With the MiFID II requirements and the ESMA Guidelines, trading venues and supervisory authorities in the EU now have a comprehensive regulatory framework for operating and supervising circuit breakers at their disposal.[43] The implementation of the new rules is set to produce new and instructive

---

[41] ESMA, 'Calibration of circuit breakers', 2017.

[42] According to the ESMA Guidelines on trading halts ('Calibration', 2017), trading venues when calibrating trading halts have to take into account the following parameters: the nature of the financial instrument; the liquidity profile and the quotation level of the financial instrument; the volatility profile of the financial instrument; any significant imbalances in the flow of orders, with the possibility of re-calibration when needed; trading venue modes and rules, whereby trading venues should have tighter circuit breaker parameters for continuous auction and quote-driven systems; internal references, whereby circuit breakers should be calibrated using static (such as opening price, closing price, or intraday auction price) and dynamic (such as the last traded price or the average price over a certain period) reference prices; external references, whereby trading venues should consider the statistical correlation between instruments, in particular in cross-asset (e.g. cash and future instrument) and cross-market (e.g. multi-listed instrument) situations; the duration of the halts, giving trading venues flexibility in deciding the time length of the volatility interruptions and introducing a certain degree of randomization in the duration of a specific halt in trading; and the number of times the mechanism was used in the previous years on their platforms.

[43] The Guidelines have applied from 3 January 2018.

evidence on the performance of circuit breakers in the coming years. Two areas of market analysis are likely to be most important from a regulatory and supervisory perspective.

12.7.1 *Circuit Breaker Calibration*

Trading venues will continue to have latitude in calibrating circuit breakers. Those circuit breakers can for instance be calibrated at the level of a class of financial instrument or, where appropriate and where necessary, at a more granular level. Our findings of current market practices suggest that circuit breaker calibrations differ widely across the EU, between trading venues, across instrument classes per trading venue, and even between individual instruments.

At the same time, it is clear that the calibration of circuit breakers by trading venues can have a profound effect on markets. The early 2016 experience of introducing a new circuit breaker regime in China provides an important example of the market sensitivities that users of circuit breakers need to take into consideration when calibrating such tools. The new MiFID II regime will facilitate the comparability of circuit breaker arrangements in future and of their performance in critical situations. It will be important to gather and evaluate the market evidence that becomes available, with the aim of learning from the experience under the new MiFID II environment.

In particular, it will be important to understand any potential performance patterns, as well as the relevance of individual elements of the calibration, for example as addressed in the ESMA Guidelines, for their effectiveness. This particularly applies to critical situations of general financial instability across instruments and market segments, liquidity dry spells in limited asset classes or wider market segments, and algorithms spinning out of control. As the technological development of infrastructure provision and access, as well as algorithmic routines, are set to continue at a fast pace, optimizing the calibration of trading-halt arrangements will remain a key concern for trading venues and supervisors alike.

12.7.2 *Market Dynamics and Circuit Breaker Interaction*

A better understanding of the complexity of potential dynamic interactions of market events is needed. Of particular future interest for market participants and supervisors are three dimensions of market interaction. The first dimension is the incidence of flash crashes and any potential feedback loops between high frequency traders and between algorithms: as algorithms become more complex and, through machine learning, more reactive to market developments, the effects that one algorithm may have on others by causing severe price movements need to be empirically investigated.

The second dimension that will require examination is the interaction between any cascading price movements and the revised regulatory landscape of circuit breakers applicable during extreme market conditions, as discussed above. This is particularly relevant given that the composition of traders around a circuit breaker event may influence the latter's effectiveness. The composition can be heterogeneous and vary over time, as HFTs typically do not participate in auction trading and may enter after a circuit breaker auction is over.

Finally, trading venues and supervisors will need to be aware of any potential feedback loops between the different circuit breakers. As we found out for the EU, there is no systematic diversion of liquidity from reference to satellite markets when a circuit breaker is triggered on the former. However, the observation of the overall decelerating effect of a reference market circuit breaker is based on an empirical analysis and may not be robust over time. If it is not robust, cascading effects triggering sequences of circuit breakers on one instrument between trading venues may result. Similarly, such cascades could not be excluded for price movements between correlated instruments.

References

Ackert, Lucy F., Bryan K. Church, and Narayanan Jayaraman. 'Circuit breakers with uncertainty about the presence of informed agents: I know what you know . . . I think'. FRB of Atlanta Working Paper, No. 2002-25, 2002.

Boehmer, Ekkehart, Kingsley Y.L. Fong, and J. (Julie) Fong. 'International evidence on algorithmic trading'. AFA 2013 San Diego Meetings Paper. Available at: https://ssrn.com/abstract=2022034, 17 September 2015.

Braun, Tobias, Jonas Andre Fiegen, Daniel C. Wagner, Sebastian Matthias Krause, and Thomas Guhr. 'Impact and recovery process of mini flash crashes: An empirical study'. Available at: https://ssrn.com/abstract=3008502, 18 July 2017.

Breckenfelder, Johannes H. 'Competition between high-frequency traders, and market quality'. NYU Stern Microstructure Meeting 2013. Available at: https://ssrn.com/abstract=2264858, 1 November 2013.

Brogaard, Jonathan, Terrence Hendershott, Stefan Hunt, and Carla Ysusi. 'High-frequency trading and the execution costs of institutional investors'. *Financial Review* 49, no. 2 (2014): 345–69.

Cespa, Giovanni, and Xavier Vives. 'High frequency trading and fragility'. ECB Working Paper no. 2020. 10 February 2017.

CESR (Committee of European Securities Regulators). 'CESR technical advice to the European Commission in the context of the MiFID Review – equity markets'. Technical Advice, CESR/10-802. 29 July 2010.

CESR. 'Impact of MiFID on equity secondary markets functioning'. Report, CESR/09-355. 10 June 2009.

CESR. 'Microstructural issues of the European equity markets'. Call for evidence, CESR/ 10-142. 1 April 2010.

CFT and SEC (Commodity Futures Trading Commission and US Securities and Exchange Commission). 'Findings regarding the market events of May 6, 2010'. Available at: https:// www.sec.gov/news/studies/2010/marketevents-report.pdf, 30 September 2010.

Clapham, Benjamin, Peter Gomber, Martin Haferkorn, and Sven Panz. 'Managing excess volatility: Design and effectiveness of circuit breakers'. Research Centre SAFE working paper. Available at: https://ssrn.com/abstract=2910977, 2 February 2017.

Davies, Ryan J., and Erik R. Sirri. 'The economics and regulation of secondary trading markets'. 20 July 2017. Presented at Initiating Conference 'New special study of the securities markets', Columbia Law School. Available at: https://ssrn.com/abstract= 3012536, 23–4 March 2017.

Draus, Sarah, and Mark Van Achter. 'Circuit breakers and market runs'. Working paper. Available at: https://ssrn.com/abstract=2081962, 22 August 2016.

ESMA (European Securities and Markets Authority). 'Calibration of circuit breakers and publication of trading halts under MiFID II'. Guidelines, ESMA 70-872942901-63. 6 April 2017.

ESMA. 'High-frequency trading activity in EU equity markets'. ESMA Economic Report, no. 1 (2014).

ESMA. 'Order duplication and liquidity measurement in EU equity markets'. ESMA Economic Report, no. 1 (2016).

ESMA. Report on Trends, Risks and Vulnerabilities. No. 1, 2017.

ESMA. 'Systems and controls in an automated trading environment for trading platforms, investment firms and competent authorities'. Guidelines, ESMA/2012/122. 24 February 2012.

European Commission. 'Impact assessment'. Commission staff working paper, SEC (2011) 1226 final. 20 October 2011.

Gomber, Peter, Björn Arndt, Marco Lutat, and Tim Uhle. 'High-frequency trading'. Working paper. Available at: https://ssrn.com/abstract=1858626, 2011.

Gomber, Peter, Martin Haferkorn, Marco Lutat, and Kai Zimmermann. 'The effect of single-stock circuit breakers on the quality of fragmented markets'. Lecture Notes in Business Information Processing, 136: 71–87. Available at: https://ssrn.com/ abstract=2221903, 21 February 2013.

Guillaumie, Cyrille, Giuseppe Loiacono, Steffen Kern, and Christian Winkler. 'Market impacts of circuit breakers'. ESMA Working Paper no. 2, 2018 (forthcoming).

Hao, Xiangchao. 'The magnet effect of market-wide circuit breaker: Evidence from the Chinese stock market'. Working paper. Available at: https://ssrn.com/abstract= 2859540, 26 June 2016.

Hasbrouck, Joel, and Gideon Saar. 'Low-latency trading'. *Johnson School Research Paper Series*, no. 35-2010. AFA 2012 Chicago Meetings Paper. 22 May 2013.

Hendershott, Terrence, Charles M. Jones, and Albert J. Menkveld. 'Does algorithmic trading improve liquidity?' *Journal of Finance* 66, no. 1 (2011): 1–33.

Kirilenko, Andrei A., Albert S. Kyle, Mehrdad Samadi, and Tugkan Tuzun. 'The flash crash: High-frequency trading in an electronic market'. *Journal of Finance* 72, no. 3 (2017): 967–98.

Kumiega, Andrew, Greg Sterijevski, and Ben Van Vliet. 'Beyond the flash crash: Systemic risk, reliability, and high frequency financial markets'. *Journal of Trading* 11, no. 2 (2016): 71–83.

Lehalle, Charles-Albert, and Sophie Laruelle. *Market Microstructure in Practice.* Singapore: World Scientific Publishing Company, 2014.

Malinova, Katya, Andreas Park, and Ryan Riordan. 'Do retail traders suffer from high frequency traders?' Working paper (2013).

Menkveld, Albert J. 'High frequency trading and the new market makers'. *Journal of Financial Markets* 16, no. 4 (2013): 712–40.

O'Hara, Maureen. 'High-frequency trading and its impact on markets'. *Financial Analysts Journal* 70, no. 3 (2014): 18–27.

Petrescu, Monica, and Michael Wedow. 'Dark pools in European equity markets: Emergence, competition and implications'. ECB Occasional Paper no. 193. 11 July 2017.

SEC (US Securities and Exchange Commission). *Equity Market Structure Literature Review. Part II: High Frequency Trading.* 2014.

Sornette, Didier, and Susanne von der Becke. 'Crashes and high frequency trading'. Swiss Finance Institute Research Paper, no. 11–63. August 2011.

Van Kervel, Vincent, and Albert J. Menkveld. 'High-frequency trading around large institutional orders'. WFA Paper. Available at: https://ssrn.com/abstract=2619686, 29 January 2016.

Wong, Kin Ming, Xiaowei Kong, and Min Li. 'The magnet effect of circuit breakers and its interactions with price limits'. Working paper. Available at: https://ssrn.com/abstract=2897328, 29 November 2016.

Zhang, Frank. 'High-frequency trading, stock volatility, and price discovery'. Working paper. Available at: https://ssrn.com/abstract=1691679, December 2010.

13

A Framework for Responsive Market Regulation

Timothy Baikie, Tracey Stern, Susan Greenglass, and Maureen Jensen

13.1 Introduction

The pace of change in the capital markets is rapid and growing ever faster. Up until late in the twentieth century, most trades in securities were undertaken the way they had been done for over 100 years: through interactions with an adviser, paper order tickets created and timestamped, and face-to-face negotiations on the floor of an exchange. Today, trading floors are a relic of a bygone age and computers make trading decisions as they buy and sell with other computers. The challenge for a regulator to keep up with, much less anticipate, changes in both market structure and practice is rapid and intense. However, doing just that is key to the regulator's purpose. Failing to look forward leaves regulators with two unappealing choices. The first would be to preserve the regulatory status quo and ban any new practice or entity that does not fit neatly into the existing framework. The second would be to decide that regulating new entrants is too difficult, which would allow an unregulated sector to operate, flourish, and perhaps begin to supplant the existing markets.

This chapter submits that a regulator's *raison d'être* is not simply to respond to market issues but to follow and understand the changes and business decisions in the market. The regulator must also have the courage to change and foster a responsive regulatory climate that allows innovation to occur, while ensuring that core principles such as investor protection are preserved and that the impact of any change is monitored. This chapter identifies drivers for responsible policy development, and cites examples of market structure issues and policy development where the Ontario Securities Commission (OSC) has used them as a basis for responsible decision-making.

13.2 Background

13.2.1 Overview of Canadian Securities Regulation

Securities regulation in Canada is done primarily at the provincial and territorial level.[1] The various securities regulatory authorities coordinate policy and rule development through an umbrella organization called the Canadian Securities Administrations (CSA) to harmonize regulation of the Canadian capital markets. This chapter describes the regulatory approach followed by the OSC and is not necessarily indicative of the approach taken by other jurisdictions in Canada; however, significant cooperation in this area has been a hallmark of Canadian securities regulation.

13.2.2 Overview of the Canadian Capital Markets

Canadian capital markets are well developed and mature. This section provides a high-level overview of market infrastructure entities regulated by the OSC. As with policy development, to avoid duplication, oversight of all of these entities is coordinated with securities regulatory authorities in other Canadian jurisdictions in which they carry on business.

(A) SELF-REGULATORY ORGANIZATIONS (SROs)

Canada has a self-regulatory system, with the Investment Industry Regulatory Organisation of Canada (IIROC) regulating the business and conduct of investment dealers in all jurisdictions, and the Mutual Fund Dealers Association of Canada regulating the business and conduct of mutual fund dealers in all jurisdictions other than Québec.[2] In addition, IIROC, acting as a regulation services provider (RSP), conducts market surveillance of all equity marketplaces and administers the various equity exchanges' timely disclosure policies.[3]

---

[1] There are provisions in the federal Criminal Code (R.S.C., ch. C-46 (1985), available at: http://laws-lois.justice.gc.ca/eng/acts/C-46/index.html), prohibiting activities such as fraud and market manipulation. The Payment Clearing and Settlement Act (1996 S.C., ch. 6, Sch., available at: http://laws-lois.justice.gc.ca/eng/acts/P-4.4/index.html) gives the Bank of Canada the ability to designate clearing agencies and oversee them with respect to any systemic risk their operations create. The federal government and the governments of five provinces (including Ontario) and one territory have announced an intention to create a single regulatory agency for the capital markets in those jurisdictions.

[2] Investment dealers, which provide a full range of services to clients, must be IIROC members. Other registered dealers, such as exempt market dealers, are limited in the business they can carry on and are regulated directly by the securities regulatory authorities in the jurisdictions in which they operate.

[3] Alternative trading systems (see text accompanying note 29) are required to use an RSP as they cannot perform regulatory functions. IIROC is the only RSP. Exchanges have self-regulatory responsibilities, and can choose to do their own member and market regulation or outsource some or all of these functions to an RSP. All of the equity exchanges use IIROC as an RSP. The derivative and commodity futures exchanges perform their own market regulation; some rely on IIROC for member regulation. The timely disclosure policies are rules of the various exchanges

IIROC has developed a body of Universal Market Integrity Rules (UMIR) and enforces UMIR violations by its members.[4] Violations by parties over which IIROC has no jurisdiction (such as clients of IIROC member firms) are referred to the relevant securities regulatory authority.

The OSC does not have a front-line role in monitoring equity trading activity, but directly oversees IIROC. Trading activity is governed both by the CSA rules and by UMIR.

(B) EQUITY AND FIXED INCOME MARKETPLACES

Equities and fixed income securities are traded on six domestic recognized exchanges[5] and 10 alternative trading systems (ATSs).[6] Aequitas NEO Exchange (Aequitas), the Canadian Securities Exchange (CSE), the Toronto Stock Exchange (TSX), and the TSX Venture Exchange (TSXV) have a listing function where they approve companies for trading and regulate their listed companies. Alpha Exchange Inc. and NASDAQ CXC Limited do not have a listing function at the time of writing. Unlike some markets, such as that in the United States, which have seen the market share of incumbent exchanges decline dramatically with the advent of competition from ATSs, the TSX and TSXV have maintained the largest share both of listed companies and trading in their listed securities (see Figures 13.1 and 13.2). As of 2 January 2018, the TSX had 1510 listings, the TSXV 1657, the CSE 345, and Aequitas 45. The TSX and TSXV's market share have declined somewhat with increased competition, but both still have most of the trading in their listed securities (55.1 per cent for the TSX and 72 per cent for the TSXV as of November 2017).

(C) DERIVATIVE AND COMMODITY FUTURES MARKETPLACES

Derivatives and commodity futures contracts are traded domestically on the Bourse de Montréal, ICE Futures Canada, and Natural Gas Exchange Inc.[7] In addition, in Ontario, a number of foreign commodity futures exchanges, swap execution facilities, and multilateral trading facilities allow access by

---

requiring their listed companies to disclose material information promptly and broadly to investors.

[4] The text of UMIR is available at http://www.iiroc.ca/industry/rulebook/Pages/UMIR-Marketplace-Rules.aspx.

[5] Aequitas NEO Exchange Inc.; Alpha Exchange Inc., TSX Inc., and TSX Venture Exchange (owned by TMX Group Limited); Canadian Securities Exchange; and NASDAQ CXC Limited. The TSX Venture Exchange is overseen by the Alberta and British Columbia securities commissions and is exempted from recognition in Ontario.

[6] CanDeal; CBID and CBID Institutional (operated by Permiter Markets Inc.); EquiLend; Instinet Canada Cross; Liquidnet Canada; MarketAxess; MATCH Now; Omega ATS and Lynx ATS (operated by Omega Securities Inc.).

[7] Bourse de Montréal is owned by TMX Group Limited. ICE Futures Canada and Natural Gas Exchange are owned by Intercontinental Exchange.

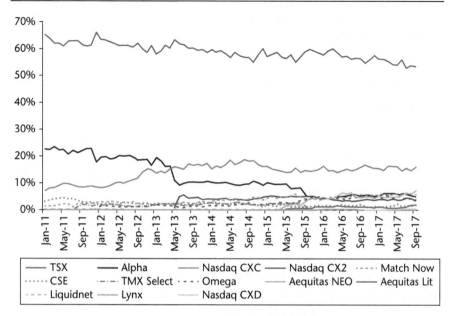

Figure 13.1. Market share of TSX-listed securities, by volume

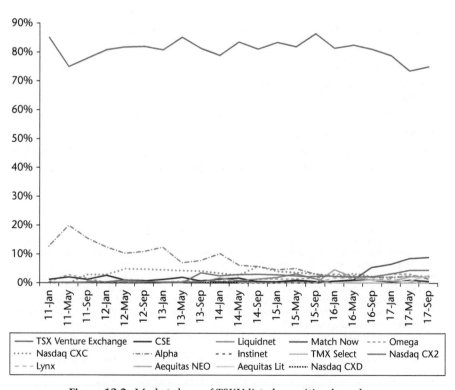

Figure 13.2. Market share of TSXV-listed securities, by volume

participants located in Ontario and are therefore considered to be doing business in Ontario.[8]

(D) OTHER INFRASTRUCTURE ENTITIES

Two information processors have been approved, one for equities (TMX Information Processor) and one for corporate debt (IIROC IP). The information processors consolidate and publish information from all marketplaces for transactions in equities and from marketplaces and dealers for unlisted debt securities. TMX Information Processor also consolidates information on displayed orders for equities.

There are four recognized domestic and foreign clearing agencies carrying on business in Ontario, with another 11 that have been exempted from recognition.[9]

Three trade repositories (the equivalent of swap data repositories)—Chicago Mercantile Exchange Inc., DTCC Data Repository (US) LLC, and ICE Trade Vault, LLC—have been designated by the Commission to receive reports of transactions in over-the-counter derivatives.

Two investor protection funds, Canadian Investor Protection Fund and MFDA Investor Protection Corporation, have been approved by the Commission. The investor protection funds are sponsored by investment dealers and mutual fund dealers respectively and cover customer losses resulting from a dealer's failure to return customer property because of bankruptcy.[10] Four credit rating agencies have been designated and are overseen by the OSC.[11]

In addition to these entities, the OSC oversees 1280 registered firms and 67,300 registered individuals, either directly or indirectly through IIROC. The OSC is also the principal regulator for over 80 per cent of all Canadian investment funds, and 1071 reporting issuers (publicly-traded companies).[12]

---

[8] All of the domestic and foreign derivatives and commodity futures marketplaces operate under exemption orders in Ontario as none are based there. An exemption order is issued when the Commission has determined that a marketplace (or other regulated entity) operates under an equivalent regulatory regime in its home jurisdiction, such that requiring it to comply fully with Ontario rules would be duplicative and unnecessary, and where the OSC can rely on the home regulator for day-to-day oversight. An exemption order will normally contain terms and conditions, such as requiring the exempted entity to report on activity by Ontario participants. For a full list of recognized and exempted exchanges, see http://www.osc.gov.on.ca/en/Marketplaces_exchanges_index.htm.

[9] For a complete list, see http://www.osc.gov.on.ca/en/Marketplaces_clearing-agencies_index.htm.

[10] The funds do not cover other losses such as change in market value, unsuitable investments, or default by the issuer of a security.

[11] DBRS Limited; Fitch Ratings, Inc.; Moody's Canada Inc.; and S&P Global Ratings Canada.

[12] OSC, 'Annual report', 2017.

13.2.3 *The Ontario Securities Commission*

The history of the OSC dates back to 1931, when the government of Ontario amended existing securities frauds legislation to allow the lieutenant-governor in council to establish 'a commission or body of persons...as a Board to administer [the] Act'.[13] The province's securities regulator, the Security Frauds Prevention Board, was renamed the Ontario Securities Commission in 1933. The OSC is a Crown corporation, accountable to the Ontario Legislature through the Minister of Finance. It operates under the direction of the Commission, which consists of 9 to 16 commissioners, including the chair and up to three vice-chairs, and is responsible for administering the Securities Act (Ontario) and the Commodity Futures Act (CFA).[14] The Commission has two independent roles. It serves as the board of directors of the OSC and also performs a regulatory function, which includes making rules and policies and adjudicating administrative proceedings. The chair is both the chair of the board and the chief executive officer of the OSC, and the executive director is the chief administrative officer.

The OSC has 16 regulatory, advisory, and corporate branches and offices, with approximately 560 employees.

The Compliance & Registrant Regulation Branch is responsible for regulating firms and individuals who are in the business of advising or trading in securities or commodity futures contracts and commodity futures options, and firms that manage investment funds in Ontario.

The Corporate Finance Branch is responsible for regulating reporting issuers other than investment funds, leading issuer-related policy initiatives, including the regulatory framework for securities offerings in the public and exempt markets, and monitoring compliance through ongoing reviews.

The Derivatives Branch is responsible for developing a regulatory framework for over-the-counter derivatives trading in Ontario and compliance oversight of derivatives market participants.

The Enforcement Branch is responsible for investigating and litigating breaches of the Securities Act and CFA, and seeking orders in the public interest before the Commission and the courts.

The Investment Funds & Structured Products Branch is responsible for regulating investment products that offer securities for sale to the public in Ontario, including mutual funds, exchange-traded funds, structured products, and scholarship plans.

---

[13] The Securities Frauds Prevention Act, 1930 S.O., ch. 39 § 2a (added by 1931 S.O., ch. 48 § 3).
[14] Securities Act, R.S.O., ch. S.5 (1990) as am. (Securities Act) § 3, available at https://www.ontario.ca/laws/statute/90s05; and Commodity Futures Act, R.S.O., ch. C.20 (1990) as am. (CFA), available at https://www.ontario.ca/laws/statute/90c20.

The Investor Office sets the strategic direction and leads the OSC's efforts in investor engagement, education, outreach, and research. The Office also brings the investor perspective to policy-making and operations.

The Market Regulation Branch is responsible for regulating market infrastructure entities (including exchanges, alternative trading systems, self-regulatory organizations, clearing agencies, and trade repositories) in Ontario, and for developing policy relating to market structure and clearing agencies.

The Office of Mergers & Acquisitions is responsible for overseeing M&A transactions and proxy voting matters involving public companies, and for rule and policy development in the areas of M&A and shareholder rights.

The General Counsel's Office is an in-house legal, policy, strategy, and risk-management resource to the OSC that also oversees organizational integrity and ethical conduct.

The Office of the Chief Accountant supports the OSC in creating and promoting a high-quality framework for financial reporting by market participants.

The Office of Domestic & International Affairs provides advice and support to the OSC in its dealings with other regulators and governments, both in Canada and internationally.

The Office of the Secretary to the Commission supports the members of the Commission in their statutory mandate as regulators and as a board of directors by providing counsel on adjudicative matters and administrative law, corporate law, and corporate governance.

The Strategy & Operations Branch leads development of OSC strategic goals and priorities as well as economic and market research initiatives and the OSC's business-planning, policy-prioritization, and risk-management processes.

The Communications & Public Affairs Branch provides strategic advice and services to ensure the timely and effective communication of OSC priorities, policies, and actions to both external and internal stakeholders.

The Corporate Services Branch supports the effective operation of the OSC through a diverse set of systems and services, including financial management (planning, reporting, and treasury), administration and office services, facilities management, information technology, library and knowledge management, procurement, and records and information management.

The Human Resources Branch provides the OSC with strategic and operational advice and services relating to the planning, acquisition, development, and engagement of OSC talent, and the planning and administration of the OSC's total compensation plan, performance management, and overall organization development.

In fiscal year 2016/17 the OSC had revenues of approximately $120 million and an excess of revenues over expenses of approximately $11.4 million.[15]

---

[15] OSC, 'Annual report', 2017, at 58.

The OSC is self-funded and operates on a cost-recovery basis. Revenue comes from activity fees (prospectus filings, recognition and designation applications, exemption applications, etc.), annual participation fees paid by reporting (public) issuers, dealers, and other regulated entities, and late fees for filings made after applicable deadlines.[16] Fines paid in connection with enforcement actions are segregated and may be (1) used to cover the OSC's costs in bringing the enforcement action, (2) allocated to such third parties as the Commission may determine, or (3) used for the purpose of educating investors or promoting or otherwise enhancing knowledge and information of persons regarding the operation of the securities and financial markets.[17]

13.2.4 *Policy Process in Ontario*

In order to give a broader context to the discussion of responsive regulation in this chapter, we will give a brief overview of the OSC's policy development and rulemaking processes. The discussion focuses on the Securities Act, but a similar approach is taken for the CFA.

Both the Securities Act and the CFA give the OSC broad authority to enact rules governing the capital markets.[18] In developing a proposal, staff identify and examine issues (either new issues or issues with existing rules) following the regulatory framework described in this chapter using qualitative and, where available and relevant, quantitative metrics. We seek input from formal OSC advisory committees, such as the Market Structure Advisory Committee, and we may receive informal feedback from stakeholders. Sometimes, particularly with respect to rule proposals that would have a significant impact on market participants, we will issue a consultation or concept paper, which sets out issues and possible alternative regulatory approaches without recommending any particular approach. We may also hold industry roundtables to solicit input more broadly.

Once staff have determined the preferred approach, rule amendments will be drafted. For market structure rules, these are, with very few exceptions, coordinated with the other provincial and territorial jurisdictions to achieve harmonized rules. Proposed new rules and amendments to existing rules, along with any related companion policies, are published for public comment.[19] Comments are reviewed and may result in changes to the proposed rule. If the changes are significant, the rule must be republished for comment.[20]

---

[16] For details, see OSC Rule 13-502 'Fees', available at: http://www.osc.gov.on.ca/en/SecuritiesLaw_13-502.htm.

[17] Securities Act § 3.4(2).   [18] Securities Act § 143; CFA § 65.

[19] A companion policy contains interpretations and explanations of a rule and guidance for compliance, but does not contain any mandatory provisions; and see Securities Act § 143.2(1).

[20] Ibid. § 143.2(7).

After a final rule is adopted by the Commission, it cannot come into force until it is approved or is deemed to have been approved by the Ontario Minister of Finance.[21]

13.3 Approach to Developing and Implementing a Regulatory Framework

The work of a regulator must always be grounded in first principles. In the case of the OSC, these are set out in our governing legislation. The purposes of the Securities Act are:

- to provide protection to investors from unfair, improper, or fraudulent practices; and
- to foster fair and efficient capital markets and confidence in capital markets.[22]

The first purpose, investor protection, lends itself to direct regulatory actions: prohibiting or regulating certain conduct, requiring certain disclosures, and taking enforcement action against fraudsters. The second is indirect. The OSC does not operate the capital markets, and while we may create an environment where fair and efficient capital markets may develop, we cannot require anyone to use them. Developing fair and efficient markets requires setting standards, but it also requires regulators to recognize when regulatory action is not needed or may be counterproductive, and when existing rules have served their purpose or have unintended consequences.

In Canada, market regulators have taken steps to be informed and responsive to market innovation. Policy analysis is both reactive and anticipatory. Most new market structure developments and practices come from marketplaces, dealers, and market participants, and regulators should ensure that developments and practices are consistent with the principles underlying the regulatory framework. Occasionally, we have anticipated changes in the market that arise due to developments in other jurisdictions or are driven by the need to accommodate innovation. All policy decisions must be regularly revisited to identify if there have been unintended consequences or market developments that necessitate a review because they were not anticipated at the time the rule or policy was made.

Policy formulation must be driven by a clear vision and set of underlying market goals.

---

[21] Ibid. § 143.4.   [22] Ibid. § 1.1.

- *Implementing a vision of the ideal market structure:* what values or attributes, such as integrity, transparency, and fair and open competition, should be maximized?

- *Identifying and addressing issues and opportunities:* what is standing in the way of the vision? What is on the horizon that may have a negative impact?

- *Fostering innovation:* does the existing regulatory framework accommodate innovation and developments in the market, or must changes be made?

- *Re-examining past decisions and their outcomes:* did previous rule and policy decisions achieve the intended outcome? Are there serious unintended consequences? Is the issue that was addressed by the rule still a concern, or is the rule outdated? Are changes required?

These drivers are discussed in this chapter with examples of concrete policy initiatives that were undertaken by securities regulators in Canada. The chapter describes the Canadian regulators' approach to developing regulatory policy to promote competition among trading venues, address inefficiencies in existing rules (order protection or trade-through), and recognize and address innovative developments that have raised potential concerns (dark trading, high frequency trading (HFT), and order processing delays). It also identifies examples where regulators revisited past decisions and made necessary changes.

13.3.1 *The Vision of an Ideal Market*

In 1999, the Canadian equity exchanges then in operation realigned their business models so that all trading in senior issuers was on the TSX, all junior issuers on the Canadian Venture Exchange (now the TSXV), and all equity options and financial derivatives on the Bourse de Montréal.[23] The CSA, led by the OSC, undertook a review of market structure with a view to creating a competitive framework where new types of marketplaces could operate. This review was taken in light of a worldwide trend of not-for-profit mutual exchanges demutualizing and becoming for-profit share corporations, which exacerbated concerns about a for-profit company having a virtual monopoly on trading. The CSA was also mindful of developments in the United States with respect to regulating new trading venues.[24]

---

[23] Both the Canadian Venture Exchange and the Bourse de Montréal were subsequently acquired by the TSX. The Canadian Venture Exchange was rebranded the TSXV.
[24] In the United States, Regulation ATS, 17 C.F.R. § 242.300–.303 (2017), created a framework for the regulation of alternative trading systems.

A broad public policy discussion on the vision of fair and efficient markets and the opportunities and issues created by new marketplaces followed. The opportunities included the potential for lower costs and the introduction of new trading methodologies more responsive to investor needs that could result from increased competition. The challenges related to the fragmentation of information, trading, and regulation,[25] a more complex market, and a risk of a regulatory 'race to the bottom' where marketplaces lower market integrity standards to compete for order flow.

To effectively engage in the policy discussion, the TSX created a Special Committee on Market Fragmentation, which in 1997 issued a report entitled 'Market Fragmentation: Responding to the Challenge'.[26] The report set out the attributes of an ideal market in the context of market fragmentation, including maximizing market integrity, ensuring fairness, maximizing liquidity, maximizing real-time transparency of orders and trades, and maximizing price discovery.

The Special Committee recognized that it is impossible to fully maximize all of these attributes at the same time, as they may conflict with market participants' needs and preferences. For example, an investor's wish not to disclose an intention to trade a large order because of potential negative market impact conflicts with the ideal of transparency. Similarly, a market participant may decide to forgo full price discovery in order to complete a trade quickly.[27]

The CSA used the work of the Special Committee as an input to develop a vision for a competitive marketplace environment that promoted fairness, transparency, market integrity, price discovery, and liquidity. This framework was developed to support the benefits of competition while minimizing the issues arising from fragmentation. The rules and policies creating a framework (Marketplace Rules) were implemented in 2001, and, as will be noted below, have been revisited and amended several times since.[28] The framework

---

[25] In a centralized market, a security trades only on one trading venue and all buying and selling interest is concentrated on that venue. There is no competition among marketplaces, but there is competition among orders. However, because the marketplace has a monopoly on trading, it does not have strong incentives to keep costs down (resulting in higher fees), nor does it have incentives to innovate. This problem is exacerbated if the marketplace operates on a for-profit basis. In a fragmented market, securities are traded on multiple venues, and buy and sell orders may be sent to any of those venues. This adds complexity, as a person entering an order (either as principal or agent) must make a decision as to where to route an order, and needs access to information on market activity and prices to make an informed decision as to where the order is most likely to obtain best execution. The trader must also have access to that marketplace, either directly or through another participant with access. However, because there is competition, marketplaces have a strong incentive to keep costs and fees as low as possible and to innovate.

[26] Toronto Stock Exchange Special Committee, 'Market fragmentation', 1997.

[27] Ibid. See also Kirzner, 'Ideal attributes', 2006.

[28] National Instrument 21-101, 'Marketplace Operation' (NI 21-101) (unofficial consolidation as of 10 April 2017), available at http://www.osc.gov.on.ca/documents/en/Securities-Category2/ni_20170201_21-101_unofficial-consolidation-forms-cp.pdf (unofficial consolidation as of 1 February

established ATSs as a new type of marketplace, distinct from traditional exchanges, and set out core principles required for all marketplaces (exchanges and ATSs).

- *A common set of rules:* all entities carrying on business as a 'marketplace' trading securities would be subject to the Marketplace Rules, with similar requirements applying, but with differentiation between exchanges and ATSs where appropriate.[29]

- *Oversight:* all marketplaces are subject to full OSC oversight.[30] Applications for recognition (exchange) or registration (ATS) and significant changes to operations, rules, and fees require approval and are generally subject to public notice and comment prior to implementation.

- *Fair access to products and services:* marketplaces may not unreasonably condition or limit access to their products and services, including by imposing fees.

- *Market integrity rules:* exchange rules must ensure compliance with securities legislation, prevent fraudulent and manipulative acts and practices, and promote just and equitable principles of trade.

- *Management of conflicts of interest:* marketplaces must maintain policies and procedures to identify and manage or avoid conflicts of interest.

- *Order and trade transparency:* a marketplace must display details of orders and trades in real time to an information processor unless it is a dark pool that does not display pre-trade order information to any participants.[31]

- *System integrity:* marketplaces must have internal controls over critical systems, make reasonable capacity estimates, perform stress tests, and have an independent systems review conducted annually. Marketplaces must also have robust business continuity and disaster recovery plans.

These rules underpin and promote the CSA's vision of ideal market attributes that promote price discovery, transparency, and liquidity by providing for the availability of trading information and fair access to all liquidity pools. They promote fairness and market integrity through compliance with a uniform

---

2017), and National Instrument 23-101, 'Trading Rules' (NI 23-101), available at http://www.osc.gov.on.ca/documents/en/ni_20170410_23-101_unofficial-consolidatation-cp.pdf.

[29] Unlike the United States, the requirements for exchanges and ATSs are largely harmonized. In addition to complying with the Marketplace Rules, ATSs must be registered as an investment dealer and be a member of IIROC.

[30] Due to the provincial nature of securities regulation in Canada, oversight responsibilities for particular marketplaces are divided among securities commissions in Alberta, British Columbia, Manitoba, Ontario, and Quebec. The CSA has a memorandum of oversight for exchanges, where each exchange is recognized by one or more lead regulators and exempted from recognition in the other jurisdictions.

[31] Dark pools must provide the same post-trade transparency as lit markets.

set of trading rules (in National Instruments and UMIR) that apply to all participants and marketplaces. Finally, they set a framework for fair and open competition among marketplaces.

These rules were successful in promoting competition, and four new equity exchanges and 10 ATSs now operate in Ontario.[32]

In addition to having a vision of the attributes of an ideal market, a regulator must also be aware of developments in the market that may impede the vision or, if left unchecked, may negatively impact capital markets or provide lower standards of investor protection. These may include developments that would be benign or even beneficial if tailored to a segment of the capital markets, but that could become problematic if they are widespread. The OSC has led policy initiatives on a number of fronts that were intended to regulate market practices before they became market problems. These initiatives, some of which are described below, were initiated and analysed through the lens of the attributes of the ideal market.

13.3.1.1 ORDER PROTECTION

Price or order protection (or the paramountcy of price priority) promotes the attributes of market integrity and fairness through policy and addresses inefficiencies. It exists in a competitive, multiple marketplace environment where a security is trading on many venues.

Price protection is a regime that ensures that the best-priced orders across multiple marketplaces are executed first. In the absence of a formal trade-through regime in an environment where multiple competing marketplaces trade the same securities, investors, including retail investors, may perceive they are not treated fairly if their orders are not executed despite being shown at a better price than the price(s) at which trades are being executed. This could lead to a decrease of market-wide confidence and withdrawal of investors and liquidity from the market, decreasing the efficiency of the price discovery process and the markets in general.[33]

In Canada, these rules long formed part of exchange trading rules, as many securities were interlisted on multiple exchanges. As noted earlier, trading in senior equities was concentrated on the TSX. However, many TSX-listed securities were also listed on US exchanges and, until 1999, on other Canadian exchanges. The trade-through rule was originally enacted to address a concern that members would trade on another, less liquid exchange to avoid having to displace better-priced bids or offers on the TSX. Because the other marketplaces were less liquid and usually had wider spreads, the trade could be reported to the marketplace as a cross, without any competing orders at

---

[32] Some ATS owners operate multiple marketplaces.　　[33] See CSA, 'Notice', 2014.

that price to interfere with the trade. The Bourse de Montréal, which traded equities at the time, had a similar rule.

The exchange trade-through rules were initially designed as an absolute prohibition on members trading through better prices on the exchange. Later, they were included in UMIR and protected visible better-priced orders on all Canadian marketplaces. This approach of an absolute prohibition proved problematic in a fast-moving, multiple marketplace environment where a trade-through might result from a change in the market that occurred between the time an order was entered and the time it arrived at a trading engine.

The complexity of the evolving market in Canada necessitated that price protection be adopted so that price discovery, liquidity, immediacy, and market integrity were maintained. The CSA enacted an order protection rule (OPR) as a policies and procedures obligation on a marketplace (or on a dealer if the dealer agreed to assume compliance responsibilities) to take steps to avoid trade-throughs.[34] The regulatory regime includes exceptions to allow for market conditions.

Specifically, OPR requires a marketplace (or dealer assuming responsibility for compliance) to have policies and procedures to prevent trade-throughs of 'protected' bids and offers. A bid or offer is 'protected' if it is displayed (i.e. is visible) on a marketplace that provides 'automated trading functionality', which is the ability to immediately execute orders against displayed volume.[35]

The implementation of OPR fostered the vision of competition and investor confidence. Together with existing pre-trade transparency requirements, it may have mitigated the impact of liquidity fragmentation across multiple marketplaces through the virtual consolidation of the order books of each visible marketplace by various market participants and vendors, helping dealers to manage orders across multiple trading venues. Many market participants believed it fostered competition at a time when virtually all trading was on the listing exchanges, but, as described below, we subsequently realized that it had unintended consequences.[36]

---

[34] NI 23-101, Part 6.

[35] Ibid. § 1.1 (definitions of 'automated trading functionality', 'protected bid', 'protected offer', and 'trade-through'.)

[36] Ibid. §§ 7.1(1) (for exchange-traded securities), 8.1(1) (unlisted government debt securities), and 8.2(1) (unlisted corporate debt securities) require marketplaces and dealers to disclose information concerning orders and trades to an information processor as required by the information processor, unless an exemption applies (see Section 13.3.1.2 of this chapter). There are currently no pre-trade transparency requirements of an information processor for unlisted corporate debt securities, and no transparency requirements for government debt securities, although the CSA is currently considering a post-trade transparency regime for government debt securities; see CSA, 'Notice', 2014, at 4880–1.

13.3.1.2 DARK MARKETS

In Canada, the framework of the Marketplace Rules permitted 'dark' trading. The pre-trade transparency requirements for marketplaces in NI 21-101 §§ 7.1 (1) (for exchange-traded securities), 8.1(1) (unlisted government debt securities) and 8.2(1) (unlisted corporate debt securities) do not apply if the marketplace only displays orders to its employees or persons or companies retained to assist in the operation of the marketplace (NI 21-101 §§ 7.1(2), 8.1(2) and 8.2 (2)). However, UMIR Rule 6.3(1) Exposure of Client Orders requires client orders of 50 board lots (5000 shares or units for securities priced at or above C\$1.00) to be immediately entered on a visible marketplace unless exempted.[37]

As dark trading developed, regulators began to consider the risk to price discovery should the volume of dark trading increase. We decided to be proactive and develop a framework to ensure that we could foster trading in the dark in particular circumstances where it was appropriate, but still maintain the principles of price discovery and transparency and ensure that market quality would not be negatively impacted by the loss of trading and order visibility in the lit market.

Our objective in undertaking a review of dark liquidity was to balance the risk that larger institutional orders could suffer adverse market impact if details were disclosed prior to execution with the need to establish limits on orders that were not transparent. These limits were needed because of the risk to the ideal market if smaller orders were removed from the visible market, were not transparent, and did not contribute to price discovery.

The CSA worked with IIROC to examine the issues created by dark trading. In 2009, a joint consultation paper (2009 Consultation Paper) was issued that discussed the emergence of dark orders and different dark order types.[38]

---

[37] An exemption from UMIR Rule 6.3(1) is available if:

- the client has instructed the dealer not to display the order;
- the order is immediately executed at a better price than is available on any visible marketplace;
- the order is returned for confirmation of its terms;
- the order is withheld pending confirmation it complies with applicable regulatory requirements;
- entry of the order would not be in the best interest of the client given current market conditions;
- the order has a value of more than C\$100,000;
- UMIR Rule 6.4 'Trades to be on a Marketplace' permits the order to be executed off a marketplace; or
- the client has directed or consented to the order being entered as a Call Market Order, an Opening Order, a Special Terms Order, a Volume-Weighted Average Price Order, a Market-on-Close Order, a Basis Order, or a Closing Price Order (all as defined in UMIR Rule 1.1 Definitions).

[38] CSA and IIROC, 'Consultation Paper 23-404', 2009.

It looked at the potential impact of dark trading on the characteristics of an efficient and effective market, with particular emphasis on the impact on liquidity, transparency, price discovery, fairness, and market integrity.[39] It solicited comment on the impact of dark trading on these market characteristics, as well as issues arising from various dark order types.[40]

The 2009 Consultation Paper was followed by a forum on 23 March 2010 that allowed commenters on the 2009 Consultation Paper to discuss their views.[41] The forum was followed by a position paper later in 2010 (2010 Position Paper). The 2010 Position Paper recommended that

- the exemption from pre-trade transparency be limited to passive orders that meet or exceed a minimum size;
- two dark orders that are at least the minimum size should be able to execute at the national best bid and offer, with meaningful price improvement required in all other circumstances;
- on a marketplace, visible orders should have priority over dark orders at the same price, but two dark orders that are at least the minimum size could be executed ahead of visible orders at that price; and
- 'meaningful price improvement' should be one 'standard trading increment' as defined in UMIR (generally 1 cent), unless the spread between the bid and offer was one standard trading increment, in which case one-half increment should be permitted.[42]

In 2011, the CSA and IIROC proposed rule amendments to create a regulatory framework for dark markets that allows IIROC as RSP to establish the minimum size for orders to be entered into a dark pool. In addition, as part of this framework, IIROC's UMIR was changed to require meaningful price improvement as recommended in the 2010 Position Paper for smaller, retail-sized orders entered in dark pools.[43] By setting these limits, the CSA and IIROC were able to proactively regulate the expansion of dark liquidity with the necessary limits, while providing flexibility.[44]

The CSA and IIROC rule amendments were adopted in 2012.[45] Dark trading as a share of overall trading declined in the months before and immediately following the enactment of the rules. From that point until the third quarter of 2017 it increased to approximately 6–7 per cent of total trading (see Figure 13.3).

---

[39] Ibid. at 7880.   [40] Ibid. at 7881–7.
[41] CSA and IIROC, 'Notice: Forum to discuss', 2010.
[42] CSA and IIROC, 'Position Paper 23-405', 2010.
[43] UMIR Rule 6.6, 'Provision of Price Improvement by a Dark Order'.
[44] CSA and IIROC, 'Staff Notice 23-311', 2011. See also CSA, 'Proposed amendments', 2011, at 7–10.
[45] OSC, 'Notice of ministerial approval', 2012.

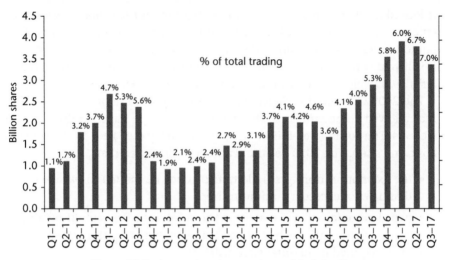

Figure 13.3. Amount and percentage of dark trading

In 2015, IIROC released the results of a study of the impact of the amend-ments.[46] The IIROC study showed an immediate and dramatic decline in dark trading upon implementation of the rule amendments. While some market-places subsequently increased their market share, as of the date of the study, dark trading had not returned to previous levels. The study also found that

- most liquidity providers on dark markets (including high frequency traders) increased their activity on lit markets;
- there was a dramatic decrease in the use of dark markets by brokers to trade with their active retail order flow;
- overall retail order flow showed no increase in costs, but active retail orders had a moderate increase in transaction costs (measured by effective spreads); and
- high frequency traders (HFTs) providing passive liquidity earned a higher effective spread in the lit markets.

The study concluded that, on balance, the benefits of the rule amendments outweighed the costs and that the amendments achieved the regulatory outcomes sought with acceptable impacts to market quality.[47]

13.3.2 *Accommodating Innovation*

Markets are continually evolving. The previous section discussed situations where a regulator must be vigilant to identify risks to achieving the regulatory

---

[46] Devani et al., 'Impact', 7 May 2015.   [47] Ibid. at 7.

vision and manage new practices to ensure they do not harm the capital markets. At the same time, regulators must be careful not to stifle new developments that do not fit neatly into the regulatory framework but that may be beneficial to the markets. The OSC has taken steps on numerous occasions to allow innovation while preserving its vision.

13.3.2.1 HIGH FREQUENCY TRADING

Electronic trading in Canada dates from 1977, when the TSX introduced the Computer Assisted Trading System (CATS), the world's first fully electronic trading system. However, because it was used to trade less liquid securities and order entry was manual, the risks it posed to the market as a whole were minimal and manageable. Later came the development of algorithmic trading, where buy and sell decisions are made by computers using preprogrammed algorithms. Increased reliance on technology by marketplaces and dealer firms has introduced new risks to the market. These include the possibility of greater volatility or errors causing sudden price movements.

The increased use of electronic trading has led to the entry of new participants such as HFTs, who rely heavily on technology to access marketplaces. HFTs have become significant players in the markets, have changed the nature of trading, and have had an impact on traditional, largely manual, market makers. Along with the risks described above, concerns have emerged about a level playing field within and between markets and whether those with better technology were unfairly trading ahead of others.

In undertaking the policy analysis of whether to regulate HFTs, the OSC focused on identifying the key risks they brought to the market. Existing trading rules, including prohibitions on manipulation, applied to their trading. Consequently, the analysis of risks focused on the use of technology, such as the risk that systems would not be properly tested, that errors would be introduced to the markets, and that improperly programmed or rogue algorithms would cause disruption in the marketplaces. This analysis suggested that the best approach was not to regulate the HFTs directly (i.e. requiring them to be registered as dealers and subject to a body of rules) but to directly address the technological risks their trading raised.

As a result, in 2012, the CSA adopted a regulatory framework for electronic trading and direct electronic access to marketplaces by clients, including HFTs.[48] Under NI 23-103, dealers must have risk management and supervisory control policies and procedures that are reasonably designed to manage the financial, regulatory, and other risks associated with accessing marketplaces

---

[48] National Instrument 23-103, 'Electronic Trading and Direct Electronic Access to Marketplaces' (NI 23-103), available at: http://www.osc.gov.on.ca/documents/en/Securities-Category2/ni_20140301_23-103_unofficial-consolidated.pdf (unofficial consolidation as of 1 March 2014).

electronically or permitting clients to access marketplaces electronically.[49] These controls must include automated pre-trade controls and post-trade monitoring, and must, among other things,

- prevent the entry of orders that do not comply with marketplace and regulatory requirements that must be satisfied before an order is entered;
- enable the marketplace participant to immediately stop or cancel orders entered by the marketplace participant or a client; and
- allow the marketplace participant to immediately suspend or terminate access to a marketplace.[50]

The controls must also ensure that order entry does not interfere with fair and orderly markets.[51]

Before giving a client direct electronic access (DEA), dealers must ensure that giving such access is in compliance with the dealer's policies and procedures, and must have a level of understanding of any order entry system used by the dealer or client to identify the risks associated with using the system.[52] Order entry systems must be tested prior to use and at least annually thereafter.[53]

Marketplaces must provide marketplace participants with access to the participant's order and trade information on a real-time basis to allow the marketplace participant to effectively implement its risk management and supervisory controls.[54] They must also have the ability to cut off access in the event an automated system is causing disorderly trading, and they must not allow execution of orders that exceed price and volume thresholds established by IIROC.[55] In all cases, the risk management and supervisory control policies must be regularly reviewed and assessed, and any deficiencies documented and addressed.[56]

NI 23-103 is a principles-based instrument that prescribes outcomes rather than setting out the steps marketplaces and marketplace participants must follow. This allows marketplaces and marketplace participants flexibility in creating their own policies and procedures based on their own business practices, provided they are reasonable and in accordance with prudent business practice. This framework imposes accountability on dealers, marketplaces, and DEA clients to ensure that when relying on technology to trade, the risks to fair and efficient markets are properly mitigated.

The electronic trading rules focus on the actual risks these new participants bring to the markets. The regulatory framework recognizes the role of HFTs in a changing market environment and the need for dealers that provide

---

[49] Ibid. § 3(1).   [50] Ibid. §§ 3(2), 3(3).   [51] Ibid.   [52] Ibid. § 5(3)(b).   [53] Ibid.
[54] Ibid. § 6(1).   [55] Ibid. §§ 8, 9.   [56] Ibid. §§ 3(6), 7(2).

them with access to be accountable for ensuring the operation of fair and efficient markets.

In 2012, IIROC released the results of a study of trading activity related to high frequency trading in Canadian equity markets.[57] IIROC identified a study group based on user IDs that had a high order-to-trade ratio (the HOT group). The study found that 11 per cent of all traders were HOT traders, accounting for 22 per cent of total share volume and 94 per cent of order messages.

In 2013, IIROC issued guidance on manipulative and deceptive trading practices in the context of the use of automated order systems and direct electronic access to marketplaces.[58] It listed certain practices that IIROC considers manipulative and deceptive, including layering,[59] quote stuffing,[60] quote manipulation,[61] spoofing,[62] and abusive liquidity detection.[63]

13.3.2.2 SPEED BUMPS

Another innovation in Canada is the introduction of order processing delays or speed bumps by two exchanges, Aequitas NEO Exchange and Alpha Exchange. Unlike the IEX Exchange in the United States, which imposes a delay on all orders, the Canadian equivalents impose targeted speed bumps. In the case of the Aequitas NEO Book, active orders of 'latency-sensitive traders' are subject to a random delay before entering the system.[64] In the case of Alpha, all orders other than post only orders (orders that are passive only) of a minimum size are subject to a random delay. The effect of the speed bumps was to allow liquidity providers to protect themselves against adverse price movements caused by HFTs (Aequitas) and large institutional orders (Alpha).

The introduction of these speed bumps raised a number of regulatory concerns, the biggest being related to quote fade. Speed bumps prevent the execution of orders against displayed volume for a limited time. During that time, liquidity-providing orders that are not subject to the speed bump may be filled, changed, or cancelled, possibly as a reaction to activity on other marketplaces.

---

[57] IIROC, Trading Review and Analysis—Analytics Group, 'The HOT Study', 2012.

[58] IIROC, 'Guidance', 14 February 2013.

[59] Placing a *bona fide* order on one side of the market while layering orders on the other side with no intention to trade.

[60] Input of excessive market data messages with the intent to flood systems and create information arbitrage opportunities.

[61] Placing orders in visible markets with no intention to trade in an attempt to affect the price at which trades will take place in dark markets.

[62] Entering non *bona fide* orders before the opening of trading with the intent to affect the opening price.

[63] Using a strategy involving entry of orders to detect the existence of a large buyer or seller with the intention of trading ahead of that buyer or seller.

[64] Aequitas also has a Lit Book which does not have a speed bump.

The introduction of speed bumps also raised issues about the applicability of OPR to these marketplaces, as speed bumps were not contemplated when OPR was developed. We examined the issues created by speed bumps in light of the underlying first principles of OPR and the potential impact on the ideal market attributes.[65] As noted in Section 13.3.1.1, trade-through protection exists for visible orders on marketplaces that provide automated trading functionality, or the ability to immediately execute against displayed volume. The issue created by marketplaces with speed bumps was whether the marketplace offered 'immediate' execution, as 'immediate' was not defined in the rule. Staff believed, and continue to believe, that the approach of not defining 'immediate' is appropriate given the speed at which technology continues to evolve. In the specific context of the application of OPR, staff believed that if orders were protected, execution against those orders should be immediate, subject to natural market or network latencies such as those caused by differences in technology or geographical remoteness.[66] Specifically, we questioned whether it was reasonable to expect participants to route orders to a marketplace for OPR compliance when, due to intentional latency, the better-priced liquidity on that marketplace may no longer exist and the participant may have missed an opportunity to trade on another marketplace.[67]

While there were concerns about the application of OPR to these marketplaces, the Commission did not want to stifle innovation. The Commission allowed the Alpha speed bump, but imposed a condition that orders on Alpha not be protected under OPR.[68] In addition, Alpha was required to provide the OSC with analyses of the impact of the speed bump, and the Commission confirmed that it could revisit its approval if there is evidence of a negative impact on the quality of the capital markets. Later, the Companion Policy to NI 23-101 was amended to clarify that the CSA does not consider any marketplace that implements an intentional systematic delay in order processing, whether for all orders or a subset of orders, to be providing automated trading functionality. This removed protected status for the Aequitas NEO Book.[69]

In allowing Aequitas and Alpha to implement speed bumps, the Commission recognized the need to foster innovation, but also recognized that there

---

[65] Canadian Securities Administrators, 'Notice and request', 2015.   [66] Ibid.   [67] Ibid.

[68] This meant that dealers would not be required to send an order to Alpha and be subjected to the speed bump, even if Alpha had a better price. Later, OPR was amended so that marketplaces imposing a speed bump would generally not be protected.

[69] Companion Policy 23-101CP to NI 23-101, § 1.1.2., available at: http://www.osc.gov.on.ca/documents/en/ni_20170410_23-101_unofficial-consolidatation-cp.pdf (unofficial consolidation as of 10 April 2017).

may be a risk that speed bumps could negatively impact fair and efficient markets. If that happens, an appropriate regulatory response should be taken.

13.3.3 *Looking Back*

Part of responsible policy analysis is recognizing that it is not sufficient to just put requirements in place. Rules and policies must be continually re-examined and assessed to ensure that they continue to achieve their objectives. This review should examine new developments in the market, identify gaps, and address unintended consequences. A regulator must have the courage to admit that a particular rule did not get it right the first time. These are a few examples where Canadian regulators adjusted and amended rules to ensure that the right outcomes were achieved efficiently and effectively.

13.3.3.1 MARKETPLACE RULES
The Marketplace Rules fostered a competitive environment for trading Canadian exchange-listed securities. Order flow was fragmented among different trading venues, but fragmentation also brought choice, with marketplaces offering different fee models, innovative technology, and new order types.[70] They have been updated several times to address changing market practices. In some instances, rules were strengthened, as when the rules for ATSs were aligned more closely with the rules for exchanges and when business continuity and disaster recovery planning were mandated. In other cases, rules were streamlined to ensure that the regulators receive the information that they need to conduct effective oversight without imposing a heavy regulatory burden. Such rules must be evergreen to ensure that they support the vision of the regulators and reflect existing market reality.

13.3.3.2 ORDER PROTECTION
In the previous section, we discussed how the OPR was reviewed in light of a new development, namely speed bumps. OPR was also revisited because its implementation led to unintended consequences and inefficiencies in the market.

The intent of OPR was to foster liquidity, immediacy, and price discovery in a competitive environment by limiting trade-throughs. Even though it was designed as a policies and procedures rule, most dealers interpreted the rule as a requirement to connect to every lit marketplace and to use all lit marketplace pre-trade data for order routing purposes. They expressed concerns that they

---

[70] CSA, 'Notice', 2014, at 4879.

were captive consumers of marketplace services and that the inefficiencies created by the rule and the costs of complying with OPR outweighed the benefits, particularly as the number of visible marketplaces grew. In light of these concerns, the OSC led a CSA initiative to review the rule, focusing on the costs and unintended consequences.

The primary focus of the review was to weigh the benefits of OPR against its possible inefficiencies. Among its benefits:

- efficiency gains from the virtual consolidation of access to fragmented marketplaces;
- an increased investor perception of a level playing field as investors' visible better-priced orders trade ahead of inferior-priced orders; and
- fostering competition among marketplaces.

Inefficiencies of OPR might arise if:

- market participants have become captive consumers of marketplace services in order to comply with OPR;
- captive consumers are generating revenues for marketplaces, supporting an otherwise unsustainable level of competition; and
- the existence of any unsustainable competition resulted in excessive complexities, costs, and inefficiencies for equity trading.[71]

As a result of the review, the CSA continued to believe that the objectives of OPR (protection of orders to foster investor confidence, facilitation of liquidity provision, and price discovery) were important. The review found a number of positive effects of OPR.[72] However, OPR also created costs and inefficiencies that needed to be addressed. The review found that the direct and indirect costs most commonly associated with OPR were marketplace fees, technology costs and risks, trading inefficiencies, and operational implications such as marketplace liability and compliance burdens.[73] With respect to trading fees, participants expressed concern that OPR required them to trade on the marketplace displaying the best-priced orders, regardless of the fee charged by that marketplace. With respect to market data fees specifically, participants expressed concerns that data fees were generally high, particularly when compared to a marketplace's contribution to overall liquidity and price discovery, and may not be subject to sufficient competitive forces to bring discipline to the level of fees charged.[74]

The CSA addressed the inefficiencies by (1) setting a minimum market share threshold for orders on a marketplace to be protected under OPR and

[71] Ibid. at 4879–80.   [72] See Section 13.3.1.1.   [73] CSA, 'Notice', 2014, at 4881.
[74] Ibid. See also CSA, 'Staff consultation paper 21-401', 2012.

(2) formalizing a data fee methodology that would be used to assess a market-place's data fees against the value of its data.[75] The goal was to maintain a high level of order protection (80–90 per cent of trades) while providing market-place participants with some flexibility with respect to trading on market-places with a low market share or speed bumps.

(a) Minimum Market Share

NI 23-101 was amended to provide that displayed orders on a marketplace offering automated trading functionality are not protected unless the market-place has a minimum market share, currently 2.5 per cent (an exchange is protected for its listed securities regardless of market share provided it offers automated trading functionality).[76] The threshold is based on volume and value traded and is recalculated for each marketplace annually.[77]

We considered using the number of trades to establish the threshold, but were concerned that this could favour a marketplace with a large number of low-volume trades. We also considered using order-based metrics, but were concerned that marketplaces could offer incentives for the placement of orders for the sole purpose of meeting the threshold.[78]

The impact of this change was to maintain a meaningful level of order protection while providing participants with flexibility to choose to trade on markets that are innovative and offer products and services that they want to use.

(b) Market Data Fee Regulation

In Ontario, fees charged by marketplaces are subject to review and approval. The OSC had been reviewing the issue of market data fees prior to the OPR review, and developed a more rigorous methodology to assess data fees.[79] Because we believed that it was important that the methodology be transparent, it was published for comment at the same time as the other OPR review proposals.[80] The methodology ranks each marketplace on its contribution to price discovery and trading activity. It uses pre- and post-trade metrics such as (1) percentage of the day for which the marketplace had orders at the national

---

[75] CSA, 'Notice', 2014, at 4887–8.

[76] NI 23-101, § 1.1. The definitions of 'protected bid' and 'protected offer' were amended to provide that the marketplace on which the bid or offer is displayed must meet the market share threshold set by the regulator (in Ontario, the Executive Director of the Commission or a delegate), or in Quebec, the Autorité des marchés financiers. It is currently set at 2.5 per cent.

[77] CSA, 'Notice', 2014, at 4889. Where a marketplace offers more than one trading facility, the calculation of the threshold is done on a facility-by-facility basis.

[78] Ibid. Specifically, we were concerned that it may be easier to successfully offer incentives for placing orders than it would be to provide incentives for actual trades.

[79] See, e.g., CSA, 'Staff Consultation Paper 21-401', 2012; CSA, 'Staff Notice', 2013.

[80] CSA, 'Notice', 2014, at 4898–9.

best bid or best offer prices for each security, (2) percentage of the day the marketplace was quoting the tightest spread of any marketplace for the security, (3) percentage of the marketplace's share of total volume and value traded and number of trades for each security, and (4) the average number of different securities traded on the marketplace compared with the number traded on all marketplaces.[81]

Once the data are compiled, several models are used to rank each marketplace's contribution to price discovery and trading, giving an estimated fee range for each marketplace. A marketplace's proposed professional market data fees or fee changes are assessed against the range and will not be approved if they are above the range. To ensure that fees remain commensurate with the marketplace's contribution to price discovery and trading, existing fees are reassessed every year.[82]

13.4 Conclusion

In fast-changing capital markets, regulators need the ability and the courage to be responsive and forward-thinking, while at the same time monitoring past decisions to ensure that the outcomes are as intended.

A regulator needs to have a vision of an ideal market, and must be able to articulate the principles that underlie this ideal market. The regulator also needs to understand what is driving change in the market, and examine it using those principles as a touchstone, and must use evidence to justify regulatory action (or inaction). Regulators must not be afraid of change, and should allow innovation unless there is clear evidence that it will have a negative impact on market integrity and market quality. Innovative practices need to be monitored to ensure there is not a negative impact, and the regulator must react quickly if there is. Regulators also need to re-examine previous decisions and address any gaps, new developments in the market, and unintended consequences. In other words, regulation must always be dynamic and forward-thinking, but also retrospective.

References

CSA (Canadian Securities Administrators). 'Notice and request for comment: Proposed amendments to National Instrument 23-101 Trading Rules'. 37 O.S.C.B. 4873, 4880. 2014. Available at: http://www.osc.gov.on.ca/documents/en/Securities-Category2/csa_20140515_23-101_rfc-pro-amd.pdf, 2014.

---

[81] CSA, 'Notice of approval', 2016, at 3281–4.   [82] Ibid. at 3284.

CSA. 'Notice and request for comment: Proposed amendments to the Companion Policy to National Instrument 23-101 Trading Rules: Application of the Order Protection Rule to marketplaces imposing systematic order processing delays'. 38 O.S.C.B. 5551. 2015, at 5554. Available at: http://www.osc.gov.on.ca/documents/en/Securities-Category2/csa_20140612_23-101_rfc-pro-amd-processing-delays.pdf, 2015.

CSA. 'Notice of approval: Amendments to National Instrument 21-101 Trading Rules and Companion Policy 23-101 to National Instrument 21-101 Trading Rules'. 39 O.S.C.B. 3237. 2016, at 3281–4, 2016.

CSA. 'Proposed amendments to National Instrument 21-101 Marketplace Operation and National Instrument 23-101 Trading Rules'. 34 O.S.C.B. (Supp-1) 1. 2011, at 7–10. Available at: http://www.osc.gov.on.ca/documents/en/Securities-Category2/rule_20110318_21-101_rfc-notice-proposed-amendments.pdf, 2011.

CSA. 'Staff Consultation Paper 21-401: Real time market data fees'. 35 O.S.C.B. 10099. 2012. Available at: http://www.osc.gov.on.ca/en/SecuritiesLaw_21-401.htm, 2012.

CSA. 'Staff Notice 21-312: Update on Consultation Paper 21-401: Real time market data fees'. 36 O.S.C.B. 10601. 2013. Available at: http://www.osc.gov.on.ca/documents/en/Securities-Category2/csa_20131107_21-312_update-21-401-rtm.pdf, 2013.CSA and IIROC (Canadian Securities Administrators and Investment Industry Regulatory Organization of Canada).

CSA. 'Consultation Paper 23-404: Dark pools, dark orders, and other developments in market structure in Canada'. 32 O.S.C.B. 7877. 2009. Available at: http://www.osc.gov.on.ca/en/25775.htm, 2009.

CSA and IIROC. 'Notice: Forum to discuss Consultation Paper 23-404 Dark pools, dark orders, and other developments in market structure in Canada', 33 OSCB 1911, 2010. Available at: http://www.osc.gov.on.ca/documents/en/Securities-Category2/csa_20100405_23-404_forum-dark-pools.pdf, 2010.

CSA and IIROC. 'Position Paper 23-405: Dark liquidity in the Canadian market'. 33 O.S.C.B. 10764. 2010. Available at: http://www.osc.gov.on.ca/documents/en/Securities-Category2/csa_20101119_23-405_dark-liquidity.pdf, 2010.

CSA and IIROC. 'Staff Notice 23-311: Regulatory approach to dark liquidity in the Canadian market'. 24 O.S.C.B. 8219. 2011. Available at: http://www.osc.gov.on.ca/documents/en/Securities-Category2/sn_20110729_23-311_dark-liquidity.pdf, 2011.

Devani, Baiju, Lisa Anderson, and Yifan Zhang. 'Impact of the Dark Rule amendments'. Available at: http://docs.iiroc.ca/DisplayDocument.aspx?DocumentID=D215AFEDA01E453D8F24BD8ED2B948BF&Language=en,7 May 2015.

IIROC. 'Guidance on certain manipulative and deceptive trading practices'. Available at: http://docs.iiroc.ca/DisplayDocument.aspx?DocumentID=02A24CF0770E4D238D32E46C4CDA32C1&Language=en,14 February 2013.

IIROC. Trading review and analysis—Analytics Group. 'The HOT Study: Phases I and II of IIROC's study of high frequency trading activity on Canadian equity marketplaces'. 2012. Available at: http://www.iiroc.ca/Documents/2012/c03dbb44-9032-4c6b-946e-6f2bd6cf4e23_en.pdf#search=HOT%20study, 2012.

Kirzner, Eric. 'Ideal attributes of a marketplace'. Available at: http://www.tfmsl.ca/docs/V4(2)%20Kirzner.pdf. (Research study commissioned by the Task Force to Modernize Securities Legislation in Canada). 2006.

OSC. 'Annual report'. Available at: http://www.osc.gov.on.ca/documents/en/Publications/ Publications_rpt_2017_osc-annual-rpt_en.pdf, 2017.

OSC. 'Notice of ministerial approval of amendments to National Instrument 21-101 Marketplace Operation and Companion Policy 21-101CP, and to National Instrument 23-101 Trading Rules and Companion Policy 23-101CP'. 35 O.S.C.B. 5316. 2012.

Toronto Stock Exchange Special Committee. 'Market fragmentation: Responding to the challenge'. 1997.

Index

Tables and figures are indicated by an italic *t* or *f* following the page number.